NEW APPROACH TO HISTORY AND GOVERNMENT

BY

PEDO G. P. OLOO

Ariba Book Publishers

ISBN: 978-9966-18180-0

Ariba Book Publishers
P. O. Box 503-40600
Siaya –Kenya
Website: www.aribatecbp.com

Printed by
Susmo Enterprises
P. O. Box 345-00511
Nairobi

Typeset by
Beatrice Adhiambo – Barons Computers (Siaya)
P. O. Box 221, **Siaya**

First published **2015**

Dedicated to

My teachers – from whom I learned

and

my students of Mbaga – from whom I continue to learn

and to my family,

most especially my sister

Cecilia Sewe

who financed my education and mentored the Pedo family,

my late parents

Joanes Pedo Aluodo and Getruda Aluoch Obwanda

and my dear wife

Beatrice

who stood by me during my most trying moments,

last but not least, my late daughter

Stacy Aluoch

who was the love of my life

TABLE OF CONTENTS

The Barons

PREFACE

The book is skillfully written and wholly covers the New History and Government syllabus succinctly. The purpose of this book is to give the form four candidates a firm foundation in the Subject. Paper 1 & 2 are covered separately and the topics are arranged according to how they are examined in the respective papers. Students, who have not covered the syllabus – from other classes, are advised to cover those topics only which are included in the syllabus of their classes. For this purpose, they should consult their teachers. This arrangement is a departure from the past practice where topics are arranged according to class level and students who cannot distinguish the topics according to respective papers get confused during their preparation for examination. Examination techniques and sample questions together with their answers are included at the back of the book to help the learners to gauge themselves and to prepare adequately for examination. A glossary of words commonly used in History and Government and an index for quick reference are also provided. This is a comprehensive book that adequately summaries the 8-4-4 History and Government syllabus for secondary schools.

The author of this book has a wealth of experience in handling History and Government, and in marking and setting exams. He is currently handling the form four candidates and heads the Department of Humanities in Bishop Okoth Mbaga Girls - Siaya.

Pedo G. P. Oloo (MBA, Bed (Hon.), Dip Ed.)
P.O. Box 221
Siaya-Kenya

ACKNOWLEDGEMENT

A large number of individuals have contributed to this project. I am thankful to all of them for their help and encouragement. Like most text books, this book has also drawn from the work of a large number of researchers and authors in the field of History and Government. My writings in this book have also been influenced by a number of standard and popular text books in the field. I express my gratitude to all of them.

I express my appreciation to all my colleagues and students of Bishop Okoth Girls Mbaga for adopting this book, or for making suggestions for the improvement of the book, or for extending their support and encouragement. I am particularly indebted to Sister Sarah Adipo who adopted the origin version of the book as a school text in Mbaga. I also owe much tribute to Elisha Otieno who encouraged me to publish the book. Without financial support from my dear sisters – Cecilia Sewe and Conslata Apul little could have been achieved in this project.

I would very much appreciate and sincerely acknowledge suggestions from academic colleagues and readers for improving the quality of the book. I shall be happy to acknowledge the support of the adopters of the book.

This book is dedicated to my sister, Cecilia, who has been a source of incessant motivation and bolster, and who has always extended her unstinted support to me. I am thankful to my wife, Beatrice as well as my sons (Bryan, Viola, Edgar, Ian and Flavio) and my daughter Joy, for their endurance through several months that I spent in writing this book.

List of abbreviations and acronyms

A.D.	After Death of Christ
ADC	Agriculture Development Corporation
AEMO	African elected members of Organisation
AG	Attorney General
AFC	Agriculture Finance Corporation
AIC	African Inland Church
ANC	African National Congress
APRM	African Peer Review Mechanism
AU	African Union
BSACo	British South African Company
CCM	Chama Cha Mapinduzi
CMS	Church Mission Society
CBK	Central Bank of Kenya
CDF	Constituency Development Fund
CID	Criminal Investigation Department
COMESA	Common Market for Eastern and Central Africa
CPP	Convention Peoples' Party
CYO	Committee on Youth Organization
DFCK	Development Finance Company of Kenya
DP	Democratic Party
DRC	Democratic Republic of Congo
EADB	East African Development Bank
ESA	European Space Agency
FRELIMO	Front for the Liberation of Mozambique
GEACo	German East African Company
HEP	Hydro electric power
IBEACo	Imperial British East African Company
ICC	International Criminal Court
ICDC	Commercial Development Corporation
ICFTU	International Confederation of Free Trade Union
ICJ	International Court of Justice
IEBC	Independent Electoral and Boundary Commission
ILO	International Labour Organization
IMF	International Monetary Fund
IUCEA	Inter-University Council for iix Africa
JSC	Judicial Service Commission
KANU	Kenya African National Union
KARI	Kenya Research Institute
KASU	Kenya African Study Union
KCC	Kenya Cooperative Creameries

KDF	Kenya Defense Forces
KFA	Kenya Farmers Association
KPA	Kenya Ports Authority
KICOMI	Kisumu Cotton Mills
KIE	Kenya Industrial Estates
KIM	Kenya Independent Movement
KLGWU	Kenya Local Government Workers Union
KNC	Kenya National Congress
KNCHR	Kenya National Commission on Human Right
KNH	Kenyatta National Hospital
KRA	Kenya Revenue Authority
LBDA	Lake Basin Development Authority
LVFO	Lake Victoria Fisheries Organization
NCWK	National Council of Women of Kenya
PAC	Public Accounts Committee
PANA	Pan African News Agency
PNU	Party of National Unity
PIC	Public Investment Committee
UAJ	Union of African Journalists
UDENAMO	National Democratic Union of Mozambique
UGCC	United Gold Coast Convention
UNAMI	African Union of Independent Mozambique
UNHCR	United Nations High Commission for Refugees
UNDP	United Nations Development Programme
UNO	United Nations Organization
NAM	Non Aligned Movement
NASA	United States National Aeronautics
NATO	North Atlantic Treaty Organization
NEPAD	New Partnership for African development
NDP	National Democratic Party
MANU	Mozambique African National Union
MP	Member of Parliament
OAU	Organization of African Unity
OATUU	Organization of African Trade Union Unity
ODM	Orange Democratic Movement
RWAFF	Royal West African Frontier Force
SAP	Structural Adjustment Programmes
SDA	Seventh Day Adventist
TUC	Trade Union Congress
UDI	Unilateral Declaration of Independence
VAT	Value Added Tax
YKA	Young Kikuyu Association
ZANU	Zimbabwe African National Union

The Barons

1 KENYAN SOCIETIES DURING THE PRE-COLONIAL TIMES

Some scholars are of the opinion that the first inhabitants of the present day Kenya were the hunter-gatherers groups, akin to the Khoikhoi and Hottentots (Bushmen) of South Africa. Dorobo which is used to refer to this group is actually not one tribe as contended by many people, but a group of closely related people. Majority of them have been assimilated by the Cushitic and Nilotic communities who joined them much later and they have now lost their culture and language.

It is reported that only about eight El Molo still speak the old language, but the rest speak either the Samburu or the Turkana language. The Njemps, who are also of the old group, speak Samburu. The same applies to the Ariaal Rendille deemed to be Eastern Cushites. Though the Ariaal are not called Dorobo, they share a similar cultural history. People who are related to them in Tanzania like the Mbugu and Iraqi speak the Southern Cushitic language. Related groups in other parts, of Africa, for instance the Sandawe and Hadzapi in Tanzania, and the Khoisan in South Africa still exhibit the same characteristics and speak with the same click sound.

The Agikuyu refer to the original inhabitants of central part of Kenya as *Athi* which translated in their dialect meant ground people after the names of Athi plains and Athi River where they lived. The Athi were probably Cushites or the original San. The word *Dorobo* was conceived by the Maasai who referred to the original inhabitants of Rift Valley as *Torobo*, translated to mean poor people who did not keep livestock. This word was taken in Swahili as Dorobo and in Kalenjin and Agikuyu as Ndorobo.

Various groups lamped together as Dorobo include: the Okiek (the largest and most distinct), the Mukogodo, the Mosiro, the Aramanick, the Mediak and the El molo. The *Dorobo* Maasai (Okiek) is the metal worker clan of the Keekonyokie Maasai. The Digiri groups of the Okiek live near Mount Kenya and some have now migrated to Maasai areas near the Tanzanian border. The El molo are an Eastern Cushite group, related to the Somali and Rendille.

Most of the Dorobo people are completely absorbed into the culture and language of their Nilotic patrons and no longer speak a unique language. The Okiek, for example are bilingual in Kipsigis and Maasai with one of the languages being more of the mother tongue and the other being the second language. Mukogodo Maasai consider themselves as a sub-tribe of the Maasai and speak their language (Maa) while the Mosiro and Mediak of Tanzania speak a language related to the one spoken by the Nandi of Kenya.

CUSHITIC SPEAKERS
There are two Cushitic communities which migrated into Kenya. These were the Eastern and the Southern Cushites.

Southern Cushites arrived earlier than the Eastern Cushites. The Southern Cushites were made up of the Boni, Iraqi and Burungi of Tanzania and the Dahallo or Sanye of the lower Tana. The Sanye (Dahallo) are the only remnants of the Southern Cushites in Kenya in the present day.

Eastern Cushites include the Borana, Somali, Oromo, Gabra, Rendille and Burji. These groups are said to have originated from either Ethiopia or Somalia and

The Barons

entered Kenya through the North Eastern part around 2,000 to 1,000 years ago.

Reasons which led to the migration and settlement of the Cushites in their present home areas included:

- The Cushites were running away from internal conflicts
- They were running away from external conflicts
- They were moving into new areas to ease population pressure in their cradle land
- They were searching for better grazing land for their animals
- They were running away from the outbreak of disease
- They migrated due to drought and famine in their original homeland
- Some migrated due to their desire for adventure

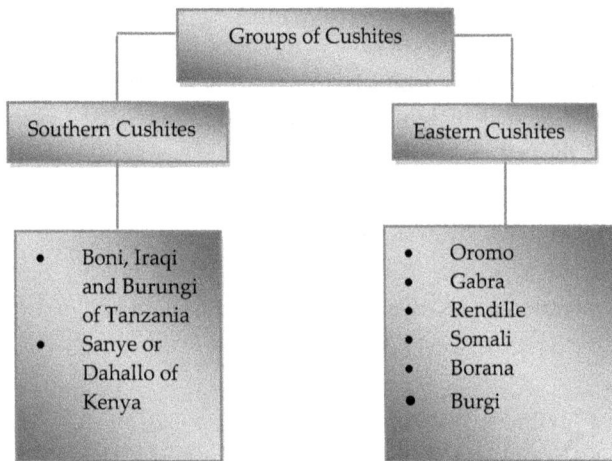

Impact of the Migration of the Cushites into Kenya during the Pre-Colonial Period included:

- The Cushites who owned livestock encouraged this practice in areas where they were settled.
- Their settlement led to increased rivalry due to ownership of land.
- Some Cushites who had been converted to Islam spread the religion in the areas where they settled.

- The Cushites attacked the Eastern Bantu Communities who had settled at Shungwaya, and forced them to move to their present homeland in Kenya.
- There was intermarried between the Cushites and the communities who found them in the region
- Trade developed between the Cushites and the communities they came into contact with - they exchanged livestock products for grains with the Bantu.
- The Bantu borrowed some of the cultural practice like circumcision and age set system from the Cushites. Iron making was also acquired from them.
- Cushites acquired mixed farming from the Bantu while the Bantu adopted livestock farming from the Somali.

Impact of the Migration and Settlement of the Somali into Kenya By 1800 included:

- The Somali people intermarried with the people they came into contact with such as Pokomo and Boran.
- The Somali formed military alliances with their cousins, Rendille - against the Turkana
- The Somali taught the Bantus the art of circumcision and age set system
- Demand for agricultural produce by the Somali led to the expansion of trade in the region.
- Their settlement led to increased conflicts between the communities over scarce resources such as water and pasture.
- Their migration and settlement led to the displacement and redistribution of people where they settled.
- There was cultural exchange between the Somali and the people they came into contact. For example, the neighbouring communities adopted Islam from the Somali.
- The Somali assimilated some communities they came into contact with, for example the Oromo.

- Their settlement in high agricultural potential areas, for example river valleys encouraged some of them to practice crop farming.

BANTU SPEAKERS

whose migration started around A.D. 1000, migrated and entered Kenya in three groups namely:
- The Western (Interlacustrine) Bantu
- The Coastal Bantu
- The Eastern Bantu

The Bantu came from their original homeland between Eastern Nigeria and Cameroon highlands (Congo Basin). They migrated southwards and eventually settled in Saba province in the present day Democratic Republic of Congo (DRC). The place became a major dispersal point. Some passed through Northern Tanzania and settled in the Taita Hills area around Mt. Kilimanjaro by 2nd century AD. From here, population pressure and Oromo attacks made them to migrate further. The knowledge of iron working greatly assisted the Bantus to migrate to different area. They used iron weapons to fight their enemies and to clear the forests to create room for their settlement.

Eastern Bantus

also referred to as the Highland Bantu, is believed to have entered East Africa between Lake Tanganyika and Lake George. They moved from Southern Congo forest, crossed the Tanganyika plateau around A.D. 1000 – 1300 and settled around Taita Hills in the present day Kenya. They dispersed from Taita Hills and Kilimanjaro areas and moved upto Shungwaya. From Shungwaya, where they were displaced by the Oromo, the ancestors of the Mount Kenya group moved into the interior along the river Tana and settled around Mount Kenya region. These people formed the Mount Kenya Group, composed of the Ameru, Agikuyu, Aembu and Kamba. The Ameru are divided into sub groups. These include the Mbeere, Tharaka and Igembe.

Impact of the Migration and Settlement of the Agikuyu
- The Agikuyu Intermarriage with their neighbours, for example the Akamba and Maasai
- Their migration and settlement resulted into expansion of trade in the region
- Some communities were assimilated by the Agikuyu, for example the Gumba
- It encouraged cultural interaction between communities, for example dressing and ceremonies
- Some communities were displaced by the Agikuyu, for example the Okiek
- There was increased warfare in the region over land for cultivation and grazing
- It led to the enrichment of language due to word borrowing

Consequences of the interaction between the Eastern Cushites and the Bantus were:
- The Eastern Cushites people intermarried with the people they come into contact such as the Pokomo and Mijikenda
- Their settlement in Kenya led to the expansion of trade in the region.
- Demand of Agricultural produce by the Somali led to the expansion of Agriculture in central and some parts of Eastern Kenya.
- Their settlement led to increased conflicts between the communities over resources such as water and pasture.
- Their migration and settlement led to the displacement and redistribution of people in the area where they settled.
- Led to cultural– exchange between the Somali and the people they came into contact with, for example the neighboring communities like Pokomo adopted Islam from the Somali
- Assimilated some communities they come into conduct with, for example Sanye and Boni
- Their settlement in high agricultural potential areas encouraged some of them to

practice crop farming, for example parts of Marsabit

- The Cushitic speaking communities brought the practice of circumcision and age-set system organization.

Western Bantus migrated directly from the Niger Congo basin and entered East Africa between Lake Albert and Lake George. They settled in the interlacustrine (Lake) region. The presence of Bantu in Western Kenya stretches back to the time of early Iron Age. The period between 1500 and 1850 A.D. saw the migration of many Bantu clans and families from Eastern Uganda into Western Kenya and the emergence of the present day Abaluhya, Abagusii and Abakuria communities.

Even though considered as one tribe, the Abaluhya is made up of a cluster of 18 sub-tribes speaking different dialects of the Luhya language. The Bukusu and Maragoli make the two largest Luhya sub-tribes. The sub-tribes include: Banyala, Banyore, Batsotso, Gisu, Idakho, Isukha, Kabras, Khayo, Kisa, Marachi, Marama, Masaaba, Samia, Tachoni, Tiriki and Wanga.

While the Bantu who lived in the North of the Winam Gulf (Abaluhya) evolved into a single community, those to South of Winam Gulf evolved into three distinct societies:

- Abagusii
- Abakuria and
- Abasuba.

This development is attributed to the expansion of the Kenyan Luo who lodged a linguistic and cultural wedge between the Abagusii and Abakuria. Abasuba were confined to Rusinga and Ngodhe Islands at the entrance of the Winam Gulf and eventually assimilated into Luo society.

The Abagusii originally migrated into Nyanza from "Misiri" (to the north of Mount Elgon) at the beginning of the 16th century. Originally a cattle keeping community, the Gusii economic and social fabrics underwent fundamental transformations in the period 1520 – 1755 A.D. as they established themselves in the lake region. There first settlement in Nyanza was made at Yimbo at the head of Goye Bay, but after prolonged cattle rusting conflicts between them and the Luo, Abagusii migrated and settled in Kano plains between 1620 and 1755. Abagusii developed most of their social institutions such as sectional totems and clanism around this epoch. They also acquired and perfected the skills of Iron technology.

Armed with better weapons, the Abagusii were able to expand at the expense of the Kalenjin, Sirikwa, Dorobo and Maasai into areas of the present day Kericho and Gusii highlands between 1755 and 1850. This expansion into the highlands from the lowland plains around Lake Victoria necessitated a change in their economic and social way of life.

To the south of the Abagusii, but separated by a corridor of Luo, are the Abakuria. They dwell in the rich and undulating savanna land along the Kenya and Tanzania border close to the Lake Victoria region. It is apparent, at least from linguistic studies that Kuria land was continously occupied from the late Stone Age. In the period upto A.D. 1500, Bantu speakers tended to occupy area bordering the Lake while the Southern Nilotes and Southern Cushites lived on their eastern flanks, in the interior. By A.D. 1700 the Bantu expanded eastwards and had absorbed most of their neighbours.

How societies interacted in the past
(a) Societies interacted through trade
(b) They intermarriage with one another
(c) There was warfare among the societies
(d) There was cultural exchange like naming and borrowing of words
(e) Some communities raided cattle from their neighbours

Coastal Bantus consisted mainly of the Mijikenda, Pokomo and Taita (Wadawida). Mijikenda are further divided in nine sub tribes. Chonyi, Kambe, Ribe, Rabai, Jibana and Giriama form the northern group while the Digo are the southern Mijikenda. The Digo are also found in Tanzania because of their proximity to the common border.

The Coastal Bantus migrated from their original homeland in the Congo Basin and settled in the Taita Hills area around Mt. Kilimanjaro by 2nd century AD. Some of them later migrated northwards along the coast to Shungwaya. From about 1459, the communities which settled in Shungwaya were forced to disperse from the area due to external pressure from the Cushites. The ancestors of the Mijikenda and Taita moved south and established their settlement along the coast while those of the Pokomo migrated into the interior and settled along River Tana. The Ameru migrated to the slopes of Mt. Kenya.

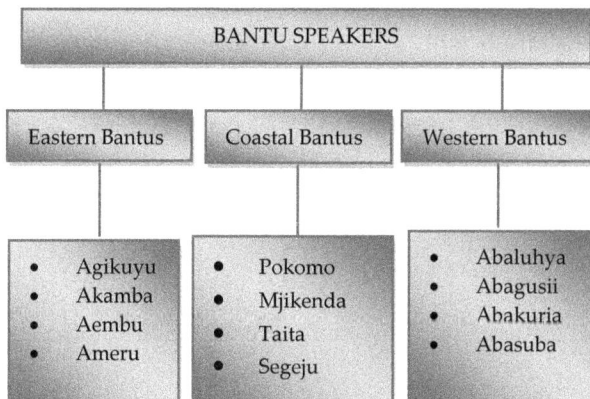

BANTU SPEAKERS

Eastern Bantu	Coastal Bantu	Western Bantu
• Agikuyu • Akamba • Aembu • Ameru	• Pokomo • Mjikenda • Taita • Segeju	• Abaluhya • Abagusii • Abakuria • Abasuba

Reasons for the Migration of the Coastal Bantu Speaking Communities included:
- Search for fertile land
- Population pressure
- Internal conflicts
- Attack by hostile neighbours
- Human and animal diseases and other epidemics
- Natural calamities like drought and famine.
- Desire for adventure

NILOTIC SPEAKERS arrived in Kenya in three distinct groups of Nilotic communities. These were the Highland Nilotes, Plain Nilotes and River Lake Nilotes.

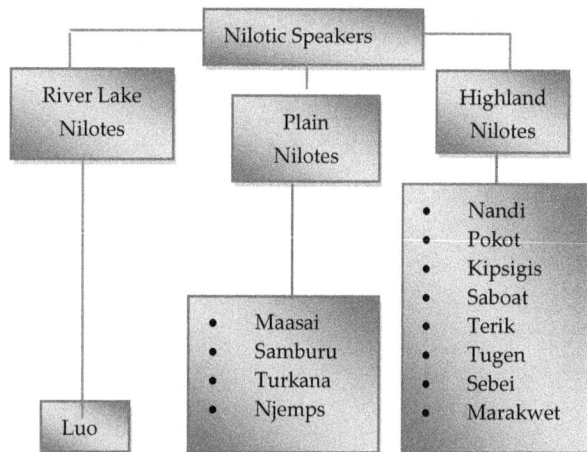

Nilotic Speakers

River Lake Nilotes	Plain Nilotes	Highland Nilotes
		• Nandi • Pokot • Kipsigis • Saboat • Terik • Tugen • Sebei • Marakwet
	• Maasai • Samburu • Turkana • Njemps	
Luo		

River Lake Nilotes are also referred to as the Luos in Kenya. They are Nilotic people who separated from other members of the Eastern Sudanic family about 3rd millennium and began migrating southwards from Bahr el Ghazal area in the early 2nd millennium A.D. This migration was probably triggered off by the medieval Muslim conquest of Sudan. The Luo temporarily settled in Northern Uganda where again they dispersed at Pabungo Pakwach region. Some of the group like Padhola, Langi and Acholi remained in Uganda while other groups moved into Kenya and Tanzania.

Reasons for the Migrations of the Luos
- Being livestock keepers, the Luos migrated to areas of new pasture and water for their animals
- They were searching for better fishing grounds
- They were escaping from either internal feuds or external conflicts.
- Population pressure from their cradle land forced them to look for new areas for settlement
- Natural calamities like drought and famine forced them to migrate
- Disease outbreak in an area made them migrate to other areas
- Some Luos were migrating to satisfy their spirit of adventure.

The Barons

The Luo were led into Kenya by Joka Jok, Joka Owiny and Joka Omolo. The Jok Luo moved deeper into the Kavirondo Gulf and forms the present day inhabitants of Kisumu and Karachuonyo. Joka Owiny moved to Got Ramogi in Yimbo before settling in Sigoma in Alego (Siaya District) while Jok Omolo settled in the present day Gem District. The last immigrants were Joka Ger who are related to Joka Omolo. They drove out the "Omiya" or Bantu group from the present day Ugenya and occupied it around 1750 A.D. The Abasuba who now identify themselves as Luos and have lost their cultural identity and language were originally Western Bantus. The Abasuba are among the hybrid communities in Kenya.

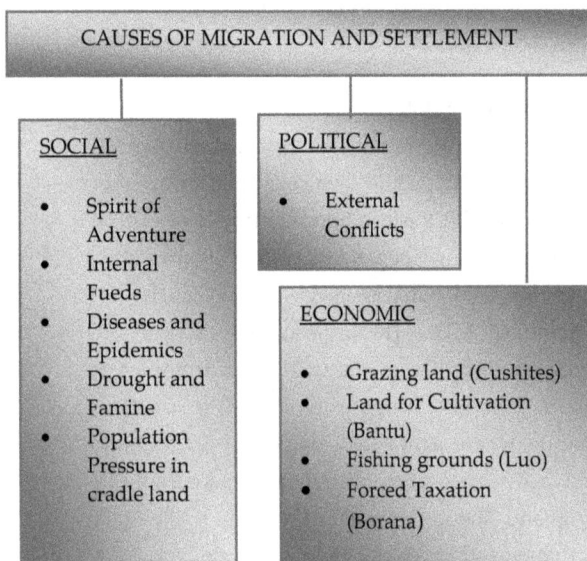

CAUSES OF MIGRATION AND SETTLEMENT

SOCIAL
- Spirit of Adventure
- Internal Fueds
- Diseases and Epidemics
- Drought and Famine
- Population Pressure in cradle land

POLITICAL
- External Conflicts

ECONOMIC
- Grazing land (Cushites)
- Land for Cultivation (Bantu)
- Fishing grounds (Luo)
- Forced Taxation (Borana)

Impact of the Migration and Settlement of the Luo in Kenya
- The luo assimilated some communities they found in the areas like Abasuba who were originally Bantus.
- They intermarried with neighbouring communities like the Abagusii and Abaluhya.
- The Luo displaced some communities – The Abagusii was displaced first from Yimbo and later from Kisumu to their present homeland.
- There were increased conflicts over the control of resources between the Luo and their neighbours.

- Expansion of trade with their neighbours– the Luo acquired iron tools from the Bantus who were skilled Iron workers.
- Occupation of fertile land influenced the Luo to adopt farming.

Plain Nilotes

The Maasai are Plain Nilotes. Other people who are closely related to them are Samburu, Turkana and Njemps.

These groups are called the *Maa* speakers. According to Maasai oral traditions, they originated from the lower Nile Valley to the north of Lake Turkana and began migrating southwards around 15th century, arriving in a long trunk of land stretching from Northern Kenya to Central Tanzania between 17th and late 18th century. Many ethnic groups that already formed settlements in the regions were forcefully evicted by the incoming Maasai while others mainly the Cushitic groups were assimilated into the Maasai society. The Maasai territory reached its largest size in the mid 19th century and covered almost all the entire floor of the Great Rift Valley and the adjacent lands from Mount Marsabit in the north to Dodoma (Tanzania) in the south.

Questions of Kenyan Societies during the Pre-colonial Time

(a) State where you would find manuscripts, stone tablets and scrolls of Kenya's history preserved

(b) Name two sources of the History of Kenyan communities during the pre - colonial period

(c) Name the main linguistic groups into which Kenyan of African origin are derived

(d) Identify two groups of the Maa speakers

(e) Identify two groups of Luos who migrated into Kenya

(f) Identify two groups of Highland Nilotes

(g) Give two examples of communities that belong to the Highland Bantu

(h) Identify three groups of Eastern Bantu

(i) Identify two hybrid communities in Kenya

(j) Name the remaining group of Southern Cushitic community

Impact of the Migration and Settlement of the Pain Nilotes

- The Maasai pushed and displaced the communities they came across
- The Maasai absorbed some groups of Southern Cushites like the Dorobo.
- They adopted some cultural practices from the Southern Cushites like circumcision and age set system.
- Some Cushites adopted Kalenjin vocabulary
- They influenced other communities such as the Nandi to adopt the institution of prophet
- A section of the Maasai acquired the practice of farming from their neighbours - the Ilolkop became mixed farmers
- The Maasai traded with their neighbours, for example the Akamba and the Agikuyu
- The Maasai intermarried with the Agikuyu and the Kalenjn
- The Maasai influenced the fighting tactics of other groups in Kenya

Highland Nilotes also known as the Kalenjin community migrated to their present location from the Southern Sudan region around 2000 years ago. They were the first group to arrive in Kenya after the Cushitic communities (Southern and Eastern Cushites). They belong to the Nilo-Saharan family. Until 1950's, the Kalenjin did not have a common name and were referred to as the Nandi speaking tribes by many scholars and the colonial administration. This practice ended in the late 1940's when a collective name was adopted.

The Kalenjin have through interactions adopted many customs and practices from the neighbouring Southern Cushitic communities. These practices include the age-set system of organization, circumcision and many words which now form their vocabulary. There are several tribal groupings within the Kalenjin community. They include: Keiyo, Elgeyo, Endorois, Kipsigis, Marakwet, Nandi, Pokot, Saboat, Terik, Tugen and Sebei

The Highland Nilotes interacted with their neighbours like the Abaluhya through intermarriage, trade, warfare, linguistic assimilation, cultural assimilation and sporting activities

---

Questions of Migration and Settlement of Kenyan societies

(a) State two environmental factors that influenced the migration of the Western Bantus
(b) What was the main reason why the Bantu migrated from Shungwaya
(c) Explain five results of the migration of the Cushites into Kenya during the pre-colonial period
(d) State two cultural practices which the Agikuyu acquired from the Gumba
(e) Explain the result of the migration and settlement of the Somali into Kenya by 1800
(f) Describe the migration and settlement of the Eastern Bantu communities in Kenya up to1800 AD
(g) What were the results of the settlement of the Luo in Kenya during the pre - colonial period?
(h) Identify the two economic activities which the Maasai acquired as a result of interacting with the Agikuyu during their settlement in Kenya
(i) Give five consequences of the interaction between the Eastern Cushites and the Bantus in Kenya.

2 ORGANIZATION OF KENYAN SOCIETIES DURING THE PRE-COLONIAL TIMES

THE AKAMBA

Economic Organization

- The Kamba practiced farming along rivers and grew crops like potatoes, yams and bananas. They also kept animals, for example cattle, sheep and goats.
- Most of them lived in hostile environments which did not favour agricultural activities hence depended on long distance trade for subsistence.
- The Kamba were skilled hunters and acquired ivory and slaves from the interior which they took to the coast to exchange with the Arabs and Swahili traders.
- Kamba women specialized in making pots using black and red soil. They also weaved baskets and mats.
- The Kamba were skilled craftsmen and curved many things, for example wooden stools.
- The Kamba harvested honey from bees which they kept.

Political Organization

- The Kamba were traditionally a decentralized society.
- The smallest political unit was the homestead (*Musyi*) and several related families formed a clan. Usually, the clans occupied same places.
- A council of elders was constituted by all male elders.
- The council settled disputes, offered advice to community when need arose and had power to declare war or make peace. They were also the custodians of the social code of ethics in the society.
- The Kamba elders were ranked according to seniority, for example junior elders defended the society, and medium elders (Nthele) assisted in administration while full elders delivered judgment. Most senior elders were involved in religious activities.
- There was a larger grouping than a clan called *Kivalo* among the Kamba which constituted the fighting unit. *Kivalo* was disbanded when there was peace

Social Organization

- The Kamba believed in a supreme god called *Mulungu* and in the existing of ancestral spirits.
- They worshiped this spirits in sacred places (shrines).
- In the society were special people, for example the traditional healers who treated the sick and the diviners who foretold the future.
- They initiated the youth into adulthood through circumcision. This involved both boys and girls. The initiates joined age-sets after circumcision.
- Senior elders presided over religious ceremonies.

Questions on Social, economic and Political Organization of the Kamba

(a) Describe the economic organization of the Akamba during the pre-colonial period

(b) Describe the political organization of the Akamba

(c) Describe the social organization of the Akamba during the pre-colonial period

(d) Give two functions of the council of elders among the Akamba during pre-colonial period

THE AMERU
Political Organization

- The Ameru had a decentralized system of government.
- The family was the basic unit and it was headed by the father. Several families made up a clan which was headed by clan elders.
- The roles of the council of elders included: - settling disputes, deliberating on day to day activities, administering justice and handling disputes affecting individuals.
- They also had a council of senior elders called *Njuri Ncheke* whose functions included solving wrangles over land and inheritance. *Njuri Ncheke* also acted as a court of appeal, advised warriors on when to go for raids, negotiated peace settlement and made laws governing the community.
- They had warriors who defended the community from external aggressions.
- Religious leaders like *Riaboni* or prophets influenced the political administration of the Ameru in a number of ways. He was a political arbitrator, a military strategist and the custodian of Ameru traditions and customs.

Social Organization

- The Ameru believed in a supreme god called *Merungu*. He lived in the sky. Prayers and scarifies were offered to him on special occasions.
- They believed that ancestral spirits existed and kept watch over them. Libations were offered to the spirits to quench their thirst and relieve their hunger.
- The family was the basic social unit and several families made up a clan. The clans were further sub-divided into three namely: *Njiru, Njeru* and *Ntuune*.
- Ameru had strong kinship ties through blood brothers. They also had a system of age-sets based on circumcision for boys and

girls. Each age set covered a period of 10 – 15 years.
- Work was divided according to gender, for example women built houses while men defended the community.
- They practiced exogamous marriages and marriage within the clan was prohibited.
- They had a class of highly respected specialists known as *Aroria* or a prophet who acted as a seer and an agent of god, and medicine men who treated the sick using herbal medicine

---

Questions on Social, economic and Political Organization of the Ameru

(a) Explain the social organization of the Ameru during the pre-colonial period
(b) Describe the political organisation of the Ameru in Kenya during the pre-colonial period
(c) State two characteristics of the Ameru Raiboni (king)
(d) State two functions of the council of elders (Njuri Ncheke) of the Ameru

---

THE MIJIKENDA

inhabit the coastal region of Kenya between the Sabaki and Umba Rivers. The outsiders called them the *"Nyika"* which was a derogatory term meaning, "bush people." They speak the Sabaki Bantu language.

Economic Activities

- The Mijikenda were farmers. They cultivated crops, for example millet, yams and beans, and also kept animals like cattle, sheep and goats.
- These were supplemented with the animals they hunted, and the fruits and honey they gathered.
- Women made clay pots which were exchanged with items from their neighbours.
- They engaged in fishing activities along the coast and in rivers. They also participated in the coastal trade with the Arabs, Swahili and the Akamba traders.

The Barons

Political Organization

- The Mijikenda had a decentralized system of government and were organized into clans made up of related families.
- These clans were governed by a council of elders called the *Kambi*.
- The *Kambi* acted as the final court of appeal and could administer punishments like imposing fines, ordering for the return of stolen property and banishing errand members of the society from the *Kaya*. The *Kambi* was also in charge of both internal and external affairs and could declare war.
- The Mijikenda lived in fortified places called *Kaya*. This was a sacred place which provided security for the group.
- Intermarriage between clans was encouraged to strengthen their political unity.
- A group of young warriors defended the community from external attack.

Social Organization

- The Mijikenda believed in one god called *Mulungu* and in the existence of spirits which they worshiped.
- They also had prophets who were referred to as *Wafisi*.
- Their ceremonies were marked with songs and dances.
- When boys and girls became of age, they underwent circumcision. The initiates then formed age-sets.
- They had clans which claimed a common ancestry and marriage within the same clan was prohibited.

- The Mijikenda were polygamous and they respected elders.
- Boys and girls specialized in different activities.

Questions on Social, economic and Political Organization of the Mijikenda

(a) Describe the economic activities of the Mijikenda during the pre-colonial era

(b) Describe the social organization of the Mijikenda during the pre – colonial period

(c) Describe the political organization of the Mijikenda during the pre-colonial period

(d) State two functions of the kambi among the Mijikenda

(e) State three punishments which could be imposed by the Kambi

---

THE AGIKUYU
Economic Organization

- Agikuyu were agriculturalists who practiced mixed farming. On one hand they grew millet, pumpkins, and yams and on the other they kept animals like cattle, sheep and goats.
- Hunting was done by men while gathering was done by the Agikuyu women.
- Agikuyu traded with their neighbours, for example the Maasai and the Akamba. They exchanged their grains and iron implements for livestock products with the Maasai.
- The Agikuyu were iron workers and produced iron tools such as hoes, spears and knives. They borrowed this iron technology from the Gumba.

Political Organization

- Agikuyu had a decentralized system of administration and each man headed his household.
- They had clans made up of several sub-clans called *Mbari*. These descended from a common ancestry and lived in the same ridge.
- Each ridge was under a spokesman called *Muthamaki*. Good personality and

leadership skills enabled one to acquire this role.
- Sub-clans were ruled by council of elders called *Kiama*.

Kikuyu council of elders

- This council performed administrative and judicial roles in the society, declared war and was also the custodians of the community customs, norms and values.
- Activities of the clan were co-ordinated by a senior elder called *muramati*.
- Several elders formed a higher council of elders which acted as a court of appeal and administration of justice.
- The age-set provided the warriors who defended the community from external attack

Kikuyu Warriors

Social Organization

- Agikuyu believed in one powerful god called *Ngai* who was all powerful and controlled life. *Ngai* dwelt on Mount Kenya and was their creator.
- They also believed in ancestral spirits who were honoured by pouring libations to appease them.

- Worship was done in sacred places like under a *mugumo* tree where they also offered sacrifice.
- They practiced polygamous marriage and this was a very important institution in the society.
- There were important people in the society like the prophets who could foretell the future, diviners who interpreted god's message to people and medicine men who cured various ailments. The medicine men acquired their art through apprenticeship.
- Circumcision was one of the rites of passage among the Agikuyu and all girls and boys were initiated together when they became of age. During this time the youths were taught societal values and customs and how to behave responsibly as future husbands and wives.
- After the initiation ceremony, presided by the council of elders, the initiates joined the age– set which were called *riika*.

Questions on Social, economic and Political Organization of the Agikuyu

(f) Describe the social organization of the Agikuyu during the pre-colonial time

(g) Give two functions of the councils of elders in the pre-colonial Kenya.

(h) Describe the political organization of the Agikuyu during the pre-colonial time

THE ABAGUSII
Economic Organization

- Both livestock rearing and crop cultivation were important economic activities among Abagusii. From the animals they got milk, meat and skins.
- Hunting and gathering were also practiced.
- The Abagusii were skilled iron workers and made spears, arrows and knives which they used to defend the society.
- Various baskets and soapstone items were also made

- Trade was conducted between them and their neighbouring communities like the Luo, the Kipsigis and the Abaluhya.

Political Organization

- The Abagusii had a decentralized political system of administration.
- Fathers took care of the management of their households.
- The society was organized into clans made up of several related families.
- Abagusii had chiefs called *omogambi* and council of elders.
- The Abagusii council of elders solved land, marital and inheritance disputes, maintained law and order, and disciplined the law breakers in the society.
- After initiation, the young boys became warriors whose duty was to defend the society in case it was attacked by neighbouring communities.

Social Organization

- The Abagusii believed in the existence of a powerful god called *Engoro* who created everything and in the ancestral spirits.
- Elders prayed to god directly or made intercessions through ancestral spirits.
- They were grouped into clans sharing a common ancestry. Though they practiced polygamy, marriage within the clan was not allowed.
- Circumcision of boys and girls formed part of their initiation rites. During this period, the initiates were taught about their customs, secretes and important values of the society.
- After this ceremony, those who had been initiated were considered as adults and could be given responsibilities which were reserved for the same.
- For greater unity, a clan associated itself with a special creature or object.
- Among the Abagusii were people with special duties. These included the diviners,

seers and priests. Witches and sorcerers who used their charm and evil spirits to cause suffering to people, eixisted among the Abagusii and were hated.

Questions on Social, economic and Political Organization of the Abagusii

(a) Explain the economic organization of the Abagusii during the pre-colonial period

(b) Explain the Socio- political organization of the Abagusii during the pre-colonial period

---

THE ABALUHYA
Economic Organization

- Both livestock rearing and crop cultivation were important economic activities, among the Abaluhya.
- Certain communities within the Luhya community had blacksmiths who made iron implements.
- The Abaluhya practiced hunting and gathering.
- They also practiced weaving of baskets.

Political Organization

- Some societies had decentralized system of government and the family was the basic political unit.
- A village was ruled by a council of elders called *Abeneng*. Several villages formed one big group called *Olukongo*. The head of Lukongo was called *Mukongo* who was both a political and religious leader.
- The Abawanga had a centralized sytem of government. Its king was known as Nabongo.
- Under the king were various councils and administrators.
- They had a group of junior warriors who graduated to elders when they retired
- The warriors defended the society against external attack.

Social Organizations

- Age-groups were the basis of organization of the Abuluhya society at the clan level.
- The Abaluhya believed in a supreme being called Were or Nyasaye.
- Intermediaries, usually ancestral spirits, assisted in praying to god.
- Boys of the same age were circumcised together to subsequently form an age group. In some clans, girls were also circumcised.
- Bull fighting and wrestling were important pass time activity among the Abaluhya.

THE NANDI
Economic Organization

- The Nandi practiced mixed economy. They kept animals, for example cattle, sheep and goats, and also grew crops like millet and sorghum.
- They depended on animals for meat, milk and skins. Having many cattle enhanced one's esteem in the society.
- Cattle raids were conducted to boost the stock held.
- Cattle were used to settle dowry and as a means of exchange.
- Hunting was a preserve for men while women did gathering.

Political Organization

- The Nandi had a decentralized political system and the family was the basic political unit.
- The father dealt with disciplinary matters and allocated land, cattle and crops to family members.
- The family was assisted by a council of elders called *Kokwet* which dealt with grazing rights.
- Above the clan was the *pororiet* which occupied a wider region and fought jointly. The *Pororiet* could negotiate for peace and declared war.

- A group of young warriors: maintained law and order in the society, defended it against external attack and above all raided other communities to acquire livestock to replenish their stock.
- *Orkoyoit* played many political roles in the society. These were:
  - ✓ Advising the council of elders on matters pertaining to the day to day running of the community.
  - ✓ Acting as an arbitrator in disputes between council of elders and between the clans.
  - ✓ Advising and blessing warriors before they went for war.

Masaai moran after the circumcision operation, cattle were slaughtered, and a ritual fire traditionally ignited by the elders of the tribe. The liver of a slaughtered ox, a choice cut, was roasted over a wood fire taken from the master fire of the elders.

Functions of Orkoiyot among the Nandi
(a) Advice council of elders
(b) Settle disputes between council of elders and between clans
(c) Advice and bless worriors
(d) Was the chief medicine man
(e) Presided over religious ceremonies
(f) Mediated between people and god
(g) Was consulted during time of crisis or calamity
(h) Had prophetic powers and could foretell the future

The Barons

Social Organization

- The Nandi worshiped one god called *Asis* who created everything.
- They also believed in the existence of spirits which were venerated through libations and sacrifice.
- Special groups of people existed among them. This included diviners, rainmakers and medicine men. *Orkoyoit* was the chief medicine man in the society.
- Boys and girls were initiated through circumcision. This ceremony was important because:
    - ✓ The boys who were circumcised together joined one age-set. Unity was enhanced among the people who were initiated together and were part of a common age-set.
    - ✓ Once it was performed the boys became warriors.
    - ✓ Circumcision made one change from childhood to adulthood. It was only then that one was allowed to marry.
    - ✓ Important secrets of the society were taught during this time.
- The initiated youths among the Nandi formed a group of young warriors who served in this capacity for 15 years before graduating to senior warriors.
- *Orkoiyot* who acted as a priest among the Nandi, presided over religious ceremonies, mediated between the people and god and offered sacrifice on peoples' behalf. He was consulted during times of crisis or when a calamity like drought befell the society. *Orkoyoit* had prophetic powers and could foretell the future, for instance success in war, impending famine and a calamity.

THE MAASAI
Economic Activities

- The Maasia were divided into two: the Purko and Kwavi. The former practiced nomadic pastoralism and kept cattle, sheep and goats. This group depended entirely on animal products like milk, meat and blood for their survival. The latter practiced mixed farming. They kept livestock and also grew crops such as grains.
- The Maasai mined salt and red ochre which they used for decoration and as a commodity for trade.
- They practiced iron-smelting and made implements like spears and arrow heads.
- Maasai were involved in craftwork, for example making pots, weaving baskets and making leather belts.
- Trade was conducted among themselves and with their neighbouring communities, for example the Agikuyu, the Abagusii and the Kalenjin community.

Political Organization

- The Maasai had a decentralized system of government.
- They were ruled by a council of elders who consisted of ritual leaders, clan heads and family heads. The council of elders: -
    - ✓ Maintained law and order
    - ✓ Made decisions about ceremonies
    - ✓ Declared war and
    - ✓ Settled disputes.
- One of their most important ritual leaders was *Oloiboni*. By the 19th century the institution of *Oloiboni* had become quite influential. The notable *Oloibons* during the near past were Lenana and Mbatian. *Oloibon's* political duties were:
    - ✓ Advising the council of elders when they were to make an important decision affecting the whole community.
    - ✓ Blessing and advising warriors before they went for war.
    - ✓ Offering pieces of advice to the community during trying moments or when there was a calamity.
- A class of warriors called *morans* existed among the Maasai. The *morans* carried out

raids to replenish their livestock and defend the community.

- The age set system was an important institution among the Maasai and they had several such sets.
- Each age-set had a leader or spokesman and the leadership role was exercised in turns.

Social Organization

- The Maasai believed in the existence of one god called *Enkai* and offered sacrifice to him under trees.
- Among them were also religious leaders who included diviners and medicine men.
- Maasai had ritual leaders whose functions were to preside over religious functions and to advise the community when there was a catastrophe. *Oloibon* was one of the most significant ritual leaders among the Maasai. His duties social duties included: -
  ✓ Seeking guidance from *Enkai* during calamities.
  ✓ Treating the sick.
  ✓ Protecting people and cattle against evil spirits.
  ✓ Conducted religious ceremonies.
- Every 15 year or so, boys of between 12 - 25 years were initiated together and they formed an age-set. This was an important way of bonding the Maasai. Cultural dances and songs were performed for a number of days to mark this occasion.

- *Eunoto* was performed immediately after this exercise. This ceremony was performed when a new generation of warriors was created to replace the old ones after circumcision. The older group graduated into junior elders.
- Young women also underwent excision (female circumcision) as part of an elaborated rite of passage called *Emuratara*.
- This was a ceremony that initiated the young Maasai girls into adulthood and then into early marriage.

Questions on Social, economic and Political Organization of the Nandi and Maasai

(a) Describe the social organisation of the Nandi during the pre-colonial period in Kenya
(b) Explain the functions of the Orkoiyot among the Nand during the pre-colonial time
(c) Describe the economic organisation of the Nandi during pre – colonial period
(d) Describe the political organisation of the Nandi during the pre – colonial period
(e) State five economic activities of the Maasai in the pre-colonial period
(f) Identify two social activities of the Maasai during the pre-colonial era
(g) Describe the political organization of the Maasai during the pre- colonial period
(h) State two social roles of the Laibon among the Maasai community in Kenya during the pre-colonial time

THE LUO
Economic Organization

- The Luos were mainly pastoralists and fishermen.
- They kept cattle, sheep and goats. Having a large stock of animals was considered prestigious in the society. Animals provided milk and blood (*riga*), but were occasionally slaughtered for meat. Luos used animal skins for their beddings (*piende*), a form of clothing and to make shield to protect them during the war.
- Dowry was paid using animals, especially cattle and goats.

- The Luos lived around swampy areas and near rivers and lakes. These areas were ideal for fishing.
- They adopted farming activities from the Bantus and grew crops like millet, sorghum and cassava. *Ugali* was their staple food.
- Luos made clay pots and weaved baskets and mats (*par*).
- Trade was conducted among them and with neighbouring communities, says the Abaluhya, Abagusii and Nandi. Hunting was done by men while women gathered wild vegetables and fruits to supplement their diet.

Political Organization

- The Luo had a decentralized form of government.
- At the lowest political level was the family headed by the father. Several related families (*anyuola*) formed a clan within which existed a council of elders called *Doho*.

Luo Warriors

- The Luo council of elders: -
  - ✓ Dealt with important matters in the society, for example murder, stock theft and boundary disputes.
  - ✓ Declared war or negotiated peace with adversaries.
  - ✓ Admitted strangers into their land or expelled the undesirable individuals in the society.
  - ✓ Was the custodian of the land.
  - ✓ Advised *Ruoth*.

  - ✓ Was the final court of appeal.
- A group of clans formed a higher council called *oganda*. This was headed by a leader who was called *Routh*. This council (*oganda*) settled major disputes in the society.

Social Organization

- The Luos were deeply religious and had one god called *Nyasaye*. They believed in the existence of spirits (*Juogi*). Some spirits were good and others were bad. The bad spirits haunted people and some diseases were attributed to them. Ceremonies like *Nyawawa* were done to cleanse the society from such spirits.
- Sacrifice and libations were performed to appease the spirits and children were named after the departed relatives. This kept the spirits of the dead relatives alive.

A Luo Medicine Man

- Among the Luo were people with supernatural powers. This included the medicine men and rainmakers. There were also witches and sorcerers who used their supernatural powers to cause harm.
- People of common ancestry made up a clan and kinship was enhanced through it.
- Marriage within the same clan was considered a taboo. Inter clan marriage was encouraged to promote good relations among the Luos.
- Polygamy was practiced and having many wives and children was considered an important virtue in the society.

- The Luo youth underwent initiation at puberty. This involved the removal of six teeth from the lower jaw. The gap between the teeth could be used to feed the terminally ill and could also be used for identification. Marriage was only allowed after this act.

- There was informal learning among them. The youth for instance, spent much time with their grand parents who told them many stories about the society and how the society expected them to behave responsibly.

Questions on Social, economic and Political Organization of the Luo

(a) Describe the Socio-political organisation of the Luos

(b) Describe the economic organization of the Luos

(c) State five functions of the council of elders among the Luos

---

THE SOMALI
Political Organization

- The basic political unit of the Somali was the clan.

- A council of elders was in charge of the day - to day affairs of the clan, for example: -
   ✓ Making major clan decisions
   ✓ Settling disputes.
   ✓ Maintaining law and orders
   ✓ The final court of appeal.

- The age set system was an important institute among the Somali and all male members of the society belonged to the age - set. Each age set performed specific duties.

- The Somali had leaders called Sultan whose role was mainly advisory

- They had warriors whose main duty was to protect the community against external attacks and acquire possessions for the community,

- They had people with special responsibilities like Sheikhs and medicine men who were highly regarded in the community and their opinions were sought before important decisions were made.

THE BORANA
Political Organization

- The Borana had a decentralized system of government and were organize into clans.

- Each clan was headed by the council of elders

- The main function was to maintain law and order, settle disputes and organized territorial defense through the warrior council called *Harriya*.

- Their clans were autonomous except in times of war or natural disasters when they would form a clan alliance

- Borana had a complex age–group and age set system which provided a military base for the society. The age set was called *gada*

- Borana were divided politically into two main sub-tribes (*moleties*) which formed basic units of political organization. *Moieties* were further divided into sub moieties through separate lineage.

- The sub tribes had a hereditary leader known as *Kallu* whose camp was the political and spiritual centre.

- The *Kallu* was a spiritual leader and his main duty was to solve conflicts between clans and in his moiety with the help of the elders.

- Handing over of leadership was done through the performance of the *butta* ceremony.

- Unity was enhanced by ownership of wells and kinship ties.

- The age – sets provided warriors who defended the community.

Social Organization

- The Borana worshiped a supreme creator god called Wak. However, in 19th century majority of them were converted to Islam.

- The whole community was divided into two sub-groups called '*moieties*.' These were further divided into sub moieties and then into *Kallu*.

- The Kallu's camp was a holy and political centre of the group
- The Borana had ritual ceremonies which united them.
- They practices exogamous marriages
- The system of inheritance was patrilineal and property was inherited from father to the son

THE CUSHITES

Economic Activities

- The Cushites practiced pastoralism. They kept camels, goats, cattle and donkeys.
- Some of Cushites who lived near oasis or along river valleys practiced subsistence agriculture. They grew grains, vegetables, dates and bananas.
- They practiced iron smelting and made iron implements like Swords, knives, bangles and arrowheads.
- They hunted wild game and gathered roots, vegetables and fruits.
- They engaged in craft industry and produced leather items such as handbags, belts and clothing.
- Some of the Cushites who lived near rivers and along the Indian Ocean practiced fishing.
- They exchanged their iron implements and leather products with their neighbours, such as the Samburu and Pokomo.

Social Organization

- The Cushites were organized according to clans which consisted of related families.
- They believed in existence of one god called *wak*
- They had religious leaders who mediated between god and the people.
- Duties were assigned to Cushites according to their gender
- They practiced exogamous and polygamous marriages

- Some Cushites adopted Islam and Islamic culture
- They circumcised of boys at teenage years

Political Organization

- Their political system was based on clannism
- Clans were headed by council of elders
- Council of elders had the following duties:
  - ✓ Presiding over religious ceremonies
  - ✓ Settling disputes
  - ✓ Acted as ritual expert
  - ✓ Maintain law and order
- They had warriors to defend the community
- They had the age-set and age group system.

Functions of age sets during pre-colonial time
(a) Defined leadership roles
(b) Provided warriors at a certain time before retirement to defend the community
(c) Created sense of comradeship and belonging
(d) Reduced conflicts between different members of the community
(e) Prepared the initiates for marriage and adult life

Questions on Social, economic and Political Organization of the Cushites
(a) Describe the economic activities of the Cushites in the pre - colonial period
(b) Describe the socio-political organization of the Cushites
(c) Discuss the social political organization of the Boran during the pre-colonial era
(d) Describe the political organization of the Somali in Kenya during the colonial period
(e) Describe the political organization of most Kenyan societies during the pre-colonial time

3 CITIZENSHIP AND NATIONAL INTEGRATION

Citizenship is the legal right of an individual to belong to a particular country. People who are legible for citizenship in the country are:

- Persons who are Kenyan citizen by descent (birth).
- Woman who are married to Kenyan men.
- Commonwealth citizen who have resided in Kenya for a period specified by law.
- Citizen of African countries which allow Kenyans to register as citizens.

Two ways are used in Kenya to acquire citizenship: birth and registration. A citizen by birth either is a child whose parents are citizens of Kenya or has been adopted. A citizen by birth does not cease to become a Kenyan citizen if he/she acquires citizenship of another country. This is because the current constitution allows Kenyans to hold dual citizenship.

Registered citizens are people from other parts who have applied for consideration and have been accepted as Kenyans. Registered citizens can be persons married to Kenyans (Naturalized), adopted children and people of good conduct who have resided in the country for at least seven years. It is important for married people who would wish to be naturalized in the country to: -

- Be above 21 years of age.
- Have lived in Kenya for at least seven years.
- Prove that they will continue living in the country after naturalization.
- Satisfy the Cabinet Secretary in charge of migration that they are of good conduct.
- Satisfy the same Cabinet Secretary that they know Kiswahili language.

The government reserves the right to deregister citizens who have acquired citizenship through registration. Conditions which may force the government to deprive one of such citizenship include:

- Showing through act or speech, disloyalty or disaffection towards Kenya.
- Direct participation in a war against the country.
- Trading or giving any other form of assistance to the enemy of Kenya.
- Imprisonment by a court of law in any country for a period of more than twelve months within a period of five years starting from the date of registration or naturalization.
- Continuously residing in countries other than Kenya for a period of seven years during which period one is neither in the service of Kenya nor in an international organization for which Kenya is a affiliated to.
- Obtaining citizenship through fraud, false representation or concealment of material fact.
- Rejection by parliament of ones citizenship.
- Being convicted of treason at any time of registration.

Children whose parents or country of origin cannot be determined become citizens by birth as long as they are under the age of eight. The government may deregister such children if:

- The age of the person become known and reveals that the person was older than 8 years when found in Kenya
- It is later determined that there was some fraud involved in the registration exercise and
- It is established that the child was of another nationality.

Elements of Good Kenyan Citizen

(a) Obedience, hard work and commitment to duty
(b) Being mindful of other people's welfare, especially those in need.
(c) Maintaining high moral and ethical standards
(d) Being loyal and patriotic to the country
(e) Proper utilization of public utilities
(f) Respecting other people's views and property

- A good Kenya citizen should be one who obeys the laws of the country in order to promote peace and harmonious relations.
- Respecting other people, their views and property is also another important virtue which would ensure a peaceful co-existence among people.
- A responsible citizen ensures that law and order is maintained in the county and this he/she does by reporting wrong doers or suspected criminals to the relevant authorities.
- Offering positive criticism to the government to promote good governance and accountability in the country.
- Individual Kenyan citizens should not remain aloof or distant themselves from government operations or organizations which are publicly held.

How public participates in the running of government

- Contesting for elections or voting for leaders of their choice. They have a duty of weeding out bad leaders instead of blaming them later.
- Attending civic meeting and debating on issues affecting the state, for example how public funds are spent, insecurity and ethnicity. By doing this citizens hold the government and public organizations accountable for their activities.
- Paying tax to enable the government fund its operations.

The constitution guarantees every Kenyan some fundamental rights which are upheld by the judiciary and are recognized both in Kenya and internationally. These include:

- The right to life: Life of a person begins at conception and continues until one dies of natural causes. Attempting to terminate another person's life or own life is a criminal offence punishable by the law.

- The right to assemble, to demonstrate, and to present petition to public authorities as long as it is done peacefully.
- The right to either individually or in a group associate with others, to acquire property and own it.
- The right to marry a person of opposite sex, based on the free consent of the other.
- Has an inherent dignity and the right to have that dignity respected and protected
- Equality before the law: has the right to equal protection and equal benefit of the law
- The right to freedom and security, for example being subjected to any form of violence, torture or corporal punishment
- The right to privacy, for example searching their home or property.
- The right to freedom of expression, for example academic freedom and freedom to seek or receive information
- Is free to make political choices, for example right to form or participate in forming a political party and to elect candidates of his/her choice.
- The right to fair labour practices, for example fair remuneration and to go on strike

---

Questions on Citizenship

(a) State two types of citizens according to the new constitution

(b) Give two conditions which must be met by one to be a registered citizen in Kenya

(c) State two conditions that one has to meet in order to be naturalized as a Kenyan citizen

(d) State two conditions under which a citizen by birth may be revoked

(e) Explain six conditions which may force the government of Kenya to deprive off a register Kenyan citizenship

(f) State two ways in which Kenya citizens participates in the running of the government

(g) Explain six responsibilities of a good Kenyan citizen

(h) State five elements of good Kenyan citizen

(i) Explain six fundamental rights enjoyed by Kenyan citizens

NATIONAL INTEGRATION

simply means cohesion (togetherness) of people in a country. Kenyans today interact in different ways. This include: -

- Working in the same workplace or region
- Learning in the same schools
- Trading together
- Participating in cultural activities like sports
- Staying in the same residential places

Symbols of national unity are used to depict this unity. According to the new constitution, the symbols are:

- Court of arms
- National Flag
- National Anthem and
- Public seal.

Official government documents bear Public Seal and the Court of Arms to make them authentic. The same applies to the National Flag which is hosted in public places to symbolize the presence of government. The president's portrait symbolizes national unity and his authority hence; it is a requirement that it is hanged in public places.

National Anthem is a special song and it is sung:

- Every time when the National Flag is raised or lowered.
- During national heads of state meetings.
- When commemorating public holidays.
- During international sports events where Kenya is participating.
- When national radio and television begins to broadcast or closes broadcasting.

Methods Used to Promote National Unity

Kiswahili has been used in the country as one of the corner stones in the government's effort to enhance unity in the country since independence. To achieve this:

- Kiswahili has been made one of the official languages of communication in the country.
- Kiswahili has been made compulsory and examinable in national examinations.

Using Kiswahili reduces misconception which would arise because of a barrier in communication between people of diverse ethnicity.

Efforts have been made to ensure equitable distributions of resources and available opportunities for Kenyan so as to bridge the gap between different regions and between the rich and the poor members of the society. To achieve this: -

- A policy of decentralization of services and industries has been put in place to enables many Kenyans to have equal access to good amenities like schools and hospitals.
- Improvements are being made in the infrastructure, for example tarmacking more roads, and availing piped water and electricity to the rural parts of Kenya.
- The policy of recruiting Kenyans across the country, for instance in the Police and Army gives many people a chance of being employed especially in the government sector and to serve in different parts of the county.
- Devolution of government enables the government to disburse equal funds to all regions. The same applies to the Constituency Development Funds (CDF) which is allocated to all constituencies.

The Kenyan constitution has been used to promote national unity in a number of ways. This includes:

- Guaranteeing equal opportunities for all
- Subjecting all citizens to the same laws
- Guaranteeing equal rights and freedom
- Protecting all citizens from all forms of discrimination
- Outlining clearly the type of government that people have chosen

- Giving guidelines on the type of leaders the people have agreed to have and the power they should be given

National unity is encouraged through sporting activities and cultural interactions among Kenyans. Promoting the latter is not only important because the activities promote unity in the country, but because they also provide: -
- Entertainment
- Education, especially the informal type.
- Create employment opportunities and
- Enhance patriotism among Kenyans.

The government has created a slot for sports and culture in one of its cabinet portfolios in recognition of this important fact. Sporting activities are encouraged in the country to rally people together. The same applies to National Drama and Music Festivals which are held annually and this brings together many students from schools and colleges all over the country.

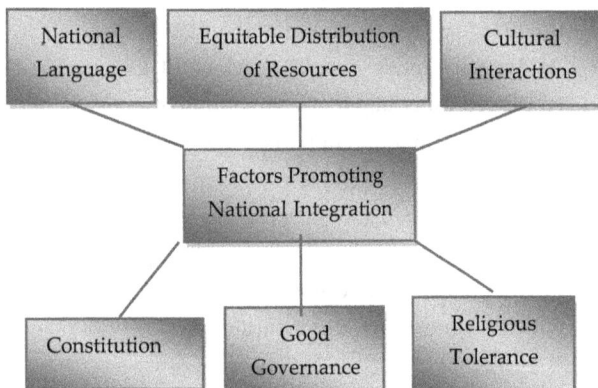

Education is used to promote national unity by:
- Encouraging students and pupils from different ethnic backgrounds to learn together in both public and national schools.
- Making students to sit for the same examination and to be taught the same syllabus.

- Teaching subjects which promote patriotism and demystify cultural differences.
- Building more schools of excellence and nationals schools across the country.
- Encouraging students to socialize in different co-curriculum activities like games and festivals like drama and music.
- Posting teachers to work in all parts of Kenya regardless of their ethnicity.

Fundamental rights of Kenyans are protected in the constitution. The citizens are free to mingle and own property in every part of the country. Protecting people's rights is important because it reduces anarchy in the country and promotes a peaceful co-existence.

Importance of National Integration
(a) Promotes peaceful co-existence among people of Kenya
(b) Enhances the achievement of national goals
(c) Reduces ethnic tension, mistrust and suspicion
(d) Enhances easier and efficient communication in the country
(e) Facilitates equitable distribution of resources in the country
(f) Promotes patriotism and cultivates a sense of identity
(g) Promotes national language and understanding of people, working towards one direction

---

Steps undertaken to promote national integration since independence in Kenya
(a) Adoption of a unitary government with one presidency to rally all Kenyan together
(b) Adoption of a constitution which guarantees individual rights
(c) Encouraging national cultural activities and festivals like Drama and Music
(d) Formulation of national philosophies like Harambee and Nyayo
(e) Adoption of education policy that stresses multi racial and ethnic integration
(f) Equitable distribution of resources and appointments in the country
(g) Making Kiswahili a national language

Factors that Discourage National Unity

Tribalism is the biggest threat to unity in the country because:

- The desire to ascend to power using all possible means is directly linked to this vice.
- People in position of leadership use the opportunity to employ their tribesmen or siblings.
- Other people feel neglected and this drives people into their tribal cocoons.
- Conflicts sometimes arise between the people who seem favoured and those who are not.

Corruption is a very bad vice and favours only the rich in the society. It creates disunity because: -

- It widens the gap between the rich and the poor in the society thus creating enmity and suspicion between the affluent groups and the less to do.
- Encourages the rich and powerful to exploit other members of the society.
- The rich bribe their way to employment and to be served at the expense of the poor who may be more deserving.
- Corrupt people use their money to bribe the poor and ascend to power. Such people promote bad governance because they are not accountable to the people who elect them and they develop tendencies of clinging to power.
- Promotes unbalanced distribution of national resources

Unequal distribution of resources creates regional inequalities. People in areas deemed to be backward feel neglected by the government and this leads to regional hostilities. In arid area of Kenya, where resources like water and grazing land are scarce, people fight to control these resources and to keep others away. Extreme poverty also makes people to develop undesirable characteristics like stealing which create antagonism in the society.

Poor governance breeds anarchy in the country. People who have lost confidence in the government become riotous, unruly and disloyal to the government. Governments become dictatorial, resort to violent means to suppress people and liquidate those perceived to be enemies of development or the establishment.

Religious intolerance segregates people into religious enclaves. Dogmatic clerics indoctrinate their faithful with anti-establishment slogans. The radicalized youths sometimes clash with the police when they take law into their hands and do mischief.

Questions on National Integration

(a) Identify three occasions when the Kenyan National Anthem is sung
(b) What is the importance of hanging the portrait of the President in public places?
(c) State five factors that promote national unity in Kenya
(d) State five factors that discourage national unity
(e) Give two ways in which corruption undermines national unity in Kenya
(f) State Two ways how the Kenyan constitution is used to promote national unity
(g) State five ways in which national integration is important in Kenya today
(h) Explain five ways in which the Government of Kenya has tried to promote national integration since independence.

CONFLICTS AND CONFLICT RESOLUTION

A conflict is a disagreement between two or more parties. It has two elements. These are the causes of the conflict and the two opposing sides involved in it. A conflict can arise between two individuals, between two groups or between states. A conflict can also arise between a state and other states. Individuals can have conflict with groups or with a state. Sometimes a state may have a conflict with a group.

Economic Causes of Conflicts

- When people attempt to control the scarce resources (minerals, water points in dry areas and arable land) a war often breaks out between them.
- Low wages cause conflicts between the employers who believe in maximizing their profits by paying less and the employees who demand for more wages and better terms of service.
- Fraudulent practices disadvantage the more deserving people who lack the means for bribery.
- Traders who sell or give arms to protagonists fuel the already volatile situations.
- Economic disparities between people lead to conflict between the rich and the poor who may resort to vices like stealing from the rich.

Political Causes of Conflicts

- Party leaders rally their ethnic groups to gunner support and this segregates the country into tribal cohorts. Ethnic clashes in Kenya are therefore more common during the electioneering periods and fizzles out immediately thereafter.
- Tribalistic tendencies breed hatred between people who are favoured by their tribesmen in leadership position and those who are sidelined.
- Poor governance and leadership makes leaders fail to respect their own laws or human rights. This causes civil strife in the country and fertile grounds for riots and protests.
- Greed for leadership makes people cling to power and this force others to use violent means to dethrone them.
- Irresponsible utterance by leaders leads to incitement of people against others.

Social Causes of Conflicts

- Religious intolerances create bad relations between people of different sects.
- Misunderstanding other peoples' norms and customary practices creates misconceptions about them.

Koffi Annan – Chief Mediator in Kenya

Peaceful Method of Conflict Resolution

- Negotiation (reconciliation) – involves having a dialogue between the two warring parties.
- Mediation – a person not involved in the conflict tries to help the warring parties to reach an agreeable solution.
- Arbitration – informal court where a neutral person is chosen to resolve the dispute. He/she listens to both sides and help them to reach an agreeable solution
- Litigation or court system – one party takes another to court
- Problem solving – where the conflicting parties talk in the presence of facilitators. The people involved in the conflict must participate in trying to work out a resolution to the problem
- Administrative process through the chief or sub chiefs to bring warring clans together

Use of force to resolve conflicts

The police and the military can also be used to quell violence in a country. This is done when:

- When law and order is broken and the alternative is the use of force.
- In case of serious unrest.
- When students or workers strike and become unruly.

Role of Parliament in Conflict Resolution

The parliament of Kenya:

- Encourage the sharing of political or executive powers. This was done during the time of coalition government when both sides of the divide agreed to work together amicably to avoid escalating the existing conflict in the country (2007).
- Encourage compensation and resettlement of internally displace people (IDPs), for example the 11th parliament allocated funds to the IDPs most of whom have been resettled in new areas.
- Participate in mediation talks, for example the Orange Democratic Movement (ODM) side was represented in the mediation talk by Musalia Mudavadi, James Orengo and Sally Kosgey while the Party of National Unity (PNU) was represented by Moses Wantengula, Mutula Kilonzo and Martha Karua.
- Engage in the negotiation process, for example members of parliament encourage warring people in their constituencies to have dialogue or disarm.
- Amendment of existing laws or constitution that is acceptable to all, for instance debating and implementing the new constitution recently promulgated
- Parliament can put in place new laws, for example the National Reconciliation Accord which put in place the Coalition government (2008) of Mwai Kibaki and Raila Odinga.

According to the National Accord singed between the President Mwai Kibaki of PNU and Raila Odinga of ODM, which ended the 2007 classes and political impasse:

- Mwai Kibaki and Raila Odinga formed a coalition government of Party of National Unity (PNU) and Orange Democratic Movement (ODM)
- Mwai Kibaki and Raila Odinga became the President and Prime Minster respectively
- The two principal leaders were to share powers equally
- Mwai Kibaki became the head of state while Raila Odinga became the Head of Government
- Each leader was to appoint equal number of ministers and assistant ministers to run the government
- The two leaders were to consult each other before making a major decision
- The two leaders were to remain in power until a new government came in place or when they both agree to dissolve.

Steps taken in Mediation Process

- A mediator is appointed who is acceptable to both parties.
- The mediator sets the rules for dialogue between the two parties in disagreement.
- The parties explain their grievances (problems) to the mediator.
- Stories from both parties are summarized by the mediator.
- Solutions are given by the mediator and the protagonists given room to ventilate their opinion on the same.
- Accepted solutions are agreed upon by the protagonists.
- Agreement is reached and each party is committed to it.

The roles of an Arbitrator in conflict resolution are to:

- Give the two conflicting parties a chance to be heard.
- Listen to the complaints of both and allow them to ask questions.
- Make clarification on some aspects which might bring conflict and allow questions on the clarification.
- Consider the facts of the matter.

Effects of Conflicts in the Society

Armed conflicts have multiple long and short term impacts on development, on environment and human well being. Conflicts:

- Lead to the loss of lives, erosion of human dignity and make people live an impoverished lifestyle.
- Affects livelihoods directly through reduced access to land and natural resources like minerals as a result of exclusion, displacement and loss of biodiversity.
- Sets in motion a cycle of degradation and human vulnerability. This refers not only to the exposure to negative environmental change, but also to the inability to cope with the change due to migration into new areas.
- Contributes to the breakdown of social cohesion and disrupts the established local governance systems.
- Increases the gap between food production and demand hence aggravating hunger and over dependence on relief food. People's health is further compromised by diminished access to health facilities and malnourishment.
- Affects the provision of essential services due to the destruction and decay of the infrastructure. In some countries essential services and relief food is airlifted to war torn areas because the roads have been destroyed or made impassable.

Questions on National Integration

(a) Identify two elements of conflicts

(b) Give five causes of conflicts among the people of Kenya

(c) Explain Five ways in which parliament is used to resolve conflicts in Kenya

(d) Describe five steps taken in mediation process

(e) Give two roles of an arbitrator during the conflict resolution process

(f) Outline two effects of conflicts in society

4 EARLY CONTACT BETWEEN KENYA AND THE OUTSIDE WORLD UPTO 15TH CENTURY

As early as 7th century traders were coming to the East African Coast to trade from different parts of the world. Notable areas where these traders came from included: Egypt, Persia, China, Rome, Greece, Arabia and India.

Trade Items

These traders brought different commodities to transact with the Africans at the coast. The Chinese brought porcelain cups and plates; the Arabs brought swords and daggers; the Indians brought brightly coloured clothes, beads and Iron ware; the Persians brought rags and glass ware; and the Maldives brought cowry shells which were used as medium of exchange.

The items of trade from the East Coast of Africa were minerals like copper and gold, which were coming from Sofala and Mwene Mutapa Empire respectively; slaves, ostrich feathers, rhinocerous horns, animal skins and ivory. For a long time, however, slaves and ivory were the dominant commodities which attracted traders from many parts of the world to the East Coast of Africa.

Documentary and Archaeological Evidence of Early Contact

A lot of documentary evidence attests to the existing trade between the East Coast of Africa and the outside world. These include: -

- Christian Topography of Cosmos Indico-Pleatustes
- The Geography of Claudius Ptolemy
- The Periplus of Erythrean Sea
- Documents of Arab Merchants such as Ibn Batuta and Al-Masudi

Archaeologists have also come with material evidence to support the documented sources. This evidence includes the remnant of ancient coins and porcelain pots, cups and plates which originated from different area, for example china.

Ancient Coins

The motive of visiting the East Coast of Africa went beyond trading activities. Some Arabs came to settle along the East Coast of Africa because they considered the place to be a safer haven than their home where there was a lot of political turmoil and religious persecutions. They were also motivated by a desire to spread their Islamic religion and culture to the coastal communities who were not Muslims. The climate and soil in this region favoured agricultural activities. Agricultural settlements therefore sprung up in the region. The desire to satisfy their curiosity also attracted others who came to explore the area.

Arab Dhow

Factors that Facilitated the Coming of Arabs include:

- The North East and South West trade (monsoon) winds propelled the Arab dhows to and from the East coast of Africa.
- New developments in marine technology aided their coming. This included making of strong sailing ships (dhows) and using compass to determine the direction of their flow.
- Presence of deep natural harbours at the coast where ships could dock (anchor) with ease also aided their coming.

- There were good ports of call along the East Coast where traders got fresh supplies of food and water.
- The East African Coast was accessible via the Red Sea and Indian Ocean.
- Rich merchants provided the funds to finance their journey and trade.

Growth of Coastal Towns

Trade which was flourishing between the East Coast and the outside world boosted revenue for the coastal towns and this led to an influx of people into this region. The Indian Ocean Trade was encouraged by: -

- Availability of items of trade
- High demand for goods from the Kenyan coast by Arabia and the outside world.
- Existence of enterprising merchants in Arabia and the Kenyan coast who funded the trade.
- Accessibility of the Kenyan coast by sea.
- The monsoon winds facilitated movement of traders
- Relative political stability of the Kenyan coastal city - states.

Settlement of Arabs and Persians sprung up along the East Coast and these developed into towns. Most of the towns were located on islands which provided security and were difficult to attack because of the water which acted as a barrier. The towns had rich hinterlands which provided enough food to feed the urban populations. Islamic religion provided unity and attracted other people who flocked into places like Kilwa for pilgrimage. Administrative work was made more efficient by use of *Sultans* or *Shieks* who used *sheria* laws.

Lifestyle of People in Coastal Towns

The coastal towns were also known as City States. Majority of the people who lived in these towns were Muslims and practiced Islamic religion. *Sheria* laws were applied and their system of education was known as *madrassa* (Islamic education). Islamic culture was dominant. This was symbolized by women who wore *bui bui* and men who wore *kanzu* and Islamic caps. Many people spoke Kiswahili, which was a mixture of Arabic and other Bantu languages. Residents of the towns were divided into classes. The rich, for instance, lived in well decorated stone houses while the poor lived in mud walled *makuti* thatched houses. Their main economic activity was trade, farming and fishing activities. The towns were autonomous and were ruled by Sultans. By 1500 A.D. most people living in the coastal town and their environs were already Islamized. This was attributed to: -

- Commercial activities between the Arabs and African.
- Arabs settlement along the coast
- Intermarriage between the Arabs and other communities.
- Islam was more accommodative to African traditional practices.
- Development of Kiswahili language

Impact of the Indian Ocean Trade by 15th Century

- The trade led to intermarriage between the Arabs immigrants and the indigenous communities at the coast. This gave rise to a hybrid type of people called the Waswahili.
- Slave trade was dominant during this era and it led to depopulation of the region.
- Kiswahili language developed as a result of the borrowing of Arabic and Bantu words.
- New crops like coconuts, mangoes, rice were introduced at the coast.
- Some Bantus copied the oriental type of building, for example stone houses.
- Some Bantus adopted Islamic religion and Islamic culture.
- Some Africans chiefs became rich due to trade like chief Kivoi of the Kamba.
- Arabic system of government, for example the Sultan and use of *sheria* laws were adopted by some communities at the coast.

- Arab settlements like those of the Mazrui and Al Basudi families sprung up at the coast.
- Better links were made with India and Goa.
- Towns like Mombasa, Malindi and Pemba came up due to the trading activities in the area.
- The trade exposed Africa to the out side world leading to colonization.
- The trade undermined the African economy.

The Decline of the Coastal Towns After 1500 A.D.

- The Portuguese invasion contributed enormously to the decline of the coastal towns: -
    - ✓ Taxes levied on the coastal settlement by the corrupt Portuguese officials weakened the economic base of their settlements.
    - ✓ Arab traders kept away from the areas which they occupied and this led to loss of revenue.
    - ✓ The constant warfare and conflict between the Portuguese and the coastal towns led to destruction of some settlements like Gedi which the Portuguese burnt down.
- Increased conflict between the City States also discouraged traders from the interior to bring trade good to the coast. For example, there was conflict between Mazrui family and the Al Busaidi family over the control of the coastal settlements.
- The towns were also affected by natural calamities like dry spell which thwarted farming activities and reduced the supply of water in the towns.
- Invasion of coastal settlements by the Zimba led to the disruption of economic activities of the coastal settlements.

Questions on Early Contact with the East Coast of Africa before 15th century

(a) Identify two documentaries of historical information about the East African coast before the seventh century

(b) Mention one way in which the monsoon winds led to the development of trade between the Kenyan Coast and the outside world

(c) State two factors that facilitated the coming of Arabs to the East African coast

(d) State five factors, which promoted the growth of trade between the Kenyan Coast and Arabia

(e) Identify two factors that led to the growth of towns along the East Coast of Africa before the 19th C

(f) Describe the ways of life in the coastal towns of Kenya before the 19th century

(g) State six result of the Indian Ocean Trade on the Kenyan Coast

(h) Identify two factors, which encouraged the spread of Islam in Kenya by 1500 A.D.

(i) Explain five factors which led to the decline of the coastal towns after 1500 AD.

The Barons

5 PORTUGUESE RULE AT THE EAST COAST OF AFRICA

Portuguese Interest in the East Coast of Africa

- The Kenyan Coast was strategically located on the way to the Far East and could act as a base for their trading activities and naval ships
- Muslims conquered and ruled their homeland for over 700. The Portuguese therefore wanted to carry out a revenge mission against the Muslims
- They wanted to spread Christianity in the area and hoped that they would trace the legendary Prester John in East Africa to help them in this endeavour.
- The Portuguese sailor like Vasco da Gama was looking for a sea route to India.
- The Portuguese wanted to participate in the Indian Ocean trade which appeared lucrative.
- They wanted to colonize the Kenyan coast in order to protect their commercial interest.
- The Kenyan Coast was of strategic importance to them in that it would serve as a resting place or where to get replenishments after a long journey.

Vasco da Gama

Portuguese Conquest of the East African Coast

- 1487 - Bartholomew Diaz reached the Cape of Good Hope raising opportunities of reaching India
- 1498 – Vasco da Gama came to collect intelligence report for the king of Portugal
- 1500 - Pedro Alveres Cabort conquered Sofala
- 1502 Vasco da Gama conquered Kilwa
- 1503 – Ray Lovenco Ravansco conquered Zanzibar
- 1505 – Fransisco de' Almelda conquered Sofala, Kilwa and Mombasa
- 1506 – Lamu surrendered to the Portuguese
- 1506 -1507 – Trivtoa da Cunna attacked Arabia, Pate and Socotra
- 1509 – the whole of the East Africa had come under Portuguese rule

The Portuguese Conquest was facilitated by the following factors:

- After Vasco da Gama's visit in 1498, the Portuguese were armed with knowledge of East African topography. They took advantage of this knowledge to launch surprise attacks on coastal communities using superior weapons like canon guns and carracks.
- Some of the communities had already been weakened by the Galla attack and offered very little resistance to the invaders.
- The Portuguese used skilled and better trained soldiers; were ruthless in their attack and this scared off most coastal communities.
- The coastal communities failed to launch an effective response because of their disunity. Some of them supported the Portuguese. Malindi, for instance assisted the Portuguese to fight Mombasa.
- The Portuguese were further aided by the weakness of the Turkish and Persian navies which could not challenge them in the Indian Ocean.

Functions of the portuguese captains

The main duty of the Portuguese captain at the coast was to collect tribute for Portugal. His other duties were:

- To supervise the ruling families in City States
- To suppress any form of resistance against the Portuguese rule in Kenya

- Control trading activities along the coast

Fort Jesus

Reasons for Building Fort Jesus

Fort Jesus was used by the Portuguese as a watchtower. It overlooked the Indian Ocean and they could use it to sight the incoming invaders. Since it was strongly built and difficult to penetrate, the Portuguese took refuge in it when they were under attack. Fort Jesus was also used as a base for initiating attacks and as an administrative centre of the Portuguese along the coastal region. They stored their ornaments and slaves in the fort before they were shipped out.

Inside view of Fort Jesus

Why the Portuguese failed to Spread Christianity
- Islam was largely accepted by most people at the coast
- Christianity was less appealing to Africans because it opposed some aspects of their traditions like polygamy.
- The Portuguese had few personnel to help them spread the evangelical work.
- The coastal communities kept away from Christianity because it was associated with the cruelty and brutality of the Portuguese.
- They remained aloof and rarely associated with the Africans.
- The Portuguese made no attempt to spread Christianity to the interior part of Kenya.

Results of the Portuguese Rule

(i) Positive Results

- The Portuguese introduced new crops such as maize, groundnuts, cassava, paw paw, pineapples and guavas.
- The Portuguese introduced the use of farm yard manure.
- The coastal communities borrowed a few Portuguese words which were incorporated into the Kiswahili language, for example, the Kiswahili word *meza* was borrowed from Portuguese.
- Portuguese built some structures along the coast, for example Fort Jesus and Vasco da Gama's Pillar in Malindi.
- The Portuguese administered the coast from Gao. This in turn contributed to the development of strong links between the coast and India.
- The Portuguese build churches along the Kenyan coast and attempted to convert some of the coastal communities to Christianity.

(ii) Negative Results

- The Portuguese rule along the coast upset trade between the Kenyan Coast, Arabia, Persia and India.
- Punitive Portuguese raids led to loss of life and destruction of coastal settlements.
- Portuguese rule along the coast upset Islam in the region. This was due to constant fighting and disruption of mosques.
- Harsh Portuguese administration led to widespread suffering of the people and some were forced to flee the area into the interior like the Mijikenda.
- Their rule led to the decline of the coastal settlements such as Gedi which was burnt down by the Portuguese.

The Ruins of Gedi

Decline of the Portuguese Rule at the Kenyan Coast

- Kenyan coast was far away from Portugal. This made it difficult for them to reinforce their soldiers when attacked. The Omani Arabs, for instance besieged Fort Jesus and the few remaining Portuguese had to commit suicide rather than surrender to the former.

- The Portuguese acquired a very large empire along the East Coast, yet they had very few personnel and soldiers to effectively control it. They therefore found it very difficult to suppress the rebellious Africans who hated them because of their aloofness and negativity towards the Africans.

- The few corrupt Portuguese officials did not help the situation. Their corrupt nature killed the Indian Ocean trade which was their main source of revenue.

- The Portuguese settlements were attacked by the Zimba from the lower Zambezi valley who looted property and killed people

- The Portuguese were constantly attacked by tropical diseases such as Malaria which killed most of their officials.

- Portuguese were challenged by other powers like the Turks and Dutch in the Indian Ocean who posed a more serious menace than the Africans and Arabs.

- The Portuguese neglected the eastern region because of their union with Spain

Questions on the Portuguese Rule at the East Coast of Africa

(a) Why were the Portuguese interested in establishing their control over the Kenya coast during 16th century A.D.?

(b) Give three reasons why the Portuguese came to the Kenyan coast by the beginning of 16th C

(c) Why did the Portuguese build Fort Jesus?

(d) Describe the Portuguese conquest of the East African Coast upto 1509

(e) State five reasons for the success of the Portuguese in conquering the Kenyan coast during the 16th Century

(f) Identify the main duty of the Portuguese captains at the coast

(g) Identify one important landmark of the Portuguese rule along the East African Coast

(h) What were the results of the Portuguese rule along the Kenyan Coast?

(i) State two benefits of Portuguese rule over the coastal settlements

(j) Give two reasons why the Portuguese failed to spread Christianity to the East Coast

(k) Explain six factors, which led to the collapse of the Portuguese rule on the Kenya Coast by the end of the 17th Century

6 THE OMANI RULE AT THE EAST COAST OF AFRICA

After vanquishing the Portuguese, the Omani Arabs who terminated their rule along the Kenyan coast did not settle in the area immediately. This was because they were preoccupied with problems at home and entrusted this responsibility to the Arab families who had established themselves in the region before.

Most of these towns, spearheaded by Mombasa, soon became problematic to the Omani Arabs. These towns craved to maintain their autonomy and were opposed to heavy taxation introduced by the Omani Arabs. In particular the, Busaidi (Omani Arabs) and Mazrui governors of Mombasa had protracted differences. These differences were attributed to: -

- The Busaidi craved to increase their control over coastal towns including Mombasa to be in command of their trading activities.
- Mombasa rebellion was encouraged by the Sultan of Oman who was more focused on enemies at home.
- The fact that Mombasa had fought hard against the Portuguese and didn't wish to be controlled by another foreigner.
- Open conflict began when Mohammed Ibn Uthman al Mazrui refused allegiance to the new Sultan in 1741.

By 18th century trade between Kilwa and the French islands of Re-Union prospered. This made the Sultan to be more determined than ever before to maintain close control over the trade at the coast. The inclination to secure direct control of the regions was motivated by the need to: -

- Control the thriving Indian Ocean trade
- Ensure that revenue from taxes were remitted to Oman
- Establish political control over the Kenyan coast
- Enlarge their commercial empire.

- Prevent rulers of coastal settlements from declaring themselves independent.

Seyyid Said chose Zanzibar to be his capital because it had been loyal to him throughout his struggle to control the region hence the need to reward them. The place was secure because it was located in an island surrounded with water thus difficult to attack. Zanzibar was strategically placed and could be conveniently used to manage the area and control the trading activities. Other factors like suitable climate and soil also favoured Zanzibar. Because of this he established large plantations of cloves in the area. Zanzibar also had the advantage of having clean fresh water and deep habours which favoured ship anchorage.

Seyyid Said

Development of Plantation Agriculture

Seyyid Said is credited with the development of plantation farming along the coastal regions. High demand for agricultural products in Arabian countries influenced Seyyid Said to introduce plantation farming to the East Coast. Seyyid realized that cloves, which were on high demand in the Far East, could do well in the coastal regions. The fertile soil and climatic conditions in places like Zanzibar and Pemba favoured this crop. At the same time slaves who would provide labour in the plantation could be easily acquired through slave trade.

Seyyid Said specifically introduced new crops like cloves and coconuts which were planted in large scale in Pemba and Zanzibar. To achieve this, he developed economic programmes that prioritized agriculture and trade. For example:

- He encouraged settlers from Oman and Zanzibar to settle in Mombasa, Malindi and Pemba.
- He acquired more land in the main land which increased agricultural activities from 1840.
- He encouraged slave trade which provided cheap labour.

Seyyid Said's contribution to International and Long Distance Trade were:

- Seyyid Said encouraged the settlement of Indian Banyans in Zanzibar whom he used to finance the caravan traders to the interior
- He levied a uniform custom duty of 5 % throughout East Africa which encouraged trade
- Seyyid Said improved monetary system by introducing small copper coins and silver currency (Indian Rupees) to facilitate transactions
- He wrote introductory letters to caravan traders going into the interior to make their identification easier.
- He provided security to the Arab and Swahili traders
- He signed trade treaties with foreign traders and this boosted trade.
- Arab and Swahili traders who went to the interior carried the flag of the sultan as symbol of his authority

SLAVE TRADE

Slaves were useful as domestic workers or solders. There was high demand for slaves as porters of ivory and other goods which were traded in, at the same time slaves were required to work in the plantations along the East Coast and in other parts of the world. Since Islam discouraged enslaving fellow Muslims, the Africans who the Arabs regarded as infidels served that purpose.

Slave caravan

How Slaves Were Captured

- The unfortunate members of the society like the mentally retarded were sold off.
- Slave raids were organized
- Criminals and debtors were sold
- War captives, for example children and women were sold as slaves
- Lone travelers were kidnapped and sold as slaves
- Children were enticed and sold

Stoppage of Slave Trade and Slavery

The British were instrumental in stopping slave trade. They signed many treaties which culminated to the abolition of slave trade and later slavery. Some of the treaties they signed were

- Moresby Treaty of 1822
- The Hammerton Treaty of 1845
- The Frere Treaty of 1873

Reasons for the Abolition of Slave Trade

Public opinion in Britain was opposed to slave trade and slavery. Philanthropists (William Wilberforce) and Missionaries (David Livingstone) exposed the horrific acts of the inhuman trade and they were of the opinion that this trade be replaced by a more legitimate one. This argument was upheld by many Europeans who contended that slaves would provide market for Europeans goods and raw materials for the European industries in Africa rather than Europe. Renowned economists like Adam Smith who argued that a free man was more economical to use than an enslaved one, upheld the same line of thought. The prevailing circumstances in Britain, say the use of machines in the 18th century, made slave trade ineffective and the independence of America, reduced the slaves market in that continent.

Impact of Slave Trade on the Kenyan Communities

- Slave trade led to death and widespread suffering among the Africans.
- The population of both people and wildlife (elephants) was greatly reduced.
- The raids led to insecurity and fear in the society, and people lost trust on their neighbours and leaders who changed their role to slave dealers rather than protectors of their subjects.
- Economic activities like agriculture and iron work were upset because able-bodied people who performed these duties were captured and sold.
- Slave trade spread Islamic faith and Kiswahili language in the interior of Kenya.
- It also opened up the interior of Kenya for European penetration and later colonization.

LONG DISTANACE TRADE

Communities which were actively involved in the Long Distance Trade in Kenya were Kamba, Giriama, Swahili and Arabs. The Arabs began making inroads to the interior because the African communities who were involved in this trade were becoming unreliable and they also brought in adequate goods. For a long time, however, this trade was dominated by the Kamba.

Why Kamba Engaged in Long Distance Trade

- The Kamba were strategically located in between the coast and the fertile highlands of central Kenya.
- Some parts of Ukambani, for instance Kitui were unsuitable for farming.
- They were skilled hunters and could easily get ivory and other animals products which they traded in.

- They established contacts with the neighbouring communities and this facilitated the trade.
- The Kamba had prosperous men, for example chief Kivoi who organized the trade.

Organization of the Long Distance Trade

- The Kamba and Mijikenda worked as middlemen who sourced for the goods from the interior while the Arabs and Swahili, based at the coast, funded their operations.
- Trade routes to the interior went up to Mount Kenya region and Lake Victoria. Areas occupied by the Maasai were bypassed to avoid their hostility.
- Traders gathered in the coastal towns and moved into the interior in groups or caravans for security purposes.
- The main mode of transport was slaves who were used as porters. They carried the goods from the interior to the coast and back.
- Centres like Taveta, Mbooni, Mumias and Lake Baringo sprung up to serve as resting points.
- Items of trade from the coast included: - guns, cotton cloths, beads, glassware, and swords while from the interior came ivory, rhinoceros horns and slaves.
- The mode of trade was barter system although towards the beginning of the 19th century cowry shells were introduced as medium of exchange. This came from Maldives Islands.

By the beginning of the 19th century the dominance of the Kamba in this trade had started to go to seed. The Kamba were increasingly replaced by the Arabs and Swahili traders who began venturing into the interior using large caravans. The nose-dive in dominance was attributed to: -

- Increased incidences of insecurity in the regions due to the Oromo and Maasai attacks on their caravans.

- The Agikuyu and Aembu who declined to trade with them because of their slave raiding activities.
- The lopsided supply they brought which could not sustain the market.
- Seyyid Said urged the Arab and Swahili traders to go into the interior and this posed challenge
- The abolition of slave trade by the British government reduced their market.
- Ivory became increasingly difficult to obtain due to the reduction of elephants

Impact of Long Distance Trade in Kenya

- The sultan of Zanzibar spread his influence to the interior of East Africa through the trade.
- Some traders like chief Kivoi of the Kamba became wealthy due to their involvement in the trade
- The trade led to the spread of Islamic religion and culture into the interior.
- There was development of trade routes that linked the coast and the interior. These routes were later upgraded by the colonial government into major roads.
- New crops, for example bananas, mangoes and rice were introduced into the interior of East Africa
- Money economy development to replace the barter system of trade which was the mode of trade in the past.
- Strong kingdoms like, the Wanga came up in the interior due to the wealth the leaders amassed from the trade
- Through the trade, Agreements were entered into between Seyyid Said and Britain. These Agreements created a more permanent link and later metamorphosed into European colonization of the region.
- Trade centres, for example Mombasa, Malindi, Pemba and Zanzibar grew up to big towns
- Kiswahili language was spread to the interior of East Africa by the traders

Economic Benefits of Omani Rule the Kenyan

- The Omani Arabs established long distance trade in East Africa which added value to the East African commodities like Rhino horns and Ivory thus leading to economic growth.
- The Omani Arabs contributed to the development of plantation agriculture along the Kenyan Coast.
- They introduced new crops in East African Coast, for example mangoes, rice and sugar cane.
- Omani Arabs introduced the money economy in Kenya which replaced the cowry shells from Maldive Islands.
- They encouraged the opening up of new lines of transport between the coast and the interior, for example trade routes.
- They linked East Coast to International trade and revitalized the Indian Ocean Trade which had collapsed during the Portuguese era.

Questions on the Omani Rule along the East Coast of Africa

(a) Why did Seyyid Said take direct control of the settlements along the coast of Kenya?

(b) State five factors which made Seyyid Said to transfer his capital from Muscat to Zanzibar

(c) State five ways how the slaves were acquired

(d) Name two treaties which were signed between the British and the Coastal Arab rulers to end Slave Trade

(e) Identify five methods employed by Seyyid Said to promote the Long Distance Trade during the 19th century

(f) Describe the organization of the long distance trade in Kenya in the 19th century

(g) State five factors which encouraged the Kamba to engage in long distance trade

(h) State five reasons which led to the decline of Kamba dominance of trade along the East Coast of Africa

(i) Describe the effects of long distance trade in Kenya during the 19th Century

MISSIONARY ACTIVITIES IN KENYA

Different mission groups operated in Kenya. They included: Church Mission Society (CMS), White Fathers, the African Inland Church (AIC), The Holy Ghost Fathers, The Seventh Day Adventist (SDA), The Methodist Church, Friends Missionaries and The Scottish Mission. These groups established different mission centres in different parts of the country.

Missionary Work

The main purpose of missionaries in Kenya was to spread Christianity in the region. African catechists were trained to assist them in this endeavour. They also felt that they were duty bond to civilize the Africans. Promoting western education was viewed as an attempt to achieve this noble course. Missionaries established schools where Africans were taught how to read and write. Hospitals were also set up to eradicate backward practices like witchcraft among Africans. The missionaries empathized with Africans and because of this; they build homes for the destitute like orphans. Centres like Frere Town were established, where freed slaves were settled and taught farming, masonry and carpentry. The missionaries were involved in exploration of Africa. They exposed the hidden treasure (fertile soils, suitable climate and minerals) of Africa to their mother governments. Missionaries also pacified the Africans and assisted them to sign treaties with European powers. This later encouraged European colonization of the country.

Missionary activities were enhanced by:
- The translation of the Bible, first to Kiswahili and later to other local dialects, made it easy to interpret and understand by the most Africans.
- The protection which the missionaries got from the colonial government in areas where they operated and the chiefs who also gave them land.
- The trust which the missionaries cultivated by living among Africans and getting involved in charity work, for example helping orphans, widows and freed slaves endeared them to many.
- The settling up of schools, hospitals and mission centres encouraged mission work
- The building of the railway line made the missionaries to penetrate to the interior of Africa easily
- The absence of any other established religion in the area, apart from Islam reduced rivalry.
- Introductory letters given to the missionaries by the sultan of Zanzibar made them to be acceptable in areas under the jurisdiction of the sultan.
- The converted Africans who assisted to spread the gospel to fellow Africans
- Independent churches which spread the gospel to other Africans
- The discovery of quinine which diminished the risk of death of missionaries who ventured into the interior

What Undermined Christian Missionary Activities in Kenya during the 19th Century?
- Islam was deeply rooted along the coastal region and winning converts there was difficult. Islamic religion was more appealing to Africans because it was more accommodative to the African traditions, for instance polygamy which is sanctioned by the Koran.
- There were a handful of evangelists to spread the gospel and missionaries were forced to train African catechist to assist them in this pursuit.
- Africans spoke different languages which missionaries could not comprehend. At the same time, they could not understand the Bible, written in foreign language. Missionaries were forced to learn the local

languages and to translate the Bible to local dialects.

- Missionaries faced hostilities from African communities who attacked their missions. They were also at loggerhead with the traditionalists who wanted to preserve their cultural practices like circumcision, deemed to be pagan practices by the missionaries. Some Christian doctrines were strict and were incompatible with traditional beliefs.
- Different mission groups competed among themselves for converts and this sometimes led to hostilities.
- Penetrating in the interior of Kenya was difficult because of the absence of roads and proper means of communication. At the same time, the harsh topical climate and tropical diseases like malaria made life very hard for the missionaries.

Contributions of Johann Kraft to the Spread of Christianity

- He build churches, for example at Rabai
- He translated the Bible to Kiswahili
- He trained catechists who later spread the gospel
- He encouraged other European missionaries to come to Kenya
- He did exploration work which led to opening of the interior of Kenya to missionary work

Results of missionary activities can be summarized as:

- The Missionaries contributed to exploration, for example Krapt was the first European to see Mt. Kenya.
- Missionaries represented Africans in the legislative council, for example John Arthur
- The missionaries spread Christianity to the people of East Africa.
- They encouraged medical services, for example building hospitals like Mukumu and Nyabondo Mission Hospitals.

- They developed agricultural and technical skills
- They led to abolition of slave trade
- They were fore runners of colonialists as they asked mother countries to give them protection.
- Their work led to the rise of African independent churches
- They spread western education
- Their work led to the establishment of independent African schools
- Their activities led to the emergence of African nationalism. This is because the nationalist were the products of mission churches
- They undermined the African culture and encouraged western civilization
- They caused disunity among the Africans between the converted and traditionalists

Questions on Missionary activities in Kenya

(a) State five factors which motivated the missionaries to come to the East Coast of Africa
(b) Why did Christian missionaries establish stations in Kenya
(c) Name two missionary societies which operated in Kenya
(d) Explain six factors which promoted missionary activities in Kenya
(e) Identify the contributions of Johann Kraft to the spread of Christianity
(f) Explain five factors that undermined Christian Missionary activities in Kenya during the 19th century.
(g) Identify the major hindrance to missionary work along the Kenyan coast in the 19th century
(h) Mention five results of Christian missionary activities in Kenya.

7 CONSTITUTION AND CONSTITUTION MAKING EXERCISE

A constitution is a set of agreed principles and rules which are used to govern a state. Its components include: The rights and duties of citizens; the composition of the executive organ of the government; the distribution of powers among the various arms of the government; the powers and duties of the head of state and the composition of the judiciary, its duties and powers.

The new constitution recognizes some specific groups of people in the country. These include:

- The old
- The youth.
- Children
- Persons with disabilities.
- Minorities and marginalized groups.

There are two types of constitutions: - Written and unwritten constitutions. In a written constitution the basic principles governing the state are clearly written down in a single document. This type of constitution has several advantages. These include:

- Provides clear guidelines on procedures to be followed when there is a crisis. This creates stability in a country.
- The constitution cannot easily be altered by politicians
- This type of constitution is fairly rigid and can only be changed after a careful consideration
- It accommodates everyone irrespective of their race, creed or ethnicity
- It provides unity in a country.

Disadvantages of a written constitution include:

- The constitution makes the judiciary to be too powerful because it is the only institution charged with the responsibility of interpreting it

- This type of constitution is too difficult to interpret by ordinary citizens
- The procedure for amending a written constitution is slow and expensive.
- It is rigid and cannot be changed easily.
- The written constitution is slow in a dynamic environment

In Unwritten constitution, the fundamental principles and rules governing a state exist, but in many scattered documents. The best example is that of Britain which is contained in many documents. The merit of this type of constitution is that: -

- It is flexible and adaptable to changing circumstances in the society.
- It is simple to amend
- It ensures continuity of a nation's traditions
- It is indigenous and hence suitable to a state

Disadvantage of the unwritten constitution

- It is open to manipulation because of its simplicity and ease in amendment.
- It does not protect the rights of the people effectively
- Its scope is indefinite hence tends to be ambiguous

It is very important to have a constitution. This is because the basis of all laws in Kenya is the constitution and it spells out the duties and rights of the citizens. This makes the citizens to know what is expected of them. The constitution ensures equality of all Kenyans and spells out the government structure and duties of each organ. It also limits the authority of those in power and spells out their responsibilities.

The roles of the constitution in governing the country include:

- The constitution protects the interest of the weak in the society from those who would like to dominate them
- It checks the powers of the would be dictatorial rulers

The Barons

- It defines how to rise to power hence preventing unnecessary power tussle
- It provides for the separation of powers between the three arms of the government
- It defines the powers of those in authority hence prevents misuse of power
- It defines relationship between Kenya and other countries
- It specifies on how a government is to be formed.
- It spells out the necessary conditions for acquisition of citizenship

A good constitution protects the rights of the citizens and offers provisions for amendments, clearly stating the procedure. It is:-
- Specific
- Contains all aspects of the government
- Flexible and can cope easily with any changes in the state
- Stable and durable to ensure that it is not easily tampered with

Prof. Yash Pal Gay

Processes involved in constitution making in Kenya include:
- Civic education is conducted based on a national curriculum to sensitize people.
- Public debate is conducted and people are requested to come up with possible suggestions or changes that they would wish to have in the new constitution.
- A commission set, writes a report based on peoples' suggestions and makes its recommendations.
- A draft constitution is written based on the suggestions and recommendations. This is published and then distributed to the public for debate.
- Special delegates (constitution) conference deliberates upon the draft and adopts it, for example the Bomas Draft.
- Certain issues that cannot be resolved by the constitutional conference are referred to people to decide through a referendum.
- If passed by the people, the draft constitution is then enacted by the National Assembly and officially gazetted.

Factors considered when making a constitution include:
- Geographical background of the area.
- Religious beliefs of the people.
- Historical background of the people.
- Culture and social background of the people.

Problems experienced in the constitution making process include:
- Many Kenyans are still illiterate and are not able to read or write. This makes only a few people to meaningfully read the draft constitution which is distributed for public debate.
- Implementing a new constitution takes a long time because of the vested interests by the politicians. They drag their feet to derail the exercise when they realize that the new changes may not after all benefit them.
- Sometimes the sitting government also lacks the good will to implement new changes and prefers the status quo. Promises in this case are not fulfilled, but continue to remain mere campaign tool to woo voters.
- There is a general apathy from the population towards many things which are related to politics in the country. Majority of people remains aloof and prefer to watch events unfold from a distance
- Constitution making exercise requires a lot of money and expertise to implement. It is often bogged down due to inadequate funds. Proper implementation requires donor funding which is sometime given, but with a lot of difficult conditions set.

• Developed countries have a lot of interest in the whole exercise and use arm twisting tendencies to force the government to implement constitutional changes which only suit their purpose. Laws are therefore made which are not relevant to the country.

A number of factors have necessitated constitutional changes in Kenya since independence. These are:

• Abolition of the Federal System of government to pave way for a Unitary Government by Jomo Kenyatta soon after independence.

• The need to indigenize (Africanize) institutions immediately after independence.

• Political ambition which created the need to consolidate power by new leaders – Moi came up with many changes to make the Kenya African National Union (KANU) more powerful and to muzzle the opposition after the attempted coup d'état in 1982.

• The need to revenge by political opponents, for example the constitutional amendment of 1966 which made it mandatory for MP who resigned from the party which sponsored them during election to forfeit their seat

• To make relevant and applicable laws to Kenyans

• Pressure from international donor communities, for example repealing Section 2A which lead to the re-introduction of multipartism.

• To enhance national unity, for example changing the constitution in 1982 to make Kenya a single party (de jure) state

CONSTITUTIONAL CHANGES IN KENYA SINCE INDEPENDENCE

The 1964 amendment

• Made Kenya a Republic with an executive president

• It provided for the appointment of the Vice President

• It reduced the powers of Regional Government

The 1965 amendment

• A simple majority in parliament was required to declare a state of emergency in the country

• Regional Government was changed to Provincial Councils

• Supreme Court was changed to high court

The 1966 amendment

• Made Common Wealth citizens eligible for Kenyan citizens

• A legislator jailed for 6 months to forfeit his/her seat in parliament

• MP failing to attend 8 consecutive parliamentary sittings without the speaker's permission to lose his/her seat

• President was given power to appoint and dismiss civil servants

• President was given power to rule North Eastern Province by decree

• MP who resigned from the party that sponsored him during election to forfeit his seat

• President to detain a citizen without trial

• President acquired power to control freedom of press

• Upper and lower house of parliament were merged to form one house

The 1968 amendment

• It abolished Provincial Councils and brought to an end Federal System of government

• All candidates for general elections to be nominated by a political party

• In the event of presidential vacancy, the Vice President to take over and elections to be held within 90 days

• 12 MPs to be nominated by the president

The 1969 amendments

• Minimum voting age was reduced from 21 – 18 years and presidential age from 40 – 35 years

- Kiswahili was included together with English as the official languages in parliament

The 1975 amendment

- Extended the prerogative of mercy by the president on the election offenders

The 1977 amendment

- The East African Court of Appeal was changed to Court of Appeal

The 1979 amendment

- Public officers who wanted to contest for seats during a General Election to resign six months prior to the proposed date of the elections.

The 1982 amendments

- Section 2A was introduced which made Kenya a one party state by law (de jure)
- Created the office of Chief Secretary as the head of public service, the post was abolished in 1987 and replaced with the office of the Secretary to the Cabinet

The 1985 amendment

- High court to work as a court of appeal on all election petitions

The 1988 amendments

- Provided for the removal of the security of tenure of office for Attorney General, the Auditor and Controller General and the Chief Secretary
- Police were given powers to hold a suspect for 14 days before taking him to court if the crime was serious. Before it was mandatory to bring all criminals to court within 24 hours.

The 1990 amendment

- Parliament reinstated the security of tenure of the office of AG and General and Controller Auditor

The 1991 amendments

- Repealing of section 2A of the constitution reverted Kenya to a multi party state
- Terms of the president was limited to 2 terms

Features of the Independence Constitution

- The independence constitution was based on West Minister's model and had two houses: Upper and Lower houses (Senate and House of Representatives)
- It provided for a position of Prime Minister to head the government and a governor to head the state
- It spelt out that a party with majority numbers formed the government (multi party)
- It contained a detailed Bill of Rights fashioned on European convention of human rights. This spelt out the right and obligation of individual.
- It provided for the establishment of a federal government. The regional (federal) governments had regional assembles and presidents
- It spelt out the powers and responsibilities of the central government and regional governments
- It set out an electoral commission which was impartial

Questions on the Constitution and Constitution Making Process

(a) State five components of a constitution

(b) Give two factors that are considered when making a constitution

(c) State five characteristics of a good constitution

(d) Give two advantages of written constitution

(e) Give two disadvantages of unwritten constitution

(f) Describe the constitution making process in Kenya

(g) Explain the problems that have been experienced in the constitution making process in Kenya

(h) Explain six factors which have necessitated constitutional amendments in independent Kenya

(i) Describe the features of the independence constitution of Kenya?

(j) Identify the major constitutional change that was implemented in 1992

8 DEMOCRACY AND HUMAN RIGHTS

Democracy is a government by the people who are for the people. The practice, which is now widespread in Western Europe and USA, was introduced by the Greeks who practiced pure democracy.

Aspects of democracy

- Political aspect – peoples' consent in the system of government is sought directly or indirectly
- Social aspect – human life is preserved and there is respect for human dignity.
- Economic aspect – equal opportunities are given to everybody and exploitation of humankind discouraged.

Types of Democracy

- Direct or pure democracy – people in the state are allowed to participate freely in making important decision of the state
- Indirect or representative democracy – people participate through elected representatives in decision making
- Constitutional (liberal) democracy – rights and powers of people are exercised, but within the confines of the constitution

Merits of Democracy

- Ensures that leaders do not ignore the citizens who give them power. Leaders become accountable to the electorate because the electorate can vote them out of office if they fail to deliver their promises.
- Promotes equality among people.
- Develops initiative among people and a sense of responsibility.
- Helps to promote patriotism and therefore lessens the chance of a rebellion.
- Promotes a peaceful co-existence among people.

Demerits of democracy

- Democracy promotes dictatorship – the views of the minority are suppressed by the majority who are not always right.
- May perpetuate incompetence because mostly dishonest characters are elected instead of the sincere and hard working type.
- Often slow and wasteful – A lot of time is wasted in rhetoric and building of consensus before useful decision is agreed on.
- Democracy encourages class struggle and competition
- Though regarded as a majority rule, in practice a few who are able to manipulate the majority remain in power.

Principles of Democracy

- People are not dictated upon but are consulted in affairs of state leadership.
- All people are treated equally irrespective of race, tribe or ethnicity
- Divergent views of people are considered when making decisions.
- People are involved in regular choice of leaders to represent them in government.
- There is control of abuse of power.
- There is openness (transparency) in the way things are done.
- There is balance of power between the governors and the governed.
- Citizens feel that they are part and parcel of the government.
- Leaders have good qualities, for example are wise, enlightened and morally right.

> **Questions on the Democracy**
> (a) Give two aspects of democracy
> (b) Identify one type of democracy
> (c) State two advantages of democracy
> (d) State two demerits of democracy
> (e) Explain five principles of democracy

KENYA NATIONAL COMMISSION ON HUMAN RIGHTS (KNCHR)

The Kenya National Commission on Human Rights (KNCHR) is an autonomous rights institution, established by the Kenya National Commission on Human Rights Act, 2011. It is a successor to the body of the same name established by an Act of parliament in 2002. The original KNCHR became operational in July 2003, and following the promulgation of the constitution of Kenya in August 2010, was legally reconstituted as the Kenya National Human Rights and Equality Commission.

The KNCHR is led by a Chairperson and four other commissioners appointed by the president of Kenya after nomination by a selected panel of governmental and non governmental interests. The current acting chairperson is Dr. Samuel Kiping'etich arap Tororei. Although established by the government, the KNCHR is an independent body. Every person has the right to complain to the commission, allegations that a right or fundamental freedom in the Bill of Right has been denied, violated or infringed, or is threatened

Functions of KNCHR

- To promote respect for human rights and develop a culture of human rights in the Republic
- To promote gender equality and equity generally and facilitate gender maintstreaming in national government
- To promote the protection, and observance of human rights in public and private institutions
- To monitor, investigate and report on the observance of human rights in all spheres of life in the Republic including observance by the national security organs
- To receive and investigate complaigns about alleged abuses of human rights and steps to secure appropriate redress where human rights have been violated.
- On its own initiative or on the basis of complaigns, investigate or research a matter in respect of human rights, and make recommendations to improve the functions of state organs
- To act as the principal organ of the state in ensuring compliance with obligations under treaties and conventions relating to human rights.
- To investigate any conduct in state affairs, or any act or omission in public administration in any sphere of government, that is alleged or suspected to be prejudicial or improper or to result in any impropriety or prejudice
- To investigate complaigns of abuse of power, unfair treatment, manifest injustice or unlawful, oppressive, unfair or unresponsive official conduct

Principles of the Bill of Rights

- Every human being has the right to life
- Every human being has the right to liberty and security
- No person shall be subjected to torture or cruel and degrading (inhuman) treatment
- Every individual is free from slavery and forced labour
- People have right to equality before the law
- People have right to peaceful assembly

Functions of the Bill of Rights

- The Bill of Rights safeguards life, freedom and security of the Kenyan citizens
- It protects one's property - If the government has to take somebody's property for public use, the person must be compensation for the loss of possession.
- It gives the citizens the freedom of worship and speech.
- It provides freedom of assembly and association.

Characteristics of Human Rights

- Human rights are universal and they apply to all.
- They are indivisible. One right cannot be applied if the other does not exist
- Rights have limitations. In the enjoyment of rights, one has a duty to respect the rights of other people
- Human rights may be suspended during crisis. For example, during war or outbreak of contagious disease

Justification of Human Rights

- Human rights are necessary for mankind to achieve a dignified life and to fulfill his potential.
- They are inherent to human beings.
- Human rights empower citizens and residents by giving them control in decision making organs of the state.
- They justify special treatment of the minority and other disadvantaged groups.
- They provide guidance to organs of state regarding the exercise of state power.
- Human rights limit internal and external conflicts and strengthen national unity.

How the bill of rights in Kenya protects the rights of individuals

- The bill of rights guarantees Kenyans the right to live. This means that taking away life (either by murder or suicide) is punishable under the Kenyan law.
- The bill of rights provides for the right to own property thus any person who interferes with another person's property is liable to prosecution in a court of law.
- It provides for the freedom of association (assembly) among Kenyans. This entitles individuals the right to assemble and associate with people of their own choice without harassment.
- It provides freedom of expression. This allows people to express their opinion freely in writing or speech without fear.
- It provides for freedom of movement of the individual. This guarantees a person the right to move freely in any part of the country at any time without fear.
- It provides for protection against slavery and forced labour. This allows the individual to choose when, where and whom to work.
- The bill of right protects the individual against arbitrary search, arrest and detention.

Incidences in which enjoyment of fundamental human rights in Kenya may be barred include:

- Declaration of the state of emergency or curfew - hinder the enjoyment of human rights, for example the freedom of movement.
- Political insecurity such as war - basic human rights is curtailed.
- Violation of fundamental human rights by the state agents like police - sometimes accused of using unnecessarily a lot of force in quelling violence or live bullets on defenseless civilians.
- Conviction to jail term by a court of law - convicts forgo certain fundamental rights like freedom of movement and association.
- Unequal distribution of resources – lead to impoverishment of some people to the extent that they are unable to enjoy their basic rights.
- Discrimination on the basis of gender, tribe, race - leads to negative enjoyment of basic freedom
- Declaration of security operation zones - limit the freedom of movement to these places
- Ignorance – makes people not to know their fundamental rights

Though human rights are fundamental to all and are entrenched into the constitution; there are times when the government may find it necessary to curtail such rights and freedoms. Such cases include:

- If one is convicted of murder in a court of law or is involved in a robbery with violence and is convicted to hang, the right to life is denied.

- If one is suspected to be a threat to the security of the state, the right to liberty and freedom of movement are denied
- If one publishes a false accusation of another person or state, the freedom of speech is denied.
- If the freedom to assemble is a threat to the security of the state or self, for instance during a violent demonstration.
- If one is not of sound mind or has an infectious disease, one is isolated or confined in a different place from others.
- If one is considered a minor (under 18 years of age), adults make decisions on their behalf
- If the government wants to develop public utility in an area, freedom to own property is denied. However, one is compensated for the loss.

Having life is important and willfully taking one's life away is not permissible constitutionally. However, there are isolated cases when this liberty cannot be guaranteed. These cases include:

- When a court passes a death sentence on a individual
- During riots and warfare – when an individual is killed it is not considered as violation
- When one kills another in self defense or defending his/her property.
- When a police officer kills one who is trying to resist lawful arrest or in the act of fighting armed criminals.
- When the life of an expectant mother is endangered – the life of the unborn baby may be terminated to save that of the mother.

There are certain groups of people in the country whose personal liberty are legally limited. These groups include:

- Convicted criminals
- People with highly infectious disease, for example Ebola.
- People of unsound mind (mad).
- People who are addicted to drugs, but are undergoing rehabilitation.
- Suspected criminals
- Young persons, under 18 years, to secure their education

RIGHTS ENJOYED BY PEOPLE IN KENYA
Political/Civil Rights
- Right to security
- Right to privacy of a person
- Right to assembly
- Right to emigration
- Right to life
- Freedom of association
- Protection from arbitrary search or detention

Social Rights
- Right to work
- Right to social security
- Right to education

Survival Rights of Children
- Right to good nutrition
- Right to shelter and clothing
- Right to be nurtured
- Right to own a name and right to nationality
- Right to medical care

Developmental Rights of Children
- Right to education
- Right to play and leisure
- Right to social security
- Right to parental love

Protection Rights of Children
- Protection from discrimination
- Protection from exploitation
- Protection from sexual abuse
- Protection from disasters

- Protection from using, making or selling dangerous drugs

Rights to Participation
- Right to express themselves
- Right to thought and opinion
- Right to contribute towards the development of the community
- Right to associate

Rights Enjoyed by Persons with Disability
- To be treated with respect and dignity
- To access educational institutions and facilities for persons with disabilities that are integrated into society
- To reasonable access to all places, public transport and information
- To use sign language, Braille or other means of communication
- To access materials and devices to overcome constrains arising from the person's disability

Rights of Older Members of the Society
- To fully participate in the affairs of the society
- To pursue their personal development
- To live in dignity and respect
- To receive reasonable care and assistance from the family and state

Rights Enjoyed by Youths
- Right to access relevant education and training
- Have opportunity to associate, be represented and participate in political, social and economic spheres of life
- To be protected from harmful cultural practices and exploitation

Questions on the Human Rights
(a) Outline the principles of the Bill of rights
(b) Explain six reasons why Human Rights are justified
(c) Give two social rights enjoyed by people in Kenya
(d) State two Survival rights of children in Kenya
(e) State two developmental rights of children in Kenya
(f) Explain circumstances which may force the government to limit the rights and freedom of the individual
(g) State five factors that might hinder the enjoyment of the fundamental rights of an individual in Kenya
(h) State two circumstances under which the killing of a person shall not be considered as a violation of fundamental rights to life

The Barons

9 EUROPEAN INTEREST IN KENYA

For along time European countries were not interested in having colonies in Africa. This perception changed in the 18th century and many Europeans began seeking for colonies in Africa. This change was attributed to:

Economic Reasons

- In order to establish a reliable market for their manufactured goods in Britain
- Wealthy industrialists wanted colonies where they could invest their excess capital
- The European nations wanted colonies as source of raw materials for their industries.
- To stop slave trade and introduce a more legitimate trade
- To control the fertile highlands
- Control the coast in order to safe guard their trade in the Far East

Social Reasons

- To protect European missionaries and other British nationals who were already settled and carrying out their work in Kenya and Uganda.
- To secure settlement for their surplus population
- To gain prestige by having colonies

Political Reasons

- To establish their control over the source of River Nile because of their interest in Egypt. To achieve this, they wanted to gain access to Uganda so as to control the River Nile.
- To prevent Kenya from being colonized by other European powers

Factors That Facilitated the Establishment of British Colonial Rule in Kenya

- Some African leaders collaborated with the Europeans, for example *Nabongo* Mumia of the Wanga Kingdom and Lenana who was a Maasai *oloibon*.
- Some African rulers were ignorant of the true implication of the protectorate treaty which they signed with the Europeans.
- The British used their superior military weapons and army to vanquish the African communities.
- The missionaries persuaded their home government to come and offer them protection
- There was disunity among the Africans – some were used to suppressed their fellow Africans
- The Europeans had worked out their strategies of occupation during the Berlin Conference. They also agreed to co-operate to deal with the Africans
- The discovery of quinine reduced European mortality. This made it possible for them to stay in Kenya long enough to impose their colonial rule.
- European traders persuaded their governments to acquire African territories which they considered as their commercial spheres.
- The construction of the Kenya- Uganda railway enabled the Europeans to send administrators and troops to the interior especially to the resisting communities.
- Establishment of administrative posts, for example Muranga, Machakos etc. assisted the Europeans to colonize Africans easily.
- Use of the chartered companies – Which pioneered the colonization by suppressing the resisting Africans.

AFRICAN REACTION TO EUROPEAN INVASION IN KENYA

Africans reacted differently to the coming of Europeans in Kenya. There are communities which immediately took up arms and attempted to drive out the intruders. These groups are said to have resisted European rule actively. They included the Nandi, the Giriama, Abagusii and the Bukusu. Notable African leaders who resisted European rule actively were Koitalel arap Samoi of the Nandi and Mekatilili wa Mwenza of the Agiriama. Other groups welcomed the Europeans and were used to impose the colonial rule in the country. These categories of Africans are called collaborators and included the Maasai and the Wanga. Leaders who collaborated with Europeans included Lenana of the Maasai, Mumia of the Wanga, Chief Odera Akang'o of Gem and Chief Kinyajui of the Agikuyu. In some communities, some sections welcomed the Europeans while other sections resisted them. These groups of people are said to have exhibited mixed reactions. They included the Kamba, the Luo and the Agikuyu.

MIXED REACTIONS

The communities which exhibited mixed reaction included:

- Akamba
- Agikuyu and
- Luo

THE AKAMBA REACTION

The onset of the British traders threatened the eminence of the Akamba as middlemen during the Long Distance Trade. The British made attempts to discontinue the Akamba raids on their neighbours like the Oromo, Agikuyu and Maasai.

Causes of Kamba Resistance

- The British failed to respect the Akamba traditions and customs. They, for example cut down their *ithembo* (shrine) tree for a flag post at Mutituni in 1891.

- The intervention of British when the Akamba attacked the Agikuyu was not taken kindly.
- The Akamba were dissatisfied with the company officials (based at Machakos) who raped their women.
- The establishment of colonial administration upset the Long Distance Trade, which was their lifeline.
- The establishment of British rule meant loss of independence for the Akamba.
- The Kamba were against the building of a British fort at Masaku in 1890.
- The British kept on disrupting their peace by sending military expeditions against them.
- The Akamba resisted forced labour.

Course of the Akamba Resistance

In 1890, Nzibu Mweu led the Akamba in boycotting to sell goods to the company agents. In the same year, prophetess Syonguu ordered the Iveti Warriors to attack the Masaku Fort as a reaction to the cutting down of their *ithembo* tree for a flagpole. The British agents were defeated during this surprise attack.

In 1894, a Warrior, Mwatu wa Ngoma ordered the Akamba warriors to again attack the British who had tried to intervene when the Kamba raided their neighbours. The British responded with devastating consequences on the side of the Akamba who were forced to collaborate with British District Commissioner, John Ainsworth. Their leader, Mwatu wa Ngoma also became a collaborator.

Another gallant fighter, Mwanamuka, led the Kangundo people to attack the colonial police at Mukuyuni and Mwala, killing six in the process. With the assistance of Maasai mercenaries, the British sent a punitive expedition against the Akamba and confiscated their livestock. Mwanamuka tried fruitlessly to blockade the Lukenya area to cut off communication between Fort Smith and Masaku. He was equally, met with devastating consequences and forced to petition for peace.

Reasons for the Akamba collaboration with the British included:

- The Kamba lost heavily to the British in 1894 and this created fear among some section of the Akamba.
- The merciless killings and looting of property by superintendent Leith against the Syonguu's forces in 1891, made many Kamba warriors to submit to the British forces.
- Some Kamba, especially the traders, collaborated with the British because they expected material rewards.
- Collaborators also wanted to gain prestige.
- They wanted to get guns to use in their hunting and raiding activities.
- The Akamba had been weakened by the 1899 famine and were therefore unable to effectively challenge the British.

Reasons for the Akamba Defeat

- Some self-serving Kamba opportunists allied with the colonial agents to enrich themselves and this weakened the resistance.
- Due to lack of territorial cohesion and centralized system of government, the Kamba were unable to co-ordinate a strong resistance against the British.
- Some sections of the Akamba community experienced severe famine in 1899 and were therefore unable to stage an effective resistance to the British.
- The missionaries pacified some sections to the Kamba who collaborated with the intruders.
- When the Akamba caravan trade and raiding activities were upset, they lost a significant source of livelihood and could not effectively sustain themselves.

Consequences of the Akamba Reaction

- The Akamba lost their independence.

- Kamba land was alienated to pave way for European settlement.
- Many Akamba warriors were killed during the confrontation with the British soldiers.
- The British interfered with the Akamba culture, for instance cutting down their *Ithembo* trees and raping their women.
- The Akamba were heavily taxed to raise revenue for the colonial administration.
- Many of the Akamba men were forcefully conscripted into the King's African Rifles (KAR) to serve as carrier corps in World War I.

THE AGIKUYU REACTION

They showed a mixed reaction against the British because they were highly fragmented and lacked territorial cohesion.

Causes of Agikuyu Resistance

- The British did not respect the Agikuyu traditions and customs. The missionaries, for example campaigned against female circumcision and Kikuyu forms of worship.
- The Agikuyu were against the raids which were conducted by the agents of Imperial British East African Company (IBEA) – for their cattle and grains.
- The conduct of some company officials like killing them and raping their women, caused fretfulness among the Agikuyu.
- The Agikuyu were revolting against the forced supply of grains and water, by their women, to the British soldiers.
- There was massive land alienation, which had left many of the Agikuyu landless or pushed to unproductive land.
- Some leaders like Waiyaki wa Hinga feared Losing their independence.
- The Agikuyu were reacting against the punishment meted on them by the British for raiding Fort Smith in 1892.

Reasons why Some Agikuyu Collaborated

• Agikuyu leaders like Kinyanjui wa Gathirimu and Karuri wa Gakure wanted to acquire personal wealth through collaboration.

• Associating with Europeans made some leaders feel recognized by Europeans and their esteem raised among their fellow Africans

• Some of their leaders hoped that by collaborating, they would be made paramount Chiefs.

• The collaborators wanted the British to protect them against their enemies.

• Some Agikuyu wanted to take advantage of the British western civilization particularly education and religion.

• They also wanted material gains from the British through trading with them.

• The Agikuyu of Nyeri realized that it was futile to resist the militarily superior Europeans.

Organization of the Agikuyu Reaction

• Captain Lugard established a fort at Dagoretti in 1890 and developed convivial relationship with Waiyaki wa Hinga who was in charge of the area. Wayaki's people supplied Lugard's men with food.

• However, when Wilson took over from Lugard who transferred to Uganda, his soldiers began looting food and livestock from the Agikuyu. They responded by setting Dagoretti Fort ablaze.

• Waiyaki was arrested by the forces sent by Sub-commissioner Ainsworth, and died enroute to Mombasa. It is alleged that he was buried alive at Kibwezi after provoking his captors.

• Kinyanjui wa Gathirimu, who succeeded Waiyaki at Dagoretti in 1899, was a collaborator.

• Fort Dagoretti was closed down due to a series of raids and Francis Hall opened another fort at Murang'a. The locals were subdued and forced to accept the British Colonial rule.

• A British trader John Boyes forged an alliance with Karuri wa Gakure, the Agikuyu leader at Fort Hall, which enabled him to subdue the resisting Agikuyu groups. He also made contacts with Wang'ombe of Gaki (Nyeri) who together with Gakure supplied the British with mercenaries in exchange for confiscated loots from resisting groups.

• Meinertzhagen, who succeeded Francis Hall in 1902, subdued the Muruku and Tetu section of the Agikuyu led by Chief Gakere.

• Chief Gakere was murdered and his associates deported to the coastal region after they wiped out an entire Asian caravan on the slopes of the Aberdares.

• The Agikuyu of Iriani (Nyeri) were defeated in 1904 and their Aembu and Ameru allies sought for peace in 1906, having seen the effects of resisting. By 1910, British rule had been established in the entire Mount Kenya region. With the Agikuyu settling peacefully in the reserves upto 1920's when they began to agitate again.

Results of the Agikuyu Mixed Reaction

• The reactions fuelled mistrust, hatred and animosity in most parts of Kikuyuland. Such feelings of skepticism continue among the Agikuyu of Murang'a, Kiambu and Nyeri to date.

• There was massive alienation of Agikuyu land by the British with the help of the collaborators like Wang'ombe wa Ihura and Gathirimu who gave land to the British for construction work. The Agikuyu lost their land and became squatters.

• Some Agikuyu leaders accumulated a lot of wealth and rose to prominence. For example, Karuri wa Gakure and Wang'ombe of Nyeri,

• The collaborators like Kinyanjui wa Gathirimu and his people received Western Education and were converted to Christianity.

- There was massive loss of lives among the Agikuyu who resisted the British rule. For example, Waiyaki wa Hinga and many Agikuyu fighters were killed.
- Both collaborators and those who resisted the colonial rule lost their independence when their territory was declared a British protectorate.
- The Agikuyu wars of resistance forced the British to shift their administrative base from Dagoretti to Fort Hall.
- There was massive destruction of property. The Agikuyu razed down Fort Dagoretti and their villages were burnt by the British.
- The Kikuyu, who collaborated, became colonial headmen and other agents of British rule in Kenya.

COLLABORATION

Some African communities in Kenya collaborated with the Europeans because:

- They needed support to defeat their rivals or traditional enemies. Lenana, for instance wanted support against his brother Sendeyo.
- Internal problems like civil wars, epidemic and hunger, drought and famine etc. weakened some communities like the Maasai. Apart from not being in a position to mount an effective challenge to a more superior group, they were in dire need for assistance.
- It was prestigious for some leaders to be associated with the superior race hence the titles like paramount chiefs being granted to some.
- They wanted to acquire western education, health and religion.
- They wanted to extend trade ties more so in fire arms.

THE WANGA COLLABORATION

Nabongo Mumia, of the Wanga Kingdom in western Kenya, exhibited bootlicking tendencies from onset. He collaborated with Arabs and later the British. In the latter's case he wanted to:

- Strengthen his position as a leader and that of his Kingdom, the Wanga.
- Get military support against the Luo of Ugenya and the Bukusu - his traditional enemies.
- Obtain material rewards from the British.
- Get modern fire arms for his army.
- Gain prestige and fame by befriending the British.
- Take advantage of western civilization, particularly education and Christianity for his children.
- Wanted to spare his people from the atrocities because he had seen the futility of resistance.

Nabongo Mumia

Nabongo knew that the British would declare Western Kenya their protectorate especially after they had declared Uganda a protectorate in 1894. He therefore sought to ally with them.

Effects of Mumai's Collaboration

- Mumias was honoured by being declared the Wanga paramount chief. He ruled as a British paramount chief upto 1926 when he officially retired.

- Mumias warriors actively became the agents of British colonialism and were used to perpetuate British rule by subduing the Luo, Bukusu and Nandi in western Kenya.
- The IBEAC was allowed to establish a base at Mumias, which became the centre of colonial administration in western Kenya upto 1920.
- Nabongo Mumia was able to enjoy the lucrative trade by having Mumias serve as major terminus for trade caravans to Uganda. He acquired firearms and other exotic commodities.
- His co-operation with the British intensified enmity and hostility between his people and other Abaluhya sub-sections. There were several attempts to kill Nabongo Mumia.
- The British employed the services of the Wanga agents to rule over Western Kenya indirectly. Mumia's half brothers were appointed chiefs of the Isukha and Idakho.
- Mumia readily provided the colonial authorities with vital information over the appointment of chief and headmen in western Kenya.
- His headquarters, Elureko became the major administrative headquarters in the British territory of western Kenya upto 1920, when Kenya was declared a colony. It was shifted to Kakamega.
- The Wanga were able to expand with the support of the British by annexing new territories in Samia, Bunyala and Busonga.
- Mumia and his people acquired some material benefits through trade, western education and religion.
- Wanga independence was compromised after the British declared Kenya their colony in 1920.

THE MAASAI COLLABORATION

They were led by Lenana when the British came to the area. He welcomed the British because:

- He wanted to consolidate his position and that of his kingdom.
- Maasai were weakened by widespread drought and famine, and Lenana required relief assistance.
- The civil war between the Purko and Kwavi Maasai had weakened the Maasai.
- The Maasai were weakened by natural calamities and diseases (Rinder pest) which affected their animals. Maasai livelihood was greatly affected by the loss of large herds of animals.
- The emergence of the Nandi as a strong power in the 18th century threatened the existence of the Maasai community.
- He wanted British support against his brother Sendeyo with whom he had a protracted engagement in a succession dispute.
- The Maasai developed fear of the British after the Kedong Massacre - Lenana was greatly impressed by the British military might and decided to be their friend.
- The Maasai wanted help to get back their women and children who had been left in custody of the Agikuyu during the 1891 famine.

Results of Maasai's Collaboration with the British

- Lenana was recognized as a paramount chief of the Maasai.
- The Purko Maasai were divided into two sections Loita and Ngong, leading to the separation of the two clans.
- There was total disruption of their cattle economy and territorial integrity – their migratory lifestyle was curtained when they were confined to Ngong
- Lenana's rival, Sendeyo was defeated and this marked Lenana's political growth among the Kenyan Maasai
- The Maasai were used by the British in colonial conquest - Maasai warriors were used in British punitive expeditions against

The Barons

the Nandi in 1906. The Agikuyu resistance was brought to a halt in 1904.

- The Maasai were given cattle as a reward for their assistance
- The British were able to build the railway across Maasai land and Nandi land without further hindrance.
- Maasai land was alienated and given to the white settlers. The Maasai were pushed into unfertile reserves, Laikipia and Ngong.

ACTIVE RESISTANCE

Africans resisted the establishment of British rule in Kenya because:

- Some communities like the Nandi overestimated their military prowess against their neighbours and believed that no other community could defeat them.
- Some communities had established strong socio-political systems which they did not want foreigners to destroy
- Some communities resisted because their socio-economic political set ups were strong enough to sustain resistance – the Nandi practiced mixed economy and could fight a protracted battle.
- They wanted to protect their independence against foreign invaders
- Most communities underestimated the military strength of the British – the colour of the White men made the Nandi to mistake them for *big babies* who could easily be defeated.
- They were against the alienation of their land

THE NANDI RESISTANCE
Causes of the Nandi Resisted
- The Nandi were confident of beating the whites because they had defeated most of their neighbours like the Abagusii and Maasai.
- They despised any intrusion of other communities into their midst and abhorred

the snobbish way in which the British invaded their land.

- The Nandi saw the Whites as devils who they had to expel
- They had a long history of resisting and fighting intruders
- They disliked the annexation of their land for railway construction and white settlement
- The Nandi did not want to lose their freedom and independence
- They had youthful warriors who were militant and ready to showcase they military prowess in opportunities like fighting the British.
- The Nandi had able leaders like Koitalel Arap Samoei who inspired them to egg on.
- The coming of the Whites had been prophesized by Kimnyole and they did not want to lose their power as envisaged.

What Made Nandi Resistance Protracted
- Nandi lived in a mountainous and forested terrain which favoured their guerilla tactics of fighting.
- The age-set system provided the Nandi with young disciplined, experienced and organized worriers.
- The office of Orkoiyot provided solidarity which enabled the Nandi to fight against the British as a single community
- The Nandi were supported by their kinfolk, the Kipsigis, to fight the British.
- The Nandi practiced mixed economy and could depend on either livestock or crops to sustain them during the war.
- The wet and cold climate caused respiratory diseases among the British troops
- The Nandi blacksmiths manufactured weapons and this ensured regular supply of arms during the resistance.
- The Nandi were naturally a war-like society. Having defeated most people, their pride would not allow them to give in easily.

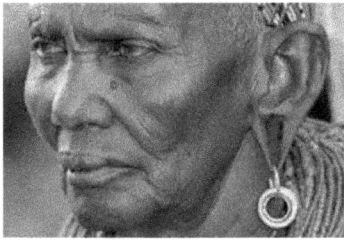
Koitalel Arap Samoei

The reasons which led to the Nandi defeat included:

- The British got reinforcement from India and among the Swahili and Somali fighters
- The Nandi traditional weapons, for example spears were no match for the British guns.
- The British army was better organized and disciplined than the Nandi warriors.

Meinertzhagen

- The British tricked the Nandi and used treacherous methods. For example, in October 1905, the commander of the British troops in Nandi territory, Captain Meinerzhagen arranged to have a meeting with the Nandi Orkoiyot, Koitalel Arap Samoei. He was killed in cold blood by the British and this demoralized and weakened the Nandi.
- The British used scorched earth military technique - They burnt down the Nandi houses, destroyed their crops and confiscated their livestock. The destruction caused by the British led to starvation and this weakened the Nandi

- Natural calamities - small pox epidemics broke out in the 1890's and killed many Nandi. This weakened the survivors.
- The Nandi fought singly and were not supported by other neighbouring communities like the Abaluyhia and Luo

Results of the Nandi Resistance

- Nandi were colonized by the British and lost their sovereignty.
- The British annexed the fertile lands belonging to the Nandi and they were pushed to the infertile reserves
- Over 1000 Nandi warriors were killed including their leader, Koitalel.
- The Nandi lost their prestige and leadership in the region.
- The Nandi military organization was disintegrated.
- The Nandi became squatters and labourers in the white farms.
- Many Nandi warriors were recruited into the colonial police.

AGIRIAMA RESISTANCE

They were motivated by the Mazrui Arabs and the Swahili who rose up against the British in 1895. They supported the Mazrui Arabs with whom they had developed long trading links. The Agiriama were also hitting back at the Busaidi Arabs who were encroaching on their territory. The British supported the Al Busaidi collaborators throughout their succession conflicts.

The British bombarded Rashid's Headquarters at Mweli forcing the Agiriama and the Mazrui to resort to guerilla technique. While the Mazrui Arabs easily capitulated, the Agiriama resorted to full scale resistance against the British infringement in 1914. The Agiriama were inspired by their prophetess, Mekatilili wa Mwenza who was joined by an elder, Wanje wa Madorika. The two were instrumental in mobilizing the community to a mass resistance against the British invasion.

The Barons

Cause of Giriama Resistance

- The Agiriama were opposed to forced labour on British plantations established on land which had been filched from them.
- They lost their land to the British due to the massive land alienation for settler farming.
- They did not want to pay taxes, especially hut tax that was hurting the traditionally polygamous group. They were forced to pay in kind (labour) rather than cash.
- The British presence had led to the loss of their ivory trade
- The British policemen at Kitengani insulted the Agiriama culture by raping their women
- They wanted to maintain their freedom and independence.
- They were forced into military conscription by the British
- They disliked the British-appointed headmen whose duties included collection of taxes and recruitment of labour.

Course of the Resistance

The immediate cause of the Giriama reaction was the forced military recruitment into the Kings African Rifles (KAR). They barred their young men from moving outside their villages to work. Mekatilili and Wanje called on the people to return to their ancestral shrine at Kaya Fungo. They offered sacrifices and denounced all appointed puppet rulers. The two administered traditional oaths to unite and inspire the people to fight on. *Mukushekushe* oath was administered to women while the *Fisi* oath was for men. When the British declared a state of emergency over the Agiriama, they resorted to a hit-and-run technique. Homes of loyalists, Europeans and collaborators were attacked and the missionaries were forced to seek refuge at Rabai.

Role of Mekatilili in the Agiriama Resistance

- She encouraged the Agiriama to face the British by administering oaths to unite them
- She presented the grievances of the Agiriama to the British.
- She rallied the Giriama together against a common enemy hence laying the basis for nationalistic struggles for independence.

The British responded to this atrocity by burning villages and crops, and driving away the Giriama livestock. The resistance fizzled out when Mekatilili and Wanje were arrested and deported to Kisii. The Arabs, under Fadhili bin Omari, mediated between the Agiriama and the British marking the end of the war under the following terms: -

- The Agiriama were to offer a specific number of labourers for European settlers and public works.
- The Agiriama were to offer a certain number of able-bodied men to serve in the King's African Rifles.
- The British would occupy all the land to the north of River Sabaki.

Results of the Agiriama Resistance

- Many people lost their lives as a result of fighting
- Many people lost their property which were destroyed by the British forces
- Their property were confiscated by the British
- The community's economic activities were upset, especially the lucrative trade at Takaungu, where they had been working as middlemen.
- The British were forced to withdraw the order which demanded that the Giriama were to be moved from their homes
- A woman leader arose to lead the rebellion, Mekatilili.
- The Agiriama were prohibited from brewing traditional liquor.

- The Agiriama lost their independence to the British

BUKUSU RESISTANCE

The resistance began with an ambush of a trade caravan passing through their land. The Bukusu stole all their rifles and when they were commanded to surrender the same in 1894, they declined. A punitive expedition was sent by the British which the Bukusu defeated. The British administrator at Elureko, Charles Hobley sought for reinforcement from Major William Grant of the Ugandan protectorate. In 1895, at the battles of Lumboka and Chetambe, the Bukusu were summarily defeated.

Causes of the Resistance
- The Bukusu wanted to safeguard their independence and cultural practices like circumcision.
- They did not want to recognize Nabongo Mumia as the overall leader of Abaluhyia.
- They were against the idea of forced payments of taxes to the British.
- The Bukusu did not want to surrender the guns their warriors possessed as demanded by the British in 1894.
- The British invaded the Bukusu when they were at the pinnacle of their military power.

Methods used by the Bukusu to resist the British
- Use of Warfare: they directly fought the British troops at Lumboka and Chetambe hills.
- Ambushes: the Bukusu ambushed a caravan of traders and stole their rifles.
- Revolting against the rule by Wanga agents: the Bukusu murdered a Wanga agent (Hamisi) who had been sent, to administer the area.

Effects of the Bukusu Resistance
- Much of the Bukusuland was alienation by the British

- They lost their independence and Bukusuland was declared part of the British East Africa Protectorate.
- Many Bukusu warriors were killed in the battle of Lumboka and Chetambe.
- A lot of Bukusu property was destroyed and their economy upset. They lost their cattle and sheep which were confiscated.
- Bukusu women and children were taken captive by the British

THE SOMALI RESISTANCE

The British declaration of Jubaland a British protectorate kindled the Somali resistance. Ahmad bin Murgan led the resistance.

Causes of Somali Resistance
- The Somali were opposed to the splitting up of Somaliland into the British and Italian spheres of influence, which separated the clans.
- The Somali were against British control of their pastureland and watering points.
- The British wanted the Somali to drop their nomadic way of life.
- The Somali were opposed to castigatory expeditions sent against them.
- The Somali were opposed to being controlled by the British whom they regarded as infidels (non believers).
- The British attempt to stop the Somali raiding activities against their neighbours exasperated them.

Course of the Resistance
The British were initially not keen on suppressing the Somali. This was because:
- It was viewed as expensive in terms of both arms and military personnel.
- Being nomadic, the group would be very hard and time consuming to suppress.
- There was no economic justification for waging a war on a highly unproductive territory.

However, when the Somali murdered the British sub-commissioner for Jubaland, Mr. Jenner (1900), the British dispatched a punitive expedition of Indian brigade against them. The Somali rose up again in 1905 against the British and the skirmishes continued into 1914 when the boundaries were changed. It finally ended in 1925 when Jubaland was put under the Italian Somaliland.

Results of the Somali Resistance

- Many Somalis were killed. Jenner, the British Sub-commissioner was also killed in the war.
- The *Darod* and *Hawiye* clans were divided by the partition of Jubaland in 1914.
- Somali cattle were confiscated.
- The Somali resistance delayed the process of colonization of Kenya.
- Ogaden was placed under Italian Somaliland.

Whether the African communities in Kenya opted to fight or collaborate, the bottom line was the same, loss of sovereignty. Communities which chose the war path were all defeated and forcefully brought under the colonial yoke. The main reason why the British were able to conquer most communities in Kenyan during the 19th century was their military might. Other reasons which contributed to these defeats were: -

- Division among Kenyan societies into autonomous units
- Local rivalry which enabled the British to play one community against the other
- The inferior weapons which were used by the Africans.
- Africans lacked disciplined force to counter the superior European army.
- Natural calamities, epidemics and famine made it difficult for most communities in Kenya to mount an effective challenge.
- Some communities assisted the enemy to fight their fellow colleagues - the British used the Maasai and Wanga to fight the Nandi

Questions on African Reaction to European Invasion in Kenya

(a) Explain the factors that facilitated the establishment of British Colonial rule in Kenya
(b) Give two terms of the Anglo German Agreement of 1890
(c) Explain why the British established control over Kenya
(d) Give five reasons which made African communities to collaborate with colonialists
(e) Identify two communities which showed mixed resistance in Kenya
(f) State five reasons for the Agikuyu Mixed Reason towards the British invasion
(g) Discuss the consequences of the Agikuyu mixed reactions.
(h) Why did Nabongo Mumia collaborate with the British?
(i) State five reasons why the Maasai collaborated with the British in the colonial period.
(j) What were the results of the collaboration between Mumia of Wanga and the British?
(k) Explain the results of the Maasai collaboration with the British
(l) State five reasons which led the Nandi to resist the British
(m) State five factors that made the Nandi to resist the British intrusion for a long time
(n) Give five reasons why the Nandi were defeated by the British
(o) Discuss factors which led to the defeat of the Nandi resistance by the British
(p) What were the results of the Nandi Resistance?
(q) Give five reasons which led to the Giriama Resistance
(r) What were the results of the Agiriama Resistance?

10 COMPANY RULE IN KENYA

The Berlin Conference, held in Germany from 1884 - 1885 paved way for the scramble and partition of Africa. The conference was held in order for the European powers (Belgium, Italy, Portugal, Spain, France and Britain) to agree on the regions in Africa that each power had the right to pursue legal ownership of land.

Carl Peters

At the conference, two European powers (Britain and Germany) expressed interest in the East African region. To resolve the dispute amicably the two powers signed a treaty in 1886 in which they agreed that Germany would lay claim to Tanganyika while the British would acquire areas where the present day Kenya and Uganda lie. Two colonial companies, one for the Germans and another for the British, were used to administer the region. The German East Africa Company (GEA) under Carl Peters was used to administer Tanganyika, Rwanda and Burundi.

The Britain did not take up direct administration of the region under its sphere of influence. This responsibility was given to a commercial company, IBEACo under Sir William Mackinnon who ran a shipping company. In 1887, the company was granted a concession to administer the area stretching from the East Coast of Africa to the kingdom of Buganda, on north eastern shores of Lake Victoria.

A charter was given to IBEACo which defined its operations. The company's broad mandate included:

- Instituting custom duties on trading activities and collecting taxes
- Establishing political authority in the area
- Pacifying the rebellious Africans
- Maintaining law and order in the region.
- Improving the area by building roads and railway line
- Civilizing the indigenous people in Kenya

The Anglo-German Agreement of 1886

Anglo-German Agreement facilitated the peaceful settlement of the German and British claims on East Africa. Its terms included:

- The Sultan was given the 16 kilometer (10 mile) coastal strip which stretched from Vanga to Lamu. Apart from towns like Kisimayu, Mogadishu, Merca, and Brava; the sultan also got the islands of Zanzibar, Pemba, Mafia, Lamu and Pate.
- Germany acquired Witu and the region between river Umba in the north and river Ruvuma in the south.
- The British got the territory north of river Umba up to river Juba in the north.

The treaty failed to determine the western boundary and this left Uganda up for grabs to any power which got there first. Uganda became the region of intense rivalry between Carl Peters who secured a treaty with Kabaka Mwanga in 1890 and Fredrick Lugard who tried in vain to sign a treaty with the same Kabaka. The tension led to the signing of Heligoland Treaty in 1890.

Terms of the Heligoland Treaty of 1890

- Germany officially recognized Uganda as a British sphere of influence.
- The western boundaries of both Uganda and Tanganyika were defined

- Britain gave up Heligoland Island in the North Sea to the Germans in return for Witu.
- Germany accepted British protectorate over Zanzibar and Pemba.
- Germany acquired a strip of land on Lake Tanganyika from Britain and the Coastal region of Tanganyika from the Sultan of Zanzibar.
- The Sultan of Zanzibar retained a 16km (10 miles) Coastal strip.
- Germany was granted Tanganyika

This treaty ended the scramble for and partition of East Africa.

The main reason why the British decided to use company rule in Kenya was because:
- She lacked adequate finance to meet the cost of effective occupation and administration of the region.
- The British tax payers were not ready to bear the burden of financing the colony, perceived as a "liability rather than an asset".
- It was convenient to use the company officials who were familiar with the region, having traded here for long.
- The government also lacked adequate personnel to use in administering this region.

The company faced many difficulties in its operations in Kenya and was compelled to windup its operations in 1894. These problems included:
- Rivalry between the company and that of the Germans over territorial boundaries.
- Lack of funds to undertake its tasks. This was because Kenya lacked strategic natural resources for export and the mismanagement of funds by corrupt company officials.
- Hostility and attacks by the local people
- Lack of experienced personnel to administer the colony
- Lack of co-ordination between the headquarters and company representatives in Kenya

- Lack of good means of transport to facilitate the co-ordination of their activities
- The officials were affected by unfavourable climatic conditions and tropical diseases

Achievements of the Company

Despite the many challenges faced by the company, there were a few good things which were attributed to it. The company: -
- Quelled local African resistances like the Nandi resistance.
- Laid the basis of colonial administration by establishing administrative bases like Fort Hall.
- Developed rubber industry along the coast and the interior
- Secured the freedom of several slaves.
- Built the first roads.

The British government dissolved IBEACo on 1st July 1885 and proclaimed a protectorate over the region. The administration was transferred to the foreign officer (Sir Arthur Henry Hardinge) based in Zanzibar.

Questions on Company Rule in Kenya

(a) Give the main reason why the British used company rule in Kenya

(b) Name two chartered companies which established spheres of influence in East Africa in the 1880's

(c) State two reasons why the British used the imperial British East Africa Company (I.B.E.A) to administer her possessions

(d) State two powers that were given to the Imperial British East African Company

(e) State two achievements of the Imperial British East Africa Company in Kenya

(f) What two reasons led to the collapse of the Imperial East African Company (IBEAC) by 1894?

(g) State five problems that the imperial British East African Company faced in administering Kenya

Hierarchy of Colonial Administration in Kenya

- Colonial Secretary: Was the top most political head of the British administration and coordinated colonial policies which were decided by the cabinet and the British parliament. He was based in London.
- Governor: He represented the British at the colony. He reported to the colonial secretary and was the head of the executive council. He gave ascent to laws from the Legislative council before they were implemented. The governor maintained law and order in the colony
- Provincial Commissioner: He represented the governor at the provincial level. The PC supervised the work of the DC and DO on behalf of the governor.
- District Commissioner: Were in charge of policy implementation in the districts. They maintained law, order and security in their areas of jurisdiction. The DC coordinated the work of the DO's and chiefs
- District Officer: Implemented the orders from the DC: They maintained law and order and coordinated the work of chiefs.
- Chiefs: Worked as links between the people and the governor at the local level. They maintained law and order and coordinated the work of the headmen.
- Headmen: They served as the link between the government and the people at the grass root level. They mobilized their people for development within their villages. Both chief and headmen collected taxes and recruited labour for public work and to work in the white farms.

The Local Government during Colonial Period

Colonial government was created during colonial time in order to: -

- Develop a sense of responsibility and duty among Africans.
- Provide a forum where educated Africans expressed themselves.
- Provide a means through which the government would understand the Africans.
- Ensure proper restriction of Africans in their reserves.
- Provide a legal forum for local people to make day to day decisions.
- Make use of locally available resources to develop native areas.
- Provide a link between the local people and the government.

The local government in Kenya faced many problems during colonial era. These problems included:

- Chronic shortage of trained personnel.
- Poor transport and communication network.
- Lack of strategic minerals limited the amount of funds required for administering the region.
- A lot of rivalry between the Africans and the settlers.
- Racial discrimination which led to poor basic amenities for the Africans.

Achievements of the Local Native Council

- Restricted the African activities especially the political agitation
- Provided Africans with basic needs like schools, cattle dips and markets
- It exploited the local resources and created a link between the local people and the government
- It encouraged the development of infrastructure and the general welfare of the Africans
- Collected taxes to finance their operations
- It assisted in arbitration of African disputes

Effects of Colonial Rule in Kenya

- Introduced western education. This education not only enlightened the Africans, but also undermined their culture.

- Built hospitals and introduced modern medicine. Other than eliminating many diseases, these facilities eroded the African's faith on traditional herbal practices and the magicians.
- Introduced Christianity which created new alliances and divisions among Africans.
- Influenced Africans to adapt to Western values and practices like new ways of dressing and a foreign language, English.
- Encouraged the construction of permanent and improved building
- Brought to halt the migration and settlement of Kenyan communities – Kipande system restricted their movement and reserves confined them to specific areas.
- Led to the expansion and improvement of transport and communication system – the railway line was built by the British.
- Improved means of transport and communication encouraged interaction between different African communities.
- They introduced new crops like coffee and tea.

COLONIAL ADMINISTRATION IN KENYA

The British used two systems to administer Kenya, the direct and indirect system of rule. Direct system was used in most parts of the country because: -

- These regions lacked centralized administrative system and colonial chiefs had to be appointed to administer them.
- Many ethnic groups in Kenya with diverse socio-cultural systems made it hard to create a unifying factor.
- Most communities resisted the British rule and had to be suppressed and controlled directly.
- The colonial government maintained a status quo by retaining the direct system and the company officials who were used to administering Kenya.

In the beginning, the British did not value Kenya, but preferred India hence used indirect rule to: -

- Cut down the cost of administrating Kenya.
- Mollify the African leaders so that they would be less rebellious.
- Make proper use of their few personnel.
- Use a system which had succeeded in other parts of the world like Uganda and India.

Effects of Indirect Rule in Kenya

- Indirect rule, pegged on the policy of "divide and rule" segregated Kenyans on tribal lines.
- Some African chiefs used their powers to stockpile wealth in terms of land and livestock.
- Colonial chiefs were hated by those who rejected the colonial rule and they were seen as traitors.
- Creation of chiefs in the former stateless societies made them mediators between rulers and the ruled
- Most chiefs lacked legitimacy because they had no traditional claim to power.

Questions on Colonial Administration in Kenya

(a) Describe the hierarchy of colonial administration in Kenya
(b) State two objectives of setting up Local Native Council during colonial era in Kenya
(c) State five factors that undermined the operations of the local government during the colonial time
(d) Explain five social effects of colonial rule to the Africans in Kenya

11 SOCIAL AND ECONOMIC DEVELOPMENTS DURING THE COLONIAL PERIOD IN KENYA

KENYA-UGANDA RAILWAY

line was built by the British with the aid of the Indian coolies. The latter were preferred because the Africans had no experience in the work and were opposed to the British. The railway line was built to fulfill the requirements of the Berlin Conference of 1884-1885, developing occupied regions to show signs of effective occupation. The railway line would also be used:

• To facilitate effective control and development of Uganda.

• To protect British strategic interests in East Africa by protecting the sources of the River Nile

• To provide a quick, safe and convenient means of transport for government administrators and troops to quell the rebellious Africans

• To open up Kenya for economic exploitation.

Indian Coolies

Problems Met by the Railway Builders

• The "man eaters" of Tsavo almost brought the construction work to a standstill. Construction work only resumed after the lions were killed by Colonel Patterson.

• Construction work was made difficult by the hilly landscape and the valleys especially in the Rift Valley where expensive tunnels and bridges had to be built.

• Many Africans were not willing to do construction work or did not have the required skills. The British had to import the Coolies from India to do the work at a more expensive cost.

• Construction work was disrupted by the Nandi raiders who terrorized the builders and stole their equipment.

• The builders faced harsh climatic conditions around the Nyika region and also lacked water and food in that dry environment.

• The Indian workers were affected by jiggers and other tropical diseases.

• It was quite problematic to transport the heavy building materials into the interior for the construction work.

Impact of the Kenya-Uganda Railway

• The railway line boosted administration, troops and colonial administrators were easily transported to different parts of the country.

• Towns like Nairobi, Nakuru and Naivasha developed along the railway lines or on terminal points like Port Florence (Kisumu).

• The railway line fast trucked the movement of heavy goods and people to the interior of Kenya.

• It encouraged trade - goods were transported efficiently to the location of business premises and to the market.

• It brought people from different parts of Kenya to work and live together. This increased their social and cultural interaction. Interacting together also increased their political awareness.

• The railway line encouraged Europeans to settle and practices their agricultural activities in the highlands of Kenya.

The Barons

- The construction of the railway contributed to the development of settler farming in Kenya
- Some of the Indian Coolies who came to build the railway line remained in the country and now form the Indian community in Kenya. They set up business premises in various locations in the country. Some of these locations developed into urban centres.
- The ease in transporting raw materials led to the development of industries in the country.
- It facilitated the spread of religion to the interior – through missionaries.
- The railway line encouraged agricultural activities in the country.
- Many people got employment in the railway industry
- The railway line was a major booster of revenue to the colonial and post colonial governments in Kenya.

Questions on Kenya – Uganda Railway

(a) State three political reasons for the construction of the Uganda Railway
(b) Give two reasons why the Uganda railway was built
(c) State five problems experienced during the construction of the railway line
(d) State six effects of the construction of the Kenya-Uganda Railway on the people of Kenya
(e) State two ways through which the construction of the Uganda railway contributed to the development of settler farming in Kenya

---

SETTLER FARMING IN KENYA

Europeans began settling in Kenya in 1890. Sir Charles Norton Eliot, a commissioner of British East Africa around 1900 – 1904, is credited with initiating the policy of white supremacy in the country. From 1902, the British government encouraged white settlers to settle in Kenya.

European settlement began in earnest after the promulgation of the Crown Land Ordinance (1902). The ordinance declared that all land belonged to the British Imperial Government.

Sir Charles Norton Eliot

Upto 1908, nearly all alienated land was found near the railway towns. This was the area between Kibwezi in the east and Fort Ternan station in the west. The second phase of European settlement was into the Uasin Gishu plateau, with major focus around Eldoret town. The third phase of European settlement started after the World War I. Land was allotted to the demobilized soldiers in the Kenya highlands under the ex-soldier settlement schemes.

The Crown Land Ordinance of 1902 provided for sale of land and leases to the settlers. According to the ordinance, the Crown had original title to the land and where Africans vacated or deserted the land, that parcel was considered waste and reverted back to the Crown. That land could be given to the settlers. The Crown Land Ordinance (1902) also provided that the settler-farmers would lease land for 99 years and not 21 years, as per the Ordinance of 1897. Each settler was to be given 160 acres free of charge as inducement to farm. In 1915 the leasehold terms were raised from 99 years to 999 years and this further stimulated the immigration of the white settlers into Kenya. From 1914 to 1950 the number of white settlers in Kenya had shot from 1,000 to 80,000.

White settlers in the early years of the 20th century were led by Lord Delemare from Chesire (England). By 1912, Delemare and his followers had shifted their base to the highlands near Nairobi where they established mixed agricultural farms. The pioneer farmers suffered a lot in their farming ventures, as little was known of crops to grow in the region. Through trial and error method they established plantations of tea, coffee, pineapples, cotton, sisal, pyrethrum and wattle trees. They also set up ranches for animals

Lord Delemare

The colonial government encouraged the European settlers to come to Kenya because:

• The colonial government wanted to make Kenya a white man's country by encouraging white settlers to form the backbone of the economy.

• The colonial government wanted to offload the British tax payer the burden of shouldering the responsibility of financing the administrative expense of the colony.

• The settlers' economic activities would help the colonial government to repay the construction costs of railway and to maintain it.

• The settlers would produce raw materials for the British industries.

• The colonial government wanted to counter the growing Asian influence in Kenya by encouraging European settlement.

• The fertile soil and cool climate in the Kenya highlands suited European settlement.

What Favoured Settler Farming in Kenya

• European settlers were provided with large tracts of land which were alienated from Africans through various land legislations

• The squatter system ensured that Africans residing in the settler farms provided required labour in return of small plots where they practiced subsistence farming

• They introduced forced labour on European farms to ensure steady supply of labour from the Africans

• The building of the railway facilitated the transportation of farm products and inputs. It also made the Kenya highlands to be more accessible.

• The government encouraged the formation of co-operatives such as Kenya Co-operative Creameries (KCC) and Kenya Farmers Association (KFA) to help the farmers to market their products.

• Extension services were rendered to the settlers to sensitive them on better animal and crop husbandry

• Through political representation in the legislative council, they managed to get many concessions from the government such as tariff barriers and removal of custom duties

• Research was done to improve the quality of animals and crops.

• Banking system and loan facilities were introduced to subsidize settlers' initiative

• Agricultural activities of the Africans were controlled. For instance, up to the 1930's, Africans were not allowed to grow cash crops.

• Establishment of agro based industries created market for their produce

• The settlers were accorded protection against possible African uprising.

Africans were barred from growing cash crops so that they do not create unnecessary competition and reduce the workforce in white farms. The excuse given by the colonial government was that:

• African crops were prone to diseases and this would spread to white farms

• Africans lacked knowledge and would lower the quality of farm produce

Africans were not willing to provide labour in settlers' farms during the colonial period. This was because:

- They were bitter that settlers had taken their land.
- Wages provided by the settlers were low and unattractive
- They were subjected to poor and harsh working conditions.
- Division of labour in African traditional society did not allow African men to leave their families

To overcome this bottleneck, the colonial government came up with new policies to ensure a steady and cheap supply of African labour to the white farms. They:

- Introduced forced labour on European farms.
- Introduced Master Servant Ordinance in 1906 which made it an offence for Africans to evade duty
- Introduced Native Registration Act in 1915 which enforced the registration of all male adult Africans and this facilitated labour recruitment
- Introduced Hut Tax in 1902 and Poll Tax in 1911 to ensured that Africans sold their labour to get money to pay tax
- Introduced the Kipande system to ensure that Africans remained in employment and did not abscond.
- Forbid Africans from growing cash crops to lower their income and force them to seek for salaried work to augment their insufficient income
- Confiscated African livestock to impoverish and force them to search for salaried employment
- Encouraged the squatter system to ensure that Africans residing on the settlers farms provided the required labour in turn for small plots where they practiced subsistence farming

- Forced Africans to settle in overcrowded and unproductive reserves. This forced some of them to work in settler farms

Different methods were used by the colonial government to acquire land for European settlement. These included:

- The colonial government got some of the land through signing of treaties with Africans. For instance, the Maasai were evicted from their land through the agreements of 1904 and 1911.
- Some of the land was acquired through the use of force. For instance, after the defeat of Nandi, large tracts of their land were alienated and they were pushed to reserves to create room for European settlement.
- Unoccupied pieces of land were declared crown land. These areas were leased, granted or sold to the settlers.

Problems Experienced by the Settlers

- Constant raids by local communities, for example the Nandi threatened their peace and security
- Africans were not willing to provide labour
- Some settlers lacked the basic farming knowledge and experience
- Shortage of capital thwarted the procurement of farm inputs
- Marketing was hard in 1930's due to the inflation caused by the World War I
- They experienced transportation problems due to inadequate railway and roads
- Their crops were affected by pests and diseases

Agricultural changes introduced by the British in Kenya included:

- The British encouraged settlers to set up plantation farms to make the colonial economy to be self reliant

- They introduced new crops, for example tea, coffee and pyrethrum
- They introduced exotic breeds of livestock into Kenya, for example dairy animals and merino sheep
- They introduced new farming methods like crop rotation
- Land consolidation was introduced
- There was a shift from subsistence farming to cash crop farming
- Farmers were encouraged to form co-operatives to facilitate their farming activities

---

Questions on Settler Farming in Kenya

(a) What factors favoured settler farming in Kenya

(b) Explain the indirect measures initiated by the colonial government to provide labour in Kenya

(c) State six ways through which the colonial government promoted settler agriculture in Kenya

(d) Give five reasons why the colonial government encouraged white settlement in Kenya

(e) Give two reasons why Africans were not allowed to grow cash crops in Kenya

(f) Give two reasons why Africans were not willing to provide labour in settler farms during the colonial period.

(g) State five problems experienced by the settlers in Kenya

COLONIAL LAND POLICIES IN KENYA

To empower the settlers to take up more arable land in Kenya, the Legislative Council passed the following Land Acts or Ordinances:

- The Indian Acquisition Act (1896): authorized the government to take possession of land for the railway, government construction and public utilities.
- The Land Regulations Act (1897): allowed the government to offer a certificate of occupation and a lease for 99 years. This Act persuaded the settlers to annex land which was given up by the Agikuyu because of drought and famine.

- The East African Land Order in Council (1901): defined crown land as all public land which was not private. The government could confiscate any land at will and either sell or lease it to the settlers.
- The Crown Land Ordinance (1902): allowed the government to sell or lease crown land to Europeans at 2 rupees per 100 acres or rent at 15 rupees per 100 acres annually.
- The Maasai Agreement (1904): led to the creation of Ngong and Laikipia reserves for the Maasai
- The Elgin Pledge of 1906: the British Secretary of State, Lord Elgin confirmed that the highlands were reserved for the settlers. This brought to an end the Asian attempt to buy land in the highlands.
- The Second Maasai Agreement of 1911: the Maasai were driven out from the lush Laikipia reserve to create room for more European settlements and large scale farming.
- The Crown Land Ordinance (1915): provided for land – registration scheme for settlers. It defined crown land as land occupied by and reserved for Africans who could be evicted at will. Farm sizes were increased from 5,000 to 7,500 acres.
- The Kenya Annexation Order in Council (1920): announced that Africans were tenants of the crown even in the reserves.
- The Land Commission (1924): fixed boundaries of the reserves, which were later legalized in 1926.
- The Native Trust Ordinance (1930): stated that African reserves belonged to the Africans unendingly.
- The Carter Commission (1932): fixed the boundaries of the white highlands and all Africans were removed from the highlands and taken to the reserves. This created overcapacity in the African reserves.
- The Kenya Highlands Order in Council (1939): fixed the boundaries of the white highlands and reserved them for white settlement exclusively.

Impact of the colonial land policies

- The displaced Africans were confined to native reserves thus leading to congestion and overuse of land.
- Africans, who lost their land, became squatters and lived in misery and hopelessness.
- The situation in the reserves and the landlessness forced Africans to supply labour to the white settlers
- The displaced Africans moved to towns to look for employment.
- The traditional socio-economic set-up of the Africans was disturbed. Communities could no longer migrate in search of better lands and pasture. Family roles also changed as women increasingly took over headship of families while men sought for paid employment.
- The large European farms suffered acute shortage of labour as many Africans were unwilling to work on them.
- It led to the introduction of the *Kipande* System enforced by the Native Registration Ordinances of 1915 and 1920, to prevent the African labourers from deserting their duties on European farms.
- Taxes which were imposed on Africans compelled them to seek for wage employment.
- Reserving of the highlands for Europeans denied Indians access to agricultural land and this forced them to resort to businesses and reside in urban areas.
- Loss of land led to bitterness and made Africans later to form political organizations to demand for their land

Problems Africans Faced in the Reserves

- Poverty and insecurity
- Restricted movement
- Congestion in the reserves
- Outbreak of diseases
- Disruption of economic activities, for example grazing and farming
- Men abandoned their families in search of employment

SWEYNNERTON PLAN (1954)

Swynnerton plan was a colonial agricultural policy which appeared as a government report in 1954. It aimed at intensifying the development of agricultural practices in the colonial Kenya. The plan was meant to expand native Kenyan's cash crop production through improved markets and infrastructure, the distribution of appropriate inputs, and the gradual consolidation and enclosure of land holding. The objective of Roger Swynnerton's plan was to create family holdings large enough to keep the family self sufficient in food production and also enable them to practice alternate husbandry hence developing a cash income.

Swynnerton plan recommended: -

- That all high-quality native land be surveyed and enclosed
- That the policy of maintaining traditional or "tribal" system of land tenure is reversed and all the thousands of fragmented holdings are consolidated and enclosed.
- The progressive farmers to be given credit facilities to improve their farms
- The new title deeds would create security of tenure which would lead to investment and rural development
- That native African farmers be allowed to grow cash crops
- Africans be given a major increase in technical assistance and have access to all market and other facilities

Though this plan was meant to placate Africans during the *Mau Mau* uprising, it created a lot of acrimony because it destroyed the *ahoi* (tenant) option of the landless Kikuyus who were the majority in central province. The plan also gave birth to a new brand of the affluent and the poverty-stricken Kikuyus. The propertied group were loyalists to the colonial regime and were hated by the down trodden who were deprived of their land and became poorer.

Questions on Colonial Land Policies in Kenya

(a) State five effects of colonial land policies in Kenya

(b) State two problems Africans faced in the reserves

(c) State two ways in which the Sweynerton Plan affected the African farmers during the colonial period in Kenya

---

DEVONSHIRE WHITE PAPER OF 1923

A number of factors prompted the issuance of the Devonshire White paper. These were:

- The influence of the Dual Mandate (a book of the League of Nations which had regulations concerning colonial mandates). Britain was committed to the principle of trusteeship whereby she was more interested on its African population than European settlers.

- The Indian opposition to the privileged position of European settlers.

- The rise of racial conflicts - African versus European dominion and also European versus Asian conflict.

- The decision by the colonial government to ban racial segregation apart from the white highlands only, disappointed the settlers who didn't want the ban to be lifted hence they sent a delegation to London to see the colonial secretary, the Duke of Devonshire .

- The Africans' general resentment of land alienation, forced labour, taxation system, *kipande* system, low wages and no political representation.

After interviewing both Europeans and Asians, the Devonshire white paper was published with certain terms. These terms included:

- The Kenya highlands were exclusively reserved for white settlers

- Indians would have five members to the Legislative Council on a communal role

- The European settlers demand for self government in Kenya was rejected

- Racial segregation in all residential areas and restrictions on immigration were abolished

- Kenya was declared a primarily African country and the African interest were to be paramount when those interest conflicted with the interest of immigrants

- The colonial secretary would exercise strict control over the affairs of the colony

- A missionary would be nominated to the Legislative Council to represent the interests of the Africans

Results of the Devonshire White Paper

- Kenya was declared an African country and the African interests were made paramount.

- The problems of Africans especially that of land and labour, were not resolved.

- European demand for self-government was rejected.

- A European missionary, Dr. J. Arthur was appointed to represent African interests in Legislative Council..

- Africans became more politically aware and began forming political groupings to address their problems

- Asians were bitter, as their demands for equality with Europeans were not considered.

- The paper intensified rivalry between the Indians and settlers.

- Local native councils were established for the Africans

- Delamere and other settlers sought assistance from Rhodesia and South Africa to enable them to establish control over the colony.

The Barons

COLONIAL EDUCATION IN KENYA

During colonial time, the formal education was provided mainly by the missionaries. Other groups which assisted the missionaries in this endeavour were the colonial government through the local councils, the Africans themselves and other communities like the Asians. Groups of Asians who provided community based education in Kenya were:

- Arya Samaj Family
- Ismaili Family
- Allidina Visram

Education provided by the missionaries and the colonial government was elementary. Religion, writing and reading were offered. There was over emphasis on industrial and technical skills. Mission education was also denominational and aimed at indoctrinating Africans. The school leavers rarely went beyond primary.

Bottlenecks were put in place to deny Africans equal access to education. The purpose of this was: -

- To produce Africans who would easily accept their inferior status and continue to provide unskilled and semi-skilled duties in the colony.
- To produce Africans who were not educated enough to begin demanding for their rights.

- To lessen competition for job opportunities with the educated Africans.
- To perpetuate racial discrimination.

The colonial government came up with two commissions to look into the educational matters in the colony. These were the Phelps-Stock Commission and the Frazer Commission.

Fraser Commission (1909)

The British government established an education board which was chaired by Henry Scott of the Church of Scotland. The establishment concurred with the time Fraser and Giround Commissions called for racial considerations in developing the British protectorate. The recommendations included a push for industrial development, technical education, and the teaching of religion as a moral foundation. Professor Fraser also recommended the establishment of a department of education.

The British began re-examining and re-evaluating education in the African territories after the World War I. In 1923, the British secretary of state established a committee chaired by the parliamentary under-secretary of state to advice on educational affairs on the African- Kenyans. This marked the beginning of the first educational policy by the British colonial government. A three tier education system was established in Kenya, for Europeans, Asians and Africans. It was also the starting point of a joint venture between the colonial government and the missionaries.

Phelps – Stock Commission

This commission aimed at promoting education for Africans in the colony. It recommended that:

- Uniform education should be given in all government and mission schools.
- More colleges to be built to provide sufficient training opportunities for teachers.
- More schools to be built in rural areas to give Africans more access to education

This commission was significant because it: -

- Established a department of education in 1911 to give grants to mission schools and government schools.
- Came up with education ordinance to control and supervise education in the colony
- Led to the building of native industrial centres, for example Kabete
- Encouraged the provision of elementary education for Africans

INDEPENDENT SCHOOLS IN KENYA

Though the educated Africans valued Christianity and western education, they were against westernizing influence by missionaries. They perceived western education as inadequate because:

- Of its elementary nature and over emphasis on vocational skills. This type of education reduced Africans to providers of unskilled labour and clerical duties.
- Of the discriminatory nature in the provision of social facilities in the schools.
- Africans were denied opportunities to head the schools.
- African children who underwent traditional rites like female circumcision were expelled from mission schools. Africans therefore wanted schools where they would inculcate traditional values.
- Missionaries were perpetuators of colonialism.

Educated Africans, mostly in central province, established Independent schools. The purpose of these schools was to:

- To provide more educational opportunities for the Africans.
- To have a control of what was taught in their schools.
- To keep away European missionary influence from their schools.
- To preserve African cultural heritage.

- To create job opportunities for educated Africans.
- To sensitize Africans on the evils of colonialism.

Independent schools experienced a lot of difficulties at the beginning. These included:

- Constant harassment by the colonial government
- Lack of trained personnel to effectively manage them
- Stiff competition for students from the more established mission schools.
- Lack of adequate funds to run the school activities

INDEPENDENT CHURCHES IN KENYA

Some African leaders came up with independent churches. Theses churches included Dini ya Msambwa, Nomia and Lego Maria among others. The leaders of these churches were ex-missionary boys and what they practiced was a blend of Christianity and African values. The dominant features about these churches were:

- The churches were headed by Africans.
- They accommodated African cultural values like female circumcision.
- They worked closely with African political associations.
- Africans were unhappy with the western mission of Christian missionaries who taught against African culture and customs
- Churches emerged as a reaction against colonial domination and exploitation, Africans resented payment of taxes, *kipande* system and forced labour
- Many Africans perceived the Christian Missionaries as agents of colonial system
- Some Africans claimed that they had received a divine calling, for example John Owallo and Elijah Masinde
- Africans were not allowed to receive offering and to preach in western churches
- Many mission churches did not accommodate traditional African expressions,

for example use of traditional instruments and dance

- Some Africans felt dissatisfied with the interpretation of the Christian scriptures

Impact of Independent Churches in Kenya

- African cultural practices and beliefs were incorporated into the Christian church.
- The churches gave African clergy leadership opportunities in the church.
- The churches gave more Africans room to train as clergy.
- They accelerated the spread of Christianity in the country.
- The churches led to the establishment of independent schools.
- The churches contributed to the growth of nationalism in Kenya.

Questions on Independent Churches and Schools

(a) Give three reasons why independent schools were established in Kenya during the colonial period

(b) Outline three characteristics of independent churches and schools

(c) Give five reasons which led to the rise of independent churches in Kenya

(d) Explain six reasons why independent churches and schools emerged in colonial Kenya

(e) State one result of the establishment of independent churches in Kenya during the colonial period

(f) State two problems experienced by the independent schools in Kenya during the colonial period

---

URBANIZATION IN THE PRE-COLONIAL KENYA

Urbanization during the colonial time in Kenya was encouraged by many factors. These factors included:

- The construction of the Kenya – Uganda Railway led to the growth of towns like Voi, Nakuru, Naivasha and Kisumu along the railway line or on terminal points. Nairobi, which was the mid point between Mombasa and Kisumu, grew up into the capital of Kenya.
- Asians established shops at different points along the railway line. These later grew up into major commercial centres.
- Administration posts like Machakos, Murang'a and Mumias also grew up into towns.
- Towns like Nakuru, Eldoret and Kitale come up as collecting centres because of the commercialization of agriculture.
- Agro based industries, for example meat processing attracted labourers
- Prospectors were attracted to the mining centres like Magadi and Kakamega.

Many Africans migrated to the urban centres during the colonial period to avoid forced labour and taxation in the villages and escape the reality of living in extreme poverty in the crowded reserves. Urban centres also created employment opportunities for Africans and alternative livelihood to those whose land were annexed. Some Africans were lured by the better amenities in towns and the potential of selling their products to a wider market.

The increasing high number of Africans in the urban centres forced the colonial government to regulate their influx. This regulation was done through:

- Taking head count of those who were supposed to live in urban centres.
- Enacting strict rules about migrations into urban centres
- Creating reserves to contain the Africans.
- Ensuring that only those who had specific activities to undertake in the urban centres lived there.
- Introducing the *Kipande* system.

CONSEQUENCES OF URBANIZATION IN KENYA

Negative consequences

- Increased cases of unemployment in towns led to low morality and increased crime rate in the urban centres
- Limited housing led to the growth of slums
- Congestion in towns led to rising cases of epidemics.
- Migration to urban centres deprived rural areas of the much needed manpower
- Urban sprawl made many people to lose their land
- Urbanization eroded peoples' customs and traditions.

Positive Consequences

- Contact between different people instilled a sense of nationhood
- Welfare associations were formed to cater for the needs of African workers. These needs included providing social security, catering for the basic needs of members and promoting unity among the group.
- Popular sporting activities cemented relations of different groups
- Many Africans were employed in gainful activities
- Many industries came up due to abundant labour
- There was increased interaction among people of different ethnic backgrounds
- Rural to urban migration in Kenya contributed to national unity in the country. This was because: -
  - ✓ A diversity of people who faced the same challenges from the colonial government was brought to live and work together in towns.
  - ✓ Employed Africans formed Trade Unions which were among the forerunners in the struggle for independence.

Questions on Urbanization in Kenya during the Colonial era

(a) Give two ways in which rural to urban migration in Kenya contribute to national unity during the colonial period

(b) Give two positive consequences of urbanization in Kenya during colonial time

(c) Identify two factors which made the Africans to migrate to urban centres during the colonial period

(d) Give two negative consequences of urbanization in Kenya during the colonial period

(e) Give two ways through which the colonial government controlled the movement of African to urban centres

(f) Explain six factors that promoted urbanization in colonial Kenya

(g) Identify two negative consequences of urbanization in Kenya during the colonial period?

12 POLITICAL DEVELOPMENTS AND THE STRUGGLE FOR INDEPENDENCE IN KENYA (1919 – 1963)

BACKGROUND INFORMATION

Increased pressure from the local White settler community, led by Lord Delemare, for more control over their destiny led to the formation of the Legislative Council in 1907. The council had no representation from the Africans and Asian communities. Lack of representation by Africans coupled with economic inequalities gave rise to political organizations in 1920's and 30's.

These political associations were upshots of the World War I when Africans became more politically aware of themselves as a distinct racial group. They also discovered the weaknesses of the Whites and even more crucial, they learnt the importance of organized resistance. It is not a wonder therefore that several African political leaders in the 1920's and 30's were ex-soldiers.

Political organizations formed during this time agitated for direct representation in the Legislative Council, but most significantly for consideration of African land claims and greater education and economic opportunities. Some of these organizations had bases which cut across the country. However, a close examination of their activities reveals that they were largely welfare organistions and were more concerned with an improvement of their members' welfare. These organizations had little impact on the masses or on the colonial government, but played a more crucial role on the post World War II political activities.

In 1940 a total ban was placed on African political organizations except the Kavirondo Tax Payers and Welfare Association (KTPWA) and the Kikuyu Provincial Association. The two organizations agitated for political rights in the colonial government.

On 5th October 1944, Eliud Mathu was nominated as the first African unofficial member of the Legislative Council. This was to endear Africans to the colonial government. Africans took this turn of events as evidence of what could be achieved through a well coordinated countrywide organization. In this pursuit, a meeting was convened in October 1944 which led to the formation of the Kenya African Union (KAU).

Jaramogi Oginga Odinga formed the Luo Thrift and Trading Corporation around this time to create an economic base for the Luo community. Other similar organizations included the North Kavirondo Central Association, Ukamba Members Association and the Taita Hills Association. Meanwhile a group of Africans who grew impatient with the colonial government's failure to solve their problems resorted to armed struggle which crystallized into what became known as the Mau Mau uprising.

The terror unleashed by this group forced the colonial government to declare a state of emergency in 1952 and to ban all political parties in the country. The leaders of these parties were arrested and detained. They included Jomo Kenyatta, Paul Ngei, Kungu Karumba, Fred Kubia, Achieng' Oneko, Kariuki Chotara and Bildad Kaggia.

The vacuum created by the ban on political parties was filled by the African Labour Federation (ALF) which was headed by Tom Mboya. Political agitation and the Mau Mau resistance forced the colonial government to lay down a framework for independence. The framework was embodied in the Lyttelton Constitution of 1954 which allowed for a limited multi-racial government. District based political organizations were allowed after 1955 except in Central province which was the bedrock of the Mau Mau resistance. Organizations which were formed around this time included Nairobi District African Congress, the Nairobi Peoples Congress, the Mombasa

African Democratic Union, the Kisii Highlands Abagusii Association, the Taita African Democratic Union and Nakuru African Progressive Party.

In spite of African opposition to the Lyttelton Constitution, the new colonial secretary Lenox Boyd applied pressure and managed to have the first African election held on a limited franchise in 1957. Eight members were elected including Daniel Arap Moi, Tom Mboya, Ronald Ngala, Oginga Odinga, J. N. Nuimi and L. Oguda. In the same year another constitution was handed over. This was the Lennox Boyd Constitution which added six more African seats to achieve parity with elected Europeans. The Africans however wanted a nonracial policy where the interest of Africans would be paramount.

Features of Political Association (1919 – 1939)

- Political associations which were formed between 1919 and 1939 were led by the few educated elites. But majority of Kenyans were uneducated and therefore less concerned with the political affairs of the country.
- These educated people were opposed to violent means of achieving their ends and mainly depended on dialogue or sending petitions to address their grievances.
- Leaders of this era focused their demands on their welfare and were more concerned with problems like discriminatory practices and poor terms of service for the employed Africans.
- The associations drew their support from their ethnic backgrounds and were mainly urban based.
- The associations addressed specific individual problems affecting their ethnic groups like land or destocking.

Kikuyu Central Association was formed in 1920 by Kikuyu colonial chiefs who were deemed loyalist. The founder members were Paramount Chief Kinyajui wa Gathirimu, Chief Koinage wa Mbui, Josiah Njonjo, Philip Karanga, Mathew Njoroge and Waweru wa Mahui.

Objectives of Kikuyu Central Association

- To advocate for the growing of coffee as a cash crops by Africans.
- To work towards the restoration of alienated African Inland.
- To have laws written in Kikuyu.
- To pressurize the colonial government to abolish racial segregation.
- The respect African culture, for example circumcision

The association was opposed to land alienation, the introduction of the Kipande system and the proposed reduction of African wages after the World War I. This association was not aggressive in its demands.

Young Kikuyu Association (YKA) was formed in 1921 by leaders like Harry Thuku, Abdalla Tairara, Mwalimu Hamisi and Mohamed Sheikh. The association adopted a more radical approach because its leaders were not happy with the activities of the Kikuyu Central Association deemed to be puppets of the colonial regime. The association demanded for:-

- A return of African land
- Better working conditions for Africans
- Withdrawal of the Kipande introduced in 1920
- Increased wages for African workers

Harry Thuku

The Young Kikuyu Association was renamed the East African Association in a meeting which was attended by George Samuel Okoth, Abdalla Tairara, Kibwana Kombo (Tanzania), Jesse Kariuki and Joseph Kang'ethe among others. Its members were drawn from all over East Africa. Thuku who was its leader was a good orator and tried to make contact with nationalists in many parts of the world. He advocated for: -

- A revocation of the colonial status of the country by the British government
- Organization of the Legislative elections based on a common roll for all races
- Abolition of Hut Tax which was paid mainly by Africans
- Increased African wages
- Provision of better education for Africans

Harry Thuku, the leader of the organization, was arrested by the colonial government in 1922 and exiled for 7 years because of his radical approach.

Kavirondo Tax Payers Welfare Association Kavirondo Tax Payers Welfare Association (KTPWA) was formed in 1921 by Jonathan Okwiri, Benjamin Owuor, Reuben Omulo, Ezekiel Apindi, George Samuel Okoth, Joel Omino and Jolmeo Okaka. Its grievances included:

- Abolition of Kipande law
- An end to forced labour
- Scrapping of high taxes for Africans
- An end of land alienation
- Better wages for Africans
- Revocation of the change of state of Kenya from a protectorate to a colony
- Separate legislative council for Nyanza with an elected African president
- Establishment of more government schools in Nyanza
- Creation of paramount chiefs for Central and South Nyanza
- Individual title deeds for African land

The colonial government was alarmed by the activities of this association and used a missionary

– Archdeacon Owen, who was close to Okwiri to tone down its activities. He was handed over the chairmanship in 1923 and had the name of the association changed to Kavirondo Tax Payers Welfare Association (KTPWA). Its objectives became better housing, food, clothing, education and hygiene for Africans. It shifted its activities from political issues to digging pit latrines, killing rats and keeping compounds clean. The movement became associated with writing memoranda to the colonial government to address their grievances.

The main grievances of early political organizations in Kenya up to 1939 were:

- An end of racialism in clubs, theatres, trains etc
- Equal educational and health facilities
- Upward social mobility for the Africans
- End to segregation in residential areas in towns and housing i.e. high and low grades.

Achievements of Early Political Organizations upto 1939

- Provided political education to the African communities
- Communicated the community feelings to the colonial government, for example memorandum, publications
- Defended African cultures against further erosion by European missionaries
- They awakened the masses by making them conscious of political situations in the country
- They played the role of trade unions by fighting for welfare of workers in the absence of formal trade unions
- They exposed the African grievances to the international community

POLITICAL ASSOCIATIONS FORMED AFTER 1939

Taita Hills Association (THA), which was a branch of the Kikuyu Central Association (KCA), was established in 1939 to address the issue of land alienation in Taita Taveta District. It was linked to land politics of Kenya. The main goals of the association were to:

- Fight for the return of alienated land to the Wataita
- Protest against de-stocking policy of the colonial government
- Get personal rights such as the removal of the *kipande* system
- Get explanation on the threat of removal of Wataita to Samburu.
- Protest against over taxation
- Protest against forced labour

Taita Hills Association was banned together with KCA and Ukamba Members Association in 1940. By this time, the association had 4000 members. These members continued to operate clandestinely unto 1950 when the Mau Mau uprising broke out. Henceforth, its activities diminished.

Ukamba Members Association was formed in 1930 by some well to do Kamba cattle owners. It was led by Muindi Mbingu, who later became an independence hero. The movement aimed at pre-empting efforts by the colonial government to settle Whites in Kamba land. This was to be achieved by reducing the Kamba herds (destocking) through obligatory purchase.

Things turned topsy turvy in Iveti when some affluent Kambas refused to accept payment for their seized 2500 cattle on the grounds that what they were offered was a mere quarter of the market value of the animals. When the government refused to cede, Muindi Mbingu led between 1,500 to 5000 men, women and children to Kariokor Market (Nairobi) to petition the governor (Sir Robert Brooke-Popham) to halt the sell of the animals. They staged a sit in until the governor held a meeting in Machakos town to address their plight. This lasted for six weeks.

During this face-off, most of the Kamba police and army, who sympathized with the demonstrators, remained indifferent. The insurgence from a people who had "dutifully" fought for the British during the World War I, and who were now being unjustly treated, made front page news in Europe. This forced the colonial government to relent and return the stock.

Ukamba Members Association later joined forces with other popular anti-colonial organizations like the Luo Thift and Trading Corporation, the Kikuyu – dominated Kikuyu Central Association, the Luhya North Kavirondo Central Association (NKCA) and Taita Hills Association.

Questions on Political developments in Kenya from 1919 - 1939

(a) Identify two features of political associations formed in Kenya between 1919 and 1939.
(b) Give three African grievances which led to the formation of political Associations in Kenya between 1919-1939
(c) State two social grievances of early political organizations in Kenya up to 1939
(d) State two objectives of the Kikuyu Central Association (K.C.A)
(e) What was the main reason for the formation of the Ukambani Members Association?
(f) State two reasons why Taita Hills Association was formed in 1939
(g) State five achievements of early political organizations upto 1939

Kenya African Study Union (KASU)
When Eliud Mathu was nominated to the Legislative Council on 10th October 1944, a number of well educated Africans led by Francis Khamisi agreed to form Kenya African Union (KAU) with the following objectives:

- To assist Mathu in his new task as the first African nominated to the legislative council.
- To create a multi-ethnic political grouping representing the interests and constitutional rights of all Africans effectively.
- To advocate for more constitutional reforms for Africans.

The Barons

- To demand for better living and working conditions.

James Gichuru

The interim officials were Harry Thuku (chairman), Francis Khamisi (Secretary) and Albert Owino (treasurer). Other members included:

- James Gichuru
- John Kebaso
- Simeon Mulandi
- Harry ole Nangurai
- S.0. Josiah
- F.M. Ng'anga
- Jimmy Jeremiah
- J.D. Otiende and
- S.D. Jakay.

Two weeks after its formation, the governor ordered its officials to change its name to the Kenya African Study Union since it was meant to help Mathu in studying African problems. In January 1945, James Gichuru became the president of KASU after Harry Thuku resigned. He was unable to cope with the radicalism in the union. Under Gichuru, KASU published a newspaper - *Sauti ya Mwafrika* that concentrated on African grievances and the proposed East African Federation which they opposed. The organization rejected proposals to give more powers to European members in the Executive Council. They refused to accept a European dominated government of the East African Federation. In 1946 KASU reverted to its former name KAU deemed to be more appropriate.

Kenya African Union (KAU) was formed in February 1946. The return to Kenya by Jomo Kenyatta in 1946 marked a new dawn in Kenya's political landscape. The party began to mobilize the population, organize public rallies and to recruit new membership. In 1947 KUA had established itself as "the first sustained effort of the Africans to create a congress organization to cover the Africans of the whole colony. On 1st June 1947, Kenyatta became president of KAU after James Gichuru stepped down in his favour. W.W.W. Awori was elected vice-president and Ambrose Ofafa and Muchohi Gikonyo were elected treasurer and secretary respectively.

OBJECTIVES OF KAU

- To unite African people towards an African nation
- To fight for the abolition of the colour bar
- To struggle for the restrictions of European and Asian migration in Kenya
- To work as an African party for unofficial representation in the Legislative Council
- To campaign for a common electoral role based on an unlimited franchise and
- To foster the social, economic and political interests of the Africans in general

The main demands (Grievances) of KAU included:

- They demanded for adequate African representation in the Legislative Council.
- They demanded for self-government for Africans.
- They were against the *Kipande* System and forced labour.
- They demanded for an improvement of the African working conditions and better wages.
- They demanded for an end to land alienation and racial discrimination.
- They demanded for an end to imposition of taxes.
- They demanded for the compensation of ex-servicemen.

- They were protesting against lack of education opportunities for Africans.

After 1947 KAU began to face the problem of a standoff between the extremist like Bildad Kaggia, Fred Kubai and Paul Ngei who wanted to use force to acquire independence, and moderates like Jomo Kenyatta who believed in dialogue. The radicals took over the KAU Nairobi branch office. When a national delegates' conference was held in 1951, Jomo Kenyatta retained presidency, Otiende became Secretary General, Paul Ngei became the Assistant Secretary General and Ole Nangurai became the Treasurer.

Problems faced KAU

- Kenyatta was too busy to run the affairs of the party because he also served as the principal of Githunguri Teachers Training Collage.
- The party faced a lot of hostility from the colonial government and the white settlers.
- KUA was dominated by the Kikuyu and this led to rampant ethnic divisions within the pecking order of the party.
- Many Kenyans were illiterate and therefore could not adequately augment the efforts of the party.
- Between 1948 and 1950, KAU faced serious financial problems and even failed to pay rent for its offices at the IBEA building.

When the *Mau Mau* movement began, the Nairobi office of Kubai, Mungai and Kaggia worked closely with it. KAU continued to expand its membership in Kenya with Ramogi Achieng' Oneko opening a branch in Kisumu in 1951, Johana Adala and Boaz Muha opened a branch in Maragoli and Muinga Chokwe opened another office in Mombasa. In 1952, KAU rallies were banned outside Nairobi after a political meeting in Nyeri. This meeting, which attracted well over 25,000 people, including Dedan Kimathi (deemed to be the leader of the *Mau Mau* Movement) alarmed the colonial government.

Walter Odede

When a state of emergency was declared in 1952, KAU leaders were arrested for being behind *Mau Mau*. Walter Odede became the acting president, Joseph Murumbi acting secretary and Awori the acting treasurer. The acting official presented a 24-point memorandum to Oliver Lyttelton, the Secretary of State for colonies who came to Kenya during the emergency period. One of their demands was the release of the Kapenguria six (Jomo Kenyatta, Paul Ngei, Kung'u Karumba, Bildad Kaggia, Achieng' Oneko and Fred Kubai).

The Kapenguria Six

Walter Odede, the acting president was later arrested on 9th March 1953 while Murumbi escaped to Bombay, India. On 8th June 1953 KAU was banned by the colonial government.

Achievements of KAU

- Party members, especially those from the Nairobi branch, gave moral and material support to the *Mau Mau* freedom fighters.
- The party provided guidance and political support to Eliud Mathu, the first African representative to the Legislative Council.
- The party acted as the spring board of the Kenya African National Union (KANU) which ushered Kenya into independence.

- Some of the members of the party like Fred Kubai and Bildad Kaggia were active members of *Mau Mau*.

Roles played by Kenya African Union in promoting nationalist struggle in Kenya (1944 - 1953)

- KAU influenced the government to increase African representation in the Legislative Council
- It opened up branches in various parts of the country to educate Africans on the need to unite against European domination
- It published its own paper, *Sauti Ya Mwafrica* to popularize its objectives throughout the country
- It supported Eliud Mathu who was appointed to the Legislative Council in various ways
- It presented the grievance of the Africans in international fora
- It supported the activities of Mau Mau freedom fighters by giving them moral and material support
- It provided leadership for the national struggle
- It laid the foundation for the formation of Kenya African National Union (KANU) which led the country to independence
- It organized rallies in most parts of the country to create political awareness
- It supported Trade Unions

Kenya African National Union (KANU) was formed after the First Lancaster House Conference of January 1960. The conference came to a verdict that nationwide political parties were essential in Kenya as a requisite for independence. On 27th March 1960, in a meeting at Kirigiti (Kiambu) convened by ex-KAU strongmen, James Gichuru and Oginga Odinga, KAU merged with Kenya Independent Movement (KIM) and the People's Congress Party to form KANU. The colonial government declined to register KANU since Jomo Kenyatta, who was its president, was still in detention.

In May 1960 James Gichuru became the president of KANU with Oginga Odinga being the second-in-command. Tom Mboya became the Secretary General and Arthur Ochwada his assistant. Ronald Ngala and Daniel Moi were elected treasurer and assistant treasurer respectively, but in absentia since they were away, attending a Commonwealth Parliamentary Association meeting in London. KANU's party constitution was drafted by Mwai Kibaki and Tom Mboya. Its objectives included:

- To attain political independence for Africans in Kenya.
- To achieve national unity through a unitary national constitution under one central government.
- To create a society based on African socialism.
- To eradicate poverty, ignorance and disease.
- To get back African land.
- To have all political detainees released.
- To unite with liberation movements in other countries in Africa in order to end imperialism and colonialism in the continent.
- To encourage good neighbourliness in the East African region.

When Jomo Kenyatta was released, he took over the leadership of the party. During the independence elections in May 1963, KANU won 73 seats against KADU's 31 and African Peoples' Party's 8. Jomo Kenyatta became the first Prime Minister of Kenya on 1st June 1963.

Achievements of KANU in the Struggle for Independence
- KANU mobilized Africans in Kenya and united them in the struggle for independence.
- Through its numerous nationwide meetings, KANU provided political education to the Africans in Kenya.
- It participated in the independence constitution making process by being part of the Lancaster House conference of 1962.

Challenges faced by KANU in the Struggle for Independence included:

- Disunity among its members was caused by the suspicion of the big communities who held key leadership positions
- The party lacked adequate funds to carry out its countrywide campaigns.
- The KANU leaders suffered from ideological differences with some opposing the unitary system of government as advocated by the party's constitution.
- Some members were dissatisfied with the way party affairs were handled especially the elections which they felt were not fair.

Kenya African Democratic Union (KADU) was formed in 1960 as a coalition of minority ethnic political groups to protect their interests against possible domination by majority groups. Its senior leaders included Ronald Ngala (President), Masinde Muliro (Vice President), Daniel Arap Moi (Chairman), Martin Shikuku (Secretary General) and Justus ole Tipis (Treasurer). KADU leaders advocated for a federal system while KANU group were advocating for a unitary system of government. KADU formed the first coalition government with the Europeans and Asians who belonged to Michael Blundell's New Kenya Party (NKP) after garnering 11 seats in the May 1961 elections. KANU refused to form a government until Jomo Kenyatta, who was still in detention, was released. In 1962, KADU and KANU formed a coalition government. Following the defeat by KANU in the May 1963 elections, KADU became the major opposition party until 1964 when it was disbanded and its members crossed over to KANU.

Roles played by the KADU in the struggle for independence included:

- KADU united the smaller communities in Kenya like the Kalenjin, Luhyia, Maasai and coastal communities.
- It mobilized Africans against the colonial domination.

- It pressed for the release of Jomo Kenyatta with a hope that he would join their side of the political divide.
- It participated in drawing up the independence constitution in the Second Lancaster House Conference.
- Within the short time, it acted as an opposition party; KADU checked the activities of the KANU government.

Achievements of KADU

- KADU united the smaller communities in the country like the Kalenjin, Abaluhya and Maasai
- It mobilized Africans against colonial domination
- It educated Africans in Kenya on the need for self determination.
- It participated in the Second Lancaster House Conference which came up with the independent constitution
- For the short time it was an opposition party, it played the role of the opposition party by ensuring checks and balances on KANU government.
- KADU proved to the colonial government that Kenyans were able to rule on their own because it had able leaders

Challenges faced by KADU in the 1960's

- The party members experienced a lot of pressure from their rivals in KANU to decamp and merge with them.
- Wrangles between senior officials undermined the party's operations
- There was suspicion that certain ethnic groups were dominating the party
- Persistent lack of funds impeded the party's activities
- Illiteracy among the majority of the members left the top leaders with too much responsibility of party affairs
- The colonial government was a major stumbling block, since it was determined to manipulate the party

- The party did not win the support of Jomo Kenyatta, already identified as an indisputable leader by the majority of Kenyans

---

Roles of Political Parties in the Struggle for Independence
- Political parties formed training grounds for future Kenyan leaders
- They fought against the colonial opposition by organizing strikes and demonstration
- Political parties sent memorandum to the governor of Kenya and colonial secretary in London where they aired their grievances
- They organized political rallies and sensitized Africans on the need to fight for their rights
- They presented candidates for general elections in 1959, 1961 and 1963

Lyttleton Constitutional Reforms (1954)

- The Lyttleton Constitutional led to the establishment of a Multi - Racial Council of Ministers. This was made up of official and non official members. It replaced the Executive Council.
- B. A. Ohanga, one of the nominated African members, was made minister for Community Development and African Affairs, hence being the first African minister in pre-colonial Kenya.
- Africans were allowed to form political organizations whose functions were confined to district levels.
- The government provided for elections of eight Africans to the Legislative Councils.
- It led to the establishment of an Advisory Council to discuss government policies.

Lennox-Boyd Constitutional Reforms (1957)

African elected members of Legislative (AEMO) presented the following demands to Lennox–Boyd:

- They demanded for an increase in the number of elected Africans to the Legislative Council to 14

- There should be special election of 4 Africans nominated to Legislative Council not representing constituencies
- A commission be set up to review and recommend the abolition of racist regulations
- That the number of African ministers to be raised to two.

The Lennox Boyd constitution increased the number of Africans in the Legislative Council from 8 and 14 members. For the first time more Africans were elected to the Legislative Council. Apart from increasing the number of African representatives in the Legislative Council, this constitution contributed to the country's independence in a many ways. The constitution:

- Allowed for the opening of up country branches which educated Africans about the importance of representation in the Legislative Council.
- Supported Eliud Mathu who was appointed to the Legislative Council.
- Represented the grievances of the Africans internationally
- Supported the activities of the *Mau Mau* freedom fighters
- Provided for leadership in the nationalist struggle.
- Laid the foundation for the formation of KANU which led Kenya to independence.
- Allowed for the organization of rallies in most parts of the country to create awareness on the rights of the Africans.
- Led to the holding of discussions with the colonial government about Kenya's political future.
- Supported the activities of the Trade Unions.

> **Constitutional Changes in Kenya (1954 - 1963)**
>
> (a) The Lyttleton constitution of 1954 led to the appointment of the first African Minister and nomination of other African leaders to the Legislative Council
> (b) In 1957 the first all races elections were held and Africans were elected in 8 constituencies.
> (c) The Lennox Boyd constitution gave more seats to Africans from 8 and 14 members.
> (d) The First Lancaster House Conference of 1960 gave Africans more seats in the Legislative Council. Thus African representation moved from 14 to 33 members,
> (e) In 1960 the state of emergency was lifted and Africans were allowed to form country wide political parties.
> (f) The Second Lancaster Conference drew up the independence constitution which made Kenya a Majimbo (federal) State.
> (g) In 1961 the first general elections were held and KANU won but refused to form the government until Jomo Kenyatta was released from jail. KADU formed the government with Ngala as leader of government business.
> (h) KANU and KADU formed a coalition government with Jomo Kenyatta as the first Prime Minister.
> (i) On December 12th, 1963 Kenya attained full independence.

AEMO members rejected both the Lyttelton and Lennox-Boyd proposals. They were opposed to these constitutional changes because: -

- The Lyttelton constitution provided for fewer elected members than nominated ones.
- The constitutions provided for rigid voting qualification requirements for the Africans.
- The AEMO demand that registration of voters be done on a common roll as opposed to the communal roll provided by the proposals.
- The proposals didn't address the state of emergency.
- The proposals gave the minority, Europeans, an advantaged position in Legislative Council.

In 1958 the AEMO members further demanded:

- For an increase of African representation in the Legislative council.
- That every African of 21 years to be allowed to vote.
- That registration of voters to be done on a common roll.
- For an end to the state of emergency.

Contributions of African Elected Members of Parliament in the Struggle for Independence included:

- Elected members formed a pressure group to demand for greater political space for Africans.
- They formed the core team which pressurized for independence.
- They made known the grievances of the Africans in international forums
- They networked with other African nationalist elsewhere, for example Ghana and Nigeria to hasten the achievement of independence in Kenya.
- They sought for the release of Jomo Kenyatta and others imprisoned or detained leaders.
- They educated and created awareness among the masses to the nationalist struggle.
- They popularized Jomo Kenyatta and made him to be accepted as the nationalist hero
- They took part in the formation of the independence constitution.

Lancaster House Conferences were called to iron out the differences which arose out of the fact that both radical Europeans and AEMO members opposed multi-racialism.

The first Lancaster House Conference (1960) which was attended by all members of the Legislative Council was convened by Ian MacLeod, the Secretary of State for colonies. The African team was led by Ronald Ngala and Tom Mboya who acted as the secretary. The conference came up with the following compromise decisions:

- The 12 elective seats in the Legislative Council would remain intact.
- There was to be 33 open seats in the Legislative Council, which were to be vied for on a common roll.
- Another 20 seats would be reserved – 10 of these for Europeans, 8 for Asians and 2 for Arabs.
- The composition of the Council of Ministers was to be altered to incorporate 4 Africans, 3 Europeans and 1 Asian.
- The conference authorized the formation of countrywide political parties for Africans. KANU and KADU were formed after this conference.

The Lancaster Conference, however, failed to entirely please both Africans and the settlers. Some settlers could not stomach the new turn of events and began to sell their property and leave the country. Africans felt that they had not been given a responsive government, but accepted ministerial positions as follows:

- Ronald Ngala- Minister for Labour, Social Security and Adult Education.
- Julius Gikonyo Kiano - Minister for Commerce and Industry.
- Musa Amalemba- Minister for Housing, Common Services, Probation and Approved Schools.
- James Nzaui Miumi - Minister for Health and Welfare.

Out of the fear of political domination by the big tribes, new alliances emerged. These included:

- The Kalenjin Political Alliance of Taita Towett.
- The Coast African Political Union of Ronald Ngala.
- The Kenya African People's Party of Masinde Muliro.

In the 1961 elections KANU won, but refused to form a government demanding for the release of Mzee Jomo Kenyatta. KADU was invited by the governor, Patrick Renson to form a coalition government with Europeans and Asians. When Jomo Kenyatta came on 21st August 1961, Kariuki Njiiri offered his Murang'a seat to Mzee Jomo Kenyatta to enable him join the Legislative Council.

The Second Lancaster Conference (1962) was convened by Reginald Maulding, the Secretary for colonies. The main aim of this conference was to draft the independence constitution which was acceptable to the two main parties, KADU and KANU. It also aimed at reconciling the differences between the two parties. KANU delegation was led by Jomo Kenyatta while Ngala led the KADU group. KANU compromised with KADU on many grounds to expedite the negotiations.

Questions on Political developments in Kenya from 1945 -1963

(k) What major reforms resulted from the Lyttleton Constitution of 1954 in Kenya?

(l) Identify two reasons why African elected members of Legislative council rejected both the Lyttelton and Lennox-Boyd proposals.

(m) In what ways did the Lennax - Boyd Constitution contribute to the constitutional changes that led to the attainment of independence in Kenya?

(n) State five grievances of the Africans which were voiced by Kenya African Union (KAU)

(o) What five roles did the Kenya African Union play in promoting nationalist struggle in Kenya between 1944 and 1953?

(p) Explain six grievances which African nationalist in Kenya had against colonial rule between 1945 and 1963

(q) State five roles played by political parties in Kenya during the struggle for independence

(r) Explain five constitutional changes which took place in Kenya between 1954 and 1963

(s) Explain the factors that hastened the achievement of independence in Kenya after 1945

(t) State five problems which the African nationalists in Kenya faced in the struggle for independence

13 LABOUR MOVEMENT IN KENYA DURING COLONIAL ERA

Prior to 1920's there was little impact of labour union movement in Kenya. This was because majority of Kenyans were illiterate and lacked knowledge to run the unions, the migratory labour system worked against the establishment of unions and the colonial government fought attempts by Africans to form workers' organizations.

The banning of political parties, subjecting Africans to poor conditions and terms of service in European farms, and the rise of African elite group (who championed rights of Africans) for example Tom Mboya, changed this situation and Trade Unions started becoming more active in the post 1920's. Many Trade Unions came into existence for instance: -

- The African Workers Federation
- Labour Trade Union of Kenya
- African Workers Union
- East African Trade Union Organization
- Kenya Federation of Labour
- The Kenya Federation of Registered Trade Union
- Domestic and Hotel Workers Union
- East African Federation Building and Construction Workers Union
- Night Watchmen, Clubs and Shop Workers Union

Demandes of the Trade Unions
- A salary increase for Africans due to the high cost of living.
- An implementation of the policy of equal pay for equal work regardless of race.
- Respect for African workers wherever they were employed.
- Payment of sufficient allowance to cater for African children and wives
- An elimination of the deliberate strategy to keep Africans in their places of work all the time

Achievements of Trade Union movement during the colonial period were:
- Trade Unions liaised with political activists and parties in the struggle for independence.
- They articulated African grievances especially after KAU was banned during the emergency period
- Trade Unions fought for the freedom of jailed nationalists
- They led to improved salaries and working conditions of the African workers
- They provided training grounds for future nationalists
- They educated African workers on their rights
- They introduced the concept of collective bargaining to the African workers
- They encouraged regional co-operation
- They encouraged co-operation between employers, employees and government

Problems Which Faced the Labour Movement in Kenya included:
- The Unions were harassed by both the settlers and colonial government
- Fear of victimization of African leaders
- Migratory nature of African workforce during the early years of colonial rule made the unions unstable
- Poor leadership affected the running of the unions, for example they lacked training on union activities
- Labour unions experienced shortage of funds since they relied on meager contributions of workers
- Choice of union leaders based on ethnicity compromised their competence
- There was constant wrangling for leadership in the unions.
- Ignorance of people on activities of the union

Achievements of Kenya Workers Federation

- Kenya Workers Federation mobilized workers from different communities to come together and fight for better wages
- It advocated for better allowances for African wives and children
- The organization kept the spirit of African nationalism alive following the banning of the Kenya African Union.
- It exposed the grievances of African workers in Kenya to the international community
- It introduced the concept of collective bargaining among the workers in Kenya
- The organization voiced African grievances in the absence of political parties.
- The organization prepared some African nationalists.
- It educated workers about their rights
- It made the colonial government to change its attitude towards labour movement

Trade Union Movement's Contributions to Independence

- Trade Union united Africans together to fight for their rights and independence
- They trained political leaders to push for independence
- Demanded for the release of arrested leaders, for example Fred Kubai
- The movement wrote memoranda to government protesting about colonization
- They replaced banned political parties in demanding for political reforms
- Demanded for independence of Kenya
- Gained international recognition through affiliations which contributed to Kenya gaining independence
- Trade Unions organized strikes under the influence of politicians
- Trade unions organized bases for political parties
- Offered education through student's airlifts to create awareness

Questions on Labour Movement in Kenya during Colonial era

(h) Give two ways in which rural to urban migration in Kenya contributed to national unity

(i) Give one reason why Africans who lived in towns formed social welfare organizations during the colonial period

(j) Give two positive consequences of urbanization in Kenya during colonial time

(k) Identify two factors which made the Africans to migrate to urban centres during the colonial period

(l) Give two negative consequences of urbanization in Kenya during the colonial period

(m) Give two ways through which the colonial government controlled the movement of African to urban centres

(n) Explain six factors that promoted urbanization in colonial Kenya

(o) Identify two negative consequences of urbanization in Kenya during the colonial period?

14 GROWTH OF NATIONALISM IN KENYA

The year 1945 witnessed many new developments in not only Kenya, but also the world all over. A wind of change blew across the world and this wind brought many changes in the country. For example:

• The labour government which came to power in Britain in 1945 was more responsive to demand for self rule in colonies. Henceforth, the colonial office began implementing changes geared towards self rule in the country. The Lyttleton Constitution of 1945, for example created a Multi-Racial Council of Ministers while the Lennox Boyd Constitution of 1958 provided for election of more Africans in the Legislative Council

• The emergence of United States of America (USA) and the former Soviet Union (Russia) as two super powers, after the end of the World War II in 1945 boosted the nationalist struggle as they urged other countries like Britain and France, which still had colonies, to liberate them.

• United Nations Organization (UNO) which came into existence at almost the same time, recommended self determination of the colonized countries as a right and urged colonial powers, for example Britain, to liberate the colonized people.

• Attainment of independence by India in 1947 gave the nationalists a strong urge to fight for their own liberation in Kenya. This urge was rekindled in 1957 when Ghana was liberated and became the first country in Black Africa to attain its independence.

• The Pan-African Movement, especially the one which met in Manchester in 1945 and was attended by many future African leaders including Jomo Kenyatta, inspired African Nationalists in their struggle for independence because this was one of its core agendum.

• The World War II which ended in 1945 was important because it made Africans who had participated in it more aware of the changes around the world and also diffused the myth of white supremacy. The ex-soldiers radicalized the nationalist movement in the country.

• Lifting of bans on political parties in 1945, 1955 and 1960 led to the formation of nationalist parties KANU, KADU and APP which intensified the struggle for the independence.

Grievances Faced by Nationalists

• The African nationalists were not happy about their land which was alienated by the white settlers. This they wanted restored.

• They complained about lack of effective representation in the Legislative council.

• Poor working conditions and poor salaries made Africans discontented.

• Imprisonment of Jomo Kenyatta and other nationalists after the declaration of the state of emergency displeased many nationalists.

• The nationalists wanted the state of emergency to be lifted to facilitate free movement and formation of political parties.

• The nationalists complained against the payment of the taxes, for instance Hut Tax, Poll Tax and *Matiti* Tax.

• The nationalist were opposed to communal labour which was used to develop public facilities.

• The African nationalists demanded for the granting of complete independence of Kenya.

• The *Kipande* system was cumbersome, humiliating and restrictive to them.

• Africans were not allowed to grow cash crops.

Methods Used in the Struggle for Independence

- The nationalists attended constitutional conferences to put forward their grievances.
- Africans in the Legislative Council put pressure on Britain to hasten her - decolonization programme.
- The nationalists used the Trade Unions to popularize the cause of the struggle among workers.
- They enlisted public sympathy through the press.
- They formed political parties to co-ordinate their activities.
- They used violence against the colonial establishment, *Mau Mau*.
- They formed independent schools and churches which popularized the need for independence
- The Africans sent petitions and delegations to the governor and to the colonial office in London
- Africans organized strikes and job boycotts to demand for better working conditions and removal of racial discrimination.
- They adopted oathing which united all the nationalist together against colonialism

Despite the prevailing changes in Kenya and in other parts of the world, the road to independence was not smooth all the way. The nationalists in the country still realized a lot of hiccups. For example:

- The nationalists were harassed, detained and jailed.
- Political organization were banned, especially during the inter war and emergence period.
- There was a lot of disunity among the African nationalists, some of whom preferred their tribal cocoons.
- The nationalists lacked adequate funds to implement their programmes.

- They were denied access to the mass media and therefore could not properly articulate their grievances.
- The colonial government used the mass media to discredit the activities of the nationalists.
- They were betrayed by other people especially the home guards or some chiefs who were loyalists to the imperial regime.
- High levels of illiteracy among most Africans made their work more difficult.
- The *kipande* system was used by the colonial government to restrict their movement.

The Mau Mau Movement

The Mau Mau Movement mainly affected the Kikuyu of central province and Nyandarua who were more adversely affected by the land alienation policy of the colonial regime than most communities in Kenya were. The murder of chief Wairuhiu in 1952 made the colonial government to take the uprising seriously and to declare a state of emergency.

Mau Mau uprising is attributed to a number of factors which caused bitterness among Africans. The factors can be summarized into:

- Land alienation in the fertile highlands, for example the central part of Kenya which made the inhabitants of these regions to be squatters.
- Poor living and working conditions of Africans in the urban area or white farms where some of them eked a living.
- Oppressive policies, for example the carrying of *Kipande* which was made mandatory for all Africans working in urban areas or European farms.
- The need to preserve their culture, for example the kikuyu women who valued circumcision very much and were bitter with the missionaries who opposed the practice.

- Delayed constitution reforms frustrated many nationalists who began agitating for change.
- The colonial regime detained many political leaders, for instance Harry Thuku, Jomo kenyatta, Bildard Kagia, Paul Ngei and Acheing' Oneko. The nationalists wanted these leaders to be released, but the government was adamant.
- Colonial brutality, for example the 1947 massacre which followed the unrest at Upland Bacon Factory caused resentment.
- Squatters were evicted forcefully, for example at Olenguruone settlement scheme and resettlement at Yatta region
- There were many youths in urban centres who were jobless and therefore quite susceptible to incitement.
- There was a lot of racism especially in job opportunities and area of recreation. This annoyed Africans.
- Brutality was also exhibited by the colonial police and African chiefs
- Most people who spearheaded the *Mau Mau* uprising were the ex–service men like General "China" and Dedan Kimathi who were disillusioned after the World War II.

Impact on World War II on the Mau Mau

The World War II had fundamental effects on the ex-service men. They developed bloated ideas when they were fighting alongside Europeans and were very much disappointed when they returned back to Kenya.

- Most of them ended up as squatters because their land had been annexed.
- They remained jobless.
- They were not adequately compensated for their services.
- Worst of all, they were treated contemptuously by the same Whites who once treated them as comrades during the war.

The ex-service men could not take this lying down because the World War II had broken the myth of European superiority and exposed their weaknesses, enabled them to be influenced by nationalists from other countries and equipped the ex-service men with the deadly art of fighting and using modern fire arms.

Mau mau fighter

The Mau Mau Uprising was favoured by many factors. These were:

- Oathing which united the fighters and made their activities secretive.
- Use of guerilla technique which made the fighters to be more elusive.
- Civilians who supplied the fighters with food, weapons and also spied on the Europeans to give the fighters the vital intelligence information.
- Inspiration by leaders, for example Dedan Kimathi, Marshall Muthoni and General "China".
- Natural forests, for example Nyandarua and Mount Kenya forest which provided ideal hide outs for the fighters.
- Easy accessibility of home made guns and ammunitions which were used by the fighters. The weapons were augmented by the guns which were stolen from the home guards by the supportive women.

Problems faced by the Mau Mau Fighters

- Fighters lacked transport and communication facilities
- Fighters succumbed to diseases and sometimes death because of the harsh climatic conditions.
- The fighters were frequently attacked by wild animals
- Fighters lacked proper fighting equipment
- Brutal killing by the British forces caused anxiety among the fighters
- Separate fighting groups lacked proper co-ordination and were easy to isolate and fight separately
- Divisions arose among fighters
- Recruitment exercise was disjointed and many Africans were unethusiastic about joinning the group.

To discourage the Mau Mau activities, the colonial government:

- Declared a state of emergency in 1952
- Banned all political organizations, for example KAU to tone down political temperature in the country
- Used military force to suppress the uprising
- Used spies to give information to the colonial government
- Removed some of the ethnic communities from Nairobi
- Put some ethnic communities to concentration camps to monitor their activities

Role of Women in the Mau Mau

Women played a very big role in the *Mau Mau* uprising. Some of them, for instance Wambui Otieno, Mary Muthoni Nyanjiru and Field Marshal Muthoni were actual combatants. Other women also took part actively though in the periphery. They for instance:

- Organized and co-coordinated the rural network which supplied the fighters with food, medicine and guns which were stolen from the home guards whom they be-friended.
- Acted as spies and gathered intelligence information from the home guards.
- Composed songs to boost the morale of the fighters and to ridicule the home guards and the cowards who were unwilling to join in the struggle.
- Mobilized men and women to join in the struggle.
- Acted as chief oathing administrators
- Refused to betray the fighters despite the inhumane treatment they were subjected
- About 8000 Agikuyu, Ameru and Aembu women were rounded up and detained.
- Endured dawn to dusk curfew and starvation, especially in Kikuyu land.

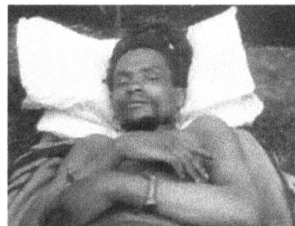

Dedan Kimathi

Results of the Mau Mau

The *Mau Mau* fight had far reaching consequences both to Kenya and abroad. It exposed the evils of British government internationally and forced her to adopt a more conciliatory approach in her management of Kenyan colony. Many reforms were made to the constitution which favoured the Africans, for example the Lenox-Boyd's constitutional reforms. These reforms were instrumental in hastening the pace towards achieving independence in Kenya.

The fight also affected Africans in a number of ways. For example:

- Many Kenyans were killed in the struggle
- Reserves were created where the Kikuyu, Ameru and Aembu, perceived by the colonial

government to bear the greatest responsibility, were taken.

- Leaders were arrested and detained in different parts of Kenya. Kenyatta, for instance was arrested and detained at Kapenguria

- The Kikuyu, Meru and Embu communities who were workers in Nairobi were sacked and replaced without rhyme or reason with other tribes.

The *Mau Mau* fight created mistrust and ill feeling among different communities. Some people joined the colonialists and were used as home guards to suppress the resistance. These people were viewed as traitors and became prime targets of the fighters. The feeling that they were a sell out has not died off in many parts of the country.

Questions on the Mau Mau Movement in Kenya

(a) Which factors favoured the Mau Mau Activities?

(b) State six problems faced by Mau Mau fighters

(c) What were the results of the Mau Mau Movement in Kenya?

(d) Give two examples of women who played a crucial role in the struggle for independence in Kenya.

(e) Give six roles women played in Mau Mau struggle in Kenya

The Barons

15 LIVES AND CONTRIBUTIONS OF KENYAN LEADERS

Mzee Jomo Kenyatta

Jomo Kenyatta was the first Prime Minister and President of the Republic of Kenya. His contributions to political developments in Kenya included:

- In 1924 Kenyatta became the Secretary General of Kikuyu Central Association
- In May 1928 he became the editor of the association's newspaper Muiguithenia where he articulated the Agikuyu culture and urged the people to take up their children to school
- In 1928 he accompanied Kikuyu Central Association (KCA) officials to give evidence to the Hilton Young Commission. Jomo Kenyatta presented the following demands to the commission: -
  - ✓ Introduction of Free Primary Education.
  - ✓ Provision of secondary and higher education.
  - ✓ Abolition of *Kipande* system.
  - ✓ Appointment of Africans to the Legislative Council.
  - ✓ Release of Harry Thuku.
  - ✓ Giving of title deeds to Africans.
  - ✓ Rejection of the proposed African federation.
- In 1929 KCA decided to send him to Britain to present African grievances to the colonial secretary in London
- On 2nd October 1931 he went back to London to present KCA grievances before the joint select committee on closer union of East African countries. He stated that Africans did not support the idea of a federation. This idea was shared by the colonial government
- Kenyatta studied political science and economics from 1932 to 1933 at Moscow University at the invitation of George Padmore. He disagreed with the Russians and his studies were cancelled and he returned to Britain for studies in anthropology and economics at the University of London
- In 1939 while in London he expressed his solidarity with Emperor Haile Selassie of Ethiopia after the Italians ousted him from power in 1935
- In 1938 he published a book "Facing Mt. Kenya" about the Agikuyu culture
- He traveled to many countries in Europe and this inspired and transformed him into a nationalist and Pan Africanist. Jomo Kenyatta made the following contributions to Pan Africanist Movement: -
  - ✓ He addressed rallies in London attacking the colonialist's policies such as the Carter Land Commission and destocking policy
  - ✓ Assisted in organizing the 1945 Pan Africanist Movement Congress in Manchester where he met other leaders. During this conference the leaders demanded complete socio-political emancipation of Africans
- In 1947 he became the chairman of Kenya African Union when James Gichuru stepped down as a chairman in his favour
- He embanked on a mission of enlightening Kenyans on the objectives of KAU in the hope of making it a political party
- He held rallies all over the country where he emphasized the need for unity for all Kenyans and for independence
- In 1952 Kenyatta's and other nationalist were arrested after a state of emergency was declared in connection with the *Mau Mau* activities. He was tried and detained at Kapenguria in 1959

- He was released in 1961 and decided to join KANU. He became president of KANU in 1961
- Kariuki Njiru, a member of Legislative Council voluntarily stepped down paving way for him to become the unopposed member of Fort Hall on February 1962.
- On April 1962, Kenyatta agreed to serve on the coalition government as a Minister of State for Constitution Making
- Kenyatta participated in the Second Lancaster Conference whose aim was to draw up the independence constitution as well as sorting out the difference between KANU and KADU
- Elections were held on 1st May 1963, Kenya gained internal self government and on 12th December 1963 it got independence with Kenyatta as the first Prime Minister
- On 12th December 1964 Kenya become a Republic with Kenyatta as the first president

---

Jomo Kenyatta's Contribution to the Nationalist Movement in Kenya Upto1963

- Jomo Kenyatta was a founder member of the KCA that fought for the rights of Africans in Kenya.
- He started the KCA newspaper *Muigwithania* in which he articulated the grievances of the Africans.
- During his study in Britain between 1929 and 1946, he presented the plight of Africans in Kenya in many international forums
- He became the president of KAU in June 1947 and endeavored to transform it into a mass party.
- His detention by the colonial government turned him into a national hero and future leader.
- In 1961, Jomo Kenyatta was elected to the legislative assembly and he attempted to reconcile KANU and KADU.
- In 1962, he led KANU delegates to the Second Lancaster House Conference to work out constitutional changes for Kenya's independence
- When KANU won election in 1963, Jomo Kenyatta became the Prime Minister

---

Challenges Faced by Kenyatta's Government

- Lack of skilled manpower to replace the expatriates in the civil service, commerce and industry who left after independence
- Imbalance in land ownership – many Kenyans were squatters while large parcels of land were owned by a few individuals.
- Tribalism became rampant during Kenyatta's time
- The fast growing population of Kenya put a lot of pressure on the few existing amenities like schools and hospitals
- The assassination of political figures like Tom Mboya and J. M. Kariuki undermined the stability of Kenyatta's government
- Corruption, especially land grabbing by the rich became widespread
- Poor transport network hampered transport of agricultural produce
- Poor quality of education and facilities to suit Kenyans who were segregated by the colonial regime
- Health and medical facilities in the country were inadequate.

Questions on Mzee Jomo Kenyatta

(a) State two contributions of Kenyatta to Pan Africanism

(b) Describe Jomo Kenyatta's contributions to political developments in Kenya

(c) Identify two demands Jomo Kenyatta presented to the Hilton Young Commission on behalf of the Kikuyu Central Association

(d) Explain six challenges Jomo Kenyatta encountered as the president of Kenya

The Barons

Tom Mboya

Tom Mboya was a renowned Trade Unionist and played a significant role in its development in the country and within the region. His contributions included the following:-

• In 1950 Tom Mboya joined the Nairobi African Local Government Servants Association and became its president in 1952.

• In 1952 he pressed for its registration as a Trade Union.

• In 1953 Kenya Local Government Workers Union (KLGWU) was formed and Mboya became its General Secretary

• In 1953 he became the Secretary General of the Kenya Federation of Registered Trade Unions (KFRTU). He fought against discrimination of African workers, low wages, detention and torture of African workers

• In 1954 he affiliated KFRTU to the International Confederation of Free Trade Unions (ICFTU) based in USA and Trade Union Congress (TUC) based in Britain. He attended various local and overseas seminars on Trade Unions

• In 1955 he organized Trade Union courses in various parts of Kenya. He also campaigned for the release of leaders

• In 1955 he mediated in the Mombasa Dock Workers Strike. He won them a 33 % pay rise

• In 1958 he was elected to the International Conference of Free Trade Unions executive board.

• Tom Mboya solicited for financial and moral support to KFL from international Trade Unions and organizations

• He played a leading role in the formation of Trade Unions in Uganda and Tanganyika

Joseph Thomas Mboya's contribution to the struggle for independence in Kenya

• Joseph Thomas Mboya condemned reservation of white highlands for white settlers

• He protested against colonial separation of Agikuyu, Aembu and Ameru from other communities in Nairobi during the state of emergency.

• He protested against government arrest, detention and torture of the African workers

• He protested restrictions of Africans to grow cash crops

• Campaigned for the release of detained Trade Unionists and political leaders such as Jomo Kenyatta

• He exposed African problems and sought assistance from other Pan Africanists

• Joseph Thomas Mboya was elected to Legislative Council in 1957 where he campaigned for the inclusion of more Africans in government affairs

• In 1960 he was elected Secretary General of KANU

• Joseph Thomas Mboya's was a member of Kenya Local Government Workers Union and Kenya Federation of Labour.

Questions of Tom Mboya

(a) Explain the role Tom Mboya played in the development of Trade Union Movement in Kenya

(b) Explain six ways through which Joseph Thomas Mboya contributed to the struggle for independence in Kenya

(c) What was the main contribution of Tom Mboya to education in Kenya

(d) What was the main contribution of Tom Mboya to Kenya

Ronald Ngala

Ronald Ngala formed the first coalition government in 1962 when KANU declined to form one because Jomo Kenyatta was still in detaintion. He played a big role in the struggle for independence in Kenya. These roles were:

- In 1947 Ronald Ngala joined the Coast African Association which articulated the problems of Mjikenda people
- In 1950 he was appointed a member of the Mombasa African Advisory Council which represented African interests to the Mombasa Municipal board
- In 1951 the organization sent a memorandum to the governor demanding that one seat in the Legislative Council be reserved for an African from the coastal region
- In 1955 he along with others, formed Mombasa Democratic Union
- In 1956 he assisted in the formation of the Kilifi African Peoples Union
- In 1957 he was elected to the Legislative Council to represent the Coast Rural Constituency
- In 1957 together with other elected African members of the Legislative Council they formed AEMO of which Ngala became the treasurer
- In 1958 Ngala and Mboya were sent to London to press for further constitutional reforms from the British government. This led to the Lennox – Boyd constitution which provided for the increase of Africans representatives in the Legislative Council (8 – 14)
- In 1960 he united the members of KIM and NIP and led them to the First Lancaster House Conference. They agreed on the type of constitution Kenya should adopt
- In 1960 when KANU was formed he was appointed treasurer, but he declined the offer because he felt it was dominated by the Kikuyu and Luo
- In 1960 together with other leaders, they formed KADU at Ngong. He was elected president. The party was formed to protect the interest of the minority
- In 1961 election Ngala was asked to form a government when KANU declined to form a government unless Kenyatta was set free
- He was appointed the Minister for Education and leader of government business in 1961
- In 1962 Ngala led KADU to the Second Lancaster House Conference which resolved that Kenya adopt a federal type of government
- In 1962 a coalition government was formed and Ngala became a minister of constitution affairs
- In 1963 election Ngala became the leader of government opposition and MP for Kilifi. He became the first President for Coast Regional Assembly
- In 1966 he was appointed Minister for Co-operatives and Social Services
- In 1972 he met his untimely death

Questions on Ronald Ngala

(a) What role did Ronald Ngala play in the struggle for independence in Kenya?

(b) Name the leaders who was elected to Legislative Council in 1957 to represent Coast Rural Constitutuency

(c) Name the first leader of opposition in the independent Kenya.

The Barons

Daniel Arap Moi

Moi became the president of Kenya in 1978 after Jomo Kenyatta's death and ruled upto 2002. During his tenure president Moi made significant contributions to Kenya's politics and national development. Some of his contributions included the following:-

- Moi Adopted the Nyayo philosophy of peace, love and unity. This became one of his pillars for development.
- He tirelessly participated in Harambee functions through which the country developed.
- Moi allowed Section 2A of the constitution to be repealed in 1991 paving way for the introduction of political pluralism in Kenya
- Through his endeavours, many schools and universities were expanded. The 8-4-4 system of education was introduced to promote self reliance. Moi promote education by: -

  ✓ Organizing *Harambees* to assist learning institutions
  ✓ Introducing the Nyayo Milk Programmed in primary schools to ease hunger among children from poverty striken regions in the country.

- He expanded the health sector by building more health institutions across the country like the Nyayo Wards.
- Assisted to set the Heart Fund and the Disaster Fund to cater for the welfare of the needy by raising money through harambee

- Moi developed the agriculture sector during his tenure. He, for instance launched programmes to curb soil erosion and establish the Nyayo Tea Zones to increase tea production.
- Moi encouraged social welfare of the people - sporting was boosted through the building of the Nyayo Stadium and Moi International Sports Complex (Kasarani) in Nairobi
- Moi launched the District Focus for Rural Development (DFRD) programme to promote balanced development throughout the country with the district as his focal point.
- Moi strengthened Kenya's international relations through a foreign policy that was liberal. During his reign Kenya was a member of the OAU, the UN, Commonwealth and NAM. He also assisted in revitalizing the EAC
- Moi initiated peace making efforts in the Eastern African region - Southern Sudan and Somalia
- He encouraged trade with the international community and East African countries
- Moi released political detainees like George Anyona, Martin Shikuku and Jean Marie Seroney

Challenges Moi Faced as President

- The Kenya Air Force led by Hezekiah Ochuka attempted to overthrow president Moi in 1982. This made him to be more authoritative and he suppressed people perceived as dissidents.
- Tribal clashes occurred in various parts of the Rift Valley, North Eastern and Coast Province during his tenure.
- Corruption and mismanagement of public utilities became widespread, for example the Goldenberg Scandal
- Assassination of Robert Ouko in 1990 brought a lot of dissatisfaction with Moi's government and riots in the country

- Poverty index in the country shot up especially when most donors withdrew aids to Kenya.
- The rate of HIV/AIDS infection became widespread and the pandemic became classified as a national disaster.
- Violation of human rights became widespread. People who were considered disloyal to the government were arrest, tortured and detained.
- Relation between Kenya and the neighbouring states like Sudan, Ethiopia and Somalia deteriorated
- Demand for political pluralism put a lot of pressure on Moi to institute political and economic reforms.

Questions on Daniel arap Moi

(a) Discuss the contribution of Daniel Arap Moi to Kenya's development between 1978 and 2002
(b) Mention two contributions of Moi to Agricultural development in Kenya.
(c) State two roles Moi played in the promotion of education in Kenya
(d) Explain six problems Moi faced as the President in Kenya?

Jaramogi Oginga Odinga

Oginga Odinga, who was the first Vice President of Kenya, played a big role in the struggle for independence in Kenya. These roles were:

- In 1946 – 1949 Oginga Odinga contested the Central Nyanza African District Council election and won

- In 1952 he mobilized the Luo Union to raise funds for the Kapenguria defense. He traveled to India and discussed the emergency with Nehru, Indian Prime Minister
- In 1954 when Ambrose Ofafa was killed by the *Mau Mau* for supporting the colonialists, Oginga Odinga moved in to calm the situation
- In 1957 Oginga Odinga contested for Central Nyanza Legislative Council and won. He joined AEMO and became its chairman. The group rejected Lennox – Boyd Constitution
- In 1958 AEMO boycotted Legislative Council demanding further constitutional reforms and release of Kenyatta
- In 1959 the elected members were joined by Asians and formed constituency elected members organization which sent a multi racial delegation to resolve the constitutional stalemate
- In 1959 AEMO split into two. The Kenya National Party (KNP) led by Ngala and Kenya Independent Movement (KIM) led by Oginga Odinga
- In 1960 he joined the delegation to the First Lancaster House Conference in London
- In 1960 Oginga Odinga and other members held a meeting in Kiambu and formed KANU. James Gichuru was elected President and Oginga Odinga became the Vice President
- In 1960 Oginga Odinga traveled extensively building relations and raising funds for KANU
- In 1961 he was elected to represent Central Nyanza. They refused to form a government unless Kenyatta was released though KANU won elections
- In 1962 he was among the delegates in the Second Lancaster House Conference
- In 1963 KANU won elections and formed the government. Oginga Odinga became the first Vice President.

Oginga Odinga's Role in Second Liberation

- In 1990 Oginga Odinga re-joined active politics and began to campaign for a new constitutional order that would embrace multi partyism
- In 1991 he announced the formation of National Democratic Party (NDP), but was denied registration since Kenya was a one party (dejure) state
- Oginga Odinga teamed up with Martin Shikuku, Masinde Muliro, Charles Rubia and Kenneth Matiba and formed Forum for Restoration of Democracy (FORD) - a pressure group, to fight political pluralism in the country.
- In 1991 FORD-Kenya became an opposition party when the government repealed section 2A of the constitution. Oginga Odinga became the interim chairman
- In 1992 they held their first rally at Kamukunji Grounds. The opposition lost to KANU in 1992 elections
- In 1993 FORD Kenya assumed the position of the official opposition. Oginga Odinga started a policy of co-operation with the ruling party.

Challenges Oginga Odinga Faced

- Jailing of other nationalists during the emergency period left Oginga Odinga isolated and pre-occupied with the role of fighting for their freedom
- He faced a lot of financial problems during colonial period.
- His approaches to issues created bitterness with his political rivals, including the late president Jomo Kenyatta.
- Reduction of his powers as the vice president in 1966 led to his resignation as a vice president.
- His political parties were outlawed on several occasions.
- He was denied the right to contest in general elections during the single party era.

- He was falsely accused by his political rivals
- Oginga Odinga as a person and his family under went a lot of mistreatment by political rivals – he was put under house arrest and his son (Raila) detained on many occasions.
- His personal ambition of leading the country was not achieved

---

Questions on Oginga Odinga

(a) What role did Oginga Odinga play in the struggle for independence in Kenya?

(b) Describe the role Oginga Odinga played in the second liberation of Kenya

(c) What was the main reason why Oginga Odinga resigned as the first Vice President of Kenya

(d) Name two leaders who formed Forum for Restoration of Democracy (FORD) in 1991

Prof. Wangare Mathai

Professor Wangare Mathai contributed a lot to Kenya's development and more particularly on environmental conservation and empowerment of women. Her contributions can be summarized as follows: -

- In 1971 she became the first African woman in East and Central Africa to acquire a doctorate degree and also the first African woman professor
- When she was employed in Nairobi University, she campaigned for equal benefit for women staff of the university.
- She was a renowned agitator in Kenya, leading protests and hunger strikes against

development on public land (Uhuru Park and Karura Forest).

- She spearheaded the Green Belt Movement which encouraged Kenyan women to plant trees as a way of empowering them.
- Wangare Mathai joined the National Council of Women of Kenya (NCWK) which campaigned for human rights and was elected unopposed.
- She campaigned for the release of political prisoners in the country.
- Mathai and other like minded opposition members formed the movement for free and fair elections in a bid to unite the fragmented opposition against KANU regime.
- She became the Member of Parliament for Tetu in 2002 and was appointed Assistant Minister for Environment and Natural Resources
- In 2004 she was awarded the Nobel Prize for her contribution in Sustainable Development, Democracy and Peace. She became the first environmentalist to win that award

Challenges Wangare Mathai Faced

- Wangare Mathai was divorced by her husband who claimed that she was strong minded and unmanageable
- She was frequently tear gassed and beaten by the unconscious police because of her participation in protests and strikes against the government
- She was denied work in Kenyan universities and struggled to bring up her two children after her divorce.
- Kenya's president (Moi) referred to her as a "crazy woman" and she was torn to pieces by the country's leading political class.
- She was arrested together with other activists and put in prison for several days

---

Questions on the Lives and Contribution of Leaders in Kenya

(a) Give the name of the Kenyan leader who was awarded the Nobel Prize for defending the environment

(b) State six contributions of Professor Wangare Mathai's to Kenya development

(c) Explain six contributions of Prof. Wangare Mathai to environmental conservation in Kenya

16 SOCIAL, ECONOMIC AND POLITICAL DEVELOPMENTS IN KENYA SINCE INDEPENDENCE

Kenya attained self rule (Madaraka Day) in 1st June 1963 with Jomo Kenyatta as the first Prime Minister. On 12th December 1964, she became a republic (Jamuhuri Day) with Jomo Kenyatta as the first president and Oginga Odinga as the first vice president. The country inherited some challenges from their former colonial masters, Britain. These challenges included:

- Lack of enough technocrats to replace the departing whites in administration because of low levels of education among Africans.
- Suspicion and jealousy between different ethnic groups, which were polarized into major tribes – who supported KANU, and minority groups who supported KADU.
- Illiterate population who were ignorant of their political obligations
- High rate of poverty among Kenyans
- Many Kenyans did not have land because of the large holdings by a few. Many Kenyans lived in crowded areas or were squatters.

Jomo Kenyatta's top priorities after assuming leadership of the country was to unit Kenyans under a unitary government, fight illiteracy and poverty, and provide medial services to Kenyans.

POLITICAL DEVELOPMENTS IN KENYA UPTO 1991

In 1964, KANU persuaded Members of KADU who were led by Ronald Ngala to cross over to KANU. Kenya African Democratic Union was dissolved and Jomo Kenyatta formed a more inclusive (unitary) government. KANU became a defacto party. Provincial administration was given more powers and this eventually replaced the federal system of government.

Sharp division soon emerged between KANU members. A group of hardliners – Oginga Odinga, Achieng' Oneko and Bildad Kaggia; deferred with Jomo Kenyatta whom they accused of being insensitive to the masses. A KANU delegate conference was held in Limuru. In this meeting, all members who were allied to Oginga Odinga were booted out of KANU and Oginga Odinga became a vice president without any portfolio. He opted to resign as a vice president and formed the first post independence opposition party, Kenya Peoples Union (KPU) in 1966.

An amendment was done to the constitution which required all members of parliament who had crossed over to other parties to seek fresh mandate from the people. A snap mini election was held in 1966 and most KPU members lost their seats in parliament. Murumbi was appointed vice president to replace Oginga Odinga, but he resigned in 1967. He was replaced by Daniel Arap Moi who served as vice president until 1978, when Jomo Kenyatta died. KPU was banned in 1969 after the Kisumu fracas.

Pio Gama Pinto

Jomo Kenyatta's regime was tinted with several assassinations which many blamed on the government. In 1965, Pio Gama Pinto, an Asian KANU member who was quite critical of Jomo Kenyatta's regime was murdered. In 1969, Tom Mboya was gunned down in Nairobi and in 1975; the badly mutilated body of JM Kariuki was discovered in Ngong Forest. This was after it was alleged in parliament by the Vice President (Moi) that JM Kariuki was in Zambia. The assassinations of the two prominent leaders led to widespread demonstrations and riots in the country.

Jomo Kenyatta became more authoritarian and many critics of the KANU regime were arrested.

Martin Shikuku, an MP of Butere and Jean Seroney – speaker of the National Assembly were arrested within the precincts of parliament and detained. Shikuku had alleged in the August House that KANU was dead and he was protected by the speaker who said that there was no need to ask Shikuku to explain what was apparent. Other leaders who were arrested and detained included Chelegat Mutai and George Anyona.

Around 1975, Jomo Kenyatta's deteriorating health alarmed those who were close to him and wielded a lot of powers like Kihika Kimani, Njenga Karume and Jackson Angaine. They wedged a spirited campaign to change the constitution so that they could bar Daniel Arap Moi from ascending to power, but Jomo Kenyatta stood his ground until his death in 1978 in Mombasa. Moi became the president of Kenya after Kenyatta's death, but in an acting capacity. Mwai Kibaki - who held the Ministry of Health portfolio, became his vice president.

In 1980, Moi who had assumed leadership and maintained that he would follow Jomo Kenyatta's *nyayo* – footsteps, banned all tribal organisations like GEMA, Luo Union and the Kalenjin Association. He also banned the Kenya Civil Servants Union and Nairobi University Staff Union. KANU became more dictatorial and was made a dejure party in 1982. KANU became increasingly unpopular and many critics of the regime emerged. In the same year – 1982, a group of junior officers of the Air Force led by Hezekiah Ochuka staged an abortive military coup against the government. Moi was temporarily overthrown and there was anarchy and jubilations in the streets of Nairobi for a brief moment.

Hezekiah Ochuka

Moi became more dictatorial and perceived enemies of the party were expelled from it by KANU's disciplinary committee led by David Okiki Amayo. Kenneth Matiba and Charles Rubia were among the leaders who were expelled from the party. In 1988, a snap election was held and the infamous queuing (*mulolongo*) system was used. Many people who were opposed to the government were rigged out in the elections. A lot of arrests were made and people who were opposed to the government were jailed. Detention without trial was introduced and many critics were tortured. Many who could escape like Koigi Wamwere and Ngugi Wathiong'o left the country and became refugees in other countries. In 1990, Robert Ouko's brutally murdered and charred remains were found at Got Alila near his Koru home. Dr. Ouko's death greatly blemished Moi's reputation both locally and internationally.

Robert Ouko

Multi Partism in Kenya
Causes of Multipartism (Political Pluralism) in Kenya included:

- The alleged rigging of the 1988 general elections led to discontent among the losers who advocated for the formation of other parties
- KANU failed to listen to criticism and the critics were either suspended or expelled from the party
- The collapse of communism in Eastern Europe made many countries like Romania and Poland to embrace democracy. This wind of change swept into Kenya.

- The events which were taking place in some African countries like Zambia, Togo and Nigeria. These countries embraced multi partism, and in Zambia a long time sitting president – Kenneth Kaunda, was defeated by the opposition candidate. This success encouraged multi partism activities in Kenya.
- Pressure from multi party activist drawn from civil society, political and legal fraternity forced the government to change, for example Martin Shikuku, James Orengo, Paul Muite, Matha Karua, Raila Odinga and Kenneth Matiba

Saba Saba activists lead by Martin Shikuku and Jame Orengo flashing the two-finger salute denoting multi-partism

- Failure by the government to adopt all recommendations forwarded by the public to the Saitoti Review Commission of 1990 led to agitation of multi partism
- Pressure on the government from the donor community to democratize as a condition for aid resumption made her to cede grounds
- The repeal of Section 2A of the constitution allowed for the formation of many parties like Forum for the Restoration of Democracy (FORD), Democratic Party (DP), Kenya National Congress (KNC)

Effect of Multipartism (Political Pluralism) Multipartism has led to many changes in Kenya. Since then:

- Kenyans are provided with an opportunity to join parties of their own choice
- The government is now more accountable and transparent in its dealings.
- Multipartism has enhanced the implementation of economic reforms in the country
- The parties have increased confidence of the international investors in the country
- The Parties have enhanced interaction among Kenyans of different ethnic backgrounds - the political parties compete for support from across the country
- The application of the rule of law in the country has been enhanced

However, multipartism has led to the formation of ethnically inclined political parties. This has tended to promote ethnic loyalties at the expense of National unity. Many divisions exist between the parties in Kenya. These divisions are caused by:

- Personality differences between leaders
- Conflicts over leadership
- Ethnic affiliations of members
- External interference
- Ideological differences among leaders

Disadvantages of Multiparty System

- Multipartism tends to divide the people on tribal, regional and sectarian lines.
- It tends to sharpen the struggle for personality and group dominance rather than policy implementation.
- Multipartism is a foreign system, which does not conform well to the aspirations of independent Africa.
- It encourages the politics of destabilization.
- Political stalemate or deadlocks on debates and tensions have become too common.
- Decisions take too long to be made and implemented due to political squabbles.
- Encourages use of violence in the state since opposition party members are regarded as traitors by the government while the

government is regarded as oppressor by the opposition.

Challenges Facing Multipartism in Kenya

- Many politicians and senior government officials are not ready for multi partism and incite their supporters against political activists
- The ruling party use state machinery, for example radio, television, police and province administration to campaign for them
- Many Kenyans are not sufficiently educated to appreciate multi partism
- Some members of civil society side with the ruling party to frustrate the opposition
- Defection from opposition parties to the ruling party weakens the latter
- The parties lack national wide support because most of them are ethnically based
- Inadequate funds make the political parties to be unsustainable
- External interference by members of the diplomatic community
- Most political parties are embroiled in leadership wrangles
- Many citizens are compromised during elections because of high levels of poverty
- Many parties lack well defined manifestoes and ideologies
- Police are often used to molest opposition leaders
- Some members of the international community openly support certain political parties

Political parties play a leading role in governance and nation building. The parties: -
- Check the excesses of the government by pointing out its weaknesses
- Formulate policies and programmes on how to run the government
- Select candidates to hold public office
- Nominate candidates to vie for various elective posts

- Mobilize people to participate in development and election
- Serve as a link between the government and the people
- Provide civic education to the electorate
- Ensure that there is an alternative government in waiting
- Provide a good avenue for association among different people
- Provide alternative approach to the management of national affairs
- Provide training grounds for leaders
- Ensure that their is availability of quality services at all levels and to all Kenyans

---

Questions on Political Developments in Kenya since Independence

(a) What factors led to the development of multi party democracy in Kenya in the early 1990's
(b) Explain six roles played by political parties in governance and nation building in Kenya
(c) State five advantages of multi - party democracy
(d) Explain five changes which have taken place in Kenya as a result of the re-introduction of multi party democracy
(e) Give two causes of division within the opposition parties in Kenya since 1992
(f) Explain five challenges opposition parties in Kenya face in their attempts to promote democracy in the country?
(g) Explain six challenges of multi party democracy in Kenya

ECONOMIC DEVELOPMENTS IN KENYA Kenya's economy (both industrial and agricultural) was dominated by foreigners and Kenyans played a very minimal role in the country's economy. The Sessional Paper No. 10 of 1965 sought to correct this glitch. The paper aimed at maintaining close ties with the industrialized nations and Africanizing Kenya's economy at the same time. Industrialization in Kenya was aimed at creating employment opportunities to the youthful Kenyans - who were unemployed, utilize locally available resources, and to generate income to the poor Kenyans and the government.

The government of Kenya took several steps to industrialize her economy. These included: -

- In 1963, Development Finance Company of Kenya (DFCK) and Industrial and Commercial Development Corporation (ICDC) were established to assist the manufacturing sector.
- In 1964, Foreign Investment Act was passed. This act allowed foreign enterprises to repatriate their profits.
- In 1966, Kenya Industrial Estates (KIE) was established to fast truck the expansion of Industries in the country.
- In 1971, the Capital Issue Committee was set up to regulate the movement of capital from Kenya

Many parastatals like Kenya Airways, Kenya Railways, Post and Telecommunication, Kenya Ports Authority, National Bank of Kenya, Agriculture Finance Corporation, Kenya Power and Lighting Company among others were established in Kenya in order to:

- Provide essential services like electricity and water
- Generate income to the government
- Create employment opportunities
- Control key sectors of the economy
- Provide loans to farmers

Factors which have favoured industrialization in Kenya since independence include: -

- Agro based industries have been encouraged by the presence of agricultural products like sugarcane which are used as raw materials.
- Availability of raw materials like trona from Lake Magadi
- Kenya has several large water bodies like Lake Victoria which provide fresh water fish

- Kenya's rivers like Tana and Sondu-Miriu are used to generate hydro electric power used by the industries
- Large population of Kenya provides both labour and market to the industries.
- Good transport network facilitates transportation of raw materials and finished products to and from the industries.
- Political stability in the country has encouraged local and foreign investment

Challenges Facing the Industrial Sector

- Widespread poverty limits peoples' purchasing power and reduces the level of investment in the country.
- Poor communication and transport systems hinder the distribution of finished products and delays the delivery of raw materials to the factories, hence loses.
- Limited industrial power and high cost of fuel (petroleum) makes Kenyan products to be expensive and less competitive.
- Mismanagement, corruption and poor management of industries lead to collapse of most industries in the country.
- Competition from developed industrial powers leads to the collapse of less competitive industries in the country.
- Poor technological advancement and limited skilled labour makes the country to rely on expensive expatriates
- Shortage of strategic raw materials and natural resources limits development of some industries
- Post– election violence created political instability and discouraged foreign investment.
- Environmental degradation by industries leads to many problems including drought and famine.

Factors which have slowed down industrialization in Kenya include:

- Most companies are owned by foreigners or multinational co-operations which siphon back their profits
- Senior management post of most firms which operate in the country are dominated by foreigners while majority of the Kenyan employees hold low cadre posts
- Most industries are located in urban centres where expansion is difficult
- Mismanagement of industries have made some of them to collapse like Kisumu Cotton Mills (KICOMI)
- Kenya Industrial Estates (KIE) lack adequate finances to support indigenous entrepreneurs
- Most industries are forced to close down due to stiff competition from industrialized countries
- Small domestic market due to low purchasing power limit expansion of industries
- Most industries produce low quality goods because of poor technology
- Kenya lacks strategic raw materials, for example petroleum
- Majority of the companies use imported kits which are already assembled in their mother countries hence low income

Effects of Industrialization

- Industrialization in Kenya has increased employment opportunities to the youths in the country
- It has assisted Kenya to diversify her economy – reduced over reliance on agriculture as the backbone of the economy.
- Industrialization has enabled the country to optimized the utilization of her resources
- It has contributed to development of roads and railway
- It has led to development of towns like Thika
- It has assisted Kenya to be self reliant

- Industrialization has opened up remote areas of Kenya like the rural parts

Land policies initiated by the Kenya government after independence include:

- Creation of settlement schemes to redistribute land to Africans
- Land consolidation and adjudication bringing together pieces of land and issuance of title deeds
- Promotion of large scale farming through the creation of Agricultural Development Corporation (ADCs)
- Establishment of research stations, for example KARI
- Promotion of irrigation schemes, for example Ahero and Bura to put more land into use
- Proper management of water catchments areas through regional development authorities, for example Lake Basin Development Authority (LBDA)
- Provision of loans to farmers through institutions like Agriculture Finance Corporation (AFC)
- Formation of marketing co-operatives to assist farmers
- Setting up of commissions to settle land issues

Challenges facing the Agricultural Sector in Kenya

- Droughts and famine, for example the 1984 drought forced the government to supply relief food to most affected areas in Kenya
- Population growth rate is faster than that of the agricultural sector making the available food to be inadequate
- World market prices for most agriculture products have dropped considerably while the price of farm input have remained high
- Corruption and mismanagement of co-operatives has led to declining income on crops, for example tea, coffee and sugarcane

- Corrupt government officials have grabbed public land and this has affected research on quality seeds and animals.
- Poor roads discourage farmers especially during the rainy seasons
- Politically instigated clashes have discouraged farming in some parts, for example Molo
- Poor technology has contributed to low yields
- Farm produce is often affected by pests and diseases
- Competition from COMESA countries, Europe and USA discourage farmers

CO-OPERATIVE MOVEMENT IN KENYA

There are three types of co-operatives in Kenya. These include: -
- Producer co-operative
- Consumer co-operative
- Saving and credit co-operative

Benefits of Co-operative Society
- Co-operatives buy and sell produce on behalf of farmers.
- They provide loans to farmers both in cash and kind (materials or inputs)
- They have extension officers who educate the members on better crop and animal husbandry
- Co-operative process produces on farmers half
- They offer transport services to members

Challenges Facing Co-operatives in Kenya
- There is a lot of political interference in their operations
- Fluctuation in the world prices affect profits of producer co-operatives
- Corruption and embezzlement of funds has led to collapse of come co-operatives
- Some co-operatives have also collapsed because of mismanagement

- Many members take less interest in the affairs of co-operatives because they have less shares

SOCIAL DEVELOPMENTS IN KENYA

Jomo Kenyatta identified poverty, ignorance and disease as the main enemies of development which his government had to tackle immediately after independence. Sessional Paper No. 10 formulated by Tom Mboya in 1965 proposed methods in which these challenges were to be addressed. Concern was raised about the poor quality education offered to Kenyans of African descent and the existing facilities in public schools. The curriculum offered was skewed towards the Europeans and did not favour the Africans. The government came up with many changes to address this concern. The initiated changes included: -
- Kiswahili was made a national language and became examinable in national exams
- Harambee strategy was adopted to create more schools and to expand the existing infrastructure.

Several Education commissions were set up to fine tune the education sector. These included: -

(i) The Ominde Commission: made education relevant to the Kenyan's need. The commission came up with 7-4-2-3 system of education.

(ii) Gachathi Commission of 1976 encouraged vocational centres like youth polytechnics to cater for the increasing number of youthful school drop outs.

(iii) Presidential working party of 1982 (Mackay Commission) introduced 8-4-4 system of education which stressed on vocational skills like home science, agriculture, crafts and carpentry. The number of examinable subjects were also raised, both in primary and secondary level

(iv) Kamunge Commission of 1988 recommended cost sharing in the education sector and reduced the number of examinable subjects in 8-4-4.

(v) Koech Commission introduced totally integrated quality education and training.

Challenges facing the education sector today

(a) High drop out rate especially for girls due to pregnancy and early marriage

(b) High HIV/AIDS infection among teachers and students

(c) Poor performance in some subjects, for examples sciences and mathematics

(d) Constant change in curriculum make education costly and discouraging

(e) High enrolment in schools which stretche the existing amenities like classrooms

(f) Frequent strikes due to poor management of schools

(g) Increasing cases of cheating in examination due to pressure to perform

(h) Inadequate funds to implement educational programmes

(i) Education is exam oriented and this give little room for exploitation of talent

---

To increase access to education president Moi introduced School milk to children in all public primary schools and created many diploma colleges and public universities. This was followed in 2002 with a declaration of free primary education to all Kenyan children by President Mwai Kibaki. Free primary education made many people, both young and old to troop back to school. This led to: -

• Overstretched facilities in the existing primary schools

• Over crowded classrooms

• Shortage of trained teachers to handle the big number of pupils

• Poor performance of children in public schools

• Over aged pupils increased cases of indiscipline in schools

• Many pupils failed to secure the few chances in secondary schools

Challenges Facing Health Sector in Kenya

• Lack of qualified medical personnel

• Congestion in government hospitals, for example in Kenyatta National Hospital (KNH), the biggest referral hospital in East and central Africa

• High cost incurred by the government in buying drugs and running health centres

• Poor infrastructure especially in rural areas. Many expectant mothers die on the way to the maternity hospitals

• Inadequate funds, for example to increase awareness on HIV/AID, environmental education, health education etc. The AIDS scourge has claimed many lives of people in Kenya.

• High infant mortality rates in some districts due to poor nutrition, high poverty levels and malaria.

• The policy of cost sharing has reduced the government's role in provision of health services and facilities

• Emerging diseases for example AIDS, heart diseases, cancer etc have claimed many lives

• Competition and embezzlement of funds in government health institutions. Most of the pharmaceutical companies are still dominated by foreigners

• Brain drain of qualified medical doctors who move to other countries where they are better paid

• Back street private clinics and chemists have mushroomed which provide poor facilities, carry out illegal abortions and give expired drugs to patients, leading to death of many Kenyans

The government of Kenya has attempted to preserve the country's cultural heritage since independence in many ways. These include:

• Through museums, Bomas of Kenya and National Archives

• Music festivals in educational institutions and other government owned colleges

- The syllabus has been tailored to include cultural studies.
- It has created the ministry of sports and cultural services to promote cultural values.
- African religious heritage is integrated into Christianity though the right of freedom of worship provided in the constitution

The government of Kenya is trying to minimize poverty among Kenyans by: -
- Providing free primary and making secondary education affordable to many Kenyans by providing grants to schools
- Loans are given to the youth and Jua Kali artisans to venture into income generating activities
- Providing education bursaries for secondary and post secondary education students
- Providing more jobs opportunities by the reviving industries, for example The Kenya Meat Commission.

Questions on Multi – Social and Economic developments in Kenya since independence

(a) State one way in which the government of Kenya is trying to minimize poverty among Kenyans

(b) Explain the challenges facing the agricultural sector in Kenya since Independence

(c) Explain six challenges facing co-operatives in Kenya since independence

(d) State five factors that have favoured industrialization in Kenya

(e) Explain six challenges facing the industrial sector in Kenya since independence

(f) State two factors that have contributed to slow industrial progress in Kenya

(g) State five effects of industrialization in Kenya

(h) Identify the challenges facing education system in Kenya today

(i) Describing challenges facing health sector in Kenya today

(j) Discuss the land policies initiated by the Kenya government after independence

17 FORMATION, STRUCTURE AND FUNCTIONS OF GOVERNMENT OF KENYA

There are two levels of government in the country. These include the National Government and County Governments. National Government is responsible for:

- Foreign affairs and international trade
- Management of international waters and water resources
- Controlling migration of people into the country and issuance of citizenship
- Controlling language policy and promoting official and local languages
- National security and defense services
- Providing internal security through police service
- In charge of courts
- Taking care of national economic policy and planning
- Regulating monetary policies, currency, banking and financial corporations
- Promoting sports and education
- Controlling ancient and historical monuments of national importance
- Monitoring national elections
- Management of public investment

Authority of the President
- The president is the head of state and government
- Is the commander in chief of the Kenya Defense Forces (KDF)
- The chairperson of the National Security Council
- The symbol of national unity
- Upholds the constitution

Executive Arm of Government

The President, the Deputy President and the Cabinet consist of the national executive arm of the Kenyan government. The President is the head of state and government, commander-in-chief of the Kenya Defence Forces, and the chairperson of the National Security Council.

The Deputy President is the president's principle assistant. During presidential elections, each presidential candidate nominates a running mate. Upon election, this running mate becomes the Deputy President.

The Cabinet comprises of the President, the Deputy President, the Attorney General and 14 -22 Cabinet Secretaries. The president appoints the Cabinet Secretaries, but the appointments must be approved by the National Assembly.

Functions of the President
- The President addresses the newly elected parliament
- Addresses a special parliamentary sitting once every year or any other time as need may arise
- Nominates Cabinet Secretaries, Attorney General, Principal Secretaries, High Commissioners and other diplomats. These nominations are subject to approval by parliament
- The President chairs cabinet meetings
- Receive foreign diplomats and other dignitaries
- Confers honours to men and women of distinguished service to the nation
- Ensures that international obligations are adhered to through respective Cabinet Secretaries

President Uhuru Kenyatta and Deputy President William Samoei Ruto

Powers of the President

Power of Mercy: depending on the advice of the Advisory Committee which include the Attorney General, Cabinet Secretary responsible for

Correctional Service and at least five other members, the President may: -

- Grant a free or conditional pardon to a person convicted of an offence
- Postpone the carrying out of a punishment, either for a specific period or indefinitely
- Substitute a less severe form of punishment
- Remit all or part of the punishment

The President has power to nominate the following: -

- The judges of the superior courts
- Public officers which the constitution requires the president to appoint
- Nominate Cabinet Secretaries
- Nominate High Commissioners and Ambassadors

Qualifications of the President

A person qualifies for nomination as a presidential candidate if the person:

- Is a citizen by birth
- Is qualified to stand for election as a member of parliament
- Is nominated by not fewer than two thousand voters from each of a majority of the counties

A person may not qualify for presidency when he/she owes allegiance to a foreign state or is a public officer.

Presidential Elections

The President is elected directly by all registered voters for a five year term. For a person to be declared winner of the presidential vote, the candidate must receive more than half of all the votes cast in the election. If no candidate meets the requirement, a fresh election is held within 30 days for the top two candidates. The candidate who receives more votes is declared the winner. Elections of a president can be challenged in the Supreme Court within 7 days after the declaration of the results. The case is determined within 14 days. The president elect is sworn into office by the Chief Justice.

The President elect can lose his office in Kenya: -

- In case of death
- In case of resignation in writing to the speaker of the National Assembly
- If an election petition against the president succeeds
- If a vote of no confidence on the president is passed by parliament. The ground of impeachment may be gross misconduct, gross violation of the law or constitution and committing a serious crime under national or international law.
- In case the president becomes incapacitated

Functions of the Deputy President

- The Deputy President is the principal assistant to the President
- Perform duties conferred to him/her by the President
- In the absence of the president the Deputy President acts as the president

The law spells out specific functions that the acting president cannot perform. These include:

- He/she cannot appoint judges or any other public officers who are appointed by the president
- He/she cannot appoint or dismiss high commissioners, ambassadors, diplomatic or consular representatives
- He/she cannot confer honours to individuals in the name of the Republic
- He/she cannot exercise the power of mercy which is a preserve for the president.

In the absence of the president the constitution allows the Deputy President to perform the following presidential functions:

- Addressing the opening of or any other special sitting of parliament

- Chair cabinet meetings
- Direct and co-ordinate the functions of the ministries and government departments
- Receive foreign diplomatic and consular representatives
- Assuming the authority of the president as the commander in chief of the armed forces
- Chairing the national security council
- Declaring with the approval of parliament, a state of emergency

Functions of the Cabinet in Kenya
- Formulate national and foreign policies to guide the country
- Advice the president on issues of national development related to ministries
- Supervise the implementation of government polices by respective ministries
- Initiate development projects by ministries in different parts of the country
- Discuss important national and international issues
- Prepare budgetary estimates for the respective ministries
- Defend government policies collectively

> **Constitutional offices in Kenya**
> (a) Attorney General
> (b) Controller and Auditor General
> (c) Electoral commissioners
> (d) The governor of the central Bank
> (e) The judges of the high court
> (f) The Chief justice
>
> Holders of these offices have security of tenure of office and cannot be removed from office any time the executive desires.

Duties of the Prime Minister in Kenya according to the National Accord were to:-
- Supervise all ministries in the government
- Answer queries in parliament regarding the function and performance of ministries

once a week when parliamentary session was in progress
- Share executive powers with the president, for example appointed ministers from his party
- Consult and advice the president on day to day activities of the government

Raila Odinga – 2nd Prime Minister

> **Why there should be separation of power**
> (a) It is a requirement by the constitution
> (b) It enhances checks and balances within the government
> (c) Promotes service delivery to all Kenyans
> (d) Ensures that each arm does not interfere with another

National holidays in Kenya according to the new constitution are Madarak Day (1st June), Jamuhuri Day (12th December) and Mashujaa Day (20th October)

Problems affecting the performance of civil service in Kenya today
- Poor remuneration and terms of service demoralizes and lowers the performance of civil servants. This has led to continuous demand for more salaries and strikes
- Rampant corruption – Most civil servants have been accused of taking bribes in order to perform their services
- Job security – retrenchment in various ministries has created fear and uncertainty hence low morale of workers
- Inadequate fund – most ministries lack enough funds to perform their duties effectively, for example they use outdated methods of keeping records

- Incompetence by some civil servants – this is due to low academic qualifications and training opportunities for the civil servants
- Lack of transparency and accountability especially in the management of finances
- Political interference – some civil servants are employed by politicians hence enjoy their patronage

DEVOLVED (COUNTY) GOVERNMENT

The Kenya constitution establishes 47 counties each with its own government. County Governments consist of a County Assesmbly and are made up of members elected from different wards in the country. Voters in each county elect their governor who appoints other members of the County Executve Committee, with the approval of the County Assembly.

The County Governments are in charge of agriculture, health services, public amenities, county trade development and regulations, county planning and development among other services that they are mandated to provide the residents of the county.

The objectives of devolution were:
- To promote democratic and accountable exercise of power
- To foster national unity by recognizing diversity
- To give powers of self governance to the people and enhance participation of the people in making decisions which affect them
- To recognized the rights of communities to manage their own affairs and to further their development
- To protect and promote the interests and rights of minorities and marginalized groups of people in the soiety
- To promote social and economic development and the provision of proximate, easily accessible services throughout Kenya
- To ensure equitable sharing of national and local resources throughout Kenya
- To facilitate the decentralization of state organs, their functions and services, from the capital of Kenya
- To enhance checks and balances and the separation of power

Principles of Devolution
- County Government is based on democratic principles and the separation of powers.
- County Government has reliable sources of revenue to enable them to govern and deliver services effectively.
- No more than two thirds of the members of representative bodies in each County Government should be of the same gender.

County Executive Committee

The County Executive Committee consists of:-
- The County Governor and the Deputy Governor
- Members appointed by the County Governor with approval of the assembly from among persons who are not members of the assembly

In the absence of the Governor, the Deputy County Governor acts as the County Governor.

Members of County Executive Committee are accountable to the County Governor for the performance of their functions and in exercise of their powers

Powers and functions of a Governor in a county government include:

- The Governor is the chief executive officer of a county. The executive branch of government, headed by the Governor, includes executive departments and advisory boards.
- The Governor is the chairman of county executive committee.
- He/ she is in charge of implementing, within the county, national legislation to the extent that the legislation so requires
- He/she ensures, through the County Executive Committee, the implementation of county legislation.
- The Governor manages and coordinates the functions of the county administration and its departments.
- He/ she provides the County Assembly with full and regular reports on matters relating to the county.
- He/ she appoints with the approval of the assembly members, members to the county executive committee.
- He/ she ensures that members of a County Executive Committee perform their functions and exercise their powers fully.
- He/ she handles on behalf of the county, all external affairs with other counties in consultation with the central government.
- The Governor prepares and submits a budget of the county for the following fiscal year.
- He/ she sets the terms and conditions of service of persons holding or working in public offices in the county.
- By virtue of his office, the Governor serves on certain boards and special commissions in the county. The Governor chairs the board of Public Works.

Removal of County Governor

A County Governor may be removed from office on any of the following grounds:

- He/she has grossly violated the constitution
- Where there are serious reasons for believing that the Country Governor has committed a crime under national or international law
- Physical or mental incapacity to perform the functions of office of county governor
- His/her election has been nullified by the High Court

Functions of County Executive Committee

- County Executive Committee implements county legislation
- Implements within the county national legislation
- Manages and co-ordinates the functions of the county administration and its departments
- It prepares proposed legislation for consideration by the County Assembly.
- It provides the County Assembly with full and regular reports on matters relating to the county.

Functions of a County Assembly

- County Assemblies make laws for the effective performance of the County Government.
- It acts as a watch dog over the County Executive Committee.
- It receives and approves plans and policies for managing and exploiting the county's resources,
- It approves policies for developing and managing the infrastructure and institutions in the county.
- It enhances legislation that may set out the structure and framework for the better administration and management of County Governments.

- It approves oversight budgets and development projects within the county.
- It approves investment decisions and loans.
- It supervises other units within the county through political authority, guidance and direction.
- Monitors the execution of projects under approved development plans, and assesses and evaluates their impact on development in the county.

Functions of the County Government
- Provides health services, for example health facilities, ambulances, licensing and control of undertakings that sell food to the public, cemeteries, refuse disposal
- In charge of planning and developing the county
- Controls education of pre-primary education, village polytechnic and childcare
- Implements specific national government policies on natural resources and environmental conservation
- Manages disaster and fight fire
- Controls agricultural activities, for example livestock sale yard and country abattoirs

Sources of Revenue for County Governments
- Licenses from business ventures
- Fees charged on services rendered
- Grants and loans from Central Government
- Rates charged on lands leased out
- Cess levy on crops like tea
- Rent from residential houses and other premises
- Rent paid by property owners or billboards
- Loans from external sources
- Parking fees paid by motorists
- Hiring facilities, for example stadiums and halls
- Fund from water bills or garbage collection
- Fine paid by the people who break the by-laws
- Sales of property owned by the country

Merits of County Governments
- Administrative services are brought closer to the people.
- Local resources are utilized effectively, for example Hospitals and piped water
- Means of transport and communication are developed
- Local people are involved in decision making
- Local priorities are identified and implemented
- Ensures equal development in all districts
- Create employment for local people

Relations between the Central Government and County Governments
- The county governments operate mainly as agents of the Central Government
- Laws laid down by the Central Government are obeyed in every area under the County Governments
- County Governments are linked to the Cabinet Secretary of County Government which has control over the activities and operations of County Governments
- All powers and responsibilities of county governments are derived from the central government
- The Central Government has powers to dissolve county governments or appoint commission of inquiry into any aspects of operation
- The Central Government appoints civil servants for example the clerk, treasurer, and engineer to the County Government.

Challenges Facing County Governments

- Many County Governments lack adequate financial base to finance their services
- Tax evasion by individuals and organization reduce the finance base of the Country Governments
- County funds are misappropriated or embezzled by corrupt officials
- Conflicts between County Representatives and chief officers derail county activities.
- Political interference in the affairs and management of County Governments
- There is duplication of roles in some activities between National Government and County Government, for example education and health
- Brain drain to the private sector due to poor remuneration leads to lack of qualified staff in areas of administration and financial management of County Governments
- Bloated employment and ghost workers in most County Governments strains their financial capability
- Sometimes illiterate county representatives are elected to manage the affairs of the County Governments
- Some counties have poor infrastructure and other amenities which can spur growth
- High population concentration strains available resources
-

ELECTONS IN KENYA

General elections are held every five years to elect the President, Governors, Senators, Members of Parliament, Women Representatives and members of County Assembly in Kenya. It is important to hold these elections because: -

- Holding elections in the country is a constitutional requirement
- Elections gives Kenyans a chance to elect leaders of their choice
- Elections gives Kenyans a chance to exercise their democratic rights
- Elections helps to generate new ideas by offering alternative government

The body that is charged with the organization of elections in Kenya is called the Independent Electoral and Boundary Commission of Kenya (IEBC). IEBC conducts General Elections, By-elections, Referedum and Civic Elections in the country. This body is empowered to:

- Conduct elections and ensures that it is smoothly done and results declared.
- Identify, recruit and deploy election officials.
- Register voters and revise the voters register to weed out ghost voters

- Set electoral boundaries of constituencies and wards
- Regulate the process by which parties nominate candidates for elections
- Settle electoral disputes
- Offer voter education to sensitize the voters of the need to vote and how to vote
- Facilitate the observation, monitoring and evaluation of elections in liaison with independent observer groups.
- Regulate the amount of money that may be spent by or on behalf of a candidate or party in respect of any election
- develop a code of conduct for candidates and parties which are contesting in the elections

Roles of Election Officials
Returning Officer
- The Returning Officer co-ordinates elections in the constituency
- Receives nomination papers from candidates at constituency level
- Receives and distributes ballot papers and boxes to all polling stations within the constituency
- Supervise the voting and counting of votes
- Appoint presiding officers in each polling station
- Announce the results of elections in the constituency

Presiding Officer
- Presiding officer is in charge of coordinating elections in the polling stations
- Ensures that voters vote only once and assists those who are illiterate
- Seal the ballot boxes after voting is complete and the counting of votes has been done
- Reports any irregularities to the returning officers

Polling Clerks
- Guide voters in the polling stations
- Identify the legible voters from the voters' register
- Issue ballot papers to the voters and direct them to the right ballot boxes
- Mark the fingers of people who have voted
- Assist the presiding officers to count votes.

Election offences can be committed by voters, the party agents or the candidates themselves. Offences which can be committed by the voters include:
- Attempting to vote more than once
- Registering more than once
- Adorning party symbols or clothes within the polling station
- Interfering with election materials and
- Causing violence to disrupt elections.

Candidates can committee offences like:-
- Campaigning before the set time or after
- Bribing voters
- Administering oath to voters and
- Organizing violence to disrupt peaceful election.

A candidate who commits an election offence may be disqualified even after being voted in. The candidate can be barred for contesting in future or be either fined or jailed depending on the gravity of the offence.

Elections officials at Bomas

ELECTORAL PROCESSES IN KENYA

- The seats are declared vacant by the speaker
- Election date is set by the IEBC
- A time span is set for the parties to nominate their candidates and present them to IEBC for authentication.
- The electoral body verifies the legibility of the candidate and issue certificates to those who have met their requirements.
- An electioneering period is set
- Campaign stops two days prior to the elections.
- Elections are held between 6.00 a.m. to 6.00 p.m.
- Counting of votes is done at the polling stations and the result for each candidate at the polling station is announced by the presiding officer there and then.
- Results of the County Representatives and Members of Parliament are announced at constituency level, that of the Governor, Senator and Women Representative at county level and that of the President at national level – Bomas of Kenya.

There are many factors which interfere with free and fair elections in the country. These factors include: -

- Ethnic loyalties – many Kenyans vote on tribal lines and easily elect candidate not because of their potentiality, but because they come from the same ethnicity or clan.
- Party affiliations – many people vote for parties rather than individuals who make the parties.
- Harassment of voters by rival groups cause voter apathy and low voter turn out because of the fear which is instilled in the voters' mind.
- Incompetent election officials who sometimes take sides and tend to favour some candidates. This compromises the legitimacy of the elections.
- Inaccessibility of some polling stations reduce the voter turn out because many people are discouraged by the distance

- Illiterate voters are easily lured to vote for candidates not of their choice.
- Insecurity and fear instilled in some candidates discourage them from the voting exercise.
- Bribery of candidates and supporters

For one to qualify as an aspirant in Kenya one should:-

- Register first as a voter and the name must appear in the voters register.
- Satisfy educational, moral and ethical requirements stipulated by the constitution. Educational requirements are higher diploma for Members of Parliament and a degree, from a recognized university, for Senators, Governors and the President.
- Be either nominated by registered parties or proposed by 1000 or 2000 people for Members of Parliament and Senators respectively if they are independent candidates. Presidential aspirants must be nominated by at least 2000 people from every county. A presidential aspirant has a maximum of two terms each of 5 year and cannot present his or her candidature beyond that term.

State officers or those who hold public offices are not legible for elections unless they resigned six months prior to the set date for elections. Those who at any time within 5 years immediately preceding the date of election, held office as a member of IEBC are also not legible for elections. The aspirant should have been a Kenyan citizen for not less than 10 years prior to the set date of elections.

Elected candidates can lose their seats if: -

- They became insane or are certified to be by a qualified medical practitioner.
- They are subjected to a sentence of at least six months imprisonment, as at the date of registration as a candidate, or at the date of election

- Elections results are nullified by court of law
- The candidate is elected as speaker of the National Assembly
- He/she resigns from the party that sponsored him/her
- He/she defects from one party to another
- He/she is declared bankrupt by a court of law
- He/she misses to attend parliamentary sessions for 8 consecutive days without informing the speaker

An elected president can lose his/her seat if: -
- He or she has already served two parliamentary terms as a president.
- One is found guilty of an election offence by court of law.
- If he or she fails to get at least 50 percent plus 1 or extra vote in an election
- He or she is not proposed by at least 2000 registered voters from each of the 47 counties for the post.
- Vote of no confidence is passed against him/her

Questions on Electoral Processes in Kenya
(a) Name the body that is charged with organization of elections in Kenya
(b) State five functions of Independent Electoral and Boundary Commission
(c) What are the roles of a Returning Officer?
(d) What are the roles of a Presiding Officer?
(e) Describe the factors that are likely to interfere with a free and fair election in Kenya
(f) State one reason why elections are held in Kenya
(g) Identify any two election offences which may lead to prosecution
(h) Identify two types of elections held in Kenya
(i) State two factors that my make a member of parliament to be disqualified
(j) Give five requirements of a parliamentary candidate in Kenya
(k) Describe the reasons that can lead to the disqualification of one as a candidate for parliamentary elections

---

PROVINCIAL ADMINISTRATION

Functions of District Commissioners included:
- Represents the president in the district
- Maintain law and order
- Interprets and explains government polices
- Supervises and co-ordinates all administration in the district
- Chairs DDC meetings
- Represents the president in district celebrations, for example Jamuhuri Day
- Ensures that the County Governments carry out their duties
- Chairman of liquor licensing board
- Chairman of trade licensing board
- Administers district revenue and co-ordinates the future of various government ministries

Functions of Provincial Administration
- Represent the president during national holidays
- They act as a link between the Central Government and the people
- It is in charge of law and order and security in the province
- It coordinates development policy and programmes
- They implement government policy and programmes
- It interprets and explains government policies to the people
- It solves minor disputes involving inheritance and land

Problems faced by the Provincial Administration in Kenya included: -
- Inadequate transport facilities such as vehicles
- Poor state of the roads in the rural areas, for example Northern Frontiers
- Some provinces are too large to administer effectively

- Frequent transfers of provincial officers prevent them from discharging their duties effectively
- Corruption of some chief officers prevents the officers form discharging their duties effectively
- Political interferences frustrates the work of the provincial chief officers
- Lack of regular in-service training for junior provincial officers for example chiefs to cope with emerging challenges for example environmental conservation, HIV and AIDS pandemic
- Tribalism and nepotism in the appointment of provincial chief officers
- Illiteracy of the masses makes the policies of the government not to be understood
- Embezzlement of funds making the development not to be carried out effectively

L EGISLATIVE ARM OF GOVERNMENT
Kenya's parliament consists of two houses: the National Assembly and the Senate. The National Assembly has: -
- 290 elected members
- 47 women members who are elected from each of the 47 counties
- 12 nominated members by political parties based on their numerical strength in the house
- A speaker who is an ex-officio member. In this category are also the Attorney General and the Sergeant at arms.

National Parliament

The National Assembly controls national expenditure and revenue allocation between the two levels of government. The National Assembly also reviews the conduct of the president and other state officers, and initiates the process of removing them from office if necessary. The Senate on the hand serves the interest of Counties and the County Governments by debating and approving bills concerning the Counties. The Senate also determines the outcome of any resolutions of the National Assembly to impeach the President or the Deputy President.

Roles of the National Parliament
- The national parliament represents the will of the people of the constituencies and special interest groups.
- Deliberates on issues of national and international importance
- Enacts legislation and makes any amends to the existing laws
- Determines the allocation of national revenue between levels of government, apportions funds for expenditure by the National Government and other national state organs and oversees national revenue and its expenditure
- Plays terminative roles as it has power to pass vote of no confidence in the president and the government.
- Checks on the executive and the judiciary so as to protect the interest of citizens and ensures that the rights of individuals are respected by those in power.
- Exercise oversight of state organs
- Approves declaration of war and extension of state of emergency
- Serves as training ground for future national political leadership

National Parliament exercises control over the executive arm of the government in the following ways: -
- Approves sources of government revenue. The Cabinet Secretary of finance

presents a budget annually to parliament and it gives its approval to this budget.

- Cabinet Secretaries are accountable to parliament for their actions - Parliamentary Select Committees have powers to summon them and ask them questions about their ministries.
- The Public Accounts Committee scrutinizes government expenditure and censors individuals or institutions that have not followed the laid down procedures.
- Only parliament has the powers to legislate the bills prepared by the Cabinet and its decisions are binding.
- Parliament can pass a vote of no confidence in the government if it is not satisfied with its performance; in that case the President and the Cabinet Secretaries have to resign.
- Parliament can pass a vote of no confidence in the government expenditure before funds can be released to various government ministries.

How Parliamentary Supremacy is realized in Kenya
- Parliament is the only body charged with makes, amending and repealing the laws in the country.
- It has powers to pass a vote of no confidence in the president and the cabinet.
- Parliament can limit the powers of the executive through the amendments
- Cabinet Secretaries are accountable to parliament for their actions.
- Bills prepared by the cabinet have to be legislated by the parliament
- Parliament has powers to approve government revenue and expenditure

---

Law Making Process
Before a bill is taken to parliament for debate proposals are made to it. These proposals are taken to the Attorney General's chambers for drafting and getting the legal framework. The Attorney General prepares a draft proposal of the intended law and notifies the members of parliament and the public about the intended bill to enable them to carry out further research. The intended law is then taken to parliament for debate.

The following are the procedures involved in law making process by parliament in Kenya:-
- The proposal of the law is drafted by the Attorney General.
- First Reading – the bill is tabled in the house not for debating but for approval by Members of Parliament
- Second Reading – bill is studied by a select committee and re-written to include suggestions made by the committee.
- Report Stage – MPs confirm recommendations of second stage now included into the bill.
- Third Reading – further debate is done and extra amendments made to the bill.
- Presidential Assent – if president signs the bill it become law. In case the bill is not signed by the president, it is amended and taken back to the house. The bill is adopted in its amended form if the House fails to garner two thirds required by law to overturn it.
- Gazetting – the act is published in Kenya Gazette and becomes law

Factors that Limit Parliamentary Supremacy
- Increased powers of the Cabinet can reduce parliamentary authority
- By-laws made by the County Government can also undermine parliamentary supremacy
- The people's traditions and customs also play an important role in influencing decisions made by parliament
- The House can not pass law that contradict the constitution of the land
- The application of international laws can also limit the supremacy of the parliament

Advantage of parliament supremacy

- Creates harmony in the country - Legislature and Executive work together
- The system allows ordinary people to participate in the governing process by electing their representatives to express their views on issues of national interest
- It allows for constructive criticism from the opposition
- It is both responsible and responsive as members of the Cabinet are controlled by parliament which consists of peoples' representatives
- Gives citizens a chance to participate in national political leadership
- It legitimizes actions taken by the government
- It enables Kenyans of ability to prove their worth in parliamentary debates

Disadvantages of Parliamentary Supremacy

- Many parties may cause division and instability in a country
- Rights of the minority may be ignored by the majority
- Where Cabinet is dominated by one political party it may become very powerful
- Opposition parties may oppose government policies for the sake of it
- Parliament weakens the Executive– Members of Parliament sometimes use their privileged position to intimidate the Cabinet Secretaries.

Parliamentary Committees

- Public Accounts Committee (PAC) - examines public accounts and ensures money is spent as budgeted
- The Committee of Supply -Verifies the estimates presented by the different ministries before approving expenditure.
- Committee of Ways and Means -Verifies the budget proposals and taxation.
- Budgetary committee
- Public investment committee

Duties of the Speaker of National Assembly
Once the speaker is elected by members of parliament he/she is sworn in by the Clerk to the National Assembly. The speaker has the following roles: -

- Is in charge of debates in parliament during sessions. The speaker organizes the order of debate and chooses which member to speak at a time
- Ensures that members observe and adhere to the rules of the House and reprimands those who violet them.
- Disciplines members who act irresponsibly during parliamentary debates
- Presides over the swearing in of Members of Parliament at the start of each parliament or after a by-election
- Maintains attendance register of members and declares their seats vacant if they fail to attend parliament eight consecutive sessions
- Receive all bills, motions and parliamentary questions intended for tabling and discussion
- Ensures that only relevant issues are deliberated on in the house
- Declares a seat vacant when a member or parliament dies or resigns
- Prevent personal attacks in parliament
- In-charge of general administration and welfare of National assembly
- Represents parliament in relation to other countries
- Chairperson of parliamentary service commission that hires parliamentary staff and remuneration

Sergeant at Arms
is responsible for all ceremonies and discipline within the precincts of parliament, is the custodian of the mace and maintains parliamentary buildings.

Role of the Attorney General

The main work of the attorney general is to advise parliament and the government on matters pertaining to the law. The Attorney General (AG) also has other duties. These are:

- Heads the Attorney General's Chamber that registers societies, for example churches and political parties
- As a member of the Cabinet, answers questions in parliament on behalf of the Cabinet Secretaries
- Answers questions on behalf of Members of Parliament as an ex-officio member of parliament
- As a member of Judicial Service Commission (JSC) advices the president in the appointment of High Court and Court of Appeal judges
- Handles matters concerning the judiciary in parliament
- Is the protector of public interest

Prof. Githu Mugai – Attorney General

SENATE

The Senate consists of: -

- 47 elected members from 47 counties in Kenya
- 16 women members nominated by political parties based on their numerical strength in the House
- 2 members (man and woman) representing the youth
- 2 members (man and woman) representing persons with disabilities
- Speaker who is an ex-officio member of the house

Function of the Senate

- Represents the counties and serves to protect the interests of the counties and their governments.
- Participates in the law making function of parliaments by debating and approving bills concerning counties.
- Determines the allocation of national revenue among counties and exercises oversight over national revenue allocated to the county government.
- Participates in the oversight of state officers by considering and determining any resolution to remove the president or deputy president from office in accordance with the law.

Questions on the Legislature

(a) Describe the composition of the National Parliament
(b) Name one ex-officio member of the National Assembly in Kenya
(c) Give one role of Sergeant at arms
(d) State two roles of the National Parliament
(e) Describe the composition of the Senate
(f) Who swears in the speaker of the National Assembly?
(g) Who swears in the president elect of Kenya
(h) Give five functions of the parliament in Kenya
(i) Explain five ways through which the parliament exercises control over the Executive Arm of the government
(j) Give five reasons why parliament is regarded an important institution in Kenya
(k) Describe the process of preparing a bill before it is taken to parliament for debate
(l) Outline the law making process in Kenya
(m) Explain how parliamentary supremacy is realized in Kenya
(n) State five factors that limit parliamentary supremacy in Kenya
(o) Explain the advantage of parliament supremacy
(p) Give two disadvantages of parliamentary supremacy
(q) Identify three committees developed in parliament to ensure that government revenue is spent well.
(r) State five ways how the speaker is of importance to the national assembly

Commission. This is subjected to the approval of the National Assembly.

Under the Kenyan constitution, the Supreme Court is the highest court in the country. The Chief Justice is the president of the Supreme Court. This court also comprises of the Deputy Chief Justice and five other judges. The Supreme Court is the only court that can hear and determine any case challenging the elections of the president. The court also attends to appeals from the Court Of Appeal, the High Court and other courts and tribunals.

The Court of Appeal is the second highest court in Kenya. It comprises of at least 12 judges and is headed by a president of the Court of Appeal. The court only has appellant jurisdiction over appeals from the High Court and other courts and tribunals.

The highest court in Kenya is the High Court. The High Court has unlimited original jurisdiction in criminal and civil matters. The court also has supervisiory powers over the subordinate courts. The consititution mandates parliament to establish special courts to determine disputes related to employment and labour relations, land and environmental matters. These special courts have equal status with the High Court. The High Court does not have any jurisdiction over matters handled exclusively by these special courts.

Prof. Willy Mtunga – Chief Justice

Functions of the Judiciary

(a) To dispense justice and settle disputes

(b) Adjudicate and make the final determination in civil and criminal cases

(c) It administers justice when one is found guilty of breaking the law and is punished according to the law

(d) It is the custodian of the constitution

(e) Ensures that the law made conforms to the constitution

(f) The legal system approves and recommends children to approved schools

(g) Arranges for the administration of deceased persons estate by appointing guardians or trustees.

(h) It also appoints receivers for bankrupt businesses, for example banks

(i) Legal representative: every accused person is entitled to legal representation by an advocate of High Court

(j) Settles disputes among political parties

The Structure of the Court System in Kenya

• The District Magistrate Court is the lowest in the structure and is found at the district level. The Kadhi's Court is at the same level, but deals only with Islamic law

• The Resident Magistrate Court is the second lowest in the court system and is based at the provincial level. Next is the Senior Resident Magistrate court

• The Chief Magistrate Court is the highest magistrate's court

• The high court is above the magistrate's court and is headed by the chief justice

• The court of appeal is the highest court in the judicial structure. It is also headed by the chief justice

• The Supreme Court is the highest court in the judicial system and is headed by the chief justice. There are six judges including the chief justice in this court. The decisions of this court are final.

- There are also special tribunals which handle specific cases like Rent tribunal, Industrial court, Business Courts and Court Martial, Children's Courts and Anti Corruption Court

Functions of the Chief Justice in Kenya

- The chief justice heads the Kenya judiciary and gives direction on how the judiciary is to determine justice in the arbitration of disputes
- Plays an advisory role in the removal of the president on ground of incapacity
- Administers oath of allegiance on the president elect.
- Chairs the Judiciary Service Commission in Kenya.
- Prescribes fee to be charged by courts
- Determines the establishment of the Kadhi's Court in consultation with the Chief Kadhi.
- He or she has jurisdiction to exercise constitutional function vested in the High Court and the Court of Appeal.

Kiriako Tobiko – Director of Public Prosecutions

The director of public prosecutions (DPP) is nominated and with the approval of the National Assembly is appointed by the president to hold the office for a non renewable term of eight years. The director does not require the consent of any person or authority to commence criminal proceedings and his/her powers may be exercised in person or by subordinate officers working under general or special instructions. For one to be appointed a DPP, he/she should have the qualifications a judge of the High Court.

The functions of the Director of Public Prosecutions include:

- The Director of Public Prosecutions has power to direct the Inspector-General of the National Police Service to investigate any information or allegation of criminal conduct.
- Exercises state powers of prosecution and may institute and undertake criminal proceedings against any person before any court (other than a court martial) in respect of any offence alleged to have been committed.
- He has powers to take over and continue any criminal proceedings commenced in any court (other than a court martial) that have been instituted or undertaken by another person or authority, with the permission of the person or authority.
- Can discontinue at any stage, before judgment is delivered, any criminal proceedings

Functions of the High Court of Kenya

- Has unlimited original and appellate jurisdiction. It deals with civil and criminal cases. It hears appeal from Court Martial, Resident Magistrate Courts and Tribunals
- It deals with criminal cases carrying death sentence or treason or civil cases involving more than Kshs. 500,000
- Deals with elections petitions for governors, senators, women representatives or members of parliament
- Exercises general supervision to the subordinate courts
- Correct any irregularities in decision by lower courts
- Has administrative jurisdiction over maritime or naval affairs
- Hears cases involving inheritance, for example administration of estates of the deceased
- Exercises divorce jurisdiction
- Has unlimited territorial jurisdiction, for example it deals with cases involving the locals or foreigners

- Deals with any case between any person from any part of Kenya
- It deals with matters of constitutional interpretation. It determines whether the issue is constitutional or not

Functions of the Chief Magistrate Courts

- The Chief Magistrate handles matters related to the welfare and professional issues affecting all magistrates
- The Chief Magistrate handles matters related to appointment of magistrates
- Chief Magistrate supervises the work of other magistrate courts
- Allocates cases to magistrates in resident magistrate courts
- Deals with civil cases of up to Khs. 120,000
- Deals with criminal cases that do not deserve capital punishment
- Deal with proceedings concerning claims under customary law for example dowry and inheritance

Functions of the Resident Magistrate Courts

The Resident Magistrate Courts have criminal jurisdiction, but cannot impose a sentence in excess of seven years or a fine of over Khs. 20,000 or corporal punishment in excess of 24 strokes. The courts have a civil jurisdiction over civil cases not exceeding Khs. 20,000 and unlimited jurisdiction in proceedings concerning claims under customary laws. The court also have appellate jurisdiction in cases from the District Magistrate Courts

Functions of the District Magistrate Courts

The District Magistrate Courts have civil jurisdiction in cases where the value of the matter in dispute does not exceed Khs. 75,000. The courts deal with customary matters related to the land and criminal cases whose sentence does not exceed 24 stokes, a fine up to Khs. 20,000 and imprisonment of up to 7 years

Functions of the Kadhi's Court

In the Kadhi's court, all parties must profess Islamic faith. The courts deals with matters relating to personal status, for example marriage and inheritance between Muslims and apply Islamic laws and rules.

Functions of the Children's Court in Kenya

The children's court can impose a fine on a child molester or on a child's parent(s). The court can also: -

- Put the young person on probation
- Commit the child to the care of a fit person or body
- Authorize that the juvenile be canned
- In rare cases, the court can sent the young person to jail.
- Send him/her for training
- Commit him/her to a youth corrective training centre
- Place him/her in a remand home

Conditions which may make a child to be taken to a Children's Court in Kenya include: -

- Being deserted by parents or guardian
- Being unable to be controlled by parents or guardian.
- Has a parent or guardian who is unable to exercise proper care and guardianship
- Is falling into bad associations or is exposed to a moral or physical danger
- Is being kept in premises which a medical officer asserts to be overcrowded, unhygienic or dangerous
- Is prevented from receiving compulsory education or is a habitual truant
- Frequents any public or gambling house or is found buying, receiving or growing drugs
- If found begging or receiving alms
- Has suffered bodily injury through the commission against him/her of certain offences in the penal code

Principals of the Independence of the Judiciary

- Independence of judiciary is spelt out in the constitution and the government has to respect it
- The judicial officers decide matters in accordance with the law, without any threat from any quarter
- There is no interference with the judicial processes nor are judicial decisions subject to revision
- The courts and judiciary must have the confidence of the communities in order to maintain their dignity
- Judges ought to be persons of high moral and ethical behaviour to win the public confidence

The independence of the Judiciary is guaranteed in Kenya in the following ways:

- There is a detached system of command for the judiciary unlike other government departments that are headed by the Public Service Commission. The Chief Justice heads the judiciary.
- Judges and magistrates are insulated from any form of victimization and molestation by the Judiciary Act.
- The judges are obligated by the oath of allegiance to perform their duties without fear or favour and malevolence.
- A judge can be removed from office only due to inability to perform the functions of his office. This means that nobody can dismiss a judge at will. His tenure of office is fairly long, the retirement age being seventy - four years.
- Salaries and allowances of judges are fixed by statues and are not subjected to be reviewed or debated upon in parliament.
- Judges and magistrates are not answerable to the executive. This allows for impartiality in making judgments.
- Appointment of magistrates is done by the Judicial Service Commission which is an independent body

- The independence of judiciary is spelt out in the constitution

Factors Limit the Independence of Judiciary in Kenya

- The courts depend on legislature for most laws which they interpret and apply
- Judiciary depends on the Executive for the reinforcement of the decisions made in courts
- The judiciary depends on the Executive for funding
- Mass media questioning the decisions of courts may undermine it autonomy

Importance of the Independence of Judiciary

- It is the basis of the rule of law
- It enables the courts to interpret the laws without fear or favour
- It safeguards the judiciary from abuse of power by the legislature and executive
- It helps in the establishment of efficient and effective commercial and financial markets
- It ensures that liberty exists. A strong independent judiciary forms the foundation of representative democracy

Challenges Facing the Judiciary include:-

- Inadequate finances to cater for its needs
- Few judicial officers in service hence the back log of cases
- Interference of the judiciary by the executive
- Corruption among judicial officers
- Information on judicial matters are not made public
- Some judges are accused of incompetence
- Lack of education on judicial affairs and ignorance of legal rights among the public
- Few courts in the country

THE RULE OF LAW

According to the rule of law, all matters are handled according to the law and suspected criminals are presumed innocent until they are proven guilty beyond reasonable doubt. All citizens are subjected to the same law irrespective of their colour, religion or creed.

Principle of the Rule of the Law

- Making of certain laws are guided by open, stable and clear general rules.
- The principle of Natural Justice must be adhered to before action is taken.

- Laws must be stable and not changing regularly
- Independence of judiciary must be guaranteed.
- Discretion of security forces should not be allowed to pervert the law
- Courts must be easily accessible
- Courts must have power to review the implementation of these principles.

Importance of the Rule of Law

The rule of law is important in a society because it promotes fairness and protects human rights in that society. The rule of law also preserves the societal values and enables law and order to be maintained in a society. It ensures that those in authority are respected and they also reciprocate. This ensures that the nation progresses and peace and stability are maintained.

How the Rule of Law is upheld in Kenya

- There is an independent court system to try offenders in the country.
- Suspected criminals are tried in a court of law and if found guilty are sentenced
- Punishment is prescribed by the law
- Those who are proved guilty are given a chance to appeal against the judgment
- Every accused person is given a chance to have his defense with the help of a legal representation
- Any law that contradicts the constitution is declared null and void
- Reviewing of law is done to make them consistent
- Ensuring the concept of the Rule Of Law is strictly adhered to

NATURAL JUSTICE

The concept of natural justice refers to the requirement that the bodies that resolve disputes adhere to at least minimum standards of fair decision making. To ensure that natural justice is upheld in Kenya:

The Barons

- Accused person are given the right to a fair and impartial trail
- Suspected criminals are presumed innocent until proved guilty
- Suspected criminals are given chance to defend themselves and call witnesses
- Accused persons are notified in advance of the impending trial and the charges facing them
- The judges carry out their duties without interference
- On reaching a decision the accused person is informed of the decision and the reason for it
- A judge cannot preside over his own case
- Mob justice is discouraged

Mob Justice

How Judiciary ensures that there is fairness in the administration of justice

- The Judicial Service Commission (JSC) ensures that judges and magistrates discharged their duties without interference.
- Suspected criminals are deemed innocent until proved guilty in a court of law, thus giving them a chance to be heard by the courts.
- Persons founds administering mob justice are liable to prosecution.
- Suspected criminals are entitled to legal representation through an advocate of High Court.
- Suspected criminals of serous crimes such as murder are guaranteed free government services of being represented by advocates.
- Persons not satisfied with a court verdict are allowed to appeal to a higher court within 14 days. However, the decisions of the Supreme Court are final.

The factors Undermining the Administration of Justice in Kenya include: -

- High incidence of crime cause delay in the hearing and determination of cases.
- Corrupt practices by some of the judicial personnel and police officers undermine fair administration of justice.
- Political interference - some suspected criminals may be freed on orders from "above" without following the laid down procedure.
- Lack of awareness by the general public on their rights and legal procedures.
- Inadequate personnel and equipment for detecting and investigation acts of crime - this may lead to inadequate evidence against acts of crime.
- Unwillingness of some members of the public to give information and to act as witness.
- Use of out-dated customary laws that have not been harmonized with current situation makes their proper interpretation difficult
- Poverty makes it difficult for some people to hire professional services of advocates.
- Low payment of lawyers in the public sector make them to move to the private sector
- There is shortage of qualified judges to handle the many cases
- Insecurity especially when handling sensitive cases.

National Security of Kenya is encouraged and guaranteed in accordance with the following principles:-

- National security is subjected to the authority of the constitution and parliament
- National security is pursued in compliance with the law and with utmost respect for the rule of law, democracy, human rights and fundamental freedoms
- In performing their functions and exercising their powers, national security organs reflect the diverse culture of the communities within Kenya
- Recruitment by the national security organs shall reflect the diversity of the Kenyan people in equitable proportions.

The Defense Council of Kenya is responsible for the overall policy, control, and supervision of the Kenya Defense Forces (KDF) and performs any other functions proscribed by national legislation. It is made up of the following: -

- The Cabinet Secretary responsible for defense - chairperson
- The chief of the Kenya Defense Forces
- The three commanders of the Defense Forces
- The Principal Secretary in the ministry responsible for defense

DISCIPLINED FORCES
are groups of people who are trained to handle firearms in their line of duty. They include: -

- Kenya Defense Forces (KDF)
- The Kenya Police Service
- The Kenya National Intelligence Service
- The Kenya Reform Service (Prisons department)

The National Intelligence Service (NIS), initially called the Special Branch, is an independent civilian government agency responsible for security intelligence and counter intelligence to enhance national security in accordance with the constitution. Functions of the national intelligence service include:

- National Intelligence Service is responsible for security intelligence and counter intelligence to enhance national security.
- It liaises with the National Police and Criminal Investigation Department (CID) to investigate threats that have criminal implications like terrorism and lay the appropriate charges.
- Gathers information which assists the government in decision–making and planning.
- The NIS in its operations protects human rights issues and the individual freedoms.

The National Intelligence Service faces a number of challenges. These include:

- The citizens are reluctant to provide information to NIS as they view it not to be any different from the former Special Branch which was known to be a tool of oppression and torture.
- The body lacks political independence. The extent to which NIS is neutral in its handling of sensitive affairs is questionable.
- There is no clear distinction between accountability and the necessary secrecy. It is

therefore difficult to audit the activities of the body due to the nature of its tasks.

- The growing volumes and complexity of communications presents a significant security challenge for national intelligence and government agencies that seek to intercept, monitor and analyze the same.
- The agency faces both external and internal threats from the Al-shabaab militia from Somalia, Merille Warriors from Ethiopia and Al-Qaeda assisted attacks. Refugees who are hosted in Kenya and the illegal migrants from Somali and Sudan are also a threat to the security of the state. They bring illicit arms and drugs into the country.
- Continuous capacity building training is necessary for the NIS officers because of the difficulty of their task.
- Limited financial and human resources hinder operations of the agency.
- Many Kenyans are ignorant on the kind of tasks the service undertakes and the advice it gives to the government. When the country is faced with tension or violence, as was the case in 2008, the public seem not to understand the role of NIS in the conflict.
- The organ does not have implementation powers. The sensitive information they give is sometimes not acted upon

The Kenya Defence Forces (KDF) have three branches. This includes the Ground Forces, the 82 Air Force and the Kenya Navy based in Mombasa. Other non combat units of the Kenya Defense Forces include: -

- Transport corps
- Medical corps
- Supplier corps
- Women service corps
- Office of the chaplain

The Kenya Defense Forces are responsible for the defense and protection of the sovereignty and territorial integrity of the republic. The land army defends the territorial borders; the air force defends the air space. The defense forces co-operate with other authorities in situations of emergency or disaster, and report to the national assembly whenever deployed in such circumstances. They can be called upon to participate in international peace keeping missions, for example in Liberia. When the police are overwhelmed – West Gate attack, the army assists police in the maintenance of law and order. The defense forces may be deployed to restore peace in any part of the country affected by unrest or instability, but only with the approval of the national assembly. The navy also protects the country from illegal docking, departure and unauthorized fishing in Kenyan waters by foreigners

Kenya Defense Forces

In addition, to military functions, the army also does some non military duties like: -

- Providing emergency services during natural disasters such as uncontrollable fire, earthquake and floods.
- Engaging in nation building activities like road and bridge constructions in hostile environments.
- The army treats the sick – Moi Referral Hospital in Eldoret
- They mount a guard of honour for dignitaries who are visiting the country and provide entertainment during national functions like Jamhuri day and Madaraka day

Challenges facing the Kenya Defense Forces include the following.

- Fraudulent practices, for example in recruitments and procurement.
- Tribalism and nepotism which demoralize hardworking officers.
- Inadequate funds for equipping the forces.
- Officers are not provided with opportunities to acquire further education.
- Use of conservative regulations e.g. gender based discrimination.
- Piracy and militia attacks on Kenyan borders and unsuspecting civilians.
- Invasion of Kenya's territorial waters.
- Human encroachment on areas occupied by the KDF e.g. the Eastleigh Moi Air Base.
- The challenges of allegation on violation of human rights as they maintain law and order.

The Kenya Police Service

The government recently merged the Regular and Administration Police to form Kenya Police Service. Other branches of the Police Service include: -

- Flying squad
- General Service Unit
- Anti Stock Theft Unit
- Criminal Investigation Department (CID)
- Traffic Police

The Functions of Kenya Police Service

- The main work of the police is to maintain law and order. The police use reasonable force to suppress riots and disperse rowdy crowds.
- The police ensure that there is enough security to the citizens and their property. They patrol residential areas and towns to arrest suspected criminals and prevent them from committing felony.
- They investigate crimes and criminal activities and arrest the perpetuators of the crimes.

- The police prosecute criminals in court. This role is increasingly being taken over by the Director of Public Prosecution
- Police conduct driving test to drivers and issue driving license to those who have qualified.
- Police conduct motor vehicle inspection and mount roadblocks to weed out unroad worthy vehicles.
- They fight cattle rustling among some communities which still engage in cattle raids and banditry.
- Police offer protection to dignitaries
- They mount guard of honour and entertain crowds during public holidays

Processes Involved in Apprehending Criminals

Suspected criminal are arrested and confined in police custody. Where a mob is involved in arresting the criminal, the police first provide security to the suspect before taking him or her to police custody. The police investigate the offence and prepare evidence for prosecution. The suspect is taken to court within 48 hours. The police prosecute the suspect in court and hand the criminal to the prisons authority. If the suspect is acquainted by court, the police set him or her free.

Factors Which Undermine the Effectiveness of the Police Service include:

- The public have negative attitude toward the police force. They are reluctant to volunteer information on insecurity to the police and this make the work of the police very difficult.
- Most criminals are armed with sophisticated weapons which they easily access from neighbouring countries. This endangers the lives of the police officers who are sometimes poorly armed.
- Corrupt judicial system demoralizes the hard-working police officers who apprehend dangerous criminals only to be released by the courts.

- Some criminals have powerful godfathers in the political class who frustrate police officers who handle their cases.
- The ratio of police officers to that of the people they are supposed to serve is not equitable. This makes the few officers to be overwhelmed.
- Police officers are poorly paid and risk their lives to serve people, yet they are poorly paid and housed. This reduces their morale.
- Rampant corruption in government institutions makes the work of the police difficult.
- Frequent road accidents add pressure to police

Current Police Reforms in Kenya

(a) A police spokesman has been employed to improve the image of the police. Customer care services are also given to people and they are encouraged to make suggestions which can lead to better services delivery.

(b) Qualifications of police officers have been raised to make them more informed and responsible.

(c) Terms of service and conditions of work have been improved to boost the morale of the police

(d) Community policing has been introduced to improve relations between police and the community

(e) The government has armed police with modern equipment to help them combat criminals who have become more sophisticated

(f) More vehicles have been allocated to the police to enable them to access trouble spot areas.

KENYA REFORM SERVICE (PRISONS)
Kenya Prisons or Reform Service can be classified into:

- Principal Institutions, for example Kamiti for hard core criminals
- District I and II prisons in various districts in Kenya
- Youth Institutions to cater for offenders between the age of 15 – 21 years
- Extra Mural Penal Employment

Functions of the Prisons Department (Reform Service)

- Confine prisoners who are convicted by courts
- Keep watch of the arrested suspects
- Implement decisions of the courts, for example giving corporal punishment and subjecting the inmate to hard labour.
- Rehabilitate prisoners
- Offer prisoners vocational training like masonry, carpentry and tailoring.
- Take care of prisoners welfare, for example food, clothing and medical care

Challenges Facing the Prisons Department

- Overcrowding due to increased number of criminals
- Disease outbreak, for example cholera and HIV/AIDS infections.
- Many inmates complain of being mistreated by prison wardens
- The inmates have inadequate food, clothing and medical care
- The wardens are poorly housed and lowly paid. This kills their morale to work and make them vent their frustrations on the inmates
- High rate of drug abuse and immorality among the prisoners
- Inadequate rehabilitation facilities

Reforms made by the government to improve the Prisons Department (Reform Service) include:

- Petty offenders are subjected to extra-mural penal employment to decongest the prisons
- Inmates are given provisions of better food, clothing and medical care

- New vehicles have been allocated to prisons department to improve transportation of inmates to the courts and health centres.
- Death row prisoners who have served for 10 years are released if they are of good conduct.
- Release of petty offenders – in December 2003, 11,500 inmates was released to reduce congestion in the prisons.
- Streamlining the hearing of cases by courts to reduce the time the inmates take in custody before their cases are determined
- Introduction of recreation facilities, for example watching television and reading newspapers
- Allowing prisoners to access human rights groups
- Improving living conditions of wardens
- Rehabilitation of drug and alcohol addicts

Questions on Disciplined Forces in Kenya

(a) Name one non combat unit of the KDF

(b) What are the functions of the KDF?

(c) Explain six challenges facing the Kenya Defense Forces

(d) Name the head of the Kenya Police Service

(e) Describe the actions taken by police officers in Kenya from the time an offence is committed to the time judgment is passed

(f) What are the functions of Kenya Police Service in Kenya?

(g) State two factors which undermine the effectiveness of the Kenya Police Service.

(h) Explain five ways how Kenya is trying to improve the effectiveness of the Kenya Police Service

(i) Identify two classes of Reform Service in Kenya

(j) What are the functions of the Reform Service?

(k) Explain six challenges that are facing the Reform Service of Kenya

(l) State five reforms made by the government to improve the Reform Service in Kenya

(m) Explain six challenges facing the National Intelligence Service in Kenya

18 NATIONAL PHILOSOPHIES IN KENYA

National philosophies which have been used in Kenya since independence are African Socialism, Harambee and Nyayoism.

Harambee Philosophy which was coined from an Indian word by the founding father of the nation, Mzee Jomo Kenyatta meant to pool resources together. The reasons why Jomo Kenyatta introduced *Harambee* were: -

- To enhance mutual social responsibility
- To enhance fairness in the distribution of resources
- To develop education
- To promote agricultural development
- To expand the transport sector
- To Extend medical services
- To assist the physically handicapped
- To enhance spiritual growth through the construction of churches
- To provide forum for leaders to educate the people
- To raise standards of living

Aims of Harambee Philosophy

- Development of the nation by pooling resources together
- Promotion of self reliance
- Promotion of national unity
- Promotion of constructive nationalism

Principals of Harambee

- Unity: co-operation of people before they settle down for common project. Participants should be involved in decision making.
- Volition: willingness of people to work whole heartedly without supervision
- Determination: the public and individuals must see the reality of the project being completed and serving the purpose required
- Sense of purpose: those involved in the project must ask the validity of the project
- In the implementation of projects, there should be maximum utilization of the local resources such as labour, materials and money.
- Participation is guided by the principles of collective good as opposed to individual gain. *Harambee* efforts should be directed towards community projects rather than individual projects.

Contributions of Harambee movement to national development include:

- Harambee movement has led to development of education in Kenya through *harambee* fundraising to construct schools and colleges.
- Funds have been collected through *Harambee* to improve infrastructural facilities such as roads, rural electrification and provision of water.
- It has given Kenyans the enthusiasm and opportunity to contribute voluntarily to national development
- It has acted as a mobilizing force which brings Kenyans of different social, economic, ethnic and moral backgrounds together to achieve a common goal in our national development
- Collective participation in development programmes by people from different groups has encouraged national unity.
- It has enhanced the spirit of patriotism
- It has boosted co-operation among individuals who, for example got their money together to buy farms, cattle, build houses etc
- Funds have been raised through *Harambee* to help the less fortunate members of the society. For example, President Moi 8th April 1989 held a mammoth rally where Kshs. 70 million was raised to help the disabled members of the society.

- It has increased the level of sharing of the national cake, for example the government help *wananchi* complete their *harambee* projects
- *Harambee* projects especially in rural areas have attracted foreign donors especially the Non Governmental Organisations (NGO's)
- Has led to re-distribution of resources as people with more funds have participated in the development projects in the less developed areas
- It has reduced the gap between the poor and the rich through the spirit of sharing wealth

---

Contributions of *Harambee* Movement to the development of education in Kenya

(a) Many learning institutions have been constructed using funds raised through *Harambee* effort.

(b) Many students are assisted to pay school fees.

(c) Physical facilities like classrooms are constructed or improved through *Harambee*.

(d) Teaching/learning materials are purchased or donated to schools to improve the quality of education.

(e) Additional support staffs in schools are paid through *Harambee* contributions by the parents.

(f) Through *Harambee* spirit, well-wishers support co-curricular activities in schools and promote individual talents of learners.

(g) School furniture has been bought through *Harambee* effort thus making learning /teaching more comfortable.

(h) Parents contribute funds to supplement the government's school feeding programmes thus improving enrolment.

Shortcomings of *Harambee*

- Misappropriation of funds, for example funds collected is used for purposes not intended.
- Coerced contribution by some government officials made people to develop negative attitude towards it

- Poverty of most Kenyans made them not to contribute as generously as expected
- It was seen as a stage show between the rich and the less to do
- Abuse of *Harambee* spirit, for example people use Harambee for their own personal gain
- Some people have conned Kenyans in the name of harambee
- Harambee puts an additional burden of taxation on the poor.

Philosophy of African Socialism is also known as sessional paper No. 10 and was written by Tom Mboya to serve as a developmental blue print. Its objectives were to:

- Enhance political equality, social justice and human dignity and freedom
- Discourage freedom from exploitation and
- Promote a high and growing income and equal distribution of wealth.

Principles of African Socialism

- Respect of individual rights and freedom
- A just and humane society
- Mutual social responsibility
- Fair distribution of wealth and income or progressive tax to bring about social equality
- Equal opportunities
- Provision of needed social services, for example education, medical care and social security
- Proper management of agriculture
- Freedom of both government and individuals to own property
- Need for Kenyans to be motivated by a service to the country and not greedy desires for personal gain

Main features of African Socialism in Kenya

- Political Democracy - all people are politically free and equal
- Allowed various forms of ownership of wealth like free enterprise, private ownership

of property, nationalization policy for key industries and partnership with the private sector

- Mutual social responsibility - the spirit of service and not greed for personal gain to motivate Kenyans
- A range of control to ensure that property is used in mutual interests of society and its members.
- Progressive taxation to ensure an equitable distribution of wealth and income
- Diffusion of ownership to avoid concentration of economic power on a few people in the society

Significance of African Socialism

- It has led to promotion of democratic process in governance. Multi-partism has been established in Kenya due to African socialism policies. Kenya has also witnessed the growth of the civil society.
- Led to the upholding of human dignity in Kenya. Human rights and private ownership of property are respected
- Has encouraged unity and peaceful co-existence among Kenyan communities
- The policy of mutual social responsibility has encouraged Kenyans to work together and this has led to economic development and patriotism
- Social development in education and health has been achieved. Discrimination in schools, hospitals and residential areas has reduced.
- A greater effort to achieve fairness and justice has been made through progressive taxation and rural development. The government has tried to achieve fair distribution of resources through the activities of the District Focus for Rural Development.
- The philosophy gave Africans the right to participate in their economy. This was through the policy of Africanization in which industrial enterprises hitherto owned by Asians and Europeans, changed ownership.

- African socialism has encouraged agricultural development through the land tenure system that was undertaken to ensure settlement of the landless in settlement schemes like Bura.
- It has led to the development of co-operatives to promote social and economic development
- Encouraged separation of power and reinforcement of fair and humane society

Problems that faced African Socialism

- Progressive taxation put additional burden of taxation on the poor hence discouraged development.
- Political interference in public projects and wrangles among leaders retarded development.
- The spirit of unity, co-operation and self-help was discouraged by misappropriation of funds.
- Corruption led to negative attitude from people towards contributing to national development.

Nyayo Philosophy was the brain child of Daniel Arap Moi who took over from the late president Jomo Kenyatta and used it as his development strategy. It was grounded on three pillars, which were peace, love and unity.

Principals of Nyayo Philosophy

- Nyayo Philosophy was guided by the need for every Kenyan to be mindful of the welfare of others
- It comprised of traditional values of peace, love and unity
- It was good for the people and condemn corruption, greed and cultural decay
- It called for honesty, commitment to duty and loyalty to the nation of Kenya
- It incorporated the spirit of African socialism

Roles Played by Nyayo Philosophy in National Development

- Mutual social responsibility has been enhanced by making people to be mindful of other peoples' welfare
- Nyayo Philosophy encouraged peaceful co-existence among Kenyans
- It led to expansion of education. Donations and the introduction of school milk led to retention of children in schools
- It led to improvement of medical facilities, for example Nyayo wards
- Nyayo Philosophy was the guiding principal in foreign affairs, for example being peaceful with neighbouring countries
- It encouraged the government to promote the jua kali sector to create employment opportunities to Kenyans
- It promoted rural development, for example district focus for rural development
- It led to the development of sports, for example Kasarani Sports Complex
- The president set up funds for the physically challenged persons
- It led to environmental conservation, for example a lot of stress was put on a forestation and wildlife conservation efforts

Challenges which faced the Nyayo Philosophy

- The government adopted a one party system which antagonized the philosophy
- It was argued that loving everybody equally was not attainable by critics
- Corruption became rampant during the Nyayo era, for example land grabbing and bribery increased during Moi's tenure
- Economic recession slowed down the pace of development, for example Nyayo Bus Project collapsed
- Poor governance, lack of transparency and accountability impacted negatively on government programmes
- Ethnic clashes were experienced in different parts of Kenya

Significance of National Philosophy

- National Philosophy served as the guiding principal in the development of the nation
- It was used to unit the diverse Kenyan communities and this was good for national building
- It inculcated the spirit of hard work and dedication among Kenyans
- National Philosophy encouraged the spirit of independence and self reliance
- It accelerate national development by mobilizing people to supplement the scarce government resources
- National Philosophy encouraged team spirit among Kenyans thereby enabling the poor to pool their resources together to initiate development projects
- The less fortunate members of the society were assisted, for example the needy and the physically challenged people
- It contributed to peace and security in Kenya which was vital for sustainable development
- National Philosophy encouraged African cultures because the concept was derived from African traditions and values

> **Questions on National Philosophies in Kenya**
> (a) Why did Jomo Kenyatta initiate the harambee philosophy after independence?
> (b) State five principals of harambee
> (c) Explain six contributions of Harambee movement to development in Kenya since independence
> (d) What were the shortcomings of harambee philosophy
> (e) State five objectives of African socialism
> (f) State five principles of African Socialism
> (g) What is the significance of African Socialism in Kenya?
> (h) Identify three pillars on which Nyayo philosophy was grounded
> (i) Explain six roles which Nyayo Philosophy played in national development
> (j) What problems faced the Nyayo Philosophy?
> (k) Explain the significance of National philosophy in development

19 GOVERNMENT REVENUE AND EXPENDITURE IN KENYA

Principles of Public Finance
- There is openness, accountability and public participation in financial mattes
- Public finance system promotes an equitable society and in particular:
  - ✓ The burden of taxation is shared fairly
  - ✓ Revenue raised nationally is shared equitably in the nation and among county government
  - ✓ Expenditure promotes the equitable development of the country, including making special provision for the marginalized groups or areas
- The burdens and benefits of the use of resources and public borrowing are shared equitably between the present and future generations.
- Public money is used in a prudent and responsible way
- Financial management is responsible and fiscal reporting is clear
- Expenditure of public finance promotes the equitable development of the country, including making special provision for marginalized groups and areas.
- There should be responsible financial management accompanied by clear fiscal reporting to ensure effective use of public funds.

Types of Public Finance
Equalization Fund: One and a half percent of collected revenue by the government is set aside for this fund. The fund is used to provide basic services like water, roads, health facilities and electricity to marginalized areas. This is done directly through grants or directly to counties with marginalized communities. Money is not withdrawn from this fund unless the Controller of Budget has approved the withdrawal.

Consolidated Fund: All money raised or received by government or on behalf of the government is paid into this fund. Public money is withdrawn from this fund and this must be approved by the Controller of Budget. If the Appropriation Act for a financial year has not been assented to or is not likely to be assented to by the beginning of the year, the National Assembly may authorize the withdrawal of money from the Consolidated Fund.

Revenue for County Government: All money raised or received by or on behalf of the County Government is paid into this fund. Money is not withdrawn from this fund unless authorized by the Controller of Budget or an appropriate legislation of the county

Contingencies Fund: The act of parliament provide for advances from this fund by the Cabinet Secretary responsible for finance if he/she is satisfied that there is an urgent and unforeseen need for expenditure for which there is no other authority

Types of Government Expenditure
- Capital (Development) expenditure: Money spent once on long term projects like roads, setting up industries or building institutions belonging to the government.
- Recurrent expenditure: Money spent continuously on regular basis like paying salaries of government workers, maintaining embassies, repair and maintenance among others.

Budget and Spending
Budget of the National and County Governments contains -
- Estimates of government revenue and expenditure

- Proposals for financing any anticipated deficit for the period to which they apply
- Proposals regarding borrowing and other forms of public liabilities that will increase public debt during the following year

When making the National Budget in Kenya, the following key areas are addressed: -

- The amount of revenue the government requires and plans to raise
- Source from which the government intends to raise the revenue
- How the government intends to spend the revenue

Reasons for the Preparation of National Budget

- To prioritize the needs of the government
- To identify sources of revenue
- Enables parliament to approve the expenditure.
- Enables the government to explain the tax structure to the public
- To make financial estimates
- For smooth running of government departments
- For accountability
- Give useful information to those organizations and individuals who may want to keep track of government expenditure

- To account for borrowed funds

Sources of Government Revenue

The body in charge of all forms of tax collection in Kenya is the Kenya Revenue Authority (KRA). The government collects revenue from: -

- Direct taxes, for example income tax and value added tax (VAT)
- Indirect taxes, for example Customs Duties and Excise Duty
- External sources, for example loans and grants
- Profits made by parastatals like Kenya Ports Authority (KPA)

- Rent from government buildings
- Business permits
- Court fines
- Charges for services rendered, for example museums
- Rent paid by plot owners in towns

Recurrent Expenditure is used: -

- To pay wages and salaries to government employees
- For general repair and maintenance of public property, for example roads and government buildings
- Serving debts from African Development Bank, World Bank and other donor countries
- Contributions to international organizations, for example United Nations Organization (UNO), COMESA and African Union (AU)
- Gives grants to county governments, parastatals, bursaries to schools and colleges
- Maintain Kenyan embassies abroad
- For supplementary expenditure

Problems Faced in Collection of Revenue

- Many individuals and companies evade paying tax. The companies declare low profits and individuals falsify information about their wealth
- Embezzlement of funds by government officials who collect revenue
- Many people lack information on how they can invest with government through treasury bills, shares etc.
- Poor economic performance lowers taxable income from Kenyans
- Many rich Kenyans stash their money in foreign accounts instead of investing it in the country
- Donors give tough conditions for the loans they advance to the country

Measures taken to ensure public funds are properly used include:

- All intended expenditure is approved by parliament before expenditure is undertaken
- Reports on expenditure must be presented to the Public Accounts Committee. This ensures that public finance is spent for the intended purpose
- The controller and the auditor general, audits all ministries and government departments and reports to parliament
- The Principal Secretary in every ministry is given the responsibility to ensure that government funds are well spent
- Government contracts are advertised for tendering and awarded on merit. All tenders are made public in line with public tendering procedures
- Parliament approves the supplementary estimates, the money set aside to deal with emergencies
- The Kenya Anti-Corruption Commission, (KACC) headed by director appointed by parliament investigate and prosecute officers involved in fraudulent deals
- Recent government directive ordered that all money collected on *harambee* basis for public projects must be audited
- Government officers who spend government money while on official duties are supposed to prove their expenditure
- At the end of its financial year, all the money that had been allocated to a ministry or a government department and which was not used is returned to the treasury and an explanation given as to why it was not used
- The accounts of parastatals, most of which are government owned are also audited by Auditor General of parastatals. His report is also forwarded to parliament
- The government has put in place mechanism to curb revenue evasion, for example the use of e-rays to verify cargo on arrival at Mombasa Sea Port
- Introduction of PIN facilitated tax collection
- Non performing parastals are being privatized to reduce loses incurred by them

---

Questions on Government Revenue and Expenditure in Kenya

(a) Name the body in charge of all forms of tax collection in Kenya
(b) Identify two factors which are addressed in the national budget in Kenya
(c) State three types of government expenditure
(d) What are the sources of revenue for the government of Kenya?
(e) Explain how the government of Kenya uses the recurrent expenditure
(f) Identity five problems faced by the government of Kenya in the collection of revenue
(g) Explain why the government of Kenya prepares the National Budget every year
(h) Explain the measures taken by the government of Kenya to ensure that public funds are properly used
(i) Describe six challenges faced in planning the National Budget in Kenya today.

Functions of the Central Bank of Kenya

- The Central Bank regulates the issue of currency to ensure that there is adequate stock of notes and coins for circulation. It also withdraws worn - out notes from the public and replaces them with new ones.
- It is charged with the responsibility of determining the denominations in which the currency should be issued.
- The Central Bank is a banker to the government. It keeps government revenue and pays for the government expenditure.
- It acts as the national centre of collection of data and general information in the field of money and banking.
- The Central Bank is given powers to inspect books of accounts of commercial banks and other financial institutions and recommend the field in which they may lend money. It also gives informal and formal advice to commercial banks.
- Foreign exchange operations - the Central Bank in liaison with the relevant government ministries administer the Country's foreign

reserves. The Exchange Control Act generally handles the financial relationship between Kenya and foreign financial institutions.

• Participates in negotiation for foreign borrowing and in handling of aid and grant funds from foreign Government and international organizations like the World Bank and international monetary fund. The repayment of capital and interests of all loans are also channeled through the bank.

• Act as a banker to all commercial banks in the country. These banks are required to maintain current account with the central banks, to use for settling claims with one another through the banking clearing house.

Challenges Faced in Planning the National Budget

• Rapid population growth leading to greater demand for government services hence straining the available resources.

• Corruption and embezzlement of funds set aside for various project by government officers.

• Tax evasion by individuals, for example businessmen deny the government revenue.

• Tough conditions by donor community.

• Frequent natural calamities, for example floods and drought.

• Price fluctuation on agricultural goods in the world market, reduce net capital flow.

• The wide spread of HIV/AIDS and other diseases affect budget.

• The devaluation of the Kenya Shilling means the cost of living will be higher and thus affect budget.

• The high cost of petroleum products.

• Wide spread poverty and high unemployment

PAPER TWO

1 INTRODUCTION TO HISTORY AND GOVERNMENT

History is a chronological account of man's past activities. It deals with events which are documented. This is different from pre-history which deals with unwritten past events of man. Pre-history relies on excavated materials and fossils. History and pre-history both make the two periods which are studied in History. Historical events:

- Contain elements of truth
- Deals mainly with the past
- Concern man
- Exist either in written or oral form
- Must have evidence for them to be construed as true.

History is divided into three major branches. These include: -

- Political History: Study governments and analyses ideas of political thinkers, leaders and their style of leadership
- Economic History: It is the way of earning a living. It deals with economic activities in different environments, for example agriculture.
- Social History: It is the study of the way people lived together, their ways of building, dressing, eating, religion and education

Types of Governments

- Democratic government: Rulers seek public mandate through popular vote. Elected leaders represent the wishes of the people.
- Aristocratic Government: A form of government in which a group from the highest social class in the society rules over others.
- Monarchial government: Power is passed from parent to children. King or Queen is the head of state. There are two types of monarchial governments. These are Absolute monarchy and constitutional monarchy.
- Dictatorial government: A system of government where the ruler has total power over subjects

Reasons for Studying History

- History helps us to understand the past, appreciate the present and predict the future.
- Helps the learners to appreciate their culture and that of others
- Helps the learners to learn about the political, social and economic organization of different people.
- Helps the leaner to understand other people and empathize with them
- History is a career subject, for example diplomacy, teaching and administration.
- Helps the leaner to know how they originated
- Gives one a sense of identity

Reasons for Studying Government

- Instills a sense of patriotism and nationalism.
- Helps the learners became responsible citizens
- Promotes international consciousness
- Makes the learner aware of their rights and obligations and prepares them for their future roles in society
- Learners learn other systems of government of other communities
- Helps the learner to appreciate the constitution and constitution making process
- Helps the learners to appreciate why they need the government

---

Questions on Introduction in History and Government

(a) Give two characteristics of a historical event
(b) Identify two periods of history
(c) Mention three branches of history
(d) Give one type of monarchial government
(e) Give two reasons for studying History

2 SOURCES OF INFORMATION ON HISTORY AND GOVERNMENT

There are two main sources of historical information: Primary and Secondary sources. Primary sources are first hand way of getting information and include sources like oral traditions, archaeology, anthropology, gentics and linguistics. Secondary sources include written (documented) and electronic sources of information.

PRIMARY SOURCES OF INFORMATION

Oral traditional

involves the study of historical information based on what has been handed down from one generation to another by words of mouth (verbally). Forms of oral traditions used in History and Government include: -

- Folk tales
- Proverbs
- Riddles
- Legends
- Myths and
- Tongue twisters

Advantages of using oral traditions

- Oral Traditions offer the most effective way of studying pre-colonial African history due to lack of written records.
- It gives a lively and enjoyable way of studying African history
- It can be used by anybody, both literate and illiterate
- Transmission is well detailed and elaborated
- It gives life experience making it interesting

Historians who use oral traditions to collect historical data encounter a lot of problems. These include:

- Information may be exaggerated. This may cause confusion because at times it's difficult to distinguish between what was real from what was made up
- Some information or facts may be forgotten or omitted since oral tradition depends on human memory
- Informants may deliberately conceal some important information, for example information based on dominant leaders may be biased since people tend to talk more of their success than their failures.
- Oral tradition may not provide dates and give correct chronology of events because it depends on human memory.
- It is an expensive method of getting information, since one has to pay for the informant's transportation, lunch, and accommodation.
- Oral tradition is time consuming, for example one has to take a lot of time to interview one individual

---

Questions on Oral Traditions

(a) Identify two forms of oral traditions used in History and Government
(b) Give five advantages of using oral traditions as a source of information on history and government
(c) Why is Oral Traditions the main source of information on African history
(d) Explain five problems experienced by historians in using oral traditions to collect historical data
(e) What is the main source of information on African history

---

Linguistics

This is a scientific study of a language. People who speak the same language or a language which is almost similar have a higher probability of being related or closely related. Historians study different groups of languages to, establish the origin and migration of different communities. Using linguistics has several advantages. These include:

- Linguistics gives information about the movement of people and their relationship. People are grouped according to the language they speak, for instance the Maa or the kwa speakers
- It helps to establish theories of peoples' origin, migration and settlement.
- Language helps those using oral traditions to gather information from various sources
- It is useful in dating the migration of people
- It helps experts to discover links between different people which were previously unknown
- It helps in the dating of the migration of people
- It is possible to know some of the cultural practices and items which were borrowed from others

Limitations of Linguistics

- It takes a long time to learn another language
- Different languages have similar words, but with different meaning
- Poor translation may distort meaning of some messages or information
- Borrowing of words may distort the meaning of the parent language
- Some languages have become extinct
- Some words may be difficult to understand because they have different meaning depending on how they are pronounced

Questions on Linguistics
(a) Give two merits of linguistics as a source of history and government
(b) Identify two limitations of linguistics as a source of history and government

Anthropology

This is the study of the human race, especially its origin, its development, customs and beliefs. To understand a group of people, the anthropologist stays in that community to empathize with them. Anthropology has several advantages. These include:

- Anthropology helps to reveal similarities in the institutions of different communities and possible interaction.
- It compliments other sources of information in gathering historical data.
- It gives a deeper understanding of a particular aspect of people culture.
- It can identify a particular community with a certain culture.

Limitation of Anthropology

- Anthropology is too expensive to use
- One may obtain inaccurate information if not properly used because people behave differently when being observed.
- It is not reliable when used alone
- Anthropology may require a well trained personnel
- It is limited to a few aspects of history, that is social and material aspects
- One may lose his culture while conducting anthropology

Questions on Anthropology
(a) State two advantages of anthropology as a source of information on history and government
(b) Identity one limitation of anthropology as a source of information on history

Archaeology

This is the study of human activity in the past, primarily through the recovery and analysis of the material culture and environmental data that they had left behind, which includes artifacts, architecture and biofacts. Archaeologist have studied the human pre-history and history from the first stone tools (about 4 million years ago) upto the recent decades.

Archaeology is the most important way of learning about the pre-historic societies, when there were no written records for the historians to study. To reconstruct the past archaeologists use the following: -

- Remains of weapons
- Remains of tools
- Remains of dwelling places
- Remains of animals bones
- Remains of plants
- Remains of works of art, for example rock paintings
- Remains of garments and beads
- Remains of traditional crafts, for example baskets

Merits of Using Archaeology

- Information is more accurate because it involves analysis of real materials and remains
- Archeology provides information not found in written records
- Archeology has a sense of time, for example where and when the fossils and artifacts where found can be determined
- Historical information on archeology are real and factual because one can feel, touch and even manipulate them
- The information got is longer lasting because the fossils and artifacts can be preserved for long.

Disadvantages of Using Archaeology

- It is pricey to hire labourers to excavate and analyze the artifacts
- It is often hard to locate a pre-historic site
- Some remains are fragile and can fall to

pieces during excavation
- It is restricted to the study of primeval period, rather than the recent history
- The information may not be accurate as it is based on conclusions and reconstruction
- The dates may not be accurate or exact as they are only estimates
- It is difficult to tell between the bones of animals and that of hominids

---

Questions on archaeology
(b) What things do archaeologists use to reconstruct the activities of people in the past
(c) Give two merits of using archaeology as a source of history and government
(d) Give two disadvantages of using archaeology as a source of history and government

---

D ATING METHODS
Resolving the age of rocks and fossils is imperative because it assists scientists to ascertain when the species inhabited the earth. Rocks and sediments form strata on the earth surface as they are deposited and unless the earth is disturbed, the oldest layers of rocks remain at the bottom and the newest at the top. By looking at each stratum one can find out what order they were deposited. However, it's hard to determine precisely the age of each layer. This method of ballpark figure is called Relative Dating. Absolute Dating not only let know which sediment was deposited first, it also gives the accurate age.

Carbon 14 Dating Method
Fossils are dated by calculating the rate of decay of radioactive elements within them which decay at knowable rates. The best known Absolute Dating technique is Carbon 14. After the demise of an organism, the proportion of carbon 14 atons begins to diminish at a predetermined rate. By studying the proportion of Carbon 14 atoms compared to

other Carbon atoms, it is possible to determine how old the rocks and fossils are.

Carbon Dating is often the most accurate way of finding out the age of a recent fossil and rock or other deposit it was found in. However, in old fossils, the proportion of Carbon 14 is so low that it is difficult or impossible to date them accurately. Carbon Dating is therefore not reliable for finds which are more than 40,000 years old.

Potassium – Argon dating Method

This is the only viable technique for dating very old archaeological materials. Geologists have used this method to date rocks as much as 4 billion years old. It is based on the fact that some of the radioactive isotopes of Potassium 40 (K-40) decay to gas as Argon-40 (Ar-40). By comparing the proportion of K-40 to Ar-40 in a sample of volcanic rock, and knowing the decay rate of K-40, the date that rock was formed can be determined.

Stratigraphy

The Principle of Stratigraphy was put forward by William Smith of England in 1800. He stated that older rocks lie below younger rocks and fossils occur in a particular predictable order. The study of stratigraphy led to Paleontology, the study of fossils. From 1830's geologists noted how fossils became more complex through time. The oldest rocks contained no fossils, and then came simple sea creatures, then more complex fishes, then came life on land, then reptiles, then mammals and finally humans.

Fission Track Dating Method

This is a radiometric dating technique based on analysis of the damage trails left by fission fragments in certain uranium bearing minerals and gases. Uranium-238 undergoes spontaneous fission decay at a known rate, and it is the only isotope with a decay rate that is relevant to the significant production of natural fission tracks. The fragments emitted by this fission process leave trails of damage in the crystal structure of the mineral that contains the uranium.

Other methods of dating are:
- Paleomagnetic variation
- Statistical method
- Lexico statistics method

Critics, say religious fundamentalists, argue that neither fossils nor dating can be trusted and that their interpretations are better. Other critics who are more familiar with the data, question certain aspects of the quality of the fossil record and of its dating. Some skeptics, especially the religious groups, believe that all fossils are the same age. How exactly they believe that all dinosaurs, mammoths, early humans, heavily armored fishes and the rest could have all lived together has never been explained. They cannot explain how marine creatures were drawn by floods. Rejecting fossil data cannot be supported by scientific proof. However, accurate dating of fossils requires specialists and advanced technology. To get the truth, repeated and careful testing and consideration of data is required. It is therefore times consuming and requires a lot of money to achieve the desired results.

Questions on Dating Methods
(a) Give two chemical dating methods used by archeologists to reconstruct history
(b) Identify two main methods which are used in dating fossils
(c) State two limitations when dating fossils by historians

WRITTEN SOURCES OF INFORMATION
Written sources are documented materials. These are information of history from known times

when people had started writing and information was put down in written form. The earliest writers were called scribes. They wrote on stone tablets, scrolls, papyrus and animal skins. Modern written sources include text books, newspapers, journals, magazines and periodicals.

Advantage of Written Source

• Written materials ensure relatively permanent storage of historical events for future reference.

• Written materials can be easily translated to different languages

• Written materials cannot be easily distorted or easily changed.

Limitations of Written Sources

• It may be rendered unreliable in case the author omit essential information

• They may be misunderstood or misinterpreted by readers to suit ones needs

• Writers are at times biased from their particular point of view

• They are only limited to literate people in the society

• Acquiring of some written records is very expensive

• Reading of written records is often time consuming

Questions on Written Sources of Information

(e) State one advantage of written materials as a source of history and government

(f) Explain the limitations of written records in reconstruction of African history

(g) Give two disadvantages of the print media

Electronic Sources

These can be films, radio and television. These sources give instant audio and visual information. They therefore appeal to a wider cross section of people – both literate and illiterate and are used to spread news or information which require immediate attention.

Limitations of Using Electronic Sources

• Information may be inaccurate, censoring of information is sometimes done to weed out what is not desired by the establishment.

• Some services may not be accessed by some people, especially those who cannot afford them.

• Films and videos may contain exaggerated information

• There is sometimes biasness in the given information depending on the motive of the reporters.

Questions on Electronic Sources

(a) List two limitations of using electronic services as a source of information on history

---

The Barons

3 THE EARLY PEOPLE

or time immemorial people have come up with Fdifferent theories to explain how human being came into existence. In many traditional societies it is believed that some supernatural being existed and he created everything on earth including human beings. Myths and legends are used to describe such events. This theory is called the mythical or traditional theory of creation. A similar version is given by major denominations like Christianity, Islam and Buddhism. According to this theory - Creation, human beings were created by God (Christians) and Allah (Muslims) at a specific time in history to fulfill God's purpose.

Charles Darwin

These theories lack firm scientific backing and have encountered criticism by some scholars who argue that human beings evolved from ape - like creatures and developed through adoption over a long period of time. This theory – Scientific or evolution theory was proposed by Charles Darwin in his book, *The Origin of Species*. According to Darwin, evolution was a gradual process and organisms evolved from simple primitive beings into more complex ones. The changing environmental conditions affected the organisms in two ways: -

- Their genetic make up changed due to mutation and this affected their physical characteristics.

- Organisms were forced to adapt to the changing environment

Organisms which were unable to mutate or adapt to the new environment were whipped out (became extinct). Darwin also contended that organism were in a constant state of competition for the scarce resources for their survival. In this competition only the fittest organisms survived and those which were unable to compete effectively died naturally. Organisms which were able to mutate, adapt to the changing environment or survive in the struggle for fitness – natural selection, multiplied in number and became dominant - Isolation. Though this theory is supported by a lot of scientific proof and archaeological evidence, it has met stiff criticism. Some of the critics question the origin of the primitive organisms and why some organisms have refused to change.

Many scholars are of the opinion that Africa was the cradle of mankind. They argue that the climate of Africa supported abundant plant and animal life. The savanna vegetation in the continent also supported luxuriant growth of grass which favoured large number of animals – both grazers and predators. Archaeological evidence also point to Africa. Many archaeological sites are located in Africa and many hominids, together with their material culture, have been found in the continent. It has been established that long before the rift valley was formed, man was roaming about in East Africa. Many hominids could have originated from Africa which was in the middle of Pangaea and moved to other continents.

Most early settlements occurred along river valleys. This was because of the availability of water for domestic use and for irrigation. Rivers were source of food and also formed ideal hunting grounds.

PRE-HISTORIC SITES IN EAST AFRICA			
Kenya	Uganda	Tanzania	Ethiopia
Rusinga	Ngongezi	Garasi	Omo Valley
Fort Tenan	Nyero	Olduvai Gorge	Hadar
Kariandusi	Napak	Isimila	
Gambles Cave	Paraa	Eyasi	
Koobi Fora	Ishango	Apis Rock	
Hyrax Hills	Mweya		
Olorgesaille	Nyabusora		
Njoro River Cave			

Aegyptopithecus

was a small, tree-dwelling and fruit- eating animal which lived about 33 million years ago. It had a stereoscopic vision and weighed about 4 kg. Aegyptopthecus somewhat resembled a modern-day lemur except for a full 32 teeth. This animal has been termed the Dawn Ape, and an important link between earlier mammals and the apes of the Miocene epoch. Aegyptopithecus was found in the Egyptian Faiyum Depression, a rich source of the Oligocene fossils.

Egyptopithecus

Proconsul

is an extinct genus of primates that existed from 23 to 25 million years ago during the Miocene era. Four species have been identified. They include:
- Proconsul *africanus*
- Proconsul *heseloni*
- Proconsul *major*
- Proconsul *nyanzae*

The four differed in body size. Proconsul sites range from forested areas to more open arid grasslands. The remains of proconsul were found in Rusinga Islands in Kenya. Proconsul had a mixture of old world monkey and ape characteristics hence their placement in the ape super family Hominoidea is tentative with some historians placing proconsul outside it, before the split of the apes and old world monkeys. Proconsul's monkey-like features include a long flexible back, curved metacarpals, and above–branch arboreal quandrupedal positional repertoire. The primary feature linking proconsul with the extant apes is its lack of a tail. Other ape-like features include its enhanced grasping capabilities, stabilized elbow joint and facial structure.

Questions on Early Hominids
(a) Identify two pre-historic sites in Kenya
(b) Give two reasons why Africa is regarded as the cradle of mankind
(c) Name the earliest hominid closer to man
(d) What were the physical changes which occurred in Early Human Beings as they evolved from ape like creatures to modern people?
(e) State two distinct features of Proconsul

Australopithecus

is an extinct hominid that lived between 3.9 and 2.9 million years ago. At least seen species of Austropithecus are generally recognized, including:
-
- Austrolopithecus afarensis
- Austrolopithecus africanus
- Austrolopithecus bahrelghasili
- Austrolopithecus anamensis
- Austrolopithecus boisei
- Austrolopithecus robustus

- Austrolopithecus aethiopicus

Austrolopithecus afarensis dating to at least 3.75 million years ago may be ancestral to all the other species of this genus, with the exception of Austrolopithecus anamensis, a hominid dating to 4.1 million years ago. Austrolopithecus afarensis is known from fossils found at a number of sites in Ethiopia and at Laetoli in Tanzania. The Postcranial skeletal remains show that Austrolopithecus afarensis was relatively small, standing 3 to 5 ft tall and weighing about 20 – 50 kg.

Remains of an Austrolopithecine of similar size and between 2 to 3 million years old have also been found in South Africa. It was known as Austrolopithecus africanus and had slightly larger molars than Austrolopithecus afarensis, but in other aspects it had decidedly more human features than Austrolopithecus afarensis, including a higher forehead, less prominent brow ridge, and shorter face.

Austrolopithecines are classified into two distinct types: gracile and robust. The robust australopithecine all became extinct between 1.5 and 1 million years ago, while one of the gracile austrolopithecines is believed to have given rise to the branch leading to the emergence of the genus home habilis 2.5 million years ago.

The physical changes which occurred in early human beings as they evolved from ape like creatures to modern people included: -
- Developed larger brain than the apes - more intelligent
- Developed a thumb to grasp objects and make tools
- Developed short feet and straight forehead
- The teeth and jaws became smaller

Questions on Austrolopithecus
(a) Identify three types of Australopithecus
(b) Mention one distinct feature of Australopithecus

Homo habilis

which lived about 2 million years ago, is a well-known, but poorly defined species. The specimen that led to the naming of this species was discovered in 1960 by the Leakey team in Olduvai Gorge, Tanzania. Louis Leakey was convinced that this was the Olduvai toolmaker he had spent his life looking for, and placed this as a direct human ancestor, with Homo erectus a dead end side branch.

This species was different from the Austrolopithecus africanus which co-existed with it due to the teeth, which fell outside the known range of the Austrolopithecus africanus, with very large incisors. Also, the large brain size and shape of hand suggested a closer affinity with the homo. In 1964, Homo habilis was announced as a new species. The name suggested by Raymond Dart, "handy man," referred to his alleged tool making prowess.

Diagnostic Features
- The brain size attributed to Homo habilis varied from 590 – 710 c.c.
- Reduced post canine tooth size

- Presence of a precision grip which provided the anatomical basis for tool making.
- It is possible that while Homo habilis was an obligate biped, it still spent some time in the trees
- It weighed about 31.7 kg.

Home erectus

meaning upright man is an extinct species of hominid that lived throughout most of the Pleistocene, with the earliest first fossil evidence dating to around 1.9 million years ago. The species originate in Africa and spread to as far as Georgia, India, Sri Lanka, China and Java. There is still disagreement on the subject of the classification, ancestry and progeny of Homo erectus, with two major alternative classifications: erectus may be another name for Homo ergaster, and therefore the direct ancestor of later hominids such as Homo heidelbergensis, Homo neanderthalensis and Homo sapiens, or it may be an Asian species distinct from African ergaster.

Charles Darwin was, however, of the opinion that human's earliest ancestors were from Africa: he pointed out that chimpanzee and gorillas, who are human relatives, live only in Africa. From the 1950's to 1970's, however, numerous fossils finds from East Africa yielded evidence that the oldest hominid originated in Africa. It is now believed that Homo erectus is a descendant of earlier genera such as Ardipthecus and Homo habilis or Homo ergaster. Homo habilis and Homo erectus co-

existed for several thousand years, and may represent separate lineages of a common ancestor.

Homo erectus

walked upright. His cranial capacity ranged from 850 – 1100 cc and the frontal bone was less sloped. Homo erectus' pointed tooth was smaller than either Austrolopithecus or Homo habilis, with large brow ridges and less prominent cheekbone. He stood at 1.79 m. He was extraordinarily slender, with long arms and legs.

It is plausible that Homo erectus communicated in a proto-language lacking the fully developed structures of modern human language, but more developed than the non verbal communication used by the chimpanzees. East African sites such as Chesowanja near Lake Baringo, Koobi Fora and Olorgesaillie in Kenya show some possible evidence that fire was utilized by early humans. At Chesonwanja archaeologists found red clay shards dated to be 1.42 million years.

Homo erectus' skull

Homo erectus was probably the first hominid to live in a hunter–gatherer society and anthropologists like Richard Leakey believed that it was socially more like human than Austrolopithecus before it. Homo erectus lived in small band-society similar to modern hunter-gatherer band societies. It is believed that Homo erectus was the first hominid to hunt in a co-ordinated group, used more complex tools and cared for the in firm or weak companions. Homo erectus had a more developed hand for grasping tools. He used tools of Oldowan technology and later progressed to the Acheulian which began around 1.8 million years ago. It is suggested that Homo erectus may have been the first hominid to use rafts to travel over oceans.

Benefits of the discovery of fire to early man

(a) The discovery and use of fire made it possible for early man to keep warm during cold nights and seasons.
(b) Fire enhanced the security of early man as it was kept burning to keep away wild animals and other possible sources of danger.
(c) It was a source of lighting at night
(d) Fire improved hunting activities of the early man as it was used to harden the tips of the tools for hunting.
(e) Early man used fire to extract poison from plants which they used for hunting.
(f) Fire was used as a source of food preservation method. For example drying meat or fish.
(g) Fire was used to attract animals towards set traps so that they were easily trapped.
(h) Fire was used to cook food and make it palatable and more easily digestable.
(i) It was used for communication.

How Homo erectus attempted to improve his way of life

- Development of upright posture using his hind limbs (bipedalism) enabled him to move fast and to widen his vision. This freed his hands and he was able to use them to manipulated tools. The upright posture reduced his surface area exposed to heat.
- Improved stone tools, for example Acheulian tools
- Created leisure activities such as work of art
- Developed speech for communication
- Migrated to warmer places

- Invented fire which was used for cooking, lighting, warming and protection against wild animals.
- Made and lived in caves for more permanent settlement and security.
- Made clothes out of animal's skins by scrapping them clean, using efficient stone tools.

How early man adopted to the environment during the Stone Age period

- Gradual use of front limbs for holding objects enabled tool making
- Improved brain capacity enhanced the level of creativity
- Developed language enhanced exchange of ideas
- Development of thumb increased grip of tools
- Discovery of fire improved his diet, security and hunting
- Domestication of plants and animals ensured prolonged food supply

Homo sapiens

There were three sub species of Homo sapiens. These included the Neanderthal man, the Rhodesian man and the Cro-Magnon Man.

Neanderthal man

A sub species of Homo sapiens, Neanderthal the species to which contemporary human beings belong, was found in the Neander valley in Germany. Many scientists classify Neanderthalas as its own species (Homo neandertalensis) pointing to the large number of anatomical differences between it and Homo sapiens.

Anatomically Neanderthals were shorter, but much more robust than the contemporary Homo sapiens were. Distinctive cranial features of Neanderthals included prominent brow ridges, low sloping foreheads, a chinless and heavy forward- jutting jaw, and extremely large front teeth. The shoulders and pelvis were wider, the rib cage more conical in shape, and the forearms and lower legs shorter. The Neanderthal anatomy gives the impression of a large and somewhat primitive homind, as though the evolutionary trajectory of Homo sapiens reversed itself. However, the brain case of Neanderthal measured 1600 cc which is larger than the modern-day Homo sapiens are.

The unique anatomy of Neanderthals probably reflects the fact that they were the first hominid to spend extensive periods of time in extremely cold environment, having evolved in Europe at the onset of the most recent glaciations of that continent. Their thick, squat built was adapted to maintaining body temperature under harsh climatic conditions while the large front teeth may have reflected a practice common among Eskimo populations of softening animal skins by chewing. Forceful chewing is also suggested by the heavy jaw and brow ridge, both of which serve to buttress powerful muscles.

Rhodesian man

The remains of the Rhodesian man were discovered in 1921 near the town of Kabwe (Zambia) by a Swiss called Tom Zwiglaar who was a miner. It is pressumed that the Rhodesian man lived between 30,000 – 40,000 years ago. The discovered skull had archaic features, being massive and flattened in profile with brow ridges that are very large and continuous across the nasal bridge. The cranial capacity of the Rhodesian man was 1280 cc.

Rhodesian man

Cro-Magnon Man

The first fossils of early modern humans to be identified were found in 1868 at the 27,000 – 23,000 year old Cro-Magnon rock shelter sites near the village of Les Eyzies in Southern France. These people, who were named the Cro-Magnon, were very similar in appearance to the modern day European people. Males were 5.4 ft, taller than Neanderthals. Their skeletons and musculature were by and large less massive than the Neanderthals. The Cro-Magnon had broad, small face with pointed chins and high foreheads. Their cranial capabilities were upto 1590 cc, which is relatively large even for people of today.

Cultural practices of Homo-Sapiens
(a) Preserved food through fire, pots and baskets.
(b) Sedentary life - constructed huts.
(c) Decorated his body using red ochre
(d) Religion beliefs, for example worshiping God and burying the dead.
(e) Used tools called microliths
(f) Settled in villages of about 1000 members
(g) Practiced rock Art

Homo sapien sapiens

All people today are classified as Homo sapiens. Our species of humans first began to evolve nearly 200,000 years ago. It is now clear that early Home sapiens or modern humans did not come from Neandertals, but were their contemporaries. However, it is likely that both modern humans and Neandertals descended from Homo heidelbergensis. Compared to the Neandertals and other late archaic humans, modern humans generally have more delicate skeletons. Their skulls are more rounded and their brow ridges generally protrude much less. They rarely have the occipital buns found on the back of Neandertal skulls. They also have relatively high foreheads, smaller faces and pointed chins.

The Barons

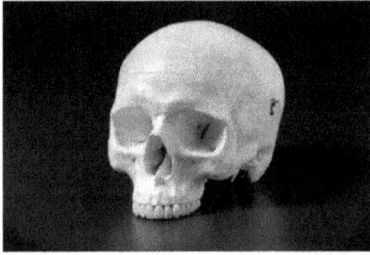
Homo sapien's skull

Current data suggests that modern human beings evolved from archaic human beings mainly from East Africa. A 195,000 year old fossil from the Omo valley in Ethiopia upholds the notion of skull changes which are linked to modern people, including a round skull case and a projecting chin. A 160,000 year old skull from Herto site in the middle Awash also seems to be at the early stages of this transition. It has a rounded skull case but retained the ridges of archaic humans. Artifactual evidence reveals that modern human beings were in Europe as early as 46,000 years ago. Dating in Asia is less concrete, but it is likely that modern human beings were present there as early as 60,000 years ago.

Since 1980's there have been two leading contradictory models which have been used to explain the evolution of modern human beings (Replacement Model and the Regional Continuity Model). The Replacement Model of Christopher Stinger and Peter Andrews purports that modern human beings evolved from archaic human beings 200,000 – 150,000 years ago only in Africa and then migrated into the rest of the old world replacing all of the Neandertals and other late archaic human beings around 60,000 – 40,000 years ago. All other lines of human beings that had descended from Homo erectus presumably became extinct.

The Regional Continuity (Multi Regional Evolution) Model was put forward by Milfod Wolfpoff. He upheld that modern human beings evolved more or less simultaneously in all major regions of the Old World from local archaic human beings. For example, modern Chinese are seen as having evolved form Chinese archaic human beings and ultimately from Chinese Homo erectus. People who uphold this school of thought believe that the ultimate common ancestor of all modern people were an early Homo erectus in Africa who lived at least 1.8 million years ago. It is further suggested that since then there was sufficient gene flow between Africa, and Asia to prevent long-term reproductive isolation and subsequent evolution of distinct regional species.

Way of life of early Man during the Stone Age period

During this period, Man used stone tools and weapons, for example scrappers. The tools were used for defense, hunting and gathering. He used the Oldowan or pebble tools. Man lived in small groups of 20 – 30 people and sheltered in caves during the day and at night he slept on trees to avoid being attacked by other animals. He ate raw food, for example meat, fruits and vegetables. Man used gestures, growling and whistling to communicate. There was division of labour: men were involved in hunting and women did the gathering of wild fruits, roots and berries.

Culture of Man during the Middle Stone Age period

During this epoch, Man used Acheulian tools. He also had aesthetic value, for example decorated his body using red ochre and made necklace using ostrich shells. Man began living in caves which had decorated walls – through drawings and painting. He hunted and lived in groups to assist others. Man developed a rudimentary language which it used to communicate with others. Fire was discovered around this time and he used it to roast meat and protect himself. Man started burying the dead – hence the beginning of his preoccupation with life after dead (religion).

Way of Life of Man during the New Stone Age period

During this time man made advanced tools with skill and precision, for example spears and harpoons. This improved his hunting. He lived in huts which had decorated walls. Apart from hunting and gathering man began to domesticate animals. He began spinning clothes using flax. Man lived a more settled life and made rules and regulations to guide his activities. He also specialized in basketry, pottery and later smelting of iron and bronze. Man practiced advanced religion, for example buried the dead.

Tool Making

Stages in the development of tools by early man included: -

- Oldowan tools: associated with Homo habilis and Australopithecus. The tools were discovered at Olduvai Gorge

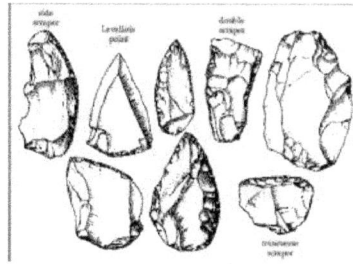

- Acheulian tools: were used during the second phase of the Old Stone Age and Middle Stone Age. These tools were associated with Homo erectus and were discovered at Acheul Valley in France
- Microliths: are associated with Homo sapiens and were made during the New Stone Age.

The early man made tools and weapons for: -

- Defense
- Cutting meat
- Scrapping skins from animals
- Grinding or pounding vegetables
- Digging roots

Hunting

Hunting methods used during the Old Stone Age period included: -

- Chasing and throwing stones and spears to injure and immobilize the animal
- Digging large pits on the paths frequently

used by animals and covering them with sticks and grass to trap the animals

- Chasing the animals over steep cliffs and forcing them to fall over and break their limbs
- Driving animals to swampy areas where they got stuck
- Waiting for animals near water points and waylaying them
- Killing animals that were injured by other others

There were hunting groups. The groups enabled the early man to jointly kill much bigger and powerful prey, It also enabled them to track and surround the prey and to protect themselves from much stronger animals

Significance of Rock Art

(a) The thought of drawing animals with arrows piercing them would give their shooting expectations great success
(b) Cave painting showed a keen observation of animal life
(c) Painting was done to decorate their dwelling places
(d) Rock art was a way of passing time
(e) It was a way of preserving man's cultural heritage through painting

Questions on Early Man

(a) List two distinct features of Home erectus
(b) Identify two sub species of homo sapiens
(c) Describe the way of life of Early Human Beings during the Stone Age period
(d) Describe the culture of man during the new Stone Age period
(e) Give two cultural practices of Homo-Sapiens
(f) State two economic activities of the Early Man
(g) Identify two aspects of the culture of the early man that had their origins in the late Stone Age
(h) State five ways in which the invention of fire changed the way of life of the Early Man
(i) Identify two ways in which man used stone tools
(j) State five ways in which Homo erectus attempted to improve his way of life
(k) Identify three hunting methods used during the Old Stone Age period
(l) Give two significance of rock art to the early man
(m) State two ways through which the Early Man adopted to the environment during the Stone Age period
(n) Give five ways in which Early Man improved his way of life during the Middle Stone Age period
(o) What were the stages in the development of tools by Early Man?
(p) Why did the early man make tools?
(q) Why did Early Human settlements occur along river valleys?

Rock Painting

4 DEVELOPMENT OF EARLY AGRICULTURE

The first animal to be domesticated by man was a dog. Man used the dog for hunting, providing security and helping to clean the homestead because it was a scavenger. A dog would also be used for herding and to drive away animals–hence prevent them from destroying the crops. Soon man started domesticating plants and other animals. This was because:

• The environment could not sustain the increased population of people

• Climatic changes, for example drought made it difficult for man to exclusively rely on hunting

• Competition between man and other animals made available food inadequate

• Hunting and gathering was becoming tiresome

• Calamities, for example bush fire destroyed vegetation and drove the wild animals away

---

Impact of Early Agriculture

(a) Early Agriculture led to increased population because of adequate food to sustain the large population.

(b) Better farm tools like sickles were invented.

(c) Man settled down and established more permanent settlements. This later grew up to urban centres.

(d) Development of Early Agriculture freed man from the tedious hunting and gathering activity.

(e) Man had adequate time to specialize in other activities like weaving and pottery.

(f) Religion also came up.

EARLY AGRICULTURE IN MESOPOTAMIA

Factors which contributed to the development of Early Agriculture in Mesopotamia were:

• Availability of indigenous crops, for example barely, wheat, grapes and onions. There were also animals like sheep, goats, pigs and cattle

• Heavy rains from the Zagggros Mountains contributed to floods in the river valley. This flooding led to deposition of fertile soil along rivers Tigris and Euphrates. The flood water was also used for irrigation.

• Invention of farming tools such as hoes, ploughs, sickles and seed drill made farming to be easy.

• Existence of transport system in the form of donkeys and canoes assisted in the distribution of farm products

• Slaves provided cheap labour in the farms.

• The settlement of the Sumerians from the Iranian plateau encouraged the flow of agricultural knowledge in the area

• The rising population created a need to feed the people.

• Political stability enabled the people to practice agriculture.

• Dykes were constructed to control floods.

Result of the Development of Early Agriculture in Mesopotamia

• The development of Early Agriculture in Mesopotamia led to the production of enough food for the population.

• The production of food enabled people to settle down and concentrate on farming activities.

• Places where people met to exchange food surpluses developed into urban centres for example Ur, Nippur, Kish, Babylon and Eridu.

• Food production allowed some people time to engage in other productive trades, for example basketry and weaving. This led to job specialization

- Surplus agricultural products led to the development of trade between the communities.
- Settled life led to the development of a centralized system of government to protect the people and their property. Hamurabi also came with laws to guide people's activities
- Need to transport agricultural products led to invention of the wheel. The wheel was used to transport grains to markets and to make pots for storage.
- Farming encouraged religious activities because of the need to give offerings to spirits who would promote their farming activities
- Need to keep records on agricultural activities led to the development of writing called cuneiform

EARLY AGRICULTURE IN EGYPT

Factors which led to the development of Early Agriculture in Egypt included the following-

- The Nile deposited fertile alluvial soil along the valley and provided abundant water for irrigation.
- The Egyptians developed different types of irrigations like the shadoof, basin and canal methods. Canal irrigation was favoured by the undulating landscape.
- Egypt was naturally protected from the enemies by the desert in the west, the harbourless coastline in the north and the cataracts in the south
- Invention of farming tools like the ox-drawn ploughs increased yields
- Contribution of Egyptian rulers in building dams on the Nile, for example Meres, facilitated proper utilization of the River.
- Proximity to the Middle East encouraged the flow of agricultural knowledge into the area.

- Knowledge of weather focusing assisted farmers to predict seasons
- By building storage facilities, they were able to preserve their output for long.
- They used free labour from slaves and this lessened their work.

Impact of the Development of Agriculture to Early Government

- People settled down in large groups. There was need for law and order among these people
- There was need to subdivide land and keep records. Those given the mandate to divide land and take care of public land became leaders
- Increased wealth led to need for security. Those given the responsibility of maintaining security became the governing body
- Health improved and population increased. With the high population there was need for a body to maintain order
- Increased wealth led to stratification of the society into employer and employee, land owners and landless, the wealthy and the poor. The wealthy class who were the land owners automatically became the governing class.

Impact of Early Agriculture in Egypt

- The availability of food led to population growth
- It led to development of towns, for example Thebes, Memphis, Aswan and Akhenaton
- Surplus food led to division of labour - the sculptures, smiths and emergence of a wealthy class of people.
- Agriculture led to emergence of small scale industries, for example weaving and pottery
- By studying the farming seasons through the moon, sun and stars, the Egyptians discovered the calendar of 365 days

- Trade developed between Egypt and her neighbours. They obtained wine and cloth from Greece and Crete in exchange of farm products.
- More land was put into production through irrigation.
- Farming encouraged formal learning, for example writing (hieroglyphics), geometry and survey which enabled them to keep records and demarcate land.
- Strong governments developed to control land, water and people
- Religious practices improved with the development of agriculture. Temples, pyramids and shrines were build

Similarities between Early Agriculture in Mesopotamia and Egypt included:

- In both case a system developed of storage and preservation of farm products
- Farmers in both case depended on flood water for farming.
- They both developed a system of irrigation.
- In both case farmers used farm implements made of stone, wood and later metal, for example ox plough
- The Egyptians and Mesopotamians both traded in farm produce.
- Both the Egyptians and Mesopotamians reared animals, cattle, sheep and chicken.
- Indigenous crops - wheat, barley, oat were planted in both Egypt and Mesopotamia
- They both used human and animal labour
- Arithmetic and writing developed in both case to keep farm records.

Questions on Early Agriculture

(a) Give five reasons which forced man to begin domestication of animals and crops
(b) Give two reasons why man domesticate a dog
(c) Explain how the development of Agriculture led to the development of government
(d) Discuss the effects of Early Agriculture on the Early Man's life
(e) Give five factors which led to the development of Early Agriculture in Egypt
(f) Mention two types of irrigation used in Egypt
(g) Outline the economic impacts of Early Agriculture in Egypt
(h) Explain five effects of early agriculture in Egypt
(i) State three factors which contributed to the development of Early Agriculture in Mesopotamia
(j) What was the result of the development of Early Agriculture in Mesopotamia?
(k) Identify two similarities between early agriculture in Mesopotamia and Egypt

---

AGRARIAN REVOLUTION IN BRITAIN
The main Features of the British agriculture before 1750 A.D. included the following: -

- Farmers used simple (crude) farm tools, for instance hoe
- They used open field system - animals were grazed collectively and farms were not fenced
- Land was left fallow for some time to regain fertility
- Communal or feudal system of land ownership was practiced.
- Farmers grew subsistence crops - mainly to sustain the family.
- Farmers owned small pieces of land which were isolated and fragmented.
- Traditional methods of farming like broadcasting were used.

- Farmers did not use fertilizer and this led to low yields

Disadvantages of Open Field System

(a) A lot of time was wasted since the plots of land were fragmented and scattered
(b) There was wastage of land because of the many paths
(c) Communal grazing encouraged the spread of diseases and pests from one animal to another
(d) Communal grazing encouraged inbreeding of animals and this lowered quality of the breeds
(e) The fields were small and this discouraged mechanisation

Disadvantages of the Traditional System of Farming were:

- Land was not fully utilized because they were left fallow
- Lands were small and fragmented and this discouraged the use of machines.
- A lot of land was wasted by cattle and foot paths that crisscrossed the farms
- Open field system allowed easy spread of livestock diseases and uncontrolled breeding in livestock.
- Broadcasting method of planting led to wastage of seeds and low yields

Agricultural problems in Britain before the Agrarian Revolution included:

- Fallow land: Most of the land was under utilized. They were also unfenced and had many through paths. This led to a lot of waste land.
- Land was owned by the king and nobles who rented it out to poor peasants
- Land was small and uneconomical to use: The pieces of land were small and scattered and a lot of time was wasted
- The peasants practiced subsistence farming, producing food just enough for the family
- Poor farming methods and tools led to low yields
- Mono cropping: Planting the same crops year after year on the same piece of land led to declining yields
- Lack of animal feeds during winter made farmers to slaughter most of their animals
- Poor quality animal and plant varieties led to low yields.
- There were uncontrolled animal and plant diseases. This was mainly attributed to Communal land ownership and grazing in open fields.

Factors that led to Agrarian Revolution in Britain

- Land consolidation and privatization of land ownership: Rich people were encouraged to buy and consolidate the small pieces of land into larger farms. The pieces were then enclosed using hedges and fences.
- Machines were introduced in farming to improve efficiency, for example seed drill was used in planting instead of the traditional broadcasting method.
- Crop rotation was introduction to improve the quality of crops and reduce the spread of diseases.
- Lord Townshed introduced the cultivation of turnips which was used as winter feed for animals
- More land was put into use by reclaiming swampy areas and irrigating dry land.
- Development of transport, for example roads and railways assisted in the transportation of agricultural products

Advantages of Enclosure System

- Consolidation of farms saved the farmer's time
- Enclosure reduced wastage of land which was due to footpaths
- Fencing of land made it possible to practice selective breeding of animals
- It was possible to control pests and diseases in animals and plants
- The large farms were more economical to cultivate and this made mechanization possible.

A number of changes marked the Agrarian Revolution in Britain. These changes included:

- Fallows were abolished and the available land was used more effectively.
- Large scale farms were established.
- Introduction and use of fertilizer in farms
- Introduction of crop rotation
- Use of farm machines like the seed drill and horse drawn hoe
- Inter cropping to retain land fertility
- Selective breeding of livestock
- Fencing of farms - enclosure system
- Use of pesticides and herbicides to crop and livestock disease and weeds respectively.
- Increased agricultural research by institutions like the Royal Agricultural Society

Agrarian Revolution in Britain greatly changed the lives of small scale farmers. These changes included:

- Due to the consolidation and land enclosure system, they were displaced from their farms and many were forced to seek for new sources of livelihood elsewhere.
- Some peasants migrated to the urban centres to look for job opportunities, while others migrated and settled in overseas countries like Canada, USA, Australia and South Africa.

- Those who lost their land resented the enclosure system.
- More land was put into utilization and this enhanced farm mechanization.
- Many farmers abandoned subsistence farming and adopted large scale farming.
- Agriculture was diversified and crop production increased.
- There was enhanced research and scientific innovation in the field of agriculture.
- Surplus production encouraged local and international trade in agricultural products.

Other things which were indirectly related to changes in farming included:

- Appreciation on value of land in Britain
- Improved transport network and
- Accelerated industrialization in Britain due to the availability of raw materials

Questions on Agrarian Revolution in Britain

(a) Give one feature of the British agriculture before 1750 A.D.

(b) State five disadvantages of the traditional system of farming in Britain before 18th century

(c) Explain the factors that led to Agrarian Revolution in Britain

(d) Explain four advantages of the land tenure system in Britain during the Agrarian Revolution

(e) State two results of land enclosure system in Britain

(f) Explain five changes that marked the agrarian revolution in Britain

(g) Explain six results of agrarian revolution in Britain

(h) Explain five ways how agrarian revolution contributed to the development of urban centres in Europe

AGRARIAN REVOLUTION IN EUROPE
Agricultural practices which were used in

Europe before the Agrarian Revolution included the following:

- Small scale farming
- Shifting cultivation
- Peasant or subsistence farming
- Use of simple tools

Factors that encouraged agriculture in Europe during the Agrarian Revolution

- Discovery of fertilizers led to high yields.
- Discovery of pesticides and fungicides facilitated control of crops pests and diseases.
- Improvement in transport especially the railway facilitated transportation of farm machinery, farm products and farm workers.
- High demand for food at the rapidly growing urban centres
- Increased demand for agricultural raw materials in the industries
- Reclamation of wasteland gave rise to more arable land.
- Increased development of new breeds of crops and animals as a result of research in agriculture.
- Migration of people to towns created room for plantation farming in the rural areas.
- The enclosure systems pushed people out of the rural areas and created room for plantation agriculture.
- The invention of machines led to intensive farming

Inventions which revolutionalised farming in Europe included:

- Invention of modern fertilizer industry by a German, Justus Leibig
- Invention of the mechanical thresher by Andrew Meikel made harvesting easier
- Invention of the seed drill by Jethro Tull eliminated seed broadcasting

- Lord Townsend recommended the use of Norfolk crop rotation system to maintain soil fertility
- Cross breeding by Robert Bakewell increased yield in animal products

Questions on Agrarian Revolution in Europe

(i) State three agricultural practices used in Europe before the Agrarian Revolution

(j) Mention two ways in which railway transport contributed to the Agrarian Revolution in Western Europe

(k) Explain six factors which promoted plantation farming in Europe during the Agrarian Revolution

(l) Mention five inventions in the field of agriculture that revolutionalised farming in Europe

(m) Explain the impact of the Agrarian revolution in Europe

(n) State two ways in which agrarian revolution contributed to the development of urban centres in Europe

Impact of the Agrarian revolution in Europe

- The use of new and improved farming methods led to the high yields and improved food security.
- Introduction of new crops such as wheat, beans, maize and turnips led to the diversification of agriculture.
- Establishment of large-scale farms and plantations farming replaced subsistence farming.
- Agricultural research finding led to the development of exotic livestock breeds and better quality crops.
- Production of sufficient food led to improved standards of living and high life expectancy.
- Abundance of food led to increase in population.

- Mechanization of farming methods led to the redundancy of manual worker (unemployment).
- Establishment of large farms encouraged the rich landlords to buy off poor farmers' land – thus creating a class of landless people; some became hired labourers on the farms.
- Displacement of the poor led to rural - urban migration.
- The price of land went up.
- Provided industries with raw materials, for example wool which led to the growth of industries.
- Those who could not own large pieces of land migrated abroad.

AGRARIAN REVOLUTION IN NORTH AMERICA

The new European immigrants to America brought many changes in the region. They not only increased population in the area, but also the demand for food. These immigrants, who were determined to eke out a living through farming, introduced new methods of farming and new crops to America. They were encouraged in this endeavor by the existence of fertile soils that supported different crops, ideal climate and presence of indigenous crops in the area. Slave labour which was cheaply available also boosted their activities.

The Homestead Act of 1862 encouraged the Agrarian Revolution by:
- legalizing individual land ownership encouraged Americans to work hard on their farms
- The Federal Government granted financial assistance and loans to farmers to purchase and develop their land

Factors that led to the Agrarian Revolution in North America included:
- The introduction of Enclosure System in Britain forced the landless peasants to migrate to North America where they introduced new farming methods.
- The increase in demand of agricultural raw materials by European industrialists encouraged expansion in agriculture.
- The mechanization of agriculture stimulated agricultural productivity, for example the steel plough and the mechanical reaper.
- The application of science and research in agriculture (for example biotechnology development of new foods from existing crops, use of fertilizers and genetic engineering in livestock production) facilitated the Agrarian Revolution.
- The development of good transport and communication network led to increased agricultural productivity as products reached markets on time.
- Increase in population created demand for food which led to expansion of agriculture.
- Government recognition of individual land ownership (The homestead Act 1860) encouraged settlers to farm.
- The introduction of slave labour ensured adequate supply of labour for farming.
- European immigrants were determined to succeed in agriculture, as there was no other source of livelihood.
- The invention of the Cotton Gin in 1793 by Eli Whitney Mark led to increase cotton acreage.
- The development of food preservation methods of canning and refrigeration encouraged farmers to produce more.
- North America was divided into several major farming zones. This zoning led to specialization and increased yields

Effects of Agrarian Revolution in North America

- Many parts were opened up for settlement in North America
- Development of towns due to population increase
- Development of industries, for example raw materials were available from farms
- There was increased wealth and high standards of living
- There was unemployment as a result of introduction of machines in farms
- Transport system improved in order to transport farm produce
- Health improved and population increased
- Trade developed between USA and Europe as they exchanged farm produce
- It gave rise to black American communities as Africans were taken to work in the plantations
- Led to diversification of agriculture

Impact of agrarian and industrial development on urbanization

- Communities became sedentary. They congregated into small settlements which grew into villages, towns and big cities
- Agrarian revolution displaced many communities who moved to urban centres to search of employment. This contributed to the expansion of urban centres
- Agrarian revolution led to adequate food supply for urban population
- Production of surplus agricultural and industrial items encouraged trading activities
- Job specialization – some people acquired various skills such as farming whiles others became craftsmen and blacksmith.
- The agrarian revolution led to the production of raw materials for industry.

Many factories were established and this drew people to towns in search of jobs
- The industrial revolution relied on mineral resources. Places where huge deposits of minerals were found developed into towns
- The developments in transport and communication enhanced peoples' mobility
- Ports which were used to export and import agricultural products and industrial products developed into towns.
- Mechanization displaced farm workers who moved into towns to look for work

FOOD SITUATION IN AFRICA

The main agricultural policy that causes continuous food shortage in third world countries is the over emphasis on growing cash crops at the expense of food crops. These eat up more space which would otherwise be used for growing food crops to sustain the population. Other factors which lead to food shortage in Africa include:

- Rapid population growth puts a lot of strain on the existing food resources and this leads to shortages.
- Poor and inadequate storage facilities lead to wastage of a lot of food reserves.
- Poor farming methods have led to low agricultural yields.
- Political instability in some African countries like Somalia and Southern Sudan undermines food production in those regions due to insecurity.
- Unpredictable weather pattern in most parts of africa discourage farmers because of the loses they incur
- Regular migrations from rural to urban areas deprive the rural areas of the vital workforce.
- Lack of sufficient capital to buy farm inputs and adequate preparation of land lessens the amount of food produced.

- Poor farming methods like broadcasting lead to low yields.
- Prevalent animal and plant diseases reduce food production.
- Destructive human activities have led to soil erosion resulting to poor yields.
- The declining popularity of indigenous and drought resistant crops has made farmers not to produce them.
- HIV/AIDS pandemic affects the productive workforce and this leads to low production

Poor transport network in Africa has largely contributed to food shortages in the continent. This includes:

- High cost of transport makes food crops unaffordable due to inflated prices.
- Poor transport lead to poor distribution of food and this causes artificial shortages.
- Poor transport lead to heavy loses of perishable products like tomatoes due to delayed delivery.
- Poor transport system undermine effectiveness of agricultural extension officers.
- Farmers are unable to get farm inputs in time due to delayed delivery

Effects of food shortage in third world countries
- Many people have lost their lives due to starvation and famine
- Many, especially children, suffer from malnourishment
- Food shortage has created social problems, for example cattle rustling and stealing
- Food shortage creates refugee problems and strain in resources in the recipient countries
- It hampers effort towards economic development
- Poor countries are forced to depend on the rich nations for provisions

- Food shortage affects the development of agro based industries

Remedies to the problem of food shortage in Africa are:

- Land reclamation to put more wetlands, for example Yala Swamp into use
- Encouraging the use of irrigation schemes to put more land especially in the arid region into use
- More research on better breeds of crops and animals to improve their yields
- Encouraging the use of pesticides and herbicides to control pests and diseases which affect crops
- Establishment of co-operatives to assist farmers, for example to acquire loans to improve their farms or to buy farm inputs
- Improve transport to ensure proper distribution of farm products and improving storage facilities to reduce waste
- Control the rate of population growth through family planning
- Improved methods of crop production and improvement of soil fertility, for example use of fertilizer and crop rotation
- Encouraging the cultivation of indigenous crops which are drought resistant

> **Questions on Agrarian Revolution in North America**
> (a) In what ways did the land enclosure system in Britain contribute to the agrarian revolution in North America?
> (b) Describe five factors that facilitated the development of agriculture in America before 1800
> (c) Discuss the factors that led to the Agrarian Revolution in North America
> (d) How did the Homestead Act of 1862 promote the agrarian revolution?
> (e) What were the effects of Agrarian Revolution in North America?
> (f) What were the effects of the Agrarian Revolution?
> (g) Describe the impact of agrarian and industrial development on urbanization

5 TRADE

Trade is the exchange of goods and services between people. One group sell and another buy the good(s) on offer. Factors which led to the development of trade include:

- Good relations among people promoted the exchange of commodities as gifts.
- Specialization in the production of specific commodities led to surplus production and a need to dispose some.
- Trade arose from the need to acquire commodities which could not be produced in one area, but could be produced abundantly elsewhere.
- Where commodities were produced in excess, disposing the surplus off through trade became a necessity.

Methods of Trade

There are two methods of trade: Barter and currency system of trade.

Barter Trade

This is the direct exchange of goods or services for other goods or services. This method is also called silent trade and it is the oldest method. Initially goods were placed at strategic points and others who were interested in the same would place theirs in the same spot and take what was there. Though dying off, this system is still preferred where there is shortfall of money.

Weaknesses of Barter Trade

- There was difficulty of determining the value of goods or services to be exchanged.
- Some goods could not be divided easily to smaller quantities
- Some goods were not easily moveable to other areas e.g. bulky goods

- Lack of double coincidence of wants – Finding two people with different commodities or services, but with similar interests was difficult.
- Lack of a common medium of communication

Money

This is any medium of exchange that is generally accepted by a group of people. In the past different commodities were used as medium of exchange. These included Gold, Copper, Cowry shells and Salt. Gold is still preferred in many places as a medium of exchange and a store of value because of its relative stability in relation to other world currencies which keep fluctuating.

Advantages of Using Money
(a) Money is not bulky and can be conveniently carried
(b) Has a measure of value for goods and services transacted
(c) It is easy to divide money into smaller denominations
(d) It can be saved for a later use (store of value)
(e) It can be used as standard of settling debts
(f) It has intrinsic value, for example coins made of precious metals

---

These items were later replaced by smaller coins. The original coins were made of copper, bronze, gold and silver and had intrinsic value. New coins are only coated with the same minerals and do not have intrinsic value. Coins were replaced with paper notes which were specially designed to reduce counterfeits.

The main draw back of using money is that it can be easily stolen, especially when one carries a large amount and because some currencies lose value more rapidly in relation to other major world currencies like US dollar, the British Pound and the

Japanese Yen. New developments like the use of cheques which are more secure and other means of payments like electronic money transfer or using smart cards have replaced the paper money in most transactions.

Type of Trade

There are three types of trade. These include Local Trade, Regional Trade and International Trade.

> **Features of Local Trade**
> (a) The trade took place within neighbouring communities or a small geographical area.
> (b) The range of goods traded in was limited and were mostly locally produced.
> (c) The trade involved less specialization, for instance there was absence of middlemen
> (d) The system of trade was mainly barter
> (e) It was conducted on set market days which were more regular

Impact of local trade in pre- colonial Africa

• People specialized in different activities, for example pottery, and Iron smelting. This led to abundant production.

• Trade made stronger the bond between people in the same locality, for example through intermarriages

• Enabled community members to satisfied their requirements through commodities produced elsewhere

• Local trade led to the improvement of transport routes

• Centralized forms of government also developed due to the local trade, for example Buganda, Ghana and Mali Kingdoms

• Local trade enhanced unity among the trading partners

Regional trade involved two areas with distinct geographical features, for example the Sudan region (West Africa) and North Africa.

> **Features of this Type of Trade**
> (a) Regional trade involved people who specialized in the trade.
> (b) Middlemen linked the buyers and sellers
> (c) Goods were transported over long distances
> (d) Goods were sold on arrival and there were no set market days.
> (e) Large number of people participated in the trade and different good were transacted.

TRANS-SAHARAN TRADE

The factors which led to the development of trade between North Africa and West Africa during the pre-colonial period included:

• The introduction of the camel as a means of transport.

• There was high demand of goods from the North and West Africa

• The Berbers provided the capital to finance the trade

• Existence of well established trade routes that made it easy for the traders to travel

• Increased contacts between North Africa, Southern Europe and Middle East led to increased demand of trade goods

• Existence of powerful kings, for example Muasa Musa of Mali, Askia Mohammed of Songai - encouraged the trade. The rulers provided security to the traders and offered financial support.

• Availability of trade goods, for example gold, kola nuts and slaves in West Africa and salt, copper, beads from North Africa

• Prior to the trade, there existed local trade among the Berber's and Tuaregs

• The conquest and settlement of North by Arabs increased the volume of trade

• Spread of Islam in the region which became a unifying factor

• The Tauregs facilitated the trade by acting as middlemen

Organization of the Trans-Saharan trade

• Traders moved in large caravans, of hundreds of camels and traders for security reasons

• Rich traders from the North provided trade goods, camels and financed the trade

• Tuaregs acted as middlemen

• Caravans left the North after the rains when sandstorms subsided.

• A number of trade routes developed between North and West Africa

• The kings provided protection along the trade routes, but imposed taxes on traders who passed through their territories

• Barter system was used since the traders lacked a common language

• It took three months to cross the desert

The major trade routes which connected the trading centers in the Western Sudan and North Africa during the Trans-Saharan Trade were:

• Fez-Marrakech-Wadan-Walata.

• From Sijilimasa in Morocco through Tuat, Gao to Timbuktu.

• From Tunisia through Ghadames and Agedes to Hausaland.

• From Tripoli through Fezzan to Bornu.

• From Cairo through Murzuk to Bilma to Kano.

• From Sijilimasa-Walata-Taghasa-Alidaghost.

Communities in West Africa benefited from Trans – Saharan Trade in the following ways:

• West African communities were able to acquire essential commodities from the trade, for example cloth, glassware, horses, firearms and salt,

• Commercial centres developed along the trade routes, for example Timbuktu, Jenne, Gao and Kano. These enhanced local trade.

• Some African leaders established strong armies with the firearms that they acquired from trade. They used the armies for defending and expanding their kingdoms,

• It stimulated the production and exchange of locally produced commodities such as gold, kolanuts, ivory and slaves

• It led to the spread of Islam.

• Islamic culture was introduced in West Africa, for example architectural designs and clothing.

• It opened up West Africa to the outside world and the establishment of diplomatic relations with North Africa.

• Iron tools acquired through trade contributed to agricultural productions.

• Revenue raised from trade taxes were used for developing the empire.

How the Trans - Saharan Trade led to development of the kingdoms

• Trans - Saharan Trade was a source of state revenue and wealth which was acquired through import and export or taxes paid by the traders.

• Kings acquired horses and firearms from North Africa which they used to establish strong armies to defend and expand the kingdoms.

• Islamic sheria which was introduced by the traders was used in the administration of kingdoms.

- The kings were able to acquire personal wealth. This assisted them to command respect. They also used it to reward their royal subjects.
- The trade stimulated local trade, which generated state wealth.
- Muslims personnel were used by the Kings as advisers and secretaries. This led to effective administration.
- The trade motivated the kings to establish diplomatic links with North Africa and countries of the Middle East.
- Islam acted as a unifying factor.

Problems Experienced by the Traders during the Trans Saharan Trade included:
- Lack of a common language made it difficult for traders to communicate.
- The journey through the desert was sometimes hazardous due to frequent sandstorms.
- Sometimes traders lost their ways through the desert.
- Traders were attacked by desert robbers.
- The journey across the desert was tedious and slow. It took the traders as many as three months to cross the desert.
- Uncomfortable weather, too hot during the day and too cold during the night.
- Attack by wild animals.
- Development of Trans-Atlantic trade diverted attention of traders to the south.

Factors Which Undermined Trans - Saharan Trade were:
- The mine fields (for gold) got exhausted
- Tuaregs started attacking and robbing traders
- Morocco invaded Western Sudan causing insecurity
- Invasion of North Africa by Turks created insecurity along trade routes
- Development of Trans Atlantic trade made some traders to begin moving southwards
- Decline of Mali and Songai kingdom left leadership vacuum in trade
- Colonization of West Africa by Europeans who took over resources in West Africa
- Anti slave trade : Pressure from the British and eventual abolition of slave trade reduced trade profits

Effects of the Trans Saharan Trade
- Trans Saharan Trade led to the growth of towns like Gao, Timbuktu, Taghaza and Kano
- Some African leaders established strong armies using the fire arms and horses acquired from the trade
- The trade stimulated the production and exchange of locally produced goods such as gold, kola nuts, ivory
- Essential commodities like clothes, glass ware, fire arms were got from the North
- The trade exposed West Africa to the outside world and this led to colonization
- A class of wealthy and powerful merchants emerged like Jaja of Opobo
- Islamic law (Sheria) was introduced in the area by the traders
- Iron tools acquired through the trade were used to develop agriculture
- It led to the introduction of camels and horse which boosted transport
- It created misery, insecurity and depopulation among Africans due to slave trade
- It led to destruction of wildlife, especially elephants due to increased demand for ivory
- Warfare increased due to slave trade
- Arabic architecture was introduced in West Africa

TRANS-ATLANTIC (TRIANGULAR) TRADE

was also known as Trans Atlantic Slave Trade or Triangular Trade. It took place across the Atlantic Ocean from the 16th through to the 19th centuries. A large number of those enslaved were transported to the New World from either west or cental Africa and were sold by West Africans slave merchants or the European traders. The South Atlantic economic system flourished on the production of crops and making of goods and clothing to sell in Europe, and the increasing number of slaves brought to the new world.

The Portuguese were the first to engage in the New World Slave Trade in the 16th century. Slaves were shipped to America as cargo to provide labour in the:

- Plantations of coffee, tobacco, cocoa, sugar and cotton
- Gold and silver mines
- Rice fields
- Construction industry
- Cutting timber for ships and
- As domestic servants

By mid 17th century, slavery had taken the shape of a racial social group with slaves and their off springs being legally regarded as property of the owners, and children born to the slave mothers were enslaved. As property, the slaves were understood to be merchandise or units of labour, and were put up for sale at markets with other goods and services.

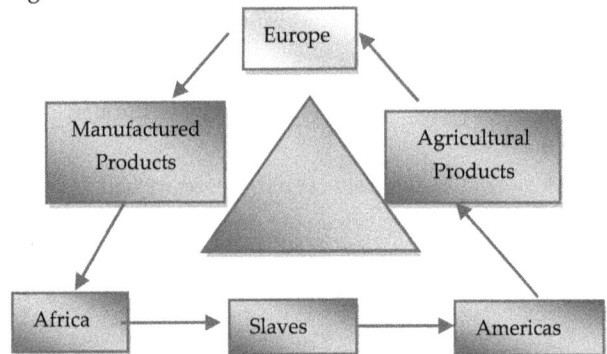

The Atlantic Slave Trade took the shape of a triangle. At the end of the triangle were exported goods from Europe to Africa. Kings and merchants from Africa took part in this trade (1440 – 1833), and for the captives they received a variety of goods like guns, ammunition and clothes from Europe. At the second side of the triangle were enslaved Africans who were exported. They were shipped across the Atlantic Ocean to the Americas and the Caribbean Islands. The third part of the triangle was the return of goods to Europe from the Americas. The goods were the products of the slaves who toiled in the plantations to produce

Cotton, Sugar, tobacco, molasses and rum. The British were the pioneers of this trade and they made profits at every stop.

Scarcity of labour in Americas and the Caribbean region directly contributed to the development of Atlantic Slave Trade. Growing, harvesting, and processing the tropical crops was energy sapping and a labour intensive activity. Initially the native inhabitants (Red Indians) of the New World were utilized as slaves, but this was brought to an end when they passed away in large numbers due to overwork and the newly acquired diseases from Europe. Alternative sources of labour such as indentured servitude, equally failed to provide enough workforce. The West African and later Central African enslave people therefore became the only answer to this dilemma.

European traders rarely entered the interior of Africa to acquired trade goods due to the fear of diseases and fierce African tribes. Although, a few African leaders like Jaja of Opobo refused to sell their criminals or captives, most Africans played a more direct role in the Slave Trade.

- They sold their war captives or prisoners of war (usually form neighbouring or enemy ethnic group or tribe) to the European buyers.
- Sometimes criminals would be sold so that they could no longer commit crimes in that area.
- Most other slaves were obtained from kidnapping or through raids that occurred at gunpoint through joint ventures with Europeans.
- People who were unable to pay debt and the weak in the society - the feeble minded, widows and children were sold as slaves.
- The slave dealers also enticed children and sold them as slaves.

The enslaved people were brought to the coastal outpost where they were traded for other goods.

Enslavement became a major by-product of internal wars in Africa, often deliberately sponsored by Europeans. Portugal, Britain, France, Span and Holland were some of the leading European countries involved in Slave Trade.

Factors which contributed to the abolition of Slave Trade

- Adam Smith, an English economist, argued that free labour was more productive than slave labour
- Use of machines in farms and industries made slave labour unnecessary
- Independence of the USA in 1776 left Britain in a quagmire. She had no colony where to take the slaves after America closed her slave markets
- The French Revolution of 1789 spread the ideas of liberty, equality and fraternity of all human kind. This made many people to question the rationale for slave trade
- The British parliament resolved in 1807 to abolish the Slave Trade. She later influenced other European countries to stop slave trade by signing anti-slave treaties
- Due to industrialization, Britain wanted to acquire raw materials from Africa. This would only be made possible if slave trade was abolished and African population remained intact to provide raw materials and market
- Humanitarians like William Wilberforce and missionaries like David Livingstone were against Slave Trade and slavery. They exposed the horrors of the trade, turned public opion against it and persuaded the government to abolish it in Britain in 1807.

Economic factors which led to the decline of Trans-Atlantic Trade

(a) Machines (invented in the 18th century) made work more efficient and faster and this replaced human labour
(b) Development of legitimate trade led to widespread condemnation of Slave Trade
(c) American civil war led to the shutting down of the American slave market
(d) Adam Smith, a British economist argued that free labour was economically more productive and paying than slave labour
(e) Some Europeans argued that African remaining at home would provide a ready market for European manufactured goods
(f) Others felt that if Africans were not enslaved they would produce enough raw materials for Europeans industries at home rather than in the far of plantations

Effects of Trans-Atlantic Slave Trade

- Trans-Atlantic Slave Trade led to the depopulation of West African region
- West Africa lost the able-bodied membes of the society and this disrupted the economic activities of the region
- The trade intensified warfare and slave raids and these made the region to be unsafe
- Growth of slave merchants – a class of slave merchants grew in West Africa
- African chiefs changed their roles from custodians of the people to slave merchants
- Some kingdoms like the Asante and Benin grew up because of the wealth acquired from their slave raiding and trading activities.
- African industries were undermined by the manufactured goods which were acquired through slave trade
- Trans Atlantic Trade undermined the Trans Saharan Trade. Most of the traders shifted southwards because of its convenience.
- Slave Trade caused widespread anguish, fear and killings in West Africa.
- Outposts which were used as collecting centes like Lagos, Porto and Elmina development in urban centres
- Roles changed in communities where women did the jobs of men who had been taken captive or sold
- The Fante Kingdom decline due to the slave raids which were conducted in the region by the Asante
- The trade led to intermingling of Africans and the Europeans and this gave rise to the Mullato population in West Africa
- The trade exposed West Africa to the outside world leading to eventual colonization
- Liberia and Sierra Leon were created as homes of freed slaves.
- Countries like Britain amassed a lot of wealth from slave trade
- Towns like Liverpool and Armsterdum grew up in Europe because of the trade
- The trade lead to the rise of Black American population in USA

Questions on Trans-Atlantic (Triangular) Trade
(a) Describe three ways which slaves were obtained during the Trans– Atlantic trade
(b) State the economic factors which led to the decline of Trans-Atlantic trade
(c) Give three factors which contributed to the abolition of slave trade
(d) Explain six effects of Trans-Atlantic Slave Trade

6 DEVELOPMENT OF TRANSPORT AND COMMUNICATION

COMMUNICATION

This is the process of passing information from one person to another. It involves the sender, the recipient and the medium through which the message is conveyed. For a message to be properly delivered it depends on: -

- Whether the sender was audible enough or not
- Whether the sender used an appropriated language understood by the recipient or not.
- Whether the sender used the correct medium of communication, used the correct time and targeted the correct recipients
- Whether the recipient coded the message correctly or not
- How the recipient perceived the sender of the message
- How relevant the message was to the recipient
- How the message was delivered to the recipient

Traditional methods of passing information
(a) Drum beating
(b) Fire and Smoke signals
(c) Horn blowing
(d) Gongs
(e) Gestures
(f) Whistling, Ululation and Crying
(g) Messengers

Drums were mostly played in the morning or evenings to relay different messages. This was because the atmosphere was quiet and the information could reach far. The messages which were sent using drums included:

- Announcement of ceremonies or festivals
- Announcement of deaths or mourning

- Declaration of war
- Arrival of strangers
- Impending danger

Advantages of Using Drum Beats
- Drum beating could be used at any time both day and night
- Drum beats communicated specific messages like death, festivals or danger.
- Drum beats could be used during all the seasons, both dry and wet seasons.
- Drum beats spread messages fast.

Gestures (sign language) are signals or deliberate body movements intended to convey a message to another or others. They can be used: -

- To put emphasis on a speech or reinforce a language
- To communicate with others where silence is required like in hospitals or schools.
- By the police traffic to communicated to motorists.
- To communicate with the deaf or partially deaf.

Fire and smoke were used mainly to send the message of danger. Using fire was more efficient at night because it could be seen far and wide while smoke was more befitting during the day. There was confidentiality in the message conveyed because it could only be coded by the sender and the person intended to receive it.

The use of fire sent wrong signals and it was difficult to decode the correct message. Fire was also not suitable during rainy seasons because of the difficulty of lighting and maintaining it.

Although fire is still used at night to alert other road users, its use has diminished remarkably in modern times. Red signs which are used to indicate danger have replaced the use of fire.

Blowing horns
Horns were blown by specialists to convey different messages depending on the event. There were unique tunes for special occasions like funerals, meetings and war. Messages using horns could not be conveyed over long distances and the tunes could only be made by specialists.

Messengers
Chiefs and kings used messengers or runners to deliver urgent messages over long distances. Marathon is a long distance race which was named after a Greek. He ran an equivalent distance, and died in the process, to deliver an urgent message to tip off the Greeks about the attack by the Spartans. Presently messages are sent directly to the recipient though Post Office or Courier Services like the G4S and Speedpost.
Messengers are still used:
- To convey not to be disclosed messages
- When the message is to be delivered formally to the recipient and
- When some explanations are to be made to the recipient

Disadvantages of Using Messengers
(a) Messengers took a long time to deliver the messages
(b) Messengers sometimes forgot the message or gave inaccurate information.
(c) Messengers were limited to short distant places.
(d) Sometimes the messengers were killed along the way
(e) Messengers sometimes deliberately distorted the messages

WRITTEN MESSAGES
Different communities use different symbols or alphabets to write messages. In the past such messages where recorded on materials like the scrolls, stone tablets, parchments and paper. The earliest forms of writings were the pictorial or ideographic types. These included the Cuneiform and Hieroglyphics of the Sumerian and Egypt respectively.

Scrolls
were rolls of paper which were rolled round rods of wood or ivory and written on. In Egypt, papyrus was used for making these rolls and they used pens and brushes, which were dipped in ink, to write. The pens were made from either hard part of feathers or reeds. Scrolls were used by the Egyptians, Greeks, Hebrews, Japanes and the Chinese.

Stone Tablets
were used in Sumerian. They wrote on wet clay tablets. These were given time to harden and form permanent impressions on the tablets. Hammurabi, the "Law giver" wrote his laws on stone pillars. The same applied to the Mosaic Laws of Moses (Ten Commandments) now contained in the Bible.

Moses and the Ten Commandments

Advantages of Written Messages

- They provide reliable information which is not very easy to forget.
- Information is stored for future reference
- Information can be interpreted into different languages.
- The messages are more accurate and can be authenticated

Disadvantages of Written Messages

- The messages could only be decoded by literate people.
- They were sometimes biased and skewed towards the mentality of the writer.
- The messages could also be misinterpreted.
- Buying written materials like newspapers is expensive
- Reading written messages is time consuming and some people have a poor reading culture

MODERN FORMS OF TRANSPORT AND COMMUNICATION

Telephone
is a communication device which is used to relay sound waves by converting them into electrical signals and then reconverting them into sound waves. Telephone was invented by a Scottish-born American called Alexander Graham Bell who was a speech teacher in 1876.

The invention of automatic switch board by Almon Brown Strowger in 1897 was a great leap forward in the telecommunication industry. By 1900 the loading coil - copper wire, had increased the communication range to about 1000 miles.

Until 1990's most telephone companies were owned by governments and telephone communications were monitored closely. The use of telephone is rapidly dying off in Kenya because many people have resorted to using mobile phones which are more convenient and affordable.

Advantages of Using Telephone

- Information is got instantaneously
- Using telephone to communicate saves time
- The communication between the sender and the receiver is directly conveyed

Disadvantages of Using Telephone

- There is no confidentiality in the messages passed
- Fixed line are not convenient for people who are highly mobile
- Telephone cost is very high and discourages many people
- Telephone lines are very easy to sabotage or put out of action and this inconveniences the users

Mobile (cell) Phone
is a type of wireless communication technology. It uses many base stations to transfer information from one station to another. Dr. Martin Cooper, a former manager of Motorola is considered to be the first inventor of a modern portable handset.

By 1982 commercial cellular phones were in use in America and Japan. Due to the crowding of the waves many improvements were made. These included increasing base stations and frequency allocations. Today many companies manufacture mobile phones – Nokia, Motorola, Samsung, and Siemens among others. There are also a number of service providers. In Kenya the leading service providers are Safaricom, Celtel and Orange.

Mobile Phone

Cell phones come in different shapes to be attracted to and sizes. The use of cell phones in the country has greatly increased of late.

Advantages of Mobile Phones
- Mobile phones are portable and can be carried everywhere
- They are affordable to many people
- Mobile phones have a wide range of coverage in the country
- They can make and receive call any time and everywhere.
- Mobile phone have many accessory services like sending and receiving text messages, accessing the internet, sending and receiving Email, taking digital photographs and videos. They also have calendars, calculators, radio, and can play music and games.

Limitations of Using Cell Phones
- Mobile phones with internal antennas have poor reception
- Mobile phones have rechargeable batteries, but some do not last for long. Such phones are difficult to use in areas without electricity.

- Continuous use of mobile phones exposes the users to radioactivity
- There is poor coverage in some parts of the country
- Handsets are easily stolen due to their small size
- They are expensive to purchase and maintain
- Using mobile phones is captivative and a lot of time is wasted on it by the youth

Television is a multipoint technology which is used to transmit news, information and entertainment to people in distant places. This technology came into being in 1920's in USA. A Scottish name Loggie Baird demonstrated in 1922 how moving images could be transmitted by electromagnetic waves and in 1931 the cathode ray tube was invented in USA. This transformed beams of electrons into visible images on the screen.

Advantages of Using Television
- Television is used to convey both audio and visual messages, news and information all over the world.
- It is a rich source of entertainment – sports, soap operas, drama, music among others are aired on television.
- A number of education programmes are aired on Television.
- Television is a powerful tool for advertisements because it captures the attention of many people.
- Events are aired live and instantly through television.

Limitations of Using Television
- Requires electricity and this limits their use to areas which are served with electricity

- Promote deviant behaviour like drug taking and alcoholism among the youth who see some displayed characters as role models.
- Pornographic programmes which are sometimes aired on television erode peoples morals, especially the youth
- Some programmes such as wrestling encourage the youth to adopt violent behaviour.
- Watching Television is addictive and many youths waste a lot of their useful time watching Television.

Radio

transmits and receives information at varying frequencies. A number of people are credited with the invention of radio. These include:

- Clerk Maxwell, an English mathematical physicist suggested that waves existed in 1864.
- Heinrich Rudolph Hertz, a German demonstrated the existence of electromagnetic waves in 1857.
- Ernest Rutheriel, an Englishman succeeded in sending radio signals in 1871
- Oliver Lodge, an Englishmen developed the basic principal of tuning a radio.
- In 1901, an Italian name Guglielmo Marconi invented the radio when he sent a radio transmission across the Atlantic. He also sent wireless messages between France and England.

Importance of Radio

- Radio is easily accessible to most people because of its affordability.
- News and information from the radio is quickly received throughout the world.
- Radio increases communication in transport systems such as motor vehicles, railways, ships and airplanes.
- Radios are used to broadcast educational programmes

- Radios are a source of entertainment
- They are used for advertisement
- Space exploration has been enhanced through radio.

Internet

is a computer based global information network system that links thousands of computers. The link enables them to share information with one another. The use of internet has resulted into the following:

- Through internet education has been facilitated. Education institutions use it for research and to conduct distant learning on line. Courses and learning materials are delivered to the students through E-mails.
- Customers are able to do shopping on line and order for the goods and services, E-commerce.
- Businessmen interact with others through internet. They are able to Shop; pay bills and do all their banking transactions electronically – E-banking.
- Individuals communicate to each other through E-mails and can chat on line.

Increasing use of internet has encouraged idleness among the youth and pornographic materials which are easily accessed through internet. Cases of electronic fraud have also increased. Some users of internet also hack sensitive information from other people's webs sites and this has made the use of internet to be quite unsafe.

Satellite

is a spacecraft or an artificial device orbiting around the earth, the moon or other planets. Satellite is used to send information back to the earth surface. The first satellite – Sputnik I, was sent into space in 1957 by the Russians. In 1961 a Russian, Yuri Gagarin went into space on board a satellite and in 1969 and American, Nel Armstrong landed on the moon in his spacecraft, Apollo II.

Different types of satellites are used to serve different purposes:

- Communication satellites send radio, television and telephone signals from one continent to another.
- Military satellites take photographs of possible enemy activities, are used for communication and to guide laser guided missiles to their target.
- Navigation satellites are used to guide ship and aircrafts in all kinds of weather.
- Satellites are also used to monitor potential disasters like floods and forest fires.
- They are also used to predict changes in atmospheric conditions (weather).

Fax is a method used to transmit text messages through a telephone network. Information is printed photo-electronically and transmitted through signals then reproduced photographically by the receiving fax machine within a span of 30 seconds. Fax machine was invented in 1902 by Arthur Korn, a German. The use of Fax machine on commercialized basis commenced as from 1926.

PRINT MEDIA is used to refer to all forms of printed or published materials and takes the form of loose or bounded leaflets, booklets, newspapers, brochures or journals.

- Newspapers are produced daily, weekly or monthly. They are usually not bounded and are printed on low quality paper called newsprints. Printing was invented by a German called Johannes Gutenberg in the 15th century and this gave the Germans a head start in the production of newspapers. Major newspapers in Kenya include *The East African Standard*, *The Daily Nation*, *Taifa Leo*, *Kenya Times* and *The People's Daily*.

- Periodicals are published at regular intervals and contain news, special features, poems and fictional stories. Periodicals aim at the general audience and may be published weekly or monthly.

- Journals are a special type of periodicals with a narrower target audience such as scholarly publications. Examples of such publications in Kenya include *Review of Political Economy*, *Canadian Journal of African Affairs* and *The Medical Journal*.

- Magazines are bounded periodicals. They are classified as general or specific interest magazines. General interest magazines deal with a wide variety of news and information which appeal to many different types of people while specific interest magazines deal with specific issues like HIV/AIDS, Women, Sports and Children. Examples of Magazines in Kenya include *Drum* and *The Parents*.

Role of Telecommunication Service in Modern Society Today

- Entertainment: Through radio, television and cinema. This has popularized creative art
- Education: Education programmes are aired by radio and television to the public and schools in many parts of the world.
- Transport: It has enhanced safe traveling by air and water through radar connections
- Exploration of outer space: Satellites sent to space are able to send information back about the outer space
- It has assisted in management through the use of computers to store and retrieve

information

- Warfare: They help in conducting warfare. They help to make precise target on the enemy
- Cultural Imperialism: Western culture has been imposed on many people through films and television
- Development of trade: It has assisted to speed up business transactions throughout the world and also advertisement of goods
- National unity: radio is used to inform people about government policies and the importance of staying together.
- It has reduced cost of management by enabling a few people to handle a lot of workload.
- Has encouraged faster transmission of information.

Questions on Communication

(a) Mention one advantage of using fire and smoke to pass information in the past
(b) Give one advantage of drum beat as a form of communication during the pre- colonial period
(c) Give one reason why drums were played in the morning and evenings
(d) Give two limitations of using messengers to send messages in the past
(e) Give two limitations of cell phones
(f) What are the advantages of the use of radio in the modern society?
(g) Discuss ways through which the modern society benefited from the development in the telecommunications
(h) Give one problem associated with the use of modern telecommunication facilities

TRANSPORT

can be defined as the movement of people and goods from one place to another. This movement can be classified according to how it took place – hence the general classification of land, water and air transport. Transport can also be grouped into two: traditional and modern means of transport.

TRADITIONAL FORMS OF TRANSPORT

Human Transport

From time immemorial man has walked from place to place sometimes carrying different item on his head, shoulders or back. Short distances were covered and limited goods transported because of the tedious nature of this form of transport. Travelers could also be kidnapped or robbed of their items.

Animal Transport

Animals used for transporting goods are referred to as pack animals and they include:

- Donkeys: were probably the first animals to be used as pack animals. They are hardy and can carry heavy loads.

- Elephants: Smaller Asian elephants are docile and are used to transport heavy logs in Burma. Their use is limited because they develop scores on their skins and feet. Loading goods on them is also difficult because of their huge size.
- Oxen: These are draught animals which are used to pull carts or heavy load and for ploughing.
- Camels: are referred to as the desert ship. They are hardy animals which are adapted to the hostile desert environment with extremely hot and cold climates. Camels survive very well in the desert because: -
  ✓ They have flappy nostrils to keep out sand during desert sandstorms.

- ✓ Camels have thick fur to regulate its body temperature and this is ideal because of the wide variation in desert climate.
- ✓ Camels can carry heavy load and move very fast on sandy surfaces because of their flat foot.
- ✓ They have fatty hump which store fat and survive on the stored reserve during scarcity.
- ✓ They can also survive with little water for a very long time.

Questions on Animal Transport

(a) Name two animals used as pack animals
(b) Give two advantages of animal transport
(c) Give two advantages of using camels in the deserts
(d) Give two disadvantages of animals transport

Advantages of Animal Transport

(a) Animals can be used in inaccessible areas, for example mountains
(b) Animals are safe from accidents
(c) Animals are cheap to maintain.
(d) Animals are environment friendly; they do not pollute the environment.
(e) Animals are capable of sensing danger

Disadvantages of Animal Transport

(a) Animals are slow and tedious
(b) Their movement is limited to day
(c) Animals can only be used for short distances
(d) Sometimes animals become obstinate and difficult to use.
(e) Animals may be affected by diseases

- Horses: are rode and were also trained to pull wagons, chariots and passenger coaches. They were used to carry soldiers during warfare (cavalry). Horses are not suitable for arid areas or semi arid regions because they require a lot of water. They are also prone to diseases.
- Dogs: are used to pull carts and sledges in the Arctic regions which experience permafrost conditions. They are also used for guiding the blind people in sports.

DEVELOPMENT OF THE WHEEL

The Sumerians invented the wheel around 3000 B.C. This development spread rapidly to other parts of the world like the Mediterranean region and Asia. The wheels were fitted into carts and wagons and were pulled by either human beings or animals. The use of horse drawn chariots was common and they were mainly used during war. The development of wheels led to the development of roads to facilitate the transportation of goods and people. In Mesopotamia, the potter's wheel was used for making pots from clay.

Significance of the invention of the wheel in road transport

- Made road transport to be faster, efficient and comfortable
- Bigger loads could be carried hence benefit of economies of scale could be enjoyed
- Commerce, both regional and international expanded
- General welfare and standard of living improved
- It made use of motor and engine driven vehicles possible

OLD FORM OF WATER TRANSPORT

Rafts are the simplest and the earliest form of water transport. These were floating structures usually made of log, stalks and papyrus which are tied together. Animal skins or air bladders were wound around logs and used as rafts. The rafts were paddled with oars or long poles across rivers to carry people and goods. The problem with rafts is that they easily capsized and needed a lot of manpower to paddle them. They were also affected by strong wind or current and this increased the risk of using them.

Canoes
The oldest canoes were made by stripping the bark from trees, bark canoes. Later "dug out" canoes were made from tree trunks. These canoes were paddled with oars. In some parts of Kenya they are still used to transport people, goods and conduct fishing in the inland lakes and rivers.

Boats
are small vessels which are paddled by oars, sail or motor. They are an improvement of canoes.

Sailing Ship
are water vessels which are propelled using wind. A piece of cloth or clothes are fixed on a pole or poles to propel the boat towards the direction of the wind. Such vessels were used by the Egyptians, Greeks, Arabs and the Portuguese to sail across oceans and to distant places. The main limitation of these vessels was that there movement depended on the direction of the prevailing wind.

MODERN FORMS OF TRANSPORT
Modern forms of transport which have undergone a lot of transformations include road, rail, water, air and space exploration.

Road transport
The invention of wheels made the developments on roads inevitable. Such changes were made by the Romans who built roads which were wide, straight and durable. The Roman soldiers dug out trenches and packed them with heavy stones and rocks. Rough and fine concrete was added to the foundation. This was followed by

layers of gravel, chalk and cement to smoothen the road surfaces. The Roman roads had curved surface and well drained trenches to facilitate drainage. They also build bridges and tunnels through hills. Roman roads facilitated administration of their vast empire and the movement of their soldiers. The roads also boosted trade in the areas occupied by the Romans.

John Macadam

By 18th century many European engineers also contributed to the development of roads. George Wade built 400 km of roads while John Metcalfe built 290 km of roads. The notable engineer was John Macadam who is credited with the development of modern day roads. He constructed roads which were laid down in three layers of broken down stones. He then added a layer of gravel which was compacted with heavy vehicles. These roads became known as Macadamized roads. These roads were later improved by adding tar to make their surfaces water proof.

Characteristics of the Macadamized Roads
- Macadamized roads were all weather type
- They were wide and straight
- The roads had good drainage
- They had smooth surface
- The roads were durable and had strong foundation

The Barons

Many developments have taken place in road transport system since 1750. These changes include: -

- Tarmacking of roads has been done to make them more durable and water proof.
- Roads have been straightened and widened
- Bridges have been constructed across rivers.
- Dual carriage ways and super highways have been constructed to fasten the flow of traffic in major centres
- By-pass have been constructed in major cites to ease congestion in the towns
- Fly overs and under passes have been built to reduce cases of accidents and fast truck movement of vehicles.

MODES OF ROAD TRANSPORT

Bicycle was and still is the most common and cheapest mode of road transport especially in rural areas. Several people are credited with the development of the Bicycle. These include:

- In 1790 de Divrack, a French made the first bicycle which was pushed with the feet hence the name "walkalong".
- Baron Karl Drais, a German invented the "walkalong" called the draisine. It had a steering bar connected to the front wheel.
- In 1860 Ernes Michaux, a French locksmith invented a bicycle which had two wheels with pedals attached to the front wheel.
- Kirk Patrick Macmillan of Scotland made the first bicycle in Britain. The "boneshaker" as it was known had iron wheels fixed to wooden spokes.
- In 1870 James Starley, also known as the father of cycle industry, invented a tension spoked wheel in which the rim and the hub were connected by wire spokes.

- In 1888 John Dunlop invented the tyre filled with compressed air.

Motor Vehicle is a power driven transport device which moves on land. They include motor cycles, trucks, cars and buses. The development of motor vehicle is credited to many people. They include: -

- In 1760 a Swiss clergyman, Genevois suggested that the wind springs would move wheels on the ground.
- Jacques de Vaucauzon demonstrated in Paris a carriage which was propelled by a large clockwork engine.
- A French army engineer, Nicholas Joseph Cugnot built a three-wheeled steam driven vehicle in 1769, but abandoned the experiment prematurely.
- In 1883 Gottlieb Daimler, a German produced a high speed petrol engine and in 1885 he fitted the engine to a wooden cycle.
- In the same year Karl Benz, a German fitted his petrol engine to a tricycle.

Gottlieb Daimler

- In 1886, Gottlieb Daimler made the first petrol driven car with four wheels. Karl Benz built the first Benz car in 1893.

- In the same year Charles Duryea, an American built the first gasoline powered automobile.
- The birth of the motor industry was attributed to a French company that bought the right to use Daimler's engine and produced the first factory produced car, Panhard-Hevassor.
- Henry Ford of USA, who formed the Ford Foundation, is credited with the mass production of cars.

Motor Cycle

is a two-wheeled device which is powered by gasoline. Daimler is credited with building the first wooden bicycle which he fitted with a petrol engine. The use of motor cycles has increased over the years. This is because:

- Motor cycles are less expensive and many people can afford to buy them.
- They are preferred in urban centres because they can easily go through traffic jams.
- Motor cycles can be used in small paths and therefore provide a flexible mode of transport especially in rural areas with poor roads.

Importance of Road Transport

- Road are flexible and can reach more places, including remote parts which are not served by other means of transport
- Roads are relatively cheap to construct and maintain.
- It is relatively fast
- It is ideal for personal use - personal cars are available and economical to run
- Motor vehicles are multi-purpose - they provide a variety of transport services
- It is convenient in terms of time
- Road transport complements other forms of transport

Disadvantages of Road Transport

- The growing number of vehicles increases pollution of the environment through emitions.
- The use of roads is limited in some areas because roads cannot go beyond seas and oceans
- Most means used in transporting goods on roads carry only limited amounts.
- It's prone to accidents because of poor and narrow roads, reckless drivers, unroad worthy vehicles and the large number of traffic.
- Large number of vehicles cause traffic jam in urban centres and this leads to wastage of time.
- Most roads become impassable during the rainy seasons.
- Construction of all weather roads is expensive

Impact of Modern Road Transport

- Has encouraged domestic and external trade
- Has enhanced exploitation of natural resources
- Has led to development of towns
- Earns industrialized countries a lot of foreign exchange through the sale of motor vehicles
- Road transportation services have created many job opportunities
- Has increased social interactions amongst the people

Questions on Road Transport
(a) Mention two limitations of road transport?
(b) Give two characteristics of the Macadamized roads
(c) Give three developments that have taken place in road transport system since 1750
(d) Explain why road transport is the most common in the world today
(e) Explain the impact of modern road transport
(f) What was the significance of the invention of the wheel in road transport?

R ail Transport involves the use of locomotive machine which move on parallel metallic rails to reduce friction. The development of steam engine greatly contributed to railway transport and this replaced the horse drawn carts, commonly used in the past. The development of railways is attributed to: -

- A British engineer, Richard Trevithick designed a steam engine that was small enough to be put on a track. In 1904, he bought a railway locomotive which was used as a cargo and passenger train.
- In 1812 Fenton, Murray and Woods of Leads build the John Blendkinsop locomotive
- In 1813 William Hedley built the puffing Billy
- In 814 George Stephenson invented a locomotive engine which he called the Blucher. This could pull eight wagons fully loaded with goods. He built the first public railway which operated between Stockton and Darlington. Together with his son, Robert – he built the most improved engine, the "Rocket" which moved at a speed of 48 km/h.

- In 1892 Rudolf, a German designed a heavy oil-driven engine. This was cheaper and more efficient than the coal-driven engines.
- Diesel engines were replaced by electric trains. The Siemens brothers and John Hopkinson built an electric engine in Britain in 1883.

Advantages of Railways Transport

- Railways provide a cheap way of transporting goods and people.
- It is a suitable means of transporting bulky and fragile goods like glass.
- Railways are less prone to accidents
- Railways reduce pressure on roads – hence reduce the damage caused by heavy moving vehicles.

Disadvantages of Railway Transport

- Constructing a railway line, and buying wagons and coaches is an expensive venture
- Railways are less flexible and must be supported by other modes of transport like roads.
- Though accidents are rare, when they occur they are fatal
- Smoke emitted from the trains pollute the environment
- The locomotives engines used in Kenya are slow and this discourages most people from using them.

Results of the Development of Railway Transport in Europe included:

- Railway transport led to the expansion of trade in Europe as goods were quickly transported from one point to another
- It facilitated the movement of people from one place to another – hence promoting greater interaction among people.

- Railway transport encouraged agricultural growth as it assured farmers of means of transporting their products.
- The railway transport provided employment opportunities.
- The development of railway transport led to growth and expansion of urban centers.
- It facilitated the development of industries in Europe by providing quick means of transporting raw materials and finished materials. Railway was also used for transporting the industrial workers.
- It led to environmental pollution through emission of large amount of carbon dioxide smoke into the atmosphere.
- Railway transport reduced the transportation costs of bulky goods.

Impact of Railway on Industrialization in Europe

- Railway assisted in the transportation of raw materials to the factories
- It assisted in the transportation of manufactured goods to the market
- Railway provided a fast inter city means of transport and assisted in the movement of workers to the industries
- The need for rail and trains led to the development of iron and steel industries which manufactured trains and wagons
- Need for sources of energy to power the train led to development of mining industry and HEP power plants
- Railway transport speeded up colonization of African countries by Europe – they were able to acquire raw materials and market their goods
- Railway transport assisted in the development of agriculture hence availability of raw materials for industries in Europe.

Questions on Road Railway Transport
(a) Mention the Scientist who discovered the Locomotive engine
(b) What were the results of the development of railway transport in Europe up to the end of 19th Century?
(c) Explain six ways through which the invention of the railway speeded up industrialization in Europe

WATER TRANSPORT

C anal is an artificial water way used to transport people and goods. The type of boat used in canals is the shallow type called the barge. The use of locks to raise the water levels in the canals enabled large ocean going vessels to go through the canals.

Examples of major canals in the world are:

- The Grand Canal: is 1,900 km long and took many years to build. It was constructed to link the Yangtze and Yellow Rivers in China.
- Erie Canal: is 845 km long and is used to link the Hudson River in New York with Lake Erie. The canal made New York City the port through which the products of the Great Lakes flow to Europe. It is now known as the New York State Barge.
- Suez Canal: is 195 km long and links the Mediterranean and the Red Sea. It was made by a French company under Ferdinand de' Lesseps between 1859 and 1869. The Suez shortened the route to India by 5000 km for European countries and therefore increased the volume of trade and amount of bulky goods transported along the region. The Suez Canal led to the occupation of Egypt by the British because Egypt was bankcraft after constructing the canal and sold her shares to the former.
- Panama Canal: was built between 1904 and 1914 by the government of USA to link the

Atlantic and Pacific Oceans. It shortened the long and dangerous trip around the southern tip of South America.

- St. Lawrence Seaway: is 3,800 km long and is used to connect the Great Lakes – Lake Superior, Huron, Ontario and Erie.

Reasons why Canals Were Constructed

- Canals were constructed to link the existing seas and oceans
- They shortened the existing trade routes, for example Suez Canal shortened route from Europe to the Far East by 5000 km
- They enabled easy transportation of raw materials and finished goods
- They were used for irrigation of farms, for example Egyptians and Sumerian farmers
- They supplied water to the urban areas, for example Rome
- Canals provided the cheapest means of transporting goods in bulk
- Canals were used to control floods.

Questions on Canals

(a) Name the chief engineer who constructed the Suez Canal
(b) Identify three major canals used in the world
(c) State two results of the construction of the Suez Canal
(d) Give two reasons why canals were constructed

Steamships

The development of steam ship is credited to many scientists who conducted many experiments. These included: -

- Dr. Denis Papin fitted a steam engine to a boat and sailed along River Fulda. But the boat broke down before he reached his destination, London.

- Comte d' Auxiron of France experimented with a steam boat, but it also broke down.
- In 1775 Perier managed for the first time in history to move a small boat by steam power on River Seine in Paris. The same was done by Marquis de Jouffrey, a Frenchman in 1783. He built and tried the first steam boat on River Saone.
- In 1807, an American inventor, Robert Fulton's double paddle-wheeled steamboat began operating on the Hudson River in New York
- In 1809 William Symington and Miller Pat made a steam boat. It was made of wood and coal was burnt to generate steam power to paddle the vessel's wheel
- In 1819 the Savanna became the first steam ship to cross the Atlantic Ocean.
- By 1830 several steam powered paddle wheelers were crossing the Atlantic and in 1840 the first regular scheduled steamship service began.

Ferries

are used to transport people, goods and vehicles over water places where building a bridge is difficult or would inconvenient other marine vessels plying the same route.

Ferry

Ferries are used to link Mombasa Island and the mainland. The same route is also used by other vessels coming to Mombasa.

Motor-driven ships

There are two types of ships based on the services they offer. Liners operate on regular schedules and defined routes. Their rates are advertised. The tramps have no regular schedule or route. They carry any suitable cargo between two negotiated points.

Modern Passenger Liners

are specially designed luxurious ships which carry as many as 2000 people, mostly tourists.

The use of liner ships were interrupted by the world wars. The use of aircrafts has also diminished the importance of passenger liners.

Military Vessels

are specialized ships which are used for battle. They include aircraft carriers, cruisers, destroyers, minesweepers and torpedo boats. Aircraft carriers are "floating" airports which can carry as many as 85 fighter jets. There are also submarines which can remain submerged for a long time and travel under water.

Aircraft carrier

Freight Vessels

are special vessels which are designed to carry large amounts of cargo. The container ship, for instance transport large sealed metallic containers which contain different types of goods. The containers are transported to destined areas where they are offloaded with giant cranes and reloaded on big trucks for further transportation.

Pipeline

are used to transport liquids, gases or semi solids from one place to another. They are mainly used to transport water or crude oil. Once the pipes have been laid, the transportation cost is low and the liquids are transported rapidly. Pipelines are also ideal for transporting liquids which are highly flammable, especially if they are dug dip underground. The danger with pipelines is that it can lead to uncontrollable fire, huge loses and death. Monitoring spillage and theft is also difficult.

AIR TRANSPORT

An aircraft is machine which is heavier than air, but uses its wings to fly in the air. They are used to transport people and goods across the sky. The following people contributed to the development of the aero planes:

- In 1783 the two brothers, Jacques and Montgolfiers succeeded in manning a flight using hot air balloons.
- Sir George Carley, an English scholar and inventor, built model gliders that could sail in the air in the 19th century.
- Carley ideas were adopted by Otto Lilienthal, a German who made over 2,500 glider fights.
- Pilcher added wheels to the gliders in order for them to be towed into the air.
- In 1850 John String, an English engineer built and designed power-driven planes.

- An American astronomer, Samuel Langleys perfected the power-driven airplane by making a full size airplane which he called Aerodrome, but it crushed before it was launched. He gave up his project due to the criticism by the press.

- Two weeks after Langley's disaster, on 17th December 1903, the Wright brothers, Orville and Wilbur produced the first manned aero plane. This was a wooden glider which was fitted with a petrol-driven engine and two propellers.

Wright brothers

- In 1909, Louis Bleriot of France became the first person to fly a biplane across the English Channel in 35 minutes.

Jet Engines

The earlier planes were limited in terms of speed and altitude. They were also small. This called for more inventions to solve the problems. A breakthrough was made by Frank Whittle of the Royal Air Force who invented the jet engine. Instead of using a propeller, the jet engine discharged gases to thrust it forward. The engine had great power and speed. Though Heinkel, a German made the first jet powered airplane, HE-178 in 1939, the first practical jet fighter, Lockheed P-8 was developed in 1944 by the Germans. After 1945 jet engines were put into commercial use.

The American Boeing 707 commercial flight was launched in 1958. The Boeing 747 Jumbo Jets which could carry 375 passengers and 20 tones of cargo and travel at a speed of 900 km/h was introduced in 1970. The French-British Concorde entered the market in 1972. This was a supersonic jet which could travel faster than sound.

Helicopters

Helicopters is a type of aircraft which is lifted by a set of rotor blades rather than fixed wings. The first helicopter was developed by the French in 1907, but was only lifted off the ground for a few seconds. The Germans made a more practical one in 1936 while the USA unveiled their version in 1942 during the World War II.

Today they are used to airlift people to hospitals, access more difficult spots and to conduct surveillance operations.

Advantages of Air Transport

• Air crafts facilitate the transportation of perishable goods , for instance flowers and fruits

• Aircrafts provide a faster mode of transport to facilitate movement of people, for instance during emergency situations

• They are used to spray pesticides so as to protect crops against pests and this has enhanced agricultural production

• Aircrafts facilitate space exploration for specific and military purpose

• Use of aircrafts has led to expansion of international trade and other business activities

• It has enhances wildlife conservation, for instance used in monitoring movement of animals or counting them

• Has facilitated movement of people to inaccessible areas, for instance mountain tops

• Has encouraged cultural interactions in the world (Tourism)

• It is used in aerial survey and cartography

Disadvantages of Air Transport

• It plays an instrumental role in modern warfare

• It has contributed to environmental pollution

• Though rare, air accidents are among the most fatal

• It has led to international terrorism

How Air Transport has Improved Trade between Nations

• The speed at which trade goods between nations, organizations or individuals has improved

• Transportation of urgent trade documents and messages has improved

• Air transport has enabled fast transportation of perishable foods

• It has facilitated trading activities

• Facilitates quick movement of people, for example Businessmen

---

Questions on Air Transport

(a) Give two ways in which air transport has improved trade between nations
(b) State two disadvantages of air transport
(c) Give five advantages of air transport

Space Exploration is an organized trip into the outer space where there are other planets, the moon, the sun and many other heavenly bodies. Man has for along time been preoccupied with the desire to venture into the known. This dream was realized when man developed space crafts which could land him to the moon and the satellites which could go round the sun on their own orbit, collect information and take photographs, and send them back to earth surface. Scientific discoveries in space have continued to fascinate man and wetted his appetite for further research. World space agencies like United States National Aeronautics (NASA) and European Space Agency (ESA) still continue to conduct studies in the outer space.

Astronauts in space

Challenges Faced in Space Exploration

- Space exploration is expensive because of the special equipment and clothing which are required.
- There are deadly hazards such as solar and cosmic radiation.
- Extreme temperatures and light ranging from extreme darkness and bright sunlight.
- Space craft accidents are deadly when they occur.
- About 1,200 satellites in space are not functioning and this has raised concern over space garbage.

Importance of Space Exploration to Man

- Space crafts continue to provide more information about the conditions in the atmosphere and outer space
- Reports derived from the weather satellites can be used to warn people of impending catastrophes e.g. floods
- Communication satellites are used to relay television programmes and telephone calls over long distances
- Information about space makes it possible to predict changes in the weather pattern
- Space exploration leads to improvement in aviation industry
- It has contributed to the development of advanced air force weapons

---

Questions on Space Exploration
(a) Mention one person who were among the first to land on the moon
(b) Describe the challenges faced in space exploration
(c) Explain six reasons why space exploration is important

7 DEVELOPMENT ON SCEINCE AND INDUSTRY

EARLY SOURCES OF ENERGY
For time immemorial human beings have depended on their muscles to work. During the early Stone Age period, they had well developed muscles to enable them to perform certain difficult tasks. Since then, a lot has changed. Human beings have developed new and increasingly more efficient tools and machines. Most of the tools and machines require few, but highly skilled manpower to operate and other sources of energy.

Wood
is consumed directly in the form of firewood or indirectly in the form of charcoal. Almost 90 % of the countries in the developing world still rely on fire wood to cook their food. The percentage is much bigger in rural areas than in urban centres where other forms of energy like gas, electricity and oil are increasingly being used to replace firewood or charcoal. Most people still prefer firewood because it is a comparatively cheaper source of energy and is also renewable. The continued use of firewood has rapidly depleted the forest reserves in most developing countries and this has become a matter of concern to the environmental conservatists.

Wind
The Monsoon or trade winds - was used in the past to propel sailing ship across the oceans. In countries like China, wind mills were used to grind maize and to process food. In Africa it was used for winnowing while in Netherlands, the Dutch used the wind mills to pump out water from the dykes. In some Scandinavian countries and Asia, wind mills are still used to generate electricity. The main advantage of wind is that it is a cheap and renewable source of energy. But it is an irregular and unreliable source of energy which keeps on fluctuating. Harnessing wind for electricity is therefore very difficult.

Water
In the past water was used to turn water wheels. They in turn moved the grindstones which were used for grinding grains. In England the water wheels were used in the textile and paper industries to turn the spinning machines. Today running water from rivers is used to turn metallic turbines which are used to generate hydroelectric power. The use of rivers to produce hydroelectricity is affected by seasonal fluctuation in water levels in the reservoirs and siltation of dams which reduce their capacity to carry enough water to turn the turbines.

NEW SOURCES OF ENERGY
Coal is a mineral which is mined from the ground or near the surface. There are three types of coal: - anthracite, bituminous and lignite. Abraham Darby invented the process of turning coal into coke in 1709. By heating coal in an oven, he was able to removed combustible and explosive gases from it. The coke formed produced intense heat which was used for smelting iron. Coal was the main source of industrial energy in Europe from the twentieth century. Apart from producing energy in the industries, it was also used to:

- Heat water which was used to produce steam
- Provide light.
- Provide raw materials in the manufacture of dye and pharmaceutical products.
- To drive locomotive engines and steamships.

The advantages of using coal as a source of energy during the industrial revolution period included: -

- Coal was a cheap source of energy.
- It was readily available in large quantities.

- Coal burnt for long hours.
- Coal was more efficient than other sources of energy at that time.

The limitations of using coal included:
- It was bulky hence difficult to transport
- Coal had low calorific value.
- Environmental hazards – produced too much smoke and this polluted the environment.
- There were many accidents in coal mines - many miners lost their lives when the mines collapsed.

Steam Power

When water is heated to the boiling point, it turns to steam. This steam has been used by human being for a long time. Steam was used to:
- Open massive doors in the ancient Egypt.
- Turn turbines which generated power for the spinning and weaving industries in Europe
- Generated energy to drive heavy machinery in the factories.
- Pump water out of the mines by the miners
- Drive steamships and locomotives.
- Turn turbines and generate electric energy.

Many people are credited for harnessing steam power in this way. They include:
- Around A.D., 100 Hero, a Greek scientist developed a steam engine for the first time.
- In the 16th century, Thomas Savery produced a steam- engine which could pump out water from the coal mines.
- In 1712, Thomas Newcomen improved Savery's steam-engine, but his new design was still too big, ineffective and wasted a lot of energy.

- In 1764, James Watt improved Newcomen's engine to make it more efficient. Newcomen's engines became very popular in Britain that by 1800, about 320 of his engines were in use in Britain.
- In 1801, Richard Trevithick installed one of the Watt's engines in a road vehicle and three years later he produced a steam-driven locomotive which ran on rails.
- In 1830, George Stephenson improved on Trevithick's work and invented the first steam locomotive, the "Rocket".

The development of steam engine contributed to the growth of industries in Europe during the 19th century in many ways. These included: -
- Steam engines facilitated faster transportation of raw materials and finished industrial products.
- Facilitated faster transportation of industrial workers.
- Provided a source of energy in the factories, for example the spinning factory.
- It was used to pump water out of the mines and this facilitated mining activity.

Petroleum

is a highly inflammable liquid which is distilled from crude oil. This oil, which is mined from the ground, is formed from the remains of organism which lived many years ago. Before it was established in the university as a lubricant and a fuel, the crude oil was taken to be a natural substance which affected farming in America.

A concerned American farmer, Bissel took the sample for analysis and commissioned Drake to drill the oil in USA. In the 19th century new methods of distilling this crude oil to separate it into petrol, paraffin, diesel, grease and natural gas came up. The use of petroleum became widespread after the invention of combustion engine by Gottlieb Daimler. Today most oil is drilled in the Middle Eastern countries like Kuwait, Iraq, Iran and Saudi Arabia. Other producers include Angola, Nigeria, Egypt, Libya, Tunisia and Algeria.

Uses of petroleum
- Petroleum is used to power vehicles, machinery, motor cycles, aero planes and ship.
- It is used to generate electricity
- It is used to run engines in industries
- Tar, a by-product of petroleum is used in tarmacking of roads
- Grease is used as a lubricant
- Certain petroleum chemicals are used in making of drugs, fertilizer, synthetic fibres and plastics.

Disadvantages of petroleum
- Petroleum is highly inflammable and leads to huge loses and death if handled carelessly
- Emition from vehicles pollute the environment
- Importing oil drain countries resources

Electricity
Michael Faraday - an English scientist, discovered electricity in 1831. His principle of electromagnetism led to the development of dynamo and electric motor. In the initial stages steam was used to drive dynamos. But later oil, coal and running water was used to drive the dynamos. Apart from Rivers - HEP, electricity is today also generated from geothermal plants, solar panels and nuclear reactors.

Electricity is a reliable source of power and a non pollutant. It is switched on and instantly begins to work. Many appliances used at home today use electricity to function. Electricity is used for:
- Lighting the homes, offices and factories
- Heating houses and cooking
- Powering machines in the factories
- Powering electric trains, trams and electric cars.
- Powering communication gadgets

Solar Energy
Is a clean, readily available and non pollutant energy obtained directly from the sun. It is traditionally used for drying clothes, firewood, fish and grains. Solar energy has been used for many activities over the years. These include:
- In 1714, Antoine Lavoiser made a solar furnace which could melt metals.
- By 1880, an engine using solar power was used to run a printing press in Paris.
- By 1900 many Americans were using solar water heaters.
- In 1954 the first solar cell was made to turn sunlight into electricity.

Uses of Solar Energy
- Heating and lighting houses
- Boiling water for domestic and industrial use
- Cooking food using solar cookers
- Evaporating salty water to produce salt crystals
- Drying agricultural products.

Atomic Energy
This form of energy is credited to Antoine Henri Beckquerel, a French physicist who in 1896 discovered that uranium produces energy waves. This process is called radioactivity, a term which was coined by a French couple – Marie and Pierre Curie. The couple discovered that two more chemical elements – radium and polonium, also produced radiation. In 1938, Hahn and Stressman discovered the process of atomic fission. Through this process atomic energy is produced when atoms of radioactive elements like uranium are split. In

1942, a group of scientists led by Enrico-Fermi – at the University of Chicago, built the first nuclear research station. This produced the first nuclear reactor and later the atomic bomb which the Americans used at Hiroshima and Nagasaki in 1945 during the World War II.

Uses of Atomic Energy
- Atomic energy is used by many countries like USA, Britain, Russia and France to develop atomic weapons
- It is used in some countries like Belgium and France to generate electricity
- The Americans and Russians use it to power submarines
- It is used to produce radioactive elements for medical use

Disadvantages of Atomic Energy
- Nuclear weapons are quite fatal if used in warfare like was the case in Japan
- Radioactivity endangers plant and animal life
- Radioactive accidents like the Chernobyl disaster which occurred in Russia in 1986 claimed many lives

Questions on Early Sources of Energy
(a) Identify the main source of industrial energy in Europe from the twentieth century
(b) State two disadvantages of the use of coal in industries during the industrial revolution
(c) Mention any four advantages of using coal as a source of energy during the industrial revolution period
(d) Mention two ways how the development of steam engine contributed to the growth of industries in Europe during the 19th Century?
(e) List two shortcoming of the use of steam engines in motor vehicles in the 19th century

USES OF METALS IN AFRICA

There are two distinct ages of metals in Africa, the Bronze and Iron Age. Prior to this era, man used stone tools. These were later abandoned because:
- Metal tools were more durable and did not break easily
- The cutting edges of metal tools could be sharpened
- Malleable metals could be melted and re-worked into different shapes and uses
- Metals were not prone to waste; broken pieces would be melted and re-worked

Gold

was often found near the surface and sometimes in pure form. Since it was relatively easy to find, gold became the first metal to be used by mankind. Gold being malleable could easily be re-worked into different shapes without melting it. Tools made from gold were too heavy and could easily break. Gold was also found in few places. In African gold was used in Wangara in Ghana, Central Africa, Egypt and Meroe.

Uses of Gold
- Gold was used to make ornaments and for decoration. It was used in Egypt for making jewellery, rings and bangles.
- It was used for making weapons like swords and knives.
- Utensils like plates, vases and drinking vessels were made of gold especially for the rich.
- Handles of swords and knives were also made from gold among the rich in Egypt.
- Gold was used for making coins in Egypt.
- It was a major item of trade in West African and Zimbabwe
- Gold was used as a measure of wealth in Egypt.

Copper

Gold was replaced with copper because the tools and weapons made from it were too soft. Copper was equally found near the surface and in fairly pure form. Though soft, the tools and weapons made from copper were more durable than those made from gold. The earliest people to use raw copper were the Egyptians. As early as 3000 B.C., they had already started smelting copper. This was done in a potter's charcoal kiln until the ore melted to liquid form. Later, copper was mixed with other metals to form alloys. A mixture of copper and zinc formed brass, while that with tin formed bronze.

Uses of Copper in Africa

- Copper was used to make tools such as axes and chisels
- It was used to make art work
- Was used for ornaments such as bangles, rings and wire chains
- Utensils and containers were made from copper.
- Copper was used as a trade item
- Copper was mixed with other metals to form stronger alloys like brass and bronze.

Bronze

was an alloy which is formed by mixing copper and tin. Tools and weapons made from bronze were much harder than those made from pure copper. The use of bronze was not widespread. It was used in Nigeria among the Yoruba; in Benin – which became the centre of bronze; Asante in Ghana and in Egypt.

In Egypt bronze was used to: -

- Cast the statues of the Pharaohs.
- Make special tools for cutting and shaping huge stones for making pyramids.
- Make tools such as hoes, chisel and adzes were made from bronze.
- Make weapons such as sword, daggers, axes and spears.
- Make items for decoration

In Benin bronze was used to: -

- Store wealth by leaders in terms of objects of art and decorations.
- Making weapons like shields, spears, swords and spear heads.
- Making sculpture and decorations of the kings' palaces.
- Making royal regalia
- Making ornaments
- Making statures for rulers

Disadvantages of Bronze

- The tools lost their sharp edge and quickly became blunt
- Bronze was expensive because the mixture was acquired through trade
- It was difficult to get appropriate proportion for the mixture.

Iron

was extracted as ore from the ground and smelted in a furnace under high temperatures to remove any impurities from it. Iron, produced from smelting ore, is the hardest and most reliable metal. It replaced bronze tools and weapons because:

- Iron was easily available.
- Iron tools and weapons were harder than bronze
- It gave a sharper cutting edge
- Iron tools did not became blunt easily

The Hittites who lived in the present day Turkey were probably the first people to smelt and use iron. This was around 1500 B.C. The idea of iron working then spread to West Asia, the Mediterranean region and Europe. It is believed that the Persians introduced this technology to North Africa before 900 B.C. By 5th century A.D. Iron work was already a common activity in Meroe (Sudan) from where it spread to Ethiopia. Around 580 B.C. iron work had spread to Taruga in West Africa from Carthage and Tunisia in North Africa.

Two theories are used to explain the origin and spread of iron working technology in Africa. These are: -

One area theory

According to this theory iron work probably developed independently in specific areas. This is evidenced by the archaeological work in Buhaya (Tanzania) which predates many sites in Africa. The Buhaya iron work is associated with a unique pottery style known as the Urewe-ware. The smelting styles used in Meroe and Taruga in West Africa were also different.

Diffusion Theory

It is said that iron work was first introduced in North Africa from the Middle East by the Phoenicians and the Assyrians. It eventually spread to west, east, central and southern Africa.

From North Africa Iron technology diffused to the south through several routes:

- From North Africa its spread was facilitated by the Pheonesians who had colonies in the western side of the Mediterranean Coast. From here the Berbers spread the technology to West Africa through trade

- It diffused from Egypt to Nubia through the Nile Valley Route. The Nubian Kingdom of Kush controlled Egypt by 722 B.C. During this time they interacted with the Assyrians who had acquired the Iron technology. When they moved to Meroe they developed large scale Iron industry at about 500 B.C.

- It spread through the Red Sea to the Horn of Africa and then to East Africa. It's argued that the Kingdom of Axum had contacts with India and China, through the Red Sea, which were using Iron.

- From West Africa to East Africa through the migration of the Bantus.

Factors which facilitated the spread of iron working knowledge in Africa include:

- Trade between Africa and Mesopotamia. The North African traders who traded across the Sahara Desert spread the iron smelting skills to the Sudan region.

- The Bantu and the Southern Cushites spread the iron working knowledge to other parts of Africa through their migration.

- It was spread through warfare by the Hittites who invaded Egypt.

- Development of agriculture led to the invention of better tools to improve food production

Uses of Iron

The following were the uses of Iron: -

- Iron technology led to increased efficiency in clearing forests for settlement and food production

- It better placed man to defend himself using iron weapons

- It enabled communities like the Bantus to expand into new areas

- Mortality rate declined leading to increased population.

- It enabled man to build ship. This increased trade
- It led to emergence of cities and towns
- Iron bars were exchanged with other commodities by the iron workers.
- It was used as medium of exchange.

The discovery of Iron working in Africa affected the peoples' lives in the continent in a number of ways. These included:

- Use of better tools – hoes and axes, enabled people to clear bushes and cultivate more land. This led to increased food production.
- Increased food production led to increased population. This forced people to migrate to find new areas for settlement and agricultural activities.
- Iron working centres grew up into town like Cairo, Meroe and Axum.
- Iron tools were used as trade goods between communities leading to expansion of trade
- Iron weapons enabled people to migrate because they could defend themselves against the enemies.
- Production of Iron weapons lead to increased warfare between communities
- Use of Iron weapons made some communities to conquer neighbouring communities and this led to creation of empires or kingdoms
- Iron smelting led to the rise of specialized people, the blacksmiths. These people gained prestige and respect in the society.

Questions on Uses of Metal in Africa

(a) Identify two earliest Iron Age sites in Africa

(b) State two factors that facilitated the spread of iron working knowledge in Africa

(c) Identify two theories which are used to explain the spread of Iron in Africa

(d) Give two advantages of iron over bronze as a raw material for making tools and weapons

(e) Explain how the discovery of iron in Africa affected the people s' lives in the continent

(f) Give two ways in which the knowledge of iron working helped in the migration of the Bantu.

SCIENTIFIC REVOLUTION (RENAISSANCE) Renaissance was a cultural movement which took place from 14th to 17th century first in Italy (Florence) and later to other parts of Europe. New insights and knowledge, which led to many innovations and inventions, were gained. This period is called renaissance or "rebirth" of knowledge.

Many theories have been advanced to account for its origin and characteristics. The focus has been on:

- The social and civil peculiarities of Florence at the time
- The political structure of Florence
- The patronage of its dominant family and
- The migration of Greek scholars to Italy following the fall of Constantinople at the hands of the Turks.

The Renaissance scholars focused on literature and historical texts. This was in contrast to the medieval scholars who concentrated on studying Greek and Arabic works of Natural Science, Philosophy and Mathematics. It was an attempt by intellectuals to study and improve the spiritual and physical world through the revival of ideas from antiquity and through novel approaches to thought.

SCIENTIFIC INVENTIONS

Agriculture

A number of people made different inventions in the field of agriculture. These included:

- Robert Bakewell (1725 – 1795) invented selective breeding of livestock. He developed new breeds of cattle like Hereford, Ayrshire and Aberdeen Angus.
- In 1843, Sir John Bennet Laws set up a super phosphate fertilizer factory in London to manufacture fertilizer
- In 1701, Jethro Tull invented the seed drill which was used to plant crops in regular rows rather than the wasteful broadcasting.
- In 1837, Cyrus McComic invented the reaper
- In 1786, Andrew Meikles made the mechanical thresher. This replaced the sickle which had been used for a long time to harvest corn.
- In 1810, Nicholas Appert developed a canning process. He stated that when food was boiled then stored in airtight tins it would last for many years without going bad.
- Louis Pasteur (1890 – 1960) discovered that most diseases are caused by bacteria and therefore sterilization of food such as milk though boiling could help to keep it bacteria free hence last longer in fresh state.
- In 1837, John Deere, invented a steel plough which was much stronger than the iron plough which had been used over the years.

Impact of Scientific Inventions on Agriculture

- Modern methods of farming like using certified seeds, fertilizer and pesticides to control pests led to increased food production.
- Scientific research in the field of agriculture has been stepped up in colleges and other institutions. Through this initiative, better quality seeds and high yielding varieties of animals, have been developed.
- Preservation of food through canning and refrigeration has encouraged farming and reduced wastage.
- Agriculture has been diversified through biotechnology
- Farming has changed from small to large scale
- Increase in consumption of chemically treated food has increased certain diseases, for example cancer

- Some pesticides are toxic and harmful to man and other organisms which inhabit the earth
- Continuous use of pesticides has led to pests which are resistant
- Increased use of fertilizer makes the soil to lose fertility
- Biotechnology is threatening traditionally produced food
- Many questions have arisen about the quality of the biotechnologically manufactured organisms and food

---

Positive Impact of Scientific Inventions

(a) The invention and use of machines in factories led to mass production of goods.
(b) The science of electronics has led to the production and use of computers in processing information
(c) The discovery of atomic power (nuclear) led to increased power generation for industrial use and electronic trains.
(d) Scientific research led to the production of alternative sources of energy for use in industries, for example gasohol, methanol, and solar energy.
(e) Scientific research has revolutionalised the transport industry through the invention of motor cars, electronic trains and supersonic jets
(f) Science has led to the development of satellites which are used for space exploration, weather forecast and spying purposes.

M edicine
In the 19th century many inventions were made in the field of medicine which greatly reduced the rate of mortality.

- Joseph Leister discovered the use of carbonic acid to sterilize surgical instruments and to kill the microbes around a wound after an operation. He also developed an antiseptic spray for cleaning the air during operations. These discoveries made operations to be much more safer

- The grouping of blood into various blood groups by Land Steiner in 1900 facilitated blood transfusion and the storage for transfusion in a later date.
- The discovery of X-ray by a German called Wilhem Roengen enabled scientists to view the bone structure and internal organs of human body to fast truck treatment.
- Penicillin, an antibiotic discovered by Dr. Alexander Fleming in 1939 prolonged life by treating bacterial infections.
- The Polio vaccine, discovered in 1954 by Jonas Edward, reduced infections by polio.
- Organ transplant surgery by Dr. Christian Barnard, A South African surgeon, in 1967 succeeded in prolonging life of kidney patients.
- The discovery of Heart valve in 1961 prolonged life through replacement of defective valves.
- The discovery of life support machines and kidney dialysis machines (1943) prolonged the life of many patients, especially those of kidney ailment
- The use of anti-retroviral drugs has prolonged the life of AID/HIV sufferers

Impact of Scientific Inventions on Medicine

- Childless couples are able to have babies through external fertilization, for example test tube babies
- Plastic surgery is used to improve the facial look of people and to repair damaged skin
- Patients with organ failure, for example heart and kidney are now able to benefit from heart and kidney transplants
- Vaccines are now used to prevent the spread of many diseases, for example polio and small pox which were once regarded as killer diseases

- Surgical operations are now done in cleaner and safer environments and they are less painful
- Bacterial germs that cause diseases, for example cholera, tuberculosis and anthrax have been isolated and this has reduce death caused by those diseases
- The causes of diseases have been identified to certain bacteria and germs, for example anopheles mosquitoes carry parasites that cause malaria. The fight to eradicate malaria has therefore shifted to the elimination of mosquitoes
- Discoveries in medicine have led to increased life expectancy of man.
- It has led to the production of advanced medical equipment.
- The manufacture of various drugs has been facilitated by scientific discoveries.

Factors which undermined scientific revolution in developing countries

(a) High level of illiteracy and ignorance
(b) Inadequate funds to invest in scientific research
(c) Political instability which undermine peace necessary for carrying out scientific research
(d) Over dependency of the developing countries on developed nations has discouraged them from being innovative
(e) Brain drain to developed world has reduced the number of trained personnel in developing countries
(f) Educational system which do no lay emphasis on science subjects inhibits scientific innovation and creativity in developing countries

Questions on Scientific Revolution (Renaissance)

(a) State two factors that facilitated scientific revolution in Europe from the 14th century
(b) State three factors that facilitated the scientific revolution in Europe in the 19TH century
(c) State one contribution of Joseph leister in the field of medicine in the 19th century
(d) State two inventions that improved textile manufacturing industry in Britain during industrial revolution
(e) State two scientific discoveries during nineteenth century which contributed to food preservation
(f) Discuss the impact of scientific inventions on agriculture
(g) What are the consequences of scientific inventions on medicine?
(h) Describe the scientific inventions of the twentieth century which have led to a reduction in death rates?
(i) Explain the positive impact of scientific inventions on industry

INDUSTRIAL REVOLUTION

Prior to the 17th century, most industries were home based (cottage) or located near sources of raw materials. Family labour and natural sources of energy like water and wind were used. Production was done in small scale.

Features of Industrial Revolution in Britain

- Increased use of machines to replace human labour
- The use of steam power to replace water, wind and animal power
- Increased exploitation and use of coal, iron and steel
- The rise of factory system in towns instead of home based (cottage) industries
- Development of other forms of transport, for example railway, road and water
- Improved living standards and human population

- Development of trade due to surplus production
- The rise of modern capitalism which increased wealth
- Growth of Trade Unions to cater for the needs of workers

Uses of Iron and Steel during Industrial Revolution
During the Industrial Revolution, a lot of iron was required for: the construction of railway lines, bridges, cars and ship; manufacture of machines; reinforcement of concrete in buildings and roofing of houses; and making of food containers and utensils. The use of Iron was, however restrictive because it was too heavy, easily got rusty and was not strong enough. This forced scientists to conduct many experiments with iron to harden it. For example:

- In 1856, Henry Bessemer, an Englishman produced steel out of iron and carbon.
- In the same year, Fredrick Siemens and his brother William invented the regenerative gas furnace
- In 1864, Pierre Emile Martin - of France, invented a method of making steel by smelting scrap steel in a bath of pig iron heated in a Siemens' regenerative furnace.

Steel which was the product of these experiments was a mixture (alloy) of iron and carbon. It was lighter, more flexible, stronger and harder than iron. Different qualities of steel could be attained by adding various metals, for instance chromium, vanadium and tungsten. To make stainless steel which is largely used for making cutlery, an alloy of steel and chromium is used. Iron was replaced by steel in the 19th century.

Industrial Revolution in Britain
first began in Britain before spreading to other parts of the continental Europe. Factors which favoured the development of industries in Britain by 1850 included:

- Britain had abundant resources of energy, for example coal.
- Existence of a large population in Britain provided steady market for the manufactured goods.
- She had wide external market for her industrial goods in her numerous colonies abroad.
- Britain had large sources of iron - ore for heavy industries.
- Existence of cottage industries which acted as a base for industrial expansion.
- Displacement of people from rural areas as a result of the Agrarian Revolutions created a large pool of labourers.
- There were many entrepreneurs in Britain who were willing to invest in the industries.
- Political stability and strong leadership which existed at the time, created conducive environment for investment.
- Well developed transport and communication network, for example railway, canals and roads facilitated distribution of raw materials and finished products.
- Agrarian Revolution increased food for industrial workers and raw materials for industries.
- Scientific innovations of the time, led to the improvement and expansions of industries.
- Existing banks and insurance systems gave financial help and security to the industrialists.
- Britain had a strong navy which protected her merchants abroad.
- Britain's policy of free trade encouraged industrialization.
- Britain had accumulated a lot of wealth from her trading activities abroad

Problems which industrial workers experienced during the industrial revolution in Britain included:-

- Low wages demoralized the workers
- The industrial workers were exposed to dangerous machines, chemicals and earsplitting noise
- Diseases like cholera, dysentery and typhoid attacked the workers due to the poor living conditions
- Environmental pollution resulted from smoke and the industrial waste matters
- Overcrowding resulted in the deterioration of health and unhygienic conditions of living
- Lack of insurance cover led to the suffering of affected workers in the risky working environments
- Long hours deprived people of leisure and rest hence reduction in their efficiency
- Children and women, who provided labour in the factories, were greatly exploited and over worked
- Industrial revolution led to social stratification between the poor working group and the rich employers

Inventions that improved textile manufacturing industry in Britain
(a) The flying shuttle (spinning machine) by John Kay.
(b) The Water Frame by Richard Arkwright
(c) Spinning Mule by Samuel Crompton.
(d) The cylindrical calico printing machine by Thomas Bell.
(e) The steam Power Loom for weaving by Edmund Cartwright.
(f) The Cotton Gin by Eli Whiney.

Questions on Industrial Revolution in Continental Europe
(a) Give two characteristic of early Industries in Britain
(b) Describe the working condition of factory workers in Britain during the Industrial Revolution
(c) Describe the characteristics of industrial revolution
(d) What factors favoured the development of industries in Britain by 1850?

INDUSTRIAL REVOLUTION IN CONTINENTAL EUROPE

Industrialization lagged behind in continental Europe because:

- Political upheavals in Germany, France and Italy created instability in those countries.
- The peasant farmers failed to provide the domestic market due to the feudal economy
- Skills in science and technology lagged behind in continental Europe
- There was inadequate capital for the industrial expansion due to the feudal economy
- There was inadequate raw materials for the industries in many parts of the continental Europe
- There was lack of enough enterprising class of people in continental Europe

Factors which favoured industrial revolution in continental Europe included: -

- Abolition of feudalism created political stability in Europe
- Agrarian Revolution ensured that continental Europe had adequate raw materials

- The rapid population growth in continental Europe provided the much needed labour force
- Existence of banking and insurance boosted the growth of industries
- There was adequate market, both locally and abroad
- Most European governments supported efforts to industrialize
- New skills in science and technology encouraged industrialization
- Countries in Europe had various sources of energy, for example coal

> **How presence of colonies contributed to industrialization in Europe**
> (a) Colonies provided an additional market for European industrial products such as cloth and spirits.
> (b) Colonies were sources of industrial raw materials like cotton, palm oil and sisal.
> (c) Colonies were used as spheres of influence where European traders sold their goods and rich merchants invested their surplus funds.

Effects of Industrialization in Europe
Economic Effects

- Machines were highly automated and this replaced the human labour
- Large scale production of a wide variety of goods led to increased trading activities, both locally and abroad.
- Transport and communication network improved to ease the movement of labourers to the factories and the transportation of both raw materials and finished products.
- Europe amassed a lot of wealth from the sales of the industrial products abroad.
- The Economies of European countries became more diversified and vibrant.
- Industrialization created job opportunities for the displaced people from the rural areas.

- Theire was increased exploitation of natural resources
- Industrialization increased demand for raw materials from within and in overseas colonies
- It led to the development of science and technology

Social Effects

- There was migration from rural areas to urban centres and this caused overcrowding in towns
- Population pressure in towns led to inadequate amenities like housing and health centres
- Pollution increased due to careless disposal of industrial effluents
- There was increased unemployment and social vices
- Industrialization led to the rise of social classes in Europe
- Industrialization was marked by increased gender inequality in Europe

Political Effects

- There was increased class struggle between the rich and the poor who were greatly exploited
- Industrialization led to eventual colonization of sources for raw materials and markets
- There was a change in political leadership from the monarchy to the rich middle class
- Trade Union movements were formed in Europe during the 19th century to fight for the welfare of workers and to enable them to collectively negotiate for better terms of service with the employers.

Impact of industrial revolution on urbanization in Europe

(a) The establishment of industrial centers created new jobs opportunities where many people were attracted to work.

(b) The industrial revolution brought in new discoveries which improved transport and communication systems, thus facilitating the movement of people to towns.

(c) The emergence of industrial centers opened up other commercial activities which attracted many people.

(d) Use of machines in production made many people to lose their jobs in the cottage industry. They migrated to urban centers to look for jobs.

(e) Industrial revolution led to enormous expansion of trade and many people were attracted to the centers of trading activities

Questions on Industrial Revolution in Continental Europe

(e) Give one main reason why trade union movements were formed in Europe during the nineteenth century

(f) State two problems which industrial workers experienced during the industrial revolution

(g) Give three reasons that led to the delay of industrialization in continental Europe

(h) State two ways how overseas colonies contribute to the expansion of industries in Europe

(i) Give one use of Iron during the Industrial Revolution

(j) Give three negative effects of the industrial revolution in Europe in the 19th C

(k) State five factors that favoured industrial revolution in continental Europe

(l) State five economic effects of industrialization in Europe

(m) State five social problems of industrialization in Europe

8 RISE OF MODERN POWERS

JAPAN

Factors which led to the emergence of Japan as an industrial power after the Second World War included: -

- Education: had emphasis on technical training.
- Japanese work ethics: discouraged idleness and encouraged hard work.
- Government policy: granted subsidies to industrial entrepreneurs to motivate them to work hard and caution them from uncertainties
- Labour: had abundant supply of skilled man power with industrial know how.
- Availability of capital from local and foreign investors, especially the USA.
- Financial support which was provided after the Second World War (the Marshall plan) stimulated industrial growth of Japan.
- Availability of energy, for example H.E.P, nuclear and solar stimulated industrial growth of Japan.
- Elaborate transport and communication system facilitated easy distribution of finished products and transportation of raw materials to the factories
- Political stability of Japan: after World War II Japan has kept away from any involvement in war and concentrated her efforts in industrialization
- Good industrial relations: she has enjoyed few strikes and industrial unrests.
- Japanese goods are cheap and attract a wide market internationally
- Open minded economic policy
- Scarce farming land and poor topography has forced Japan to concentrate in industries.
- Foreign investments, for example Japan invest in foreign countries and this earns her a lot of revenue which she has injected in her industries at home.

GERMANY

Prior to 1871 Germany was referred to as Prussia and the German speaking people were scattered in different small states with weak economies. After the defeat of France in the Franco-Prussian war (1870 – 71) Otto Von Bismarck united all the German states and formed a much more powerful state called Germany. She grabbed Alsace and Lorraine, which were rich in minerals and embanked on an aggressive industrialization programme. Factors which enabled Germany to attain an industrial status by the start of 20th century included:

- Establishment of customs union eliminated trade barriers and encouraged free trade among the German states. The creation of the union also facilitated the transportation of goods in the region.
- Presence of energy source, for example coal from the Ruhr region, H.E.P. and atomic energy to power the industries.
- Abundant mineral resources such as coal and iron. These were used to spur the development of heavy industries like the steel rolling.
- Improved railway lines and canals ensured easy distribution of finished products and raw materials to the factories
- West Germany was given a lot of foreign aids from USA after the 1st World War to reconstruct her economy
- High population of skilled and wealthy citizens who offered labour and market
- Mechanization of agricultural production – left people free to offer labour in industries
- After unification of German states in 1871, she enjoyed a long period of stability under the able leadership of Otto Von Bismarck

- Government supported local and international investors
- She enjoys large external market in Europe because of her centrality and quality products.

UNITED STATES OF AMERICA

Industrialization began in the mid 19th century and by the mid 20th century USA had emerged not only as one of the major industrial powers, but the only super power after the disintegration of USSR in 1990. The factors which led to the emergence of USA as an industrial power included: -

- Existence of large mineral deposits, for example coal, iron and tin for use in industries.
- Labour - both skilled and unskilled - was readily available from immigrant workers
- The development of efficient transport and communication network enhanced economic growth.
- Existence of enterprising entrepreneurs who have invested in the country enabled the United States of America to enjoy a monopoly of the world's economic systems.
- Existence of ready market at home and abroad for American products stimulated industrial growth.
- The USA has experienced relatively fewer strikers and industrial growth.
- The aggressive foreign investments policy has enabled her to dominate world economic system and also to attract foreign investment.
- The collapse of European economies during the 2nd World War enabled the USA to extend here influence to Europe and other parts of the world.
- Technological advancement has enabled the USA to dominate world economy. Scientific innovations prompted industrialization

- Long periods of political stability gave investors security and confidence.
- Availability of energy, for example coal, oil and natural gas etc.
- Stable banking and insurance services supported the entrepreneurs.
- USA philosophy of capitalism encouraged investment and hard work.

Questions on Emergence of Modern Powers

(a) Identify one main drawback to industrialization in Germany before 1870

(b) Give two ways in which World War II contribute to industrialization in Japan

(c) Explain six factors which led to the emergence of Japan as an industrial power after the Second World War

(d) Give five factors which led to the rise of Germany as an industrial power

(e) Explain six factors which led to the emergence of USA as an industrial power

---

INDUSTRIALIZATION IN THE THIRD WORLD COUNTRIES

Third world countries are also known as developing countries. They form the bulk of the poor nations and are mostly found in Africa, Latin (South) America and some parts of Asia. Though a good number of these countries are now almost in an advanced stage of industrial take off, some - especially those found in Africa, have continued to stagnate. This is attributed to the following: -

- Lack of capital to invest in industries due to high level of poverty
- Lack of skills and technological knowledge because majority of the people in third world countries are illiterate or semi illiterate.
- Industries from developed countries have a competitive edge over those in developing

countries and this has made most of them to collapse.

- Lack of market due to low purchasing power of the citizens
- Political instability creates unhealthy environment for local and foreign investment.
- Poor government economic policies like over protecting their industries have stalled their growth and made most of the industries to be uncompetitive.
- Colonialism – over exploitation of their economic resources during colonial era and relegating most of them to producers of cheap raw materials and consumers of expensive goods from the west has greatly contributed to their backwardness.
- In a bid to fight poverty and sustain their fast growing populations, the governments have diverted their resources to providing basic services rather than investing in industries.
- Corruption and mismanagement of industries leads to collapse of the already existing industries
- Many countries lack adequate sources of energy
- Poor disaster management strategy
- HIV/AIDS pandemic which is claiming the lives of many workers.

Poor transport network is a major bottleneck to industrialization in the 3rd world countries. This is because the poor infrastructure: -

- Causes delay in marketing goods, especially the perishable type.
- Causes delays in supply of industrial raw materials.
- Increases the cost of supplying industrial raw materials to the factories.

Impact of Industrialization in 3rd World Countries

- Industrialization has enabled most third world countries to manufacture their own goods
- It has created job opportunities in those countries and this has led to high standards of living
- Encouraged external trade between the 3rd world countries of the world as well as internal trade
- Facilitated acquisition of foreign exchange through the exportation of manufactured products
- Facilitated the diversification of the economy of the 3rd world countries
- Encouraged urbanization
- Led to the development of transport and communication, for example roads
- Increased agricultural production because farmers are assured of a ready market in the agro based industries
- Has led to the provision of social amenities such as schools and hospitals

BRAZIL is the fourth largest country in the world after Canada, China and USA. Among the third world nations, she is leading in terms of industrial development. Her industries can be grouped into the following sectors:

- Petroleum and petrochemical industries.
- Motor vehicle industry.
- Aircraft and aerospace industry.
- Electricity generation industry.

Factors which led to industrialization in Brazil included: -

- Development of agriculture: coffee processing has been Brazil's leading industry and export earner for a long time
- Natural resources: vast forest belts provide raw materials for lumbering industry. Other minerals are iron ore, manganese and coal

The Barons

- Capital: the state provided capital for investment in transport and energy sector. This increased industrial investment
- Good transport and communication: there are good roads and railway network connecting different towns
- Foreign aid: Brazil received financial aid from USA which she invested in Iron and Steel Industry. She also encouraged foreign investment
- Government policy: Between 1930 and 1945 President Vargas nationalized major industries so that the state could supervise them effectively
- Banking facilities: They provided loans to industrialists
- The out break of World War II forced Brazil to manufacture its own goods because of the difficulty in importation
- Market: Her large population provided ready domestic market
- Development plan: 1956 -60 five year plan emphasized increased production of energy for example coal, oil and HEP.: It also encouraged the starting of new industries and expansion of the old ones

Problems that Hinder Industrial Expansion in Brazil include:

- Lack of labour: Population is low in the south hence Brazil's inability to fully exploit her resources
- High poverty level: Majority of her people are poor and have no capital to invest in industries or to purchase goods
- She faces stiff competition from developed nations for markets
- The economy of Brazil is monopolized by multinationals which take back profits to their countries
- Huge foreign debts: a lot of money in Brazil is used to service existing loans
- The country lacks enough people with the required technical skills
- Poor transport hinders distribution of finished products and raw materials to the market.
- Historical background: Brazil is still Exploited by her colonial masters

INDIA is one of the most populous nations in the world after China. For along time industrialization stagnated in India because Britain used India as a source of her raw materials and political disunity in India. This scenario changed in the 1850's and industrialization began to take root. Today India boosts of industries like Iron and steel, chemical industries, textile, leather making, ship and motor vehicle building among others. Reasons which have contributed to industrialization in India include:

- Capital: Indians in foreign countries are making money through which they are steadily investing in their country. The government also provides funds through the banking system
- Political Stability: India has enjoyed considerable peace since independence
- Labour: India has high population which provides cheap labour. The government also strengthens education system which produce technical experts in industry
- Market: Her large population provides internal market while her cheap goods are also popular in other parts of the world
- Sources of energy: India has energy sources like coal, HEP and nuclear energy
- Natural resources: India is endowed with minerals, for example coal, iron ore and manganese
- Cottage Industries: Many Indians set up

small cottage (textile) industries at home. This advanced local India textile industries

• Transport and communication: The British government built roads, railway and postal services in the country.

The Government of India contributed to industrialization in many ways. These included:

• Restriction on importation of goods to give Indian factories a chance to stabilize

• Encouraged technical and scientific education

• Development of heavy industries by the government

• Emphasis on industrialization in the five - year development plan.

• Encouragement of foreign investment in the country.

Challenges facing India in its desire to industrialize

• Competition from goods manufactured in the developed world

• More resources are concentrated in the agricultural sector to feed the large population

• Poor transport network

• Natural calamities – floods and cyclones

• Political upheavals with Pakistan

• Indian caste system is too conservative and they are unable to exploit the modern opportunities

• High population and poverty: This leads to low purchasing power.

• Lack of funds: They have to rely on loans, grants and aids from developed countries

• Lack of technical skills to exploit her resources fully

SOUTH AFRICA attained majority rule in 1994 with Nelson Mandela as the first Black African president. The country is one of the most industrialized countries in the Africa continent. Most industries in South African were started by the Apartheid Regime. The industries include iron and steel industries, engineering, locomotive, chemical, textile, cement and light industries among others. The factors which have encouraged industrialization in South African include:

• Natural resources: South Africa is endowed with minerals, for example lead, zinc, iron ore, uranium, gold and diamond

• Market: Her goods are of high quality and compete favourably with those from developed countries

• Entrepreneurship: The Europeans in South Africa were willing to invest in industries

• Agriculture: Her rich agricultural resources such as grains, fruits, sugar cane – provide raw materials for agro-based industries

• Labour: The South African's black population supplied cheap labour in the industries

• Source of energy: S. Africa has coal deposits and HEP

• Good transport and communication system: Roads, railway and water transport are greatly developed linking major cities and extending to neighbouring countries

• Government support: South Africa's government provided funds which boosted and encouraged local investment. The government also imposed heavy taxes on imports

• Political stability: The post Apartheid government of South Africa has been relatively calm

Problems facing industrialization in South Africa

• South Africa had a long history of inter racial conflicts and wars which affected industries

• Due to the Apartheid policy UNO imposed economic sanctions on South Africa which prohibited other nations to trade with her

- Due to racial labour policies there were frequent riots, strikes and demonstrations by the blacks
- Development of transport, communication, banking and insurance was inadequate in areas where blacks lived
- Majority of the blacks are poor and this led to low purchasing power
- High level of insecurity discouraged foreign investment
- HIV/AIDS ravaged the country's labour force

Questions on industrialization in Developing Countries

(a) Explain five factors which have encouraged industrialization in South African

(b) Explain five problems facing industrialization in South Africa

(c) Explain five reasons which led to industrialization in India

(d) Explain five challenges facing India in its desire to industrialize

(e) Explain six factors which have contributed to industrialization in Brazil

(f) State five factors that have undermined scientific revolution in developing countries

(g) Explain five ways in which industrialization in 3rd world countries has affected them

(h) Give one way in which poor transport hinders industrialization in the 3rd world countries

(i) State five factors that hinder industrialization in 3rd world countries

9 URBANIZATION

EARLY URBANISATION IN AFRICA

Urbanization is the process whereby large settlement of people are formed or attracted to cities of urban centre. Towns which grew up in Africa during the pre-colonial time include Timbuktu, Meroe, Axum, Cairo, and Thababosiu. A number of factors led to the development of urban centers in Africa during the Pre-colonial period. These include: -

- Trading activities led to the rise of convergent centers which later developed into towns.
- The existence of local industries led to population concentration in places that were developed into towns,
- Existence of trade routes which linked various places led to the development of towns at major cross - roads.
- Administration centers later developed into towns, for example Kumasi and Addis Ababa.
- Development of centers of learning later became urban centers, for example Timbuktu.
- Development of Agriculture led to availability of food which in turn encouraged people to establish permanent settlements.
- Religious centers developed into town, e.g. Ife and Kumasi.
- Places that were secure attracted population concentration and later developed into towns, for example Thababosiu the capital of Basuto land
- Most urban centres developed along river valleys. This was because the rivers provided adequate water supply and encouraged accessibility

CAIRO

which is the capital city of the present day Egypt was started around 969 A.D. The growth of Cairo can be attributed to:

- The Nile valley provided fertile soil and water for irrigation. This led to increased population and settlement.
- Strategic location of Cairo attracted caravan traders who crisscrossed the region from the North, Central and West Africa.
- The Suez Canal opened in 1869 linked Egypt and the Far East and increased traffic from Europe. This greatly enhanced the growth of Cairo
- Cairo was a cultural centre and the origin of the ancient civilization.
- The town served as a religious and an educational centre. Many universities in the town contributed to its growth.
- The construction of the Aswan High Dam in 1902, boosted irrigation and agricultural production in Egypt.

Functions of Cairo

- Cairo is the national capital of Egypt and a political centre of the Arab world
- It is a major commercial and transport centre for both North Africa and the Middle East
- Cairo serves as a recreational centre
- It is an industrial centre
- It is of historical importance to Egypt because of the ancient monuments which continue to attract many tourists in the country.

Challenges facing Cairo

- Unemployment: The city of Cairo has not been able to generate many jobs as its rapidly growing populations requires. Unemployment is therefore high.

- High population: It is the largest city in Africa and has a very large population, about 11 million (1988). Feeding this population and providing enough socio-economic amenities has remained a big challenge.
- Housing problem: has led to the development of slums in the city
- Inadequate infrastructure: It has not been possible to develop the city's infrastructure as fast as the city's population growth. As a result roads are congested and many areas of the city are poorly served with water, electricity and telephones services.
- Social dislocation: Cairo suffers from all the social dislocations of very large cities. Crime and prostitution, insecurity and inequality are widespread. This takes a heavy toll on the lives of many residents of the city.
- Pollution: increased number of vehicles and industries has polluted the air in town due to the emitions form vehicles and smoke from the industries.

MEROE

was situated on the bank of River Nile to the north of Khartoum. The city which is believed to have emerged around 650 B.C. was an industrial centre, started by the Nubians. These were former rulers of Egypt who fled to this region when Egypt was conquered by the Assyrians around 8th century B.C. Meroe established itself as an important iron working centre and produced many farm tools, weapons and hunting tools. The growth of Meroe was attributed to: -

- Meroe was a mining centre. Iron smelting started in this region around 500 B.C. and it is believed that from here the technology spread to other parts of Africa. Meroe was a heavily forested area and this formed the basis for smelting.

- It served as a religious centre and had many temples for worshipping and tombs for burial
- It was a trading centre
- Major trade routes converged in the place thus making it a transport hub
- It was an administrative centre

Factors which were responsible for the decline of Meroe as an urban centre included: -
- The decline in mining activities due to exhaustion of mineral
- The rise of Axum in the modern day Ethiopia denied Meroe access to the Red Sea.
- Malarial attack in the region
- Desertification in the region reduced timber for iron smelting and also led to the decline in agricultural activities.

Impact of Meroe
- Meroitic language developed and this replaced the Egyptian language which was used by the founder Nubian people.
- Some hieroglyphic writings have been discovered in the region.
- New architectural designs like tombs - where leaders were buried, temples and palaces for the rulers came up in the region.

KILWA

is one of the city states which sprung up along the East Coast of Africa around 10th century A.D. The rise of Kilwa is accredited to the Shirazi rulers. Ali Ibn Hassan in particular conquered most of the city states between Pemba and Kilwa and brought them under his rule. These states were forced to pay tribute to Kilwa. Around Kilwa was built a stone citadel to protect it from enemies and a big mosque. Factors which contributed to its growth included:

- Kilwa was ruled by able leaders who kept the enemies at bay and forced other city states to pay tribute to her.
- Strategic location of Kilwa attracted many Merchants who used it as a port of call to replenish their stock
- By 1300 A.D. Kilwa had taken control of the Gold trade along the East Coast. The gold originated from Mwene Mutapa Empire, present day Zimbabwe.

Functions of Kilwa
- Kilwa served as a trading centre (gold)
- The town was heavily fortified and served as a defense centre
- It was a religious town (Islam)
- The town was an administrative centre

By 14th century Kilwa began to lose its glory because of the disruption of the gold trade which she had monopolized for a long time. This trade was upset by the civil wars among the communities which were producing gold.

Most early urban centres in Africa declined because of the: -
- Impact of malaria, for example Meroe and Axum
- Decline of trading activities, for example Trans-Saharan
- Wars of conquest, for example Gedi and Kilwa were burnt down by the Portuguese
- Decline in Empires, for example Gao and Mali
- Change in trade routes, for example Timbuktu and Sijimasa
- Water shortages which caused outbreak of epidemics, for example Gedi

EARLY URBANISATION IN EUROPE

Athens is one of the Greek city states which flourished between 490 – 480 B.C. after the Persian wars. Athens is famous for: -
- Many great thinkers and philosophers like Plato, Socrates, Aristotle, Archimedes and Pythagoras
- Democracy evolved in Athens among the Greeks who were great debaters in open fields
- Massive temples and statues of gods and goddess
- Great debates which were conducted in an open place, Agora.
- Development of many theories in the field of education and medicine

The Athenians were stratified into four distinct classes. This included:
- The first class: the richest and most heavily taxed.
- Second Class: provided cavalry for the army
- Third Class: provided solders for the infantry
- Fourth Class: consisted of the poorest and paid no tax

Those who were captured in wars were enslaved, but they were not mistreated. Some who served their masters well were freed and others would even be allowed to inherit their property. No Athenian was enslaved.

Factors which contributed to the growth of Athens as an urban centre included:
- Strategic Position – It was a port and main city.
- The Athenians depended on trade and commerce because they inhabited an infertile area.
- Security: was surrounded by rivers and mountains which made it difficult for external enemy attack.
- Culture like drama and games, led to its growth.

- Religion – It was a center of worship, for example goddess Athena.

Functions of Athens included:
- Cultural centre: they liked watching plays and this contributed to the development of theatre
- Educational centre: believe in giving their children a good education base.
- Sports centre: Athens is associated with the origin of the Olympics where they participated in events like jumping, discus throwing and wrestling.
- Religious centre: there were temples for worshipping and statures of many gods and goddess in town.
- Commercial centre: depended on trading activities for their survival
- Transport centre: It was a port and a city
- Administrative centre

L ONDON which sprung up around 43 A.D. after the conquest by the Romans is the capital city of England. The Romans are given credit for the development of London. The original inhabitants of London are Celtics from whom the name of the town, Llyn Dun which means "Celtic Lake Fort" is derived. The town faced a lot of calamities during its initial stages of growth. These included:
- In 60 A.D. it was looted by the Romans following a rebellion.
- In 120 A.D. the town was razed down by fire

Medieval London attracted many people of different nationalities who established their own settlements because the English excluded them from their unions or guilds. This gave London a unique characteristic. By the 18th century, London had emerged as one of the modern cities in the world. Factors which contributed to the growth of London included: -
- Trading activities: trading and commercial activities contributed to the growth of London
- Industrialization: it was the centre of industrial activities like textile, ship building, and metal work among others
- Improvement in transport: London was served with good transport and railway network
- Shipping activities: loading and offloading at the port of London attracted a large number of people to the port

Functions of London

The city of London served many functions. These included:
- Transport and communication centre: it is served with roads, railway and airports
- London is a political and administrative capital. It houses the Prime Minister, all Cabinet Offices and the Monarchy
- It is a commercial centre: has many financial institutions like banks
- An industrial centre e.g. textile was the oldest industry in town.
- An educational centre: it has some of the oldest universities in the word like Oxford and Cambridge.
- Serves as a historical centre.

Problems facing London
- Poverty: poor people were exploited by the rich especially in the initial stages of the growth of London
- Rural-Urban migration: large number of people came to London to seek for employment and this led to congestion in the town
- Housing problem: the large number of people in the town led to the development of

slums because not everybody would be properly housed

- Unemployment led to increased cases of crime and social vices like prostitution and robbery
- Air pollution continues to be a major challenge

Results of Urbanization in Europe in the 19th Century

- Migration of people to urban centres which led to high population in urban centres
- Inadequate housing due to high concentration of people in urban centres
- Concentration of people in urban areas led to shortage of food which resulted to malnutrition
- Frustration and suffering in urban life led to anti social behaviour, for example alcoholism, drug abuse and prostitution
- Poor sewage and sanitation facilities exposed people to diseases, for example cholera
- Increase in crime rate and violence created fear and insecurity
- Poor working conditions, for example child labour and long working hours
- High concentration of people in urban areas strained the social amenities, for example schools and hospitals

---

Questions on Early Urbanization in Africa and Europe

(a) Identify two reasons why most urban centres developed along river valleys

(b) What factors led to the development of urban centers in Africa during the Pre-colonial period

(c) What was the main reason which led to the decline of Meroe

(d) Give five factors that contributed to the decline of most early urban centres in Africa

(e) Give two contributions of the ancient city of Athens to the world civilization

(f) State three ways in which the industrial revolution contributed to urbanization

---

MODERN URBAN CENTRES IN AFRICA

Johannesburg owes its existence to the discovery of gold in Witwatersrand in 1886. In a span of three years the town had blossomed into a major city. People flocked from far and wide to prospect for gold in the region. The rise of Johannesburg to a modern city is attributed to: -

- River Vaal which provided water for both domestic and industrial use
- Sitting in a plain which facilitated the building and construction work
- Existence of minerals like Gold, iron ore, chromite, diatomite and fluorspar greatly facilitated its growth
- Coal was mined in areas like Benoni, Vereeniging and Witbank. This provided energy for the industries.
- Areas around Johannesburg are fertile and provided enough maize and wheat to feed the town.

Functions of Johannesburg as a City

- Johannesburg is a transport and communication centre
- The city plays host of international meetings like the United Nations Summit meetings
- It is a mining centre: gold greatly contributed to its growth
- It's a sports and cultural centre: it hosts international world cup rugby tournaments
- It is an industrial and manufacturing centre
- Johannesburg is a commercial centre
- Educational centre: Several institutions of higher learning are located in Johannesburg

Problems Facing Johannesburg as a Modern City

- Racial discrimination is still a great challenge among the mine workers
- Inadequate housing has led to the mushrooming of slums

The Barons

- Traffic congestion especially at rush hours
- Poor sanitation and careless disposal of waste products
- Inadequate social amenities like hospitals and schools
- There is a lot of pollution by the industries in the city
- The level of unemployment is high among the educated youth in the city
- HIV/AIDS pandemic is a serious health issue in the city
- A large financial gap exist between the affluent class of Europeans and the Blacks who are the majority

Solutions to the Problems
- The end of apartheid policy also marked the end of racial discrimination. Now people mingle and live freely in places of their choice.
- Slums are being upgraded by the post apartheid government and better housing estates established.
- Many social vices like crime and unemployment are reduced by the creations of many job opportunities.
- By creating awareness about HIV/AIDS and its dangers, the government hopes to reduce the impact of the pandemic.

NAIROBI

The town owes its name to the Maasai community who called it *enkare nairobi*, translated to mean a "place of cool waters". It started as a small centre where the Maasai and the Agikuyu met to transact trading activities. Nairobi grew into prominence during the construction of Kenya-Uganda Railway (1899) when it became a railway depot and a camp.

The growth of Nairobi into a modern day city is attributed to: -

- There was adequate water both for domestic and industrial use
- The place was located in a region with ideal landscape which facilitated the construction of buildings, stores and workshops.
- Areas around Nairobi had fertile soil and climate which favoured agricultural activities.
- The cool climate of Nairobi favoured European settlement.
- Trading activities between the Agikuyu and Maasai, and the Swahili-Arab traders favoured its growth.
- Nairobi was at the centre and therefore formed an ideal place for the constructors of the railway and a resting point during the long voyage from Mombasa to Kisumu.

Functions of Nairobi
- Nairobi is the government of Kenya's administrative headquarters and capital city. Parliament, the President and all Cabinet Secretaries are based in Nairobi.
- It is a commercial and financial centre
- Nairobi is a transport and communication centre
- Regional headquarters of various international bodies are located in Nairobi like UNEP
- It is a tourist attraction centre: it has Nairobi National Park, National Museum and the Bomas of Kenya

Problems Facing Nairobi

- Unemployment: many Kenyans from rural areas are attracted to Nairobi, but few of them succeed in securing jobs. The many unemployed youths who are easily lured to bad practices like prostitution and robbery have become a major problem in the city.
- Poor Housing: the rising population in Nairobi has led to the mashrooming of unplanned structures and slums with inadequate amenities like water and proper sanitation
- Inadequate socio-economic infrastructure: the large population strains the existing amenities like schools and hospitals.
- Traffic Jam: this is caused by the large number of vehicles especially at rush hours
- Pollution of the air and water due to emitions from the vehicles and factories and careless dumping of waste matter.
- HIV/AIDS pandemic takes a heavy toll on the youthful population in Nairobi
- There is an increasingly high number of street families and children in the streets of Nairobi
- Water shortage is a common problem in many parts of Nairobi.

Solutions to the problems

- Construction of by-pass and increasing packing fees in the centre of the city is aimed at decongesting the city centre.
- Dual carriage ways and super highways like Thika have been constructed to increase the flow of traffic to and out of Nairobi.
- City railway is being re-introduced to ease traffic problems in the city.
- The government is placing more stress in promoting the informal sector like the Jua Kali to create more job opportunities to Kenyans and increase their source of income.

- Community policing – *Nyumba Kumi* initiative, has been introduced to reduce the rate of crime in the city.
- Street children are being rehabilitated by taking them to schools and other vocational centres where they can learn new skills like carpentry, tailoring and masonry
- The third Nairobi water project from River Chania is hoped will alleviate water problem in Nairobi
- Slums like Kibera and Mathare are being upgrades and affordable buildings erected.

Questions on Modern Cities in Africa

(a) Discuss the problems of urbanization in Cairo
(b) State two factors that led to the rise of Johannesburg
(c) Mention two functions of Johannesburg
(d) Explain five problems which face Johannesburg
(e) State five factors that led to the rise of Nairobi as a modern city in Kenya
(f) Mention two factors that led to the rise of Cairo
(g) Explain five problems which face Cairo City

---

10 SOCIAL, ECONOMIC AND POLITICAL ORGANIZATION OF AFRICAN SOCIETIES

THE SHONA (MWENE MUTAPA KINGDOM) is a linguistic term that is used to describe the Karanga, Rozwi, Kore Kore, Zezuru and Manyika sub-tribes who live between Limpopo and Zambezi rivers. It is believed that the Mwene Mutapa Empire was established by the Rozwi dynasty.

Factors which led to the rise of shona state
(a) The Shona had able rulers like Chikura Nyatsimba, Mutola and Matope.
(b) They had a strong economy based on agriculture and pastoralism.
(c) The area was rich in minerals like gold, copper and Iron ore which they mined and trade on.
(d) The Shona traded with the coastal people and this brought in lot of wealth.

Economic Activities of the Shona
- The Shona took part in long distance trade
- They cultivated crops like grains and cassava.
- They kept cattle from which they got milk and meat
- The Shona practiced hunting and gathering to supplement their diet.
- They were skilled iron workers and also carried out craft
- They were fishermen

Social Organization
- The Shona had faith in one supreme God who they called Mwari
- The Shona had sacred places of worship (shrines) and communicated to their spirits through oracles.
- The Shona were organized into clans and their elders were very much respected
- Priests presided over religious functions among them
- They stayed in circular houses made of stones
- The Shona practiced polygamy and exogamy

Political Organization
- The Shona were ruled by a king called *Mwene Mutapa* (Emperor) whose position was hereditary.
- The emperor had a standing army which was used for defense and expansion of the kingdom and he was its commander-in chief.
- *Mwene Mutapa* controlled trading activities in the kingdom.
- The Emperor administered his kingdom in partnership with the queen mother, the head drummer, the king's sister, the king's nine principal wives, the head cook and the head door keeper.
- The king was in control of religion which was deeply entertwined with politics
- The Royal Fire was lit throughout the reign of the king. It was carried by the vassal chiefs to their states to make obvious their loyalty to *Mwene Mutapa*
- The Kingdom was divided into provinces each under a lesser chief who were directly answerable to the emperor.
- The emperor controlled trading activities and the revenue collected was used to keep the empire and the army going.
- Religion was used to enhance peace and stability in the empire

Factors Which Led to the Decline of Mwene Mutapa Empire included:

- The rulers who succeeded Nyatsimba and Mutola, who were the founders of Mwene Mutapa Empire, were not powerful enough to keep up the empire.
- Civil wars and insurgence by the priests made Mwene Mutapa empire to fall apart
- Forays by the Matabele into Mashona land contributed to the decline of empire.
- Mashona land was brought under British rule and this led to its collapse.

Questions on Social, Economic and Political Organization of the Mwene Mutapa

(a) What factors led to the rise of the Shona state in the pre-colonial period
(b) State two political roles of Mwene Mutapa
(c) Name two principal assistants to Mwene Mutapa during pre-colonial time
(d) State the social organization of the Shona (Mwene Mutapa) Kingdom
(e) What was the main significance of the royal fire in Mwene Mutapa Empire?
(f) Describe the political organization of the Shona during the pre-colonial period
(g) Identify five economic activities of the Shona before the colonial period
(h) State five factors which led to the decline of Mwene Mutapa Empire

---

THE BAGANDA

are a Bantu speaking group who at the moment live in Uganda. Some folk story points out that they were the offsprings of Kintu while another maintains that the founder of the Baganda Kingdom was Kimera, a brother of Isingoma Mpunga Rukidi of the Luo Babito dynasty.

The rise of Baganda Kingdom is linked to three rulers. These were Kibugwe, Katerragga and Mutebi. Katerraga, to be precise, increased the size of Baganda twofold and extended the kingdom to the north and northwest. These areas were up to that time controlled by Bunyoro-Kitara dynasty.

The rise and expansion of Buganda Kingdom was associated with:

- The fall of Bunyoro-Kitara Kingdom created a vacuum which was filled by Buganda Kingdom.
- The fact that power was consolidated in the hands of the Kabaka enabled him to rule effectively and encountered minimal dissent.
- The Kingdom was capably administered by Kabaka Kkyabagu, Kabaka Junju and Kabaka Suna.
- The Baganda developed a hereditary system of chiefs appointed by the Kabaka. This made them loyal to the Kabaka
- Buganda had a navy with war canoes, which patrolled the waters of the lake and were also used for faster transportation of troops
- Buganda had fertile soils which provided ample food for her population
- Buganda got fire arms from Arab and Swahili traders which were used in wars of conquest
- A lot of wealth was acquired from conquered areas like Buddu, Kyagwe and Busoga. Ivory, slaves, iron ore and livestock were obtained from these areas.
- Political stability of Buganda encouraged the development of trade, which enriched the kingdom
- Buganda was small and centralized. This made the control of the Kingdom easy. Power was concentrated at Kabaka's court in Mengo.

Symbols of royal authority in Buganda included the Throne, Royal Drum, Roral Spears and Royal Stools.

Economic Organization

• The Baganda were mixed farmers who grew crops like bananas (staple food) and they also kept animals from which they got milk and meat.

• They were skilled iron workers. The Baganda acquired iron from her neighbouring communities through warfare and used it to make spears, arrows and agricultural tools.

• They practiced hunting and gatherering to supplement their diet. They hunted elephants for their ivory which they sold.

• They exchanged their commodities with the Arabs and Swahili traders from the coast.

• They practiced fishing in Lake Victoria

• The Baganda made clothes from fibres and animal skins

• They weaved basket and made pots

Social Organization of the Baganda

• The Kingdom was divided into several social classes – the royal family of the Kabaka, the chiefs and the commoners (Bakopi) and at the bottom were the slaves (Badu)

• The Baganda believed in the existence of many gods, for example Katonda (god the creator) and Kiibuuka (god of war or thunder).

• They believed in the existence of ancestral spirits whose responsibility was to maintain discipline in the clans.

• They had religious leaders who included the Kabaka, prophets and medicine people.

• Baganda had shrines where they could worship their deities.

• Labour was divided according to sex i.e. women tilled the land, while men engaged in warfare.

• They had rites of passage which went together with ceremonies.

• They had age set system where the initiated young men belonged.

Political Organization of the Baganda

• Buganda was a centralized monarchy headed by the Kabaka. The office of the Kabaka was hereditary

• The Kabaka was assisted in running the government by a Prime Minister known as the Katikiro.

• There was a Council of Ministers consisting of the Prime Minister (Katikiro) Treasurer (Omuwanika) and Chief Justice (Omulamuzi)

• The kingdom had a legislative body known as Lukiko made up of Kabaka's nominees.

• Buganda had a stranding army which was used in defending the kingdom

• The kingdom was divided into counties called Sazas. These were headed by Saza chiefs

• The counties were divided into sub-counties called Gombolola. They were headed by Gombolola chiefs

• Gombololas were divided into smaller divisions known as Miluka. These were headed by Miluka chiefs

• Bataka were minor chiefs in charge of

Functions of the Lukiko

(a) Formulated laws for the kingdom.
(b) Advised the Kabaka on matters affecting the country
(c) Directed the collection of taxes
(d) Represented peoples' grievances to the Kabaka
(e) Settled disputes in their areas
(f) Acted as the final courts under them

Functions of the Katikiro

(a) Organized the collection of tax.
(b) Organized public work.
(c) Informed the Kabaka of the decisions to make on court matters.
(d) Gave permission to those who wanted to see the Kabaka.

Functions of the Bataka Chiefs

(a) Were in charge of the gombolola and clan
(b) Gave guidance to their respective clans on political matters
(c) Collected taxes
(d) Maintained law and order
(e) Supplied men for military services
(f) Send their sons to serve as pages
(g) Settled disputes in their areas

Questions on Social, Economic and Political Organization of the Baganda

(a) State one way in which centralization of the authority contributed to the Success of the Buganda kingdom
(b) Identify two symbols of authority among the Baganda
(c) State two functions of the Katikiro
(d) Give two functions of the Buganda traditional parliament
(e) State two functions of the Lukiiko
(f) Give five factors that led to the rise and expansion of Buganda kingdom
(g) Give two functions of the Kabaka of Buganda during the pre-colonial period
(h) Describe the social organization of the Baganda during the pre-colonial period.
(i) Describe the political organization of the Baganda

THE ASANTE are the Akan speaking group of people who at this point in time live in southern part of Ghana. It is upheld that the Oyoko clan, under the leadership of Osei Tutu, were instrumental in the establishment of the Asante Empire.

The Rise of the Asante Empire

• The empire was a centralized state divided into three divisions namely: Kumasi, Amato (Provincial) and conquered states. Centralization of government provided unity in the empire.
• The Asante had powerful rulers, for example Osei Tutu who introduced the Golden Stool and Odwira festival to unite the people
• Asante was made up of several related families which supported each other during crisis.
• They had a strong permanent army with modern weapons
• They Asante occupied an area which was suitable for mixed farming. This supported a strong agricultural base.
• The region was the centre of the Trans Saharan Trade which brought in a lot of wealth to the people.
• They had a variety of items which they sold, for example Gold and Kolanuts to raised income

Economic Organization of the Asante

• The Asante cultivated yams, vegetables and fruits
• They also kept livestock.
• They traded in slaves, ivory and gold in return for guns
• They practiced iron working activity
• Gold mining was an important activity among them
• They practiced hunting and gathering

- They raided their neighbours for slaves and ivory

Social Organization of the Asante
- The Asante were divided into clans and the original Oyoko clan formed the ruling class.
- At the lowest level of the society were the slaves who provided labour
- They practiced polygamy
- The Asante worshiped many gods
- They had a golden stool which was a religious symbol and provided unity
- They organized traditional dances and songs annually in a festival called the Odwira festival.

Importance of Odwira Festival
(a) The Omanhene took advantage of the Odwira Festival to pay homage to Asantehene
(b) It gave people an opportunity to venerate the dead
(c) Asante were able to resolve disputes among themselves during the festivals
(d) Enhanced unity among the Ashanti states

Political Organizations of the Asante Empire
- The Asante Empire was a centralized state divided into three divisions namely: the nucleus: (Kumai) states outside Kumais (amatoo) and the conquered states.
- The overall ruler of the empire was Asantehehe and Kumasi was under his direct control.
- The conquered states were ruled by their kings, but treated as provinces of Asante. Asantehene appointed representative in each of these conquered state.
- The Asantehene ruled with the help of a confederacy of kings (Omanhehe). They took an oath of allegiance to ensure loyalty to the Asantehene.
- The Omanhehe represented the king in the provinces. They were allowed some autonomy but were expected to pay tribute to Asantehene and provide soldiers in time of need.

The role of Omanhene
(a) Pay tribute to the king
(b) Recruit soldiers
(c) Settle disputes
(d) Represent Asantehene in their provinces
(e) Collect taxes

- The empire had a standing army which defended it, conquered other states and maintained law and order in the empire.
- The sacred Golden Stool which was introduced in the 18th century by Asantehen Osei Tutu, strengthened unity in the empire. It was kept at the headquarters, Kumasi. Each Omanhene was given a symbolic black stool to signify the unity of purpose in the provinces.
- The empire had a well established judicial system based at Kumasi and was headed by the king. The Omanhene were given powers to try minor cases at the provinces.
- The empire had a strong economic base that depended mainly on taxes and profits derived from the long distance trade.
- There was a national festival known as Odwira where all Omanhene assembled every year to pay tribute to Asantehene and to resolve their disputes.

Factors that Led to the Decline of Asante Kingdom
- The Asante experienced succession disputes since she had matrilineal inheritance system
- Decline of the Trans Saharan Trade

reduced the income of the kingdom

- Rivalry between the Fante and Asante weakened the Asante
- The coming of the British colonialists led to Anglo-Asante wars which resulted in the defeat of the Asante
- The expansiveness of the empire led to internal revolt from the vassal states which wanted to preserve their autonomy

Questions on Social, Economic and Political Organization of the Asante

(a) Identify the role of Omanhene among the Asante

(b) What was the importance of the Odwira Festival?

(c) Give the main reason why the Golden stool was important for the Asante Empire?

(d) Mention two roles of the Asantehene

(e) State five factors that led to the rise of the Asante Empire

(f) Describe the social organization of the Asante

(g) Describe the economic organization of the Asante

(h) Describe the political organizations of the Asante Empire during the 19th century

(i) State five factors that led to the decline of Asante Kingdom

11 SCRAMBLE AND PARTITION OF AFRICA

European powers which took an active part in the scramble and partition of African included Britain, France, Germany, Portugal, Italy and Belgium. For along time these countries did not have colonies in Africa and their interests were taken care of by their traders, missionaries and companies. They were not interested in having colonies because: -

- Colonies were considered expensive to manage and a burden to the tax payers.
- Little was known about the interior of Africa hence the notion that colonies were of no value
- West Africa was considered as a "death bed" to the European race because of the prevalent malarial attack and subsequent death
- Penetrating Africa was hard because of the hostile tribes and lack of effective means of transport and communication.

This perception changed in the 18ᵗʰ century and many European nations began developing a keen interest in Africa. The scramble to own spheres of influence led to the partitioning of Africa among the European powers.

FACTORS THAT LED TO THE SCRAMBLE FOR COLONIES IN AFRICA

Economic Reasons

(a) The Industrial Revolution in Europe:
- Industrialization created a desire for markets for European manufactured goods in Africa.
- Europeans came to Africa to search for raw materials like cotton, palm oil, copper and iron ore.
- Abolition of slave trade created a large pool of cheap labour in Africa.

- Africa provided an avenue for investing surplus funds acquired from industrialization.
- Development in transport system, especially the railway, facilitated colonization.
- Firearms manufactured during the revolution enabled Europeans to conquer African territories.
- Discovery of quinine enabled Europeans to survive the African conditions and protect themselves from diseases such as malaria.
- Those who were rendered unemployed in Europe due to invention of machines moved to Africa to find alternative ways of living.
- There was increased rivalry among traders and a desire to lock out other traders from their spheres of influence

(b) Speculation about the availability of large deposits of minerals in Africa: The discovery of Diamond at Kimberly in the 1860's and Gold in the 1870's increased the European inclination to search for colonies in the southern and central parts of the African continent. The Ndebele war of 1893 was fought because of the assumption that Lobegula occupied a mineral rich area.

Political Reasons

(a) Unification of Germany under Otto Von Bismarck after the Franco-Prussian war of 1870 - 71: The rise of Germany upset the balance of power in Europe and there was need to re-establish this balance in Africa through acquisition of colonies. Having lost her mineral rich provinces of Alsace and Lorraine to

Germany, France had to restore her lost glory by forcefully acquiring colonies in Africa.

(b) Public opinion in Europe

With the rise of democracy in the 19th century in Europe, it was fatal for any government to ignore public opinion, which was in favour of colonies.

- In 1882, due to public demand, the French assembly ratified De Brazza's treaty with Chief Makoko and created a French colony in Congo.
- German took over South-West Africa (Namibia), Togo and Cameroon due to what Bismarck termed as public demand.
- In Britain, the public demanded that Britain had to maintain her leading position as a colonizing power in Africa.

(c) Militarism

Army officers in Europe favoured colonial domination to show case their military prowess.

In Sudan, it was the military officers, in search of glory, and not the French government who spearheaded French colonization in the region. British soldiers like Wolseley Kitchener supported the expansion of the British Empire in Africa.

(d) The rise of Nationalism

There was a general feeling of European civilians that their nations should acquire overseas colonies to satisfy their national pride. The Germans, in particular developed a feeling that they belonged to a superior race and had to acquire colonies in Africa like other European powers (Britain and France).

Strategic Reasons

(a) Construction of the Suez Canal (The Egyptian Question)

- The construction of the Suez Canal, which shortened the link between Europe and the Far East, encouraged international trade and made Egypt strategically import to most Europeans.
- The failure of Khedive Ishmael (1863-1879) to pay for the cost of the construction of the Suez Canal forced Britain to fully occupy Egypt in 1882.
- The disappointed French planned diversions of the Nile waters, and make Egypt a desert, by occupying territories to the south of Egypt.
- It was against this backdrop, that Britain claimed Uganda (source of the Nile) in 1894, Kenya (the gateway to Uganda) in 1895 and Sudan (where the Nile passes) in 1898.

(b) French activities in West Africa and Congo: The activities of France in Congo and West Africa, through their Italian agent Savorgnan de Brazza alarmed other powers. Germany in particular, was encouraged to join in the scramble and acquired Togo, Cameroon, Namibia and Tanganyika in the process.

King Leopold II

(c) Personal activities of King Leopold II of Belgium

- In 1876, Leopold convened the Brussels Geographical Conference where he formed a business company, the International African Association made up of explorers and traders to enlighten Africans, bring an end to slave trade and introduce legitimate trade in the Congo region.
- The Congo Free State, which Leopold changed to his personal empire in 1884, was the brain child of Henry Morton Stanley who acted as his agent in the area.
- The Berlin Conference of 1884 was held because of the activities of King Leopold in Congo which led to intense rivalry among the European powers.

Social Reasons

(a) The work of Christian missionaries

- They created an aura of trust by giving Africans gifts and introducing valuable economic activities like farming, carpentry and clerical work.
- When put in danger, missionaries persuaded their home governments to give them protection.
- Missionaries had direct contact with the people of the interior of Africa and paved way for the colonialists.
- They preached peace, love and hard work. These virtues made Africans submissive and more receptive to the Europeans.
- Some of them wrote exaggerated reports about untapped potential in Africa and the horrors of slave trade to convince their nationalities to be more interested in Africa.

(b) Population explosion in Europe in the 19th century led to the quest for new outlets to re-settle surplus population. Britain settled some of her people in Australia, New Zealand, USA, Canada and South Africa. Germany, Portugal and Holland also had to find places in Africa to settle some of their people.

(c) Anti-Slave Trade Campaigns:
Humanitarians in Europe (William Wilberforce and Granville Sharp) and the missionaries (David Livingstone) led a crusade against the Slave Trade and advocated for colonization of Africa. This was to stop the inhuman Slave Trade and replace it with a more legitimate trade. When Slave Trade was abolished, many European nations used it as an excuse to remain in some parts of Africa, control the region, enforce the anti-slavery treaties, and promote a legitimate trade in those areas.

The Pull Factors

- Natural resources like minerals and ivory attracted Europeans in Africa. This was particularly true in Gold Coast (Ghana) and Ivory Coast in West Africa.
- Well developed trade routes which were used to penetrate the interior of Africa.
- Navigable Rivers like Congo and Niger made transportation easy
- Most African communities were decentralized and had no military structures. This weakened their resistance to European invasion.
- Frequent inter tribal wars weakened African communities and made them ill prepared for a more serious challenge by the Europeans.

Causes of the Scramble and Partition of Africa

Pull Factors
- Developed routes
- Navigable rivers
- Natural calamities weaken Africans
- Natural resources

Strategic Reasons
- Egyptian Question
- Activities of King Leopold in Congo
- The French activities in West Africa

Causes of the Scramble and Partition of Africa

Political Factors
- Having colonies to boost national pride e.g. France
- Public opinion in Europe favoured colonial domination
- Military leaders desired to show of their might

Economic Factors
- Protecting sources of raw materials
- Protecting markets
- Protecting traders
- Investing surplus funds

Social Factors
- Missionary activities
- Settling excess people
- New discoveries e.g. quinine
- Anti-Slavery crusade

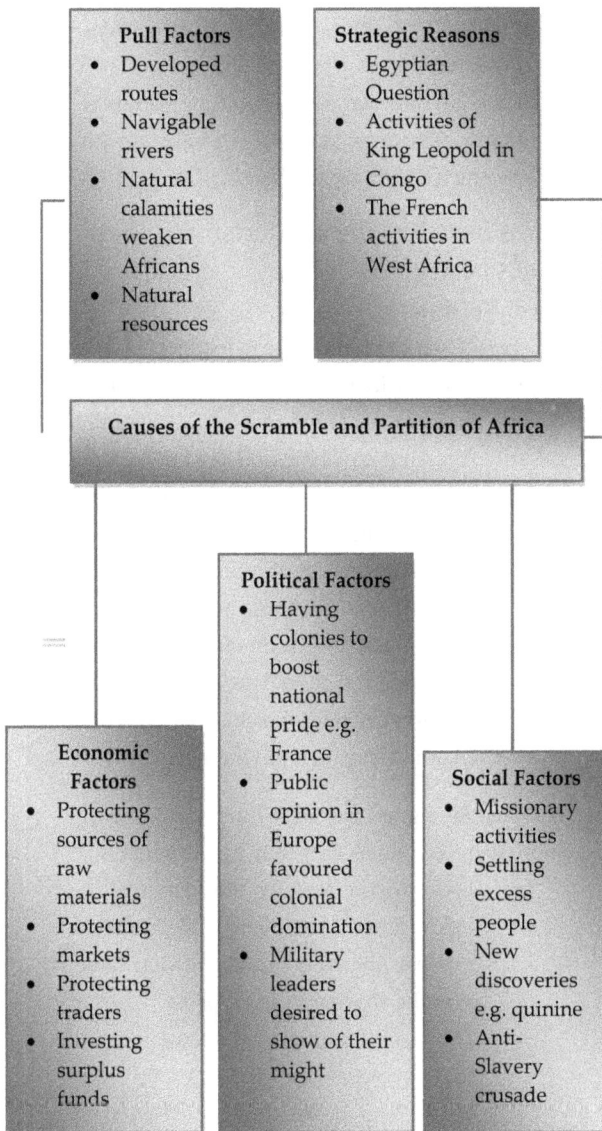

THE PROCESS OF PARTITION

The fore–runners to the process of partitioning Africa were the early explorers, missionaries and traders. Their activities were succeeded by the treaties and agreements made in various parts of Africa between trading companies and the locals leaders. Such agreements included the Buganda Agreement, the Heligoland Treaty and the Berlin Act of 1884-1885. Boundaries were drawn along the physical features like rivers and mountains.

African interests were paid no attention to and communities were set apart by artificial boundaries which only favoured the colonialists.

Berlin Conference of 1884-5

The main reason why the Berlin Conference of 1884-5 was convened by Otto Von Bismarck was to set up rules to allow the colonial power to divide Africa without resorting to war. Other reasons were-

(a) To lay down the rules for Africa's partition

(b) To forestall conflicts amongst European powers during Africa's partition

(c) To settle differences of opinion over the Congo-Niger region

(d) To synchronize European perception on Slave Trade

Otto Von Bismarck

Terms of the Berlin Conference of 1884 -5

- Any European power making claim of territory in Africa to inform other European nations so that the claim could be endorsed

- Signatories to declare their spheres of interest

- Land behind areas claimed became the sphere of influence of the claimant

- King Leopold's claim in the Congo was acknowledged.

- European nations making claims of territories had to effectively occupy the areas

- Occupying powers had to develop transport and communication in the areas

- The Congo, Zambezi and Niger Rivers and their tributaries were left open for use by all European powers
- Occupying powers had to commit themselves to abolition of Slave Trade, promotion of freedom of trade and protection of missionaries in the region occupied.

Factors which facilitated European colonization of Africa in 19th century included:

- Some Africans rulers were ignorant of the true implications of the protectorate treaties which they signed with the European imperialists.
- Some Africans collaborated with the imperialists and were used as mercenaries against fellow Africans
- The European imperialists used superior military weapons against the African communities who were poorly armed.
- The imperialist used missionaries who were friendly with some African leaders to persuade them to accept European rule. For example, in Buganda, kabaka Mwanga had refused to sign a protectorate treaty with Captain Fredrick Lugard in 1890, but was swayed by the Christian missionaries to do so.
- European traders operating in Africa convinced their respective governments to acquire territories which they would take over as their commercial bases
- The discovery of quinine during the first half of the 19th century reduced the European mortality rate in Africa. This made it possible for Europeans to stay in Africa and impose their rule on the Africans.
- Europeans mapped out strategies of occupation in Berlin Conference and co-operated with one another against Africans.

- Political weakness of African states favoured European colonization
- Lack of material and financial resources made Africans unable to sustain a protracted military onslaught

METHODS USED BY EUROPEANS TO ACQUIRE COLONIES IN AFRICA

Signing of Treaties

(a) Treaty signing with African leaders
- The British signed the Maasai Agreements (1904 and 1911), Buganda Agreement of 1900 and the Lewanika-Lochner Treaty with Lozi. The Royal Niger Company had by 1884, signed 37 treaties through George Goldie, with African leaders in Niger delta, Yorubaland and Gambia.
- Carl Peters signed treaties on behalf of Germany with the chiefs of Uzigua, Ukami, Usagara and Ungulu.

(b) Treaties signed amongst European power. These were known as Partition Agreements.
- The Anglo-Germany Agreements of 1886 and 1890 and Heligoland between the British and the Germans over the sharing of East Africa.
- The Anglo Italian Treaty signed in 1891 between the Italians and the British over possession of Eritrea and the Somali coast.
- The treaty between the British and Portugal and France in 1890 on the sharing of Madagascar (France) Mozambique and Angola (Portugal).

These treaties facilitated the acquisition of those areas for colonization.

Military Conquest

Europeans employed outright war against those societies that resisted their invasion. For example:

- The French war against the Mandinka of Samori Toure (1870-1899) and their conquest of Western Sudan from Senegal to Chad
- The British used military force in the Nandi Resistance from 1895-1905 and the Chimurenga Wars involving the Shona/Ndebele from 1896 -7
- The Germans fought the Maji Maji Wars from 1905- 1907.
- The Italians were defeated during their Ethiopian campaign, by Menelik II in the battle of Adowa in 1896.
- The Portuguese forcefully established their rule over Angola, Guinea Bissau and Mozambique.

Use of Missionaries as Frontrunners

The Europeans used missionaries to convince Africans to be submissive to colonial domination. For example:

- In Buganda, where there were religious conflicts between Catholics, Protestants, Muslims and Traditionalists, they manipulated local quarrels and took sides to champion European course.
- They went to war against each other and against the Africans. In the Franza-Ingeleza war of 1892, between the Protestants (British) and the Catholics (French), Fredrick Lugard intervened on the side of Protestants.
- In Bulozi, Father Francois Coillard convinced Lewanika of the benefits of British protection.
- In Nyasaland (Malawi), depicted as Livingstone's country, the missionaries shaped public opinion to favour imperial control.

Treachery and Divide and Rule Policy

Europeans instigated inter-tribal wars in which they supported one of the warring communities against another.

- The Wanga were used against the Luo of Ugenya and the Bukusu while the Maasai were used against the Nandi, both in Kenya.
- The Italians lied to Menelik II that he was signing a treaty of friendship while the Italian version of the same indicating that Ethiopia had agreed to become an Italian protectorate.
- The Maasai agreement was written in a language that the Lenana never understood.

Use of Company Rule

The British and the Germans used chartered companies to acquire and rule their colonies.

- The British South African Company (BSACo) of Cecil Rhodes was used to occupy much of Central Africa (Malawi and Zimbabwe)
- Imperial British East African Company IBEACo) of Sir William Mackinnon was used to occupy British East Africa (Kenya and Uganda)
- The German East Africa Company (GEACo) of Carl Peters was used to occupy Tanganyika (Tanzania).
- The Royal Niger Company of George Goldie was used to occupy areas around the Niger delta

Enticements

Europeans gave gifts such as cloth, weapons and drinks to African chiefs, for instance Lewanika of the Lozi and Mwanga of Buganda to lure them into collaboration.

Diplomatic Skills

Good relations were maintained with African leaders, who later, gave up their areas. The British used this method in Maasailand and Yorubaland.

A Blend of Diplomacy and Force

The British initially signed treaties with the Ndebele (Moffat and Rudd treaties), but again they fought them during the Ndebele war of 1897.

IMPACTS OF THE PARTITION OF AFRICA

Political effects

- Colonial government structures inherited by most independent African states have continued to be models of governments in African countries.
- It gave rise to African nationalism to fight against colonialism.
- Europeans gained fame, prestige and national glory by having colonial possessions.
- Colonialism led to the collapse of African traditional political systems and leadership.
- It led to development of strong African leadership and beginning of state formation.
- Divide and rule technique of administration encouraged ethnic disunity that still continues to haunt Africa.
- Introduction of European administration minimized inter tribal wars and civil strife.
- The colonial boundaries split many African communities. For example, the Somali are found both in Kenya and in Somalia, the Maasai in Kenya and Tanzania and the Ewe in Ghana and Togo.
- Communities which were economically and culturally mismatched found themselves horded together and this has created conflicts in Africa.

Social Impacts

- Towns like Nairobi and Machakos grew up as centres of administration. Other towns like Kisumu grew up as a railway terminus.
- Through the protection offered to missionaries, it stimulated the spread of Christianity to various parts of Africa.
- Some Africans benefited from western education and health facilities introduced by the Europeans.
- European languages were introduced in Africa.
- Partitioning created landlessness among Africans as European settlers appropriated their land.
- Many Africans lost their lives through resistance.
- Africans acquired Western culture and lost their cultural values.

Economic effects

- Roads, railway and other forms of infrastructure were constructed to open up the interior.
- Colonialism widened the market for African produce especially the local industries.
- Africans acquired European manufactured goods and this improved their way of life.
- The partition speeded up the economic growth of European nations like Britain.
- Forced labour and exploitation of African resources left many parts of Africa impoverished and underdeveloped.
- Africans were exposed to heavy taxation and economic exploitation

---

Questions on the Scramble and Partition of Africa

(a) Name two colonies in N. Africa which were colonized by France during the 19th Century

(b) What three economic reasons made Britain to acquire colonies in Africa?

(c) Identify the economic factors that contributed to the Scramble and Partition of Africa

(d) State five factors that led to the Scramble and Partition of Africa

(e) What methods did European powers use to acquire colonies in Africa?

(f) What was the main reason why the Berlin Conference of 1884 -5 was convened by Otto Von Bismarck?

(g) Give two reasons why the Berlin Conference of 1884-5 was convened

(h) Give the terms of the Berlin Conference of 1884 - 5

(i) Explain the impact of the partition of Africa to both Europe and Africa

(j) Explain the effects of partition of Africa among European powers in the 19th C

(k) Explain six factors which facilitated European colonization of Africa in 19th Century

12 AFRICAN RESPONSE TO EUROPEAN INVASION

COLLABORATION

Lewanika who was originally known as Lubosi, ascended to the throne in 1876, but was briefly ousted in 1884. After he recovered the kingship in 1885, Lubosi took the name Lewanika and ruled until his death.

Lewanika expanded Lozy control over the neighbouring Ila and Toka peoples, raiding them for cattle and slaves. His main enemies to the south were the Ndebele under king Lobengula. He was also fearful of attack from the Portuguese in Angola to the west. These fears made him to put Barotseland under the British protectorate. He was motivated to collaborate with the British by a number of factors. These included:

- Lewanika collaborated in order to protect his kingdom from the Germans, Portuguese and the Boers who were encroaching into his land
- He wanted the British to protect him against internal enemies, for example the Kololo chiefs. In effect he wanted to safeguard his position as the king of the Lozy
- Lewanika desired western education and medical facilities.
- Lewanika was encouraged to collaborate by his friend, king Khama of Gwato who had already sought British protection
- Lewanika saw the futility of resisting a much more stronger power like the Britain
- Lewanika wanted the British to protect his kingdom against attacks by other African communities like the Ndebele
- He was influenced by a European missionary, Coillard to accept the British
- He collaborated to preserve economic structure of his people
- He desired to promote trade between his people and Britain

Lewanika

Although Lewanika sought friendship and protection with the British, he was led into signing the Lochner Concession in June 1890 which assigned mineral and trading rights of Barotseland to the British South African Company (BSAC). He believed he was signing an agreement with the British government and was unhappy to learn otherwise.

Terms of the Lochner Treaty of 1890
- The BSACo. got the right to all the minerals in Barotse land
- Lewanika was to receive £ 2000 a year and a royalty of 4 % of all the minerals mined
- Lewanika received an income of £ 850 p.a.
- The BSACo was to build schools, promote trade and install telephone services
- Lewanika would retain his position as king, but his power were to be reduced

Missionaries of the Paris Evangelical Missionary Society led by Francois Coillard were given permission to set up stations in Barotseland. Lewanika consented to abolishing the Slave Trade in the 20th century, but he lamented the failure of the missionaries and the BSAC officials to provide him with weapons he felt were owed to him and means to develop the local economy in order to compensate for the lost Slave Trade revenue. His popularity fell when he was not able to prevent his people from being subjected to taxation by the BSAC or the loss of parts of western Barotseland to the Portuguese Angola in 1905.

Lewanika also signed the Coryndon Treaty with the British. Its terms included:

- The treaty gave BSAC administrative and judicial rights over white men in Lewanika's territory
- The company would provide education to Lewanika's people as well as telegraphic, postal, transport and communication services.
- Lewanika promised to end slavery and witchcraft in his kingdom
- The company would have right over the Balozi
- Company was not to mine in the Lozy traditional iron mines and farm in areas which were cultivated by the Lozy

Results of the Lozy collaboration

- The Lozy lost their power and were ruled by the British
- Lewanika was made a paramount chief
- The Lozy land was alienated by the British
- The British were given mining rights in Lewanika's kingdom
- Lewanika was protected from his enemies like the Ndebele
- Taxation and forced labour was introduced in Barotseland
- The Lozy culture was interfered with. Christianity was spread in the kingdom and witchcraft checked
- The Lozy were used as mercenaries to defeat other Africans
- Some of the Lozy were used as administrators by the British

---

Questions on Collaboration by Lewanika of the Lozy

(a) Give two terms of Coryndon Treaty
(b) Give two terms of the Lochner –Lewanika Treaty of 1890
(c) Explain the results of the Lozy collaboration with the British
(d) Explain six factors which made Lewanika to collaborate with the British

---

THE BAGANDA

Kabaka Mutesa I welcomed Stanley, an explorer into his kingdom. The latter accompanied the Kabaka in his expeditions and highly impressed him during his short stint in the palace. When Stanley departed he challenged him to encourage other Europeans to visit his kingdom. Specifically, Mutesa I expected the missionaries who followed Stanley's lead to:

- Help his people to acquire western education, medicine and technology
- Counter the growing influence of Muslims and traditionalists in his palace
- Help him fight his traditional enemies like Mukama of Bunyoro who was a threat to his position and trade
- Protect him against Khedive Ismail of Egypt who wanted to expand his kingdom into Buganda
- Use them to consolidate his power as the king of Buganda
- Promote trading activities with the Europeans so as to get their goods, especially fire arms

Suspicious of their motives, Mutesa confined the missionaries to his court. The first crops of convertees were therefore his royal chiefs and pages. The two religious groups developed conflicting interests immediately they began advancing their agenda. They had many disputes and failed to provide the arms Mutesa expected.

To improve their foot hold, the Arabs took advantage of these conflicts to spread Islam, expand trade and discredit the Christian factions who were invited by the Kabaka. Mutesa lost confidence in the missionaries and consequently, the Catholics decided to remove themselves and established a station at Kagei, south of Lake Victoria in 1882.

By the time he died in 1884, Mutesa was a disenchanted man. The missionaries whom he welcomed in his court were more interested in winning converts than assisting him in his expeditions or supplying him with weapons. The pages started giving respect to the preachers; they started questioning Kabaka's wisdom; denouncing his authoritative rule and preaching what they regarded as democracy.

Kabaka Mwanga

Kabaka Mwanga (1884-1898)

Mwanga's main predicament when he ascended to kingship was religious discord which in the end degenerated into political instability. In January 1885, he executed three Church Missionary Society (CMS) convertees. In October 1885, he had Bishop Hannington killed. In May 1886, 30 young convertees were burnt to death at Namugongo for refusing to denounce their Christian faith.

In 1888, under the influence of the traditionalists, he fruitlessly made an attempt to expel all foreigners whom he blamed for causing chaos in his kingdom. Instead, Mwanga was ousted by a combined force of Muslims, Catholics and Protestants and replaced by his brother Kiwewa who agreed to share authority with the foreigners. In 1890, Mwanga recaptured the throne through the assistance of Christians and Kabalega of Bunyoro Kingdom.

> **Why Mwanga collaborated**
> (a) He wanted to acquire protection from internal and external enemies.
> (b) He wanted to secure his position and safeguard the Baganda from interference.
> (c) He wanted the British to help him gain regional supremacy over the surrounding kingdoms of Bunyoro, Ankole and Toro.

Mwanga signed a protectorate treaty with Carl Peters for the Germans and rejected a treaty offer by Fredrick Jackson of IBEACo. In 1891, Mwanga was swayed by the Protestants to sign a treaty of collaboration with Fredrick Lugard. All through the religious turmoil which ensued in Uganda between the Protestants and the Catholics, Kabaka Mwanga always backed up the Catholics to the chagrin of the British administrators.

Kabaka Mwanga was unseated in 1894 when Lugard captured his palace (Mengo). He declared war on Britain on July 6, 1897 and was defeated at the battle of Buddu. Mwanga fled to the German East Africa where he was arrested and detained at Bukoba. He later escaped and led a rebel army to retake the kingdom, but was defeated once again in 1898. Mwanga was deported to Seychelles where he spent the rest of his life. He died in 1903 and his remains were repatriated and buried at Kasubi in 1910.

THE BUGANDA AGREEMENT agreement was signed in 1900 between Sir Harry Johnstone (British Official) and Apollo Kagwa, representing the Baganda. Reasons for signing of the Buganda agreement included:

- To define the position of Buganda in the country.
- To introduce law and order in the country.
- To reduce the cost of British administration since Buganda was to meet the cost of administration.
- To define the relationship between Buganda and the British government.

Terms of the Buganda Agreement of 1900

- The Buganda laws remained in effect as long as they did not interfere with the protectorate laws which were applied to Buganda Kingdom. Buganda kingdom was to be ruled by the Kabaka with the assistance of Katikiro. The Lukiko was to be the legitimate making laws body of Buganda.
- Kabaka was recognized as the king of Buganda but with lesser powers
- The Kabaka, his ministers and chiefs were to be paid since they were now considered as employees of the British government.
- Buganda boundaries were defined to include parts of Bunyoro (the ten sazas she had acquired from Bunyoro). The kingdom was expanded to twenty counties and to ease administration, each county was placed under a Saza Chief.
- Though Buganda became a province within the protectorate, Ganda system of government was recognized, but modified. It was to have three ministers (Katikiro, Treasurer and Chief Justice.). The Lukiko had fixed number – 20 -saza chiefs, 60 notables and 6 Kabaka's appointees.

- Land tenure system was changed to include land on freehold basis (*Mailo* land) and crown land. The crown land was for the protectorate government while the *Mailo* land was particularly for the kabaka, his ministers and his chiefs.
- A British resident was to stay in Buganda

Results of the Buganda agreement

- British authority was confirmed over Buganda.
- Buganda was reduced to a status of a mere province.
- The position of the king was reduced – he lost his power to give or withhold land as well as the power to appoint or transfer chiefs.
- The 1900 Agreement gave birth to early nationalistic movements in Buganda. The Bataka Opposition Movement of the 1920's was as a result of the conflict between the landless class and the land-owning group.
- Modern economy and western education were introduced in Uganda with Buganda taking the lead.
- Buganda was used as the spring board of the British administration and the Baganda were used as British administrators in the region.
- It strengthened the special position of Buganda in relation to other communities in Uganda.
- Sazas were increased from 10 to 20 and Saza Chiefs got land and right to impose land rent.
- It led to expansion of Christianity and decline of Islamic influence in Buganda.
- Bunyoro kingdom became aggrieved as a result of the loss of part of their territory that was transferred to Buganda by the British.

Impact of Buganda collaboration

- The collaboration enhanced the spread of Christianity in Buganda
- It intensified religious conflicts in Buganda after the death of Mutesa I
- Buganda was able to fend off her enemies like Bunyoro
- The powers of Kabaka were snipped and more authority was given to his court officials and the Lukiko
- Buganda become a British base and was used to spread out the British influence in the region
- Buganda community got advantage over other tribes by getting a head start in western education and being involved in the British administration
- The Buganda community advanced materially more than the rest of the tribes in Uganda
- It created political crisis in Buganda, when Kabaka Mwanga was dethroned and replaced with Daudi Chwa who was an infant.

Impact of Collaboration

(a) Collaboraters lost their independence to Europeans.
(b) Some leaders gained recognition although their powers were greatly reduced.
(c) Collaborating leaders were protected from their traditional enemies.
(d) Europeans used collaborating leaders to colonize other African societies.
(e) Collaborating communities got some benefits from the Europeans like western education and modern medicine.
(f) Collaboraters were economically exploited by the Europeans through land alienation, mining, taxation and forced labour.
(g) There was increased trade between them and Europeans.

Questions on the Baganda reaction to the British Invasion

(a) What was the main reason why Lugard was opposed to Kabaka Mwanga
(b) Give three reasons which led to the signing of Buganda agreement of 1900
(c) Why did the Kabaka Mutesa II collaborate with the British in 1890
(d) Give the main reason why Kabaka Mutesa confined the missionaries to his palace
(e) What were the terms of the Buganda Agreement of 1900?
(f) What was the impact of Buganda collaboration with the British?
(g) Discuss the results of Africa collaboration

ACTIVE RESISTANCE

Samori Toure was born around 1830 in Sanankaro, a village southwest of Kankan in the present day Guinea. He chose war path and diplomacy to counter the French incursion into West Africa and established himself as a leading African opponent of colonial imperialism.

Samori's parents were traders and he followed their footprints until when he as 20 years. After finding out that his mother was captured in a slave raid, Samori offered to serve in her captor Sori Birima's army in exchange for his mother's release. Accomplishing the position of a commander and displaying extraordinary military skills, Samori and his mother were as a result released. Coupled with his experience as a trader, these two qualities were to later on serve him in a good way as he put together his army and built his empire across West Africa.

Samori Toure

Samori Toure observed that the Mandinke people were disorganized and that there was no single chief with the ability to unite them. Having left Sori Birama's army, Samori gained the support of an increasing number of Mandinke chiefs to fulfill his vision of bringing together the Mandinke and patiently began to craft his empire.

What enabled Samori Toure to build a strong empire?

(a) He used Islam to unify the people

(b) He acquired wealth through his trading activities which he used to buy weapons, horses and pay his professional soldier

(c) He used his military experience to create a strong army which he led

(d) He used diplomacy to buy time and reorganize his forces

(e) He used minerals from Bure mines to acquire wealth

The army formed the corner stone of his empire, with Samori Toure as both commanders-in-chief and the head of state. His innovativeness enhanced loyalty to the state, with primary allegiance to him. Between 1852 and 1882, Samori Toure had created the Mandinke Empire.

Samori Toure built a powerful, virtually proficient army equipped with modern repeater rifles and trained in modern methods of warfare. The army was divided into two flanks, the infantry (sofa) with 30,000 to 35,000 men and the cavalry (Sere) of 3,000 men. Each wing was further subdivided into permanent units, fostering comradeship among the members and loyalty to both the local leaders and Samori himself.

In the second half of the 19th century, colonial powers were setting up colonies in West Africa and could not put up with strong states like the Mandinke Empire and able leaders like Samori Toure. In 1882, the French got the chance they yearned for when Samori declined to withdraw from an important market centre (Kenyeran) which his army had cordoned.

Causes of the Franco – Mandika War of 1891 – 1898

(a) Samori wanted to uphold the sovereignty of his empire

(b) Samori was not willing to lose the rich Bure mines to the French

(c) The French came when Samori had reached his peak and did not want his expansionist policy jeopardized

(d) Samori did not fear an encounter with the French

(e) The French activities of selling arms to his enemies upset him

(f) Samori was disturbed by the failure of his scheme of playing off the British against the French

---

Between 1882 and 1885, Samori fought with the French and only halted briefly in 1886 and 1887 by signing a temporary truce. In 1888, Samori took up arms again when the French broke a promise on the treaty by making an attempt to stir up insurgence within his empire. In 1890, Samori acquired modern weapons for his army by concluding a treaty with the British in Sierra Leone. He changed tactics and concentrated on defending his empire and using guerilla technique.

Samori Toure's resistance against the French colonization in West Africa lasted between 1882 and 1898. The protracted resistance was attributed to:

- Samori Toure had a large well- organized army which was a formidable force even for the well drilled French troops.
- He equipped his army with modern weapons which he acquired through trade and also manufactured some locally.
- He used Mandinka nationalism and Islam to rally the soldiers together.
- He had adequate food supply which sustained the army.
- He used guerilla warfare and scorched earth policy which proved effective against the French.
- Some of his soldiers had served in the French colonial army and were thus familiar with the French war tactics.
- Use of horses by Samori during the war enhanced his soldiers' mobility.
- Samori's soldiers were familiar with the terrain. This enhanced effective assignment of duties.
- He was a competent leader who inspired his soldier.
- He used diplomacy, for example he signed the Bisandongou Treaty (1886) to get more time to re-organize his troops.
- Samori shifted his empire and capital further inland to give him more time to re-organize his forces.

In 1891, armed with modern weapons and a re-organized army, Samori defeated the French, only to be thoroughly trounced in 1892 by the French forces. In 1893, Samori transferred his capital from Bisandongou to Dabakala and decide to expand his empire eastwards. In 1898, Samori Toure coerced to combat against insurmountable odds was captured and deported to Gabon, where he died two years later.

Samori Toure was defeated by the French because:

- He Lacked support from British who did not want to be in disagreement with the French
- His involvement in Slave Trade made him unpopular
- He Lacked support from other African rulers, for example Seku Ahmed of Tukolor and Tiebba of Sikasso who instead supported the French
- His sources of military supplies of horses and weapons were stopped because he moved further East
- Non – Muslims in his empire sided with the French since they saw them as protector of fellow Christians
- Scorched-earthed policy destroyed everything on the way to the east and made him unpopular to his subjects who became unpatriotic
- His wealth was reduced due to loss of Bure gold mines
- French were supreme militarily and were determined to defeat Samori Toure
- Samori Toure's policy of converting his subjects to Islam caused revolt in 1888 which weakened the empire
- He became old and was unable to control large armies he had built.
- His army was constantly on the move and could not engage in economic activities
- Samori's retreat to Liberia was blocked and his capital was besieged

Results of Samori Toure's resistance against the French

- The Mandika Empire disintegrated as the French established their rule
- Property was destroyed due to the use of scotch earth policy causing famine and

suffering to the people

- Some Mandika fled to other countries, for example Ghana and Ivory Coast to avoid the French rule
- Many people lost their lives due to prolonged war
- Samori was captured and exiled to Gabon in 1889

Why Samori Toure second empire was not suitable

(a) He was cut off from his gold mines at Bure.
(b) He was cut off from Freetown where he bought firearms
(c) The Southern frontier of the empire was open to French attacks from Ivory coast
(d) He was surrounded by enemies (France and Britain) from all sides
(e) He was at war with the communities which he had attacked in his expansion campaign.

Questions on Samori Toure of the Mandinke Empire

(a) Identify the empire which was ruled by Samori Toure
(b) Give the main reason why Samori Tuore resumed fighting the French after the Bisandugu Treaty
(c) State two results of Samori Toure's resistance against the French in West Africa between 1882 -1898
(d) State three factors that enabled Samori Toure to build a strong empire
(e) What were the causes of the Franco – Mandika War of 1891 – 1898?
(f) What factors enabled Samori Toure to resist French colonization in West Africa between 1882 and 1898?
(g) Explain five factors that led to Samori Toure's defeat by the French
(h) Outline five reasons why Samori Toure second empire was not suitable.

The Ndebele Resistance of 1893

In 1821, Mzilikazi differed with Shaka Zulu and took flight to the north where his Kumalo clan became known as Ama-ndebele, which means "people of the long shields." They established themselves in the present day Zimbabwe. The death of Mzilikazi triggered off a succession crisis resulting amidst disagreement, in his son Lobengula ascending to the throne. The succession crisis sharpened Lobengula's political skills which, while it brought together the Ndebele, led to an unavoidable clash with the Europeans.

Caught between the insubordinate military *indunas* and Europeans in search of gold, Lobengula put a stop to the internal dissent by signing a number of treaties with the Europeans without making vulnerable his sovereignty. He restricted the number of whites in his territory and the duration of their stay.

In 1880's the Scramble for Africa was in full swing as the Boers, British, Germans and Portuguese were all trying hard to out compete each other on the riches of the interior. The Matabele land was directly in the path of the only viable route to the interior and Lobengula had no illusion that he could hold back the Europeans indefinitely.

Lobengula

On February 11, 1888 the beginning of the end came when Lobengula signed the Moffat Treaty, believing it to be the renewal of a limited treaty signed by his father. Moffat Treaty placed Matabela land directly in the sphere of British influence with an associated influx of Europeans. On October 30th 1888 the death knell was sounded when Lobengula signed the treacherous Rudd Concession, which through the intrigues of Cecil Rhodes and his cohorts, was then used to obtain a royal charter. BSAC which was controlled by Rhodes became the sole British concessionaire.

The Rudd Concession was unique in that it was not a treaty between sovereign states, but a concession granted to a commercial company. The oral and written version of the treaty differed. Realizing that he was hoodwinked, Lobengula appealed to the Queen (Victoria) to no avail.

In July 1893, a Ndebele party which which was raiding the Shona for cattle and grains, was shot by Europeans near Port Victoria. Lobengula, his diplomacy and patience exhausted, his honour and dignity affronted, realized that he had to retaliate. He tried to avoid war, but the European's design on his land was not to be denied. The Anglo-Ndebele War, the similarity of the schemings leading to the Anglo-Zulu War not being purely coincidental, began. The Ndebele never got within the range. Lobengula's *assegais* were no match for the machine gun.

In October 1893, Lobengula in a final act of desperation fled northwards where he died in January 1884. His people, whose livelihood was based on farming and livestock, were deprived of land and were frequently conscripted to work in the British gold mines

Lonbengula was defeated by the British in 1893 because:

- Of the superiority of the British weapons
- The British had created enmity between the Shona and the Ndebele. Therefore the Shona could not help the Ndebele
- The British suppressed the revolt ruthlessly and this created fear among the warriors
- Small pox attacked and weakened a section of the Ndebele warriors
- The Ndebele used poor fighting strategies, for example use of open– pitched battles
- Ndebele operated under a caste system – the less privileged class, for example Enhla and Holi refused to participate in war
- The British were supported by some African warriors against the Ndebele.
- The British soldiers were better trained and organized
- The fleeing and final death of Lobenguela in exile demoralized the Ndebele.

The results of the British – Ndebele war of 1893
(a) The British occupied the Mashona land
(b) The Ndebele were pushed to the reserves of Gwaai and Shangani
(c) The Ndebele were subjected to forced labour and taxation
(d) Many Ndebele lost their lives during the war
(e) The war created hostility between the Africans and the Europeans which later led to

Questions on the Ndebele Resistance of 1893
(a) State three reasons which caused the Ndebele resistance of 1893
(b) Identify two agreements signed between Lobengula and the White men
(c) Give three reasons why Lobengula was defeated by the British in 1893
(d) What were the results of the British-Ndebele war of 1893?
(e) Explain six negative results of African resistance against the Europeans in the 19th century.

REBELLION

Chimurenga Wars of 1896 -1897

Chimurenga is a word in Shona language roughly meaning "revolutionary struggle." In specific historical terms, it refers to the Ndebele and Shona insurgence against the BSAC during the late 1890's.

Mlimo, the Matebele spiritual leader is credited with drumming up much of the resentment that led to this confrontation. He convinced the Ndebele and Shona that white settlers were to blame for the drought, locust invasion and rinderpest which were creating havoc in the country at the time. He claimed that Mwari hated the Whites and promised them immunity from British bullets if they united against them.

Only a few months earlier the BSAC Administrator General for Matabeleland, Leander Starr Jameson, had send most of his troops and armaments to fight the Transvaal Republic, under Paul Krugger, in the ill-fated Jameson Raid. This left the country's defenses in disarray.

Causes of the Chimurenga wars of 1896 -1897

- The Ndebele did not fully accept the defeat of 1893
- The British took away the best land and put them to reserves which were infertile
- Chiefs and their subjects were punished together and forced to work in the farms and mines
- Hut tax was introduced and was forcefully collected
- The British took most of the Ndebele cattle making them to suffer
- The British disregarded the Ndebele customs, for example the class system where the Holi were regarded as slaves, but all of them were now given the same treatment and subjected to the same work
- The British stopped the Shona from trading with other countries and traded with them at lower rates
- Natural calamities, for example rinder pest and drought were blamed on the whiteman
- The failure of the British, under Jameson, to defeat the Boers (1895-6) made them to realize that the British were not indomitable

Course of the Rebellion

The Ndebele began their revolt in March 1896. In June, Mashaykuna led the uprising of the Zezuru Shona people located to the south west of the Capital (Salisbury). He worked with the local spiritual leader Kagubi and during this period a British farmer Norton and his wife were killed at Porta Farm in Norton. The third phase of the Chimurenga was joined by the Hwata dynasty of Mazoe. They succeeded in driving away the British settlers from their land on 20th June 1896. Three months later, the British South African police regrouped and established control over the Hwata people after their Mambo (king) surrendered together with his spiritual medium, Nehanda Nyakasikana. They were both sentenced to death and executed. Mlimo was eventually assassinated in his temple in Matobo Hills by the American Scout, Fredrick Russell Burnham.

Cecil Rhodes

Cecil Rhodes persuaded the "troublemakers" to lay down their arms and the uprising came to an end in October 1897. Matabeleland and Mashonaland were unified under company rule and renamed Southern Rhodesia.

Role of Religion in the Organization of the Shona–Ndebele Resistance

- Religion united the Shona and Ndebele who had hitherto been bitter rivals.
- It boosted and sustained the morale of the fighters and gave them spiritual strength to fight a mighty force.
- Religion provided the resistance with a common ideology much of which was derived from *Umlugulu,* the chief priest of the Ndebele; *Nyamanda,* Lobengula's eldest son and Mlimo, the medium of Mwari Cult
- Religious leaders provided leadership to the war against white aggressors who were considered immoral and brutal.
- The Mwari Cult provided an important organization link between the Ndebele and shona since it was widespread.
- The most important representatives of the Mwari Cult were Mkwati and Singinyamatse who were the backbone of the spiritual unity of the Ndebele.

The Ndebele and Shona were defeated because:

- The Ndebele and Shona fought as different groups
- The British had more superior weapons than the Africans who depended on magic
- The British got reinforcement from Botswana and South Africa
- Cecil Rhodes was determined to win the war and used all methods, for example negotiation and battle
- British soldiers were better armed and trained

- The executed African leaders demoralized the fighters
- The African economy was too week to support the military expedition
- The Ndebele social class did not favour them against the British
- The magic failed to protect the people against the bullets
- Rhodes negotiated with the Ndebele to end the war and easily defeated the isolated Shona

---

Effects of Chimurenga War
(a) Many people lost their lives in the war
(b) A lot of property was destroyed
(c) Political and economic reforms were initiated
(d) More land and cattle were taken away
(e) Ndebele were reallocated to new land at the lowlands
(f) The Ndebele *Indunas* were recognized
(g) Failure of Mwari cult made many people to be converted to Christianity
(h) The war united the Shone and Ndebele who had been traditional enemies

---

Questions on the Chimurenga Wars of 1896 -1897
(a) Name two people who organized the Chimurenga uprising of 1896 -1897
(b) Identify the main reason why the Shona fought a more protracted war against the British than the Ndebele during the Chimurenga War of 1896 - 1897
(c) What were the causes of Chimurenga wars of 1896 -1897?
(d) Why were the Ndebele and Shona Defeated?
(e) State the effects of Chimurenga War

Maji Maji Rebellion of 1905 -7

*M*aji *Maji* rebellion was a vicious reaction by Africans in the southern part of Tanganyika against the German tyrannical rule in the German East African colony. It was the only one of its kind in the region because:

- It was fought after the already established Germans who had squashed African opposition to their colonial rule
- The reaction consisted of different African tribes who came together against a common enemy
- *Maji Maji* was the first organized reaction against the Germans in Tanganyika to regain independence
- It was a protracted resistance and had many casualties

Maji Maji was an uprising against the German policy intended to coerce Africans to grow cotton in the southern part of Tanganyika for export. The tribes which were involved in the skirmish included the Zaramo, Wamwera, Ngindo, Bunga, Bena, Mpunga, Matumbi, Pogoro, Luguru and Ngoni.

After the scramble for Africa among the major European powers in the 1880's, Germany reinforced its hold on several formal African colonies. These were German East Africa (now Tanzania, Rwanda, Burundi and parts of Mozambique) and German South West Africa (presently Namibia, Cameroon and Togo). Her hold on the German East African colony was relatively weak, but she maintained a system of forts throughout the interior and was able to assert some sort of control over it.

Germany resorted to using violent repressive tactics to control the population in areas where her hold was weak. She began levying Head Tax in 1898, and relied heavily on forced labour to build roads and accomplish various other tasks. In 1902, Karl Peters ordered villages to grow cotton as a cash crop. A quota of cotton was set for each region and the village headmen were held accountable for the set target. This set the Akidas and Jumbes, who were used by the Germans to accomplish the Herculean task, against the rest of the population.

The German policies were not only unpopular, but also had serious effects on the lives of the natives. The social fabrics of the society were changed. Women increasingly began to assume the traditional roles of their men who were forced away from their homes to work for the Germans.

These effects created a lot of animosity against the then government. In 1905, a drought threatened the region. Coupled with the opposition to the government's agricultural and labour policies, an open rebellion against the German rule ensued in July.

The Causes of the *Maji Maji*

(a) They needed to regain their lost independence to the Germans

(b) Germans were harsh and quite brutal to the Africans

(c) Africans were forced to work especially in public utilities

(d) Christians disregarded African traditional beliefs

(e) A lot of land was forcefully grabbed from the Africans

(f) Africans resented the failed cotton growing programme in the south

(g) Ngoni wanted to revenge against the Germans who had killed many of them in 1896 and took away their property

(h) The use of Arabs and Waswahili as Jumbes and Akidas by the Germans was resented by the people of Southern Tanzania.

(i) The Germans showed disrespect for African culture, for example they raped and slept with Ngindo women which was a crime punished by death.

(j) Germans treated African rulers contemptuously, e.g. flogging them in public.

Course of the *Maji Maji*

The insurgents turned to magic water to drive out the German colonizers and used it as a unifying force in the rebellion. A religious leader called Kinjinkitile Ngwale, who claimed to be possessed by a snake spirit called Hongo, organized the rebellion. He called himself Bokero and developed a belief that the people of German East Africa had been called upon to eliminate the Germans.

German anthropologists recorded that he gave his followers "war medicine" that would turn German bullets into water. This "war medicine" was in fact water (*maji* in Swahili) mixed with castor oil and millet seeds. Empowered with this new liquid, Bokero's followers began what later become known as the *maji maji* rebellion. They were poorly armed with sticks, spears and arrows. Nevertheless, they were numerous and of the opinion that German bullets, which would turn to water, would be harmless.

Initially, Bokero's followers attacked small outposts and damaged cotton plants, but on 31st July 1905, Matumbi tribesmen destroyed the cotton crops as well as a trading post. On 14th August 1905, Ngindo tribesmen attacked a small party of missionaries on a *safari* and speared all the five, including Bishop Spiss. Throughout August, the rebels moved from the Matumbi Hills in the southern part and attacked German garrisons throughout the colony. The Ngoni people decided to join the revolt with a force of 5000. However, when confronted by the German troops, armed with machine guns from Malenga on 21st October 1905, the Ngoni worriers fled. They threw away their bottles of "war medicine" and cried, "The *maji* is a lie."

Upon the outbreak of the fighting Count Gustav Adolf Von Gótzen, governor of German East Africa requested for reinforcement from the German government. Kaiser Wilhem immediately dispatched two cruisers to the troubled colony. The Germans also got reinforcement from as far as New Guinea. Gótzen used 1000 regular German soldiers and other reinforcements to destroy villages, crops and other food sources which were used by the rebels. He made effective use of his fire power to break up rebel attacks. German advance to the south west was temporarily halted by the Bena who made a successful ambush of a German column which was crossing the Rufiji River.

Not until August 1907, were the last embers of rebellion extinguished in most parts of Southern Tanganyika. The rebellion was crushed because:

- The Germans used superior weapons and well trained soldiers
- The arrest, imprisonment, deportation and execution of some leaders demoralized the fighters
- Africans were not well organized in their resistance. Each Community fought on its own.
- The magic water failed to protect Africans from German bullets leading to death of many African worriers in the battle.
- The Africans did not unite to face the common enemy, for example major tribes like the Hehe, Chagga, Yao and Nyamwezi did not join the revolt.
- The Germans received reinforcement from Germany and other colonies and their number overwhelmed the African worriers.
- The ruthlessness of the German soldiers in crushing the rebellion, for example use of scorched earth policy scared many people.

Role of religion in the Maji Maji rebellion

- Religion gave people courage, loyalty and confidence to fight the Germans.
- Religious cults like bokero promised people the destruction of the white man.

- Through religion, suspicions among communities were wiped out.
- Many people joined the maji maji regardless of their tribe because of the religion.
- Religion provided the ideology, which guided the war efforts.
- It sustained the morale of the warriors.
- It gave spiritual strength to fight a superior force.
- It provided a common plan of action based on mass action
- Religion provided leadership during the war.
- It was used, to address the so many African grievances emanating from the harsh German rule.

Results of the *Maji Maji* Rebellion

In its wake, the *maji maji* rebellion left 15 Europeans and 389 native soldiers, and tens of thousands of the insurgents and innocent bystanders dead. Many leaders were captured and hanged. The rebellion broke the spirit of the people to resist and for a long time Tanzania has remained calm. Lions in the area developed a taste for human flesh in the wake of the slaughter and Songea region is still plagued by the "man-eaters".

The famine following the *maji maji* rebellion was partly deliberate. Von Gótzen was willing to pardon the common soldiers as long as they gave up their weapons, leaders and witchdoctors. However, he also needed to flush out the remaining rebels and famine was the chosen weapon.

After the war, the imperial government instituted reforms so that, by the outbreak of the World War I, Tanganyika was one of the best administered European colonies in Africa. Later Tanzanian nationalists used *maji maji* as an example of the first stirring of Tanzanian nationalism, a unifying experience that brought together all the different people of Tanzania under one leader in an attempt to establish a nation free from foreign domination.

Effects of the Maji Maji

(a) There was massive destruction of property

(b) The war upset economic activities of the people, for example farming was neglected leading to famine and starvation

(c) Many people were displaced and their houses burnt down by the Germans

(d) The war made people to lose faith in their traditions and the magicians

(e) There was ill feeling among the communities some of whom felt betrayed

(f) Africans learnt the importance of unity against a common enemy

(g) Africans realized the futility to use force against the Germans

(h) Germans were forced to reform their administration

Maji Maji rebellion was an eye opener to the German administrator in Tanganyika and they initiated many reforms after the rebellion. These reforms included:

- Communal cotton growing was stopped and Africans were encouraged to plant their own cotton and get profits from it
- Forced labour in settler farms was abolished
- Corporal punishment was forbidden and settlers who mistreated African workers were punished
- Extra taxation for Africans was abolished
- Africans were involved in administration of the region instead of the Akidas and Jumbes
- The new governor censured newspapers that supported settlers against the Africans
- A colonial department of Germany was formed in 1907 to closely investigate the affairs of German East African Company
- Kiswahili was accepted as the official

language

- Colonial administration was tailored to suit African interest
- Harsh leaders like Karl Peters were recalled.
- A new governor was brought who was more sympathetic to African cause

Generally, European colonization of Africa was influenced by:

- Disunity among African communities
- Military superiority of Europeans
- Illiterate African leaders failed to figure out the true intentions of the white men
- Berlin conference came up with a formula for effective occupation of Africa
- Missionaries play an important role of encouraging African chiefs to sign treaties with the colonialists
- Ruthless attack by the Europeans made most Africans to fear taking them head on
- Collaboration by some African communities made the work of the colonialists easy
- The colonial powers got reinforcement from their home countries or other colonies

Questions on the Maji Maji Rebellion of 1905 -7

(a) Name two tribes who took part in the Maji Maji Rebellion

(b) State two contributions of religion to the Maji Maji uprising

(c) State two ways how the Maji Maji uprising was different from other resistances against the Germans in Tanganyika

(d) State five causes of the Maji Mai rebellion of 1905 -7

(e) What factors led to the failure of the Maji Maji rebellion of 1907

(f) What were the results of the Maji Maji Rebellion?

(g) Explain five reforms that were introduced by the German Administration after the Maji Maji

The Barons

13 COLONIAL ADMINISTRATION IN AFRICA

BRITISH SYSTEM OF COLONIAL RULE IN AFRICA

British Direct Rule in Zimbabwe

The British used direct rule in Zimbabwe because:

- There were many Europeans in the colony who could serve as administrators
- British had lost confidence in African leadership after Chimurenga wars
- They wanted to fully utilize mineral resources in Zimbabwe
- The British South African company had enough funds to pay the administrators
- Zimbabwe traditional chiefs were unco-operative and wanted to retain their independence
- The existing traditional system of administration and indigenous institutions such as the *Indunas* had been destroyed or upset during the British occupation period

---

Features of direct rule in Zimbabwe

(a) There was a large number of Europeans and the system was designed to give them an edge over Africans

(b) The settlers believed that the region belonged to them

(c) Upto 1923 the place was administered by a commercial company, BSACo.

(d) The European government made all the important decisions

(e) They had a Legislative Council which was dominated by whites

(f) Europeans acquired large tracks of land

(g) There was racial segregation

(h) The administration was quite authoritative and managed by white minority

---

The BSAC administrative structure in Southern Rhodesia (1905-1923)

At the helm of the government was a Resident Commissioner who was appointed by the company and below him were various European commissioners in charge of the districts then African Chiefs whose duty included:

- Collecting tax
- Recruiting labour and
- Maintaining law and order

In 1898, a Legislative Council, which was heavily dominated by the European settlers, was established. An Executive Council, consisting of the Resident Commissioner and 4 nominees of company was also established. In 1902, a Native Affairs Department, headed by a European Native Commissioner was created. The duty of the commissioner was to:

- Allocate land to Africans
- Collect taxes and
- Recruit labour.

Due to lack of enough valuable minerals in Zimbabwe, the Europeans acquired large tracts of land from African communities as compensation.

Effects of British rule in Zimbabwe

- Africans were displaced from their ancestral lands to pave way for European settlement.
- The establishment of white settlement exposed Africans to abject poverty and suffering. Africans were subjected to extreme economic exploitation through taxation and forced labour.
- African traditional economy was greatly undermined.
- The Africans were highly discriminated

- The day-to-day running of the colony was rested on the hands of whites without much reference to the African interest.
- African traditional rulers lost their autonomy and became mere puppets of British administration.
- African culture was undermined, for example through the separation of families as people sought alternative livelihood.
- White settlement enhanced the production of cash crops, development of infrastructure and encouraged trade and industry in Zimbabwe.
- Africans were denied freedom of movements by being confined to the reserves and required to carry identification cards
- Oppressiveness of the Whites led to the rise of nationalism in Zimbabwe.
- British South African Company was given too much powers in the administration of the colony

Crown Colony Rule (1923-1953)
In 1923, the company relinquished its control and Zimbabwe became a crown colony. The settlers favoured a crown colony over a merger with South Africa because:
- The merger would have led to domination by Afrikaners in their political matters.
- Their economic interests would have been neglected in favour of those of Afrikaners.

A Governor was appointed in 1923 to represent the Queen of England. Though the British government was empowered by the constitution to veto any discriminatory legislation, in practice this did not happen. A parallel development policy (A two tier pyramid) which was characterized by widespread prejudice against Africans was established.

At the bottom of the pyramid were Africans who were the majority, but were consigned to their demeaning role of serving as "hewers of wood and servants" of the white race. At the apex were the whites who were the minority. They took the lion's share in the economic and political system. To legitimize the two pyramids policy, two Acts were passed in 1930 and 1934.

Land Apportionment Act of 1930
The Act established rigid territorial separation and land was apportioned into African reserves and European enclaves. No African was permitted to obtain land outside their designated areas. The whites, who were the minority, acquired more than half of the prime land while Africans, who were the majority, were given the discarded areas. The Act categorized land into four:
- Native reserve areas for African population. This land was over populated and unproductive.
- Native purchase area: Africans could buy land from such areas, though they were located in areas with harsh climatic conditions.
- European Area: This land was set aside exclusively for the whites.
- Unassigned Area. This land was designated for government expansion.

Effects of the Land Apportionment Act on Africans
- Many Africans became migrant labourers. They moved to the mines, towns and European farms to provide cheap labour since their land was unproductive.
- Large tracts of African land were alienated and a big chunk was allocated to the whites while Africans were given a very small portion.
- Prime land, which was strategically located near roads and market centres were dished out to the whites while Africans were

The Barons

placed in remote areas which were likely to be affected by drought.

- The rapid population increase in the reserves made poverty to grow deeper among Africans in rural areas.
- The state agricultural policy and legislation of the 1930's firmly gave preference to European agricultural practices and sought to trivialize the African production.
- Africans were racially segregation in provision of social amenities in the urban centres.
- Societal social fabrics were disrupted and women began to engage in roles which were traditionally designated for men who moved to towns and settler farms and left their women and children in the reserves.
- Africans were over taxed to drive them to the settler farms where they would provide labour to earn wages and pay tax.
- Land apportionment Act became the focal point of African nationalism in Zimbabwe

The Industrial Conciliation Act of 1934 was a pre-emptive measure for the white workers against African competition. Through the act, Africans were prohibited from setting up Trade Unions and forced to provide cheap labour to the whites. Skilled and well paying jobs were set aside for Europeans while Africans were downgraded to clerical and unskilled duties.

The two acts created humiliating conditions for the Africans and promoted the spirit of nationalism among them. To thwart African agitation, the government encouraged more Europeans to settle in the region and gave them large tracts of land. The settlers on the other hand, began to agitate for the formation of a federation of the three Central African territories which included Southern Rhodesia, Northern Rhodesia and Nyasaland. In 1953, the British government gave approval for the formation of the Federation of Central African Countries.

THE CENTRAL AFRICAN FEDERATION

The first Prime Minister of the Federation was Garfield Todd. Since he was sympathetic to the Africans who were protesting over the formation of the federation, Garfield Todd legalized Trade Unions and funded the African education and Agriculture. But when Todd was replaced in 1958, all his programmes were abandoned. In 1963, the federation was dissolved and shortly afterwards Malawi and Zambia became independent. Southern Rhodesia remained the only a self-governing colony.

How the federation was organized
(a) Each territory had its own government responsible for local administration.
(b) Each territorial government was responsible for all aspects of native affairs within its boundaries.
(c) The British government was directly involved in the administration of the two northern protectorates.
(d) An African Board was established to ensure that no racist legislation against the Africans was passed in the Federal Parliament.
(e) The Federal Parliament was given powers to deal with all matters involving more than one territory and foreign affairs.

The Reign of Ian Smith

Ian Smith's Rhodesian Front Party, controlled by the white extremists won the 1962 elections. On 15th October 1965, Smith led the settlers in the "Unilateral Declaration of Independence" (UDI) from Britain. This meant that political leadership was now completely in the hands of the extremist white settlers who had no regard for Africans. The declaration provoked instant protest not only within Africa but also from the international community. United Nations Organization (UNO) declared sanctions against Southern Rhodesia, but countries like South Africa and Portugal still continued to trade with her. This made the sanctions to be ineffective.

Ian Smith

In 1970, UDI declared itself a Republic under a new constitution which entrenched European supremacy in Zimbabwe. It spelled the following:

- Voting qualifications for Africans were revised and were now based on income. This automatically disenfranchised the majority of Africans.
- The land tenure system was revised to enable the Europeans to purchase land from the government.

A violent struggle for independence began in Zimbabwe around 1966 in earnest. This war was provoked by the 1965 UDI declaration. A patriotic front, formed by Zimbabwe African National Union (ZANU) of Mugabe Robert and Zimbabwe African People's Union (ZAPU) of Joshua Nkomo waged guerilla warfare. Zimbabwe became independent in 1980, with Robert Mugabe as the first Prime Minister and later president.

Questions on the British Policy of Direct Rule in Zimbabwe

(a) State two reasons why British used Direct Rule in Zimbabwe

(b) Describe the features of Direct Rule as applied by the British in Zimbabwe

(c) Explain the effects of British Direct Rule in Zimbabwe

(d) Mention two Central African Territories which formed a federation during the colonial time

(e) Mention two reforms which favoured Africans that were introduced by Garfield Todd in Central African federation

(f) Name the white leader who led the settlers in the unilateral declaration of independence from Britain in Central Africa

(g) Mention one reason why the sanctions which were declared by UNO against Southern Rhodesia were less successful

(h) Mention two parties which fought for independence in Zimbabwe

(i) Explain five effect of Land Apportionment Act on the African in Zimbabwe

British Indirect Rule in Northern Nigeria
Fredrick Lugard, who took up the position of High Commissioner of the protectorate of Northern Nigeria in 1900, has often been looked upon as the model British colonial administrator. Trained as an army officer, Lugard had served in India, Egypt and East Africa, where he expelled Arab slave traders from Nyasaland and established the British presence in Uganda. Joining the Royal Niger Company in 1884, Lugard was sent to Borno to counter the inroads made by the French. In 1897 he was assigned the responsible for raising the Royal West African Frontier Force (RWAFF) from local levies to serve under British officers.

Captain Fredrick Lugard

During his six year tenure as the High Commissioner, Lugard was pre-occupied with transforming the commercial empire inherited from the Royal Niger Company into a viable territorial unit under effective British political control. His objective was to conquer the entire region and to obtain recognition of the British protectorate by its indigenous rulers, especially the Fulani Emirs of the Sokoto Caliphate.

Lugard's campaign systematically subdued local resistance, using armed force when diplomatic measures failed. Burno capitulated without a fight, but in 1903 Lugard's FWAFF mounted assault on Kano and Sokoto. From Lugard's point of view, clear cut military victories were essencial because their surrenders weakened resistance elsewhere.

Lugard's success in Northern Nigeria has been attributed to his policy of Indirect Rule, which he called for governing the protectorate through the rulers who had been defeated. If the Emirs accepted British authority, abandoned the Slave Trade, and co-operated with the British officials in modernizing their administration, the colonial power was willing to confirm them in office. The Emirs retained their Caliphate titles, but were responsible to the British district officers, who had final authority. The British High Commissioners could depose Emirs and other officials if necessary.

Lugard reduced sharply the number of title holders in the Emirates weakening the ruler's patronage.

Why the British used Indirect Rule

(i) The British did not have enough manpower to administer the vast territory

(j) Britain had inadequate funds to facilitate administrative expenses of the protectorate

(k) The British wanted to win the confidence and the support of all the people by giving them the impression that they were still under the governance of their leaders

(l) The existing well centralized system of administration based on Islamic law under the Emirs was ideal for Indirect Rule

(m) Success was already realized elsewhere within the empire, for example in Uganda and India

(n) Poor transport and communication network made it difficult for the British officials to effectively administer parts of the colony

(o) Britain had inadequate soldiers to quell revolts which would have erupted from Muslims

(p) The North Nigerian Emirs were willing to co-operate so long as they were allowed to exercise their Islamic law

(q) The officials sent to Northern Nigeria Africa were affected by tropical diseases

(r) Natives of Northern Nigeria were used to paying taxes thus could not rebel over taxes

The Islamic institutions in the Northern Nigeria influenced Lugard's decision to use indirect rule in the region. These institutions included:

• Institution of the Emirs who were the traditional rulers

• Existence of a police force which maintained law and order

• An effective taxation system which made the natives less resentful to paying tax

• Existence of sheria laws which guided peoples' activities

Under Indirect Rule, Caliphate officials were transformed into salaried district heads and became in effect agents of the British authorities responsible for maintaining law and order, recruitment of labour, supervising communal work and tax collectors. The traditional rulers were negatively affected by their new role. Their duties, for example collecting tax and recruiting labour made them quite unpopular among their subjects. They also lost their independence to the British and became mere puppets.

The old chain of command was merely capped with a new Lordship, the British High Commissioners. The protectorate required only a limited number of colonial officers scattered throughout the territories as overseers. Depending on local conditions they exercised discretion in advising the Emirs and local officials, but all orders from the High Commissioners were transmitted through the Emirs. Although the High Commissioners possessed unlimited executive and legislative powers in the protectorate most of the activities of the government were undertaken by the Emirs and their local administration, subject to British approval. A dual system of law functioned – the Sheria Courts continued to deal with matters affecting the personal status of Muslims, including land disputes, divorce, debt and slave emancipation.

As a consequence of indirect rule, Hausa-Fulani domination was confirmed and in some instances imposed on diverse ethnic groups, some of them non- Muslims, in the so called middle belt. In the north, Lugard and his successors limited the activities of missionaries in order to maintain Muslim domination. Consequently, the north lagged behind those in the south.

> **Why Indirect Rule was less successful in the South**
>
> (a) Southern Nigeria did not have Centralized Government suitable for the application of Indirect Rule
> (b) Southern Nigeria had many ethnic groups with diverse culture and language, making it difficult to unite them under one rule
> (c) The Yoruba Obas were given excessive powers and this caused friction, resentment and discontent among the people
> (d) The warrant chiefs were unpopular because they had no traditional claim to office and were imposed on the people by the British administration
> (e) The educated were ignored by Lugard and were given minor positions
> (f) The people of the Southern Nigeria were opposed to direct taxation and forced labour
> (g) The use of excessive force to suppress any form of resistance provoked resentment, for example the shooting of women during a demonstration against the British
> (h) The British administrators failed to understand the social economic and political systems of Southern Nigeria

Some, progress were made in economic development in the north. Railroad lines, for instance were constructed to: -

- Transport tin from Jos Plateau and northern grown peanut and cotton to the ports on the coast.
- Promote trade in the country.
- Facilitate the movement of colonial administrators.
- Facilitate the exploitation of natural resources in remote parts of the country.
- Speed up communication between Nigeria and Britain.
- Raise revenue for administering the country.

Effects of Indirect Rule in Nigeria
Positive effects

- There was introduction of Common Law in Nigeria
- Modern facilities, for example hospitals and schools were spread in the southern Nigeria
- It assisted in the spread of modern currency
- Emirs backed by the British had more powers than before
- It led to the rise of nationalism because educated Africans were ignored by Indirect Rule and they were not happy
- Indirect Rule assisted to preserve African culture, unlike assimilation
- Indigenous system of administration and justice was modernized by the British
- African chiefs were able to accumulate a lot of wealth at the expense of their people, for example land and livestock

Negative effects

- Northern Nigeria remained backward and conservative because Muslims did not accommodate change.
- Many administrative jobs in the north were taken over by educated southerns, for example Igbo
- The role of the traditional chiefs changed, for example they collected taxes and recruited Africans in forced labour. This made them unpopular
- Local rulers lost their independence and power to the British and became puppets
- Europeans lacked a language to communicate with African chiefs and their instructions were not clearly understood by them. Chiefs often disregarded what was not familiar to them and gave more attention to what they understood, like Christianity and forced labour. This made it difficult to apply Indirect Rule
- Chiefs, whose rule did not conform to the British expectation, were replaced.

Questions on the British Policy of Indirect Rule in Northern Nigeria

(a) State three functions of the chiefs and Emirs
(b) Why did the British use Indirect Rule in Northern Nigeria
(c) Explain why Indirect Rule failed in Southern Nigeria
(d) What were the effects of Indirect Rule in Nigeria?
(e) Mention two ways in which Indirect Rule negatively affected traditional leaders in Nigeria
(f) Why did the British improve transport and communication in Northern Nigeria?

FRENCH SYSTEM OF COLONIAL ADMINISTRATION

Assimilation

The French practiced Assimilation policy mainly in Senegal and Association in areas outside the four communes. Assimilation aimed at detribalizing Africans and producing Europeans in black skins who spoke, dressed and behaved like the French. Africans who had undergone this transformation were considered French citizens and could enjoy certain privileges.

Conditions to be meet before being assimilated

(a) Knowing how to read, write and speak the French language
(b) Being converted to Christianity
(c) Knowing and practicing French legal system
(d) Having distinguished record in the French military service
(e) Accepting French mannerism like eating and dressing habits
(f) Serving in the French Civil Service for a long time
(g) Being born within the four communes in Senegal

The French policy of assimilation was more successful in the four communes in Senegal which included St. Louis, Dakar, Goree and Rustsique. This success was attributed to:

- A high percentage of *Mulato* population in the area who readily accepted the French due to their long term intercourse with the French system
- Africans in the four communes were familiar with the Europeans because of their trading activities in the past
- Many people from the four communes had already been converted to Christianity

The French policy of assimilation was not successful in the areas outside the French communes in Senegal. This was due to:

- Opposition by local people who did not want the French to interfere with their culture
- People who had been converted to Islam resisted the French attempt to convert them to Christianity
- There was opposition by the French traders in West Africa who feared competition from the assimilated Africans
- The French government found it expensive to implement the policy because it required building many schools and employing teachers
- It was opposed by the French because they feared that Africans would out number them in the French Chamber of Deputies
- Traditional rulers did not want to lose their authority
- Vastness of the French colony made it difficult to supervise the system (adequate personal)
- The French imperialists opposed the policy in Senegal
- The system of land ownership in Senegal differed from that of France.

Assimilated Africans in the French colonies enjoyed certain benefits. These benefits included:

- They were allowed to send representatives to the French Chamber of Deputies
- They were exempted from forced labour
- They were provided with education rights like the French people
- They were allowed to vote like the French people and could be voted for
- They were allowed to serve in the French Civil Services
- They were provided with the same trading rights like the French people
- They were allowed to operate their own municipalities and county governments

Effects of the French policy of assimilation in Senegal included:

- Assimilation undermined the authority of the traditional rulers as they were replaced by the assimilated one.
- Senegal was incorporated in French Republic and was regarded as an overseas province
- It undermined the spread of Islam in the same communities where Africans had adopted Christianity
- It created a class of privileged Africans who were regarded to be equal with French people. Some Africans became citizens while others became subjects
- It led to the rise of nationalism in Senegal as Africans in Senegal fought for their cultural identity
- There was a great rift between assimilated Africans regarded as French men and the rest of African communities who were subjected to forced labour and heavy taxation
- The policy of assimilation undermined African culture as many adopted the French culture.

Africans from Senegal were allowed to participate in the political affairs of France. Some of them became deputies and minister in the French government.

Hierarchy of French colonial administration

- The French colonial administration was highly centralized with a minister who was based in Paris
- It was a federal system of government where the 8 French colonies were grouped together to form a federation called Dakar
- Each colony was headed by Lieutenant General
- The colonies were divided into provinces which were under a Commandant
- The provinces were divided into districts which were under a Chief
- The districts were divided into divisions under a Chief de Village

BRITISH AND THE FRENCH SYSTEM OF ADMINISTRATION

Differences

- French colonies were ruled as provinces of France while British colonies were treated as separated political entities under the rule of the governor on behalf of the British government
- The British allowed African traditional customary law to be applied while the French never gave regard to customary law
- In French colonies, the African rulers took orders from the French but in British colonies the chiefs retained their authority under supervision of colonial administration except in Zimbabwe where Direct Rule was used
- While the French wanted to assimilate the Africans, the British left them on their own so long as they accepted the British rule
- Laws used in French colonies were made in France while in British colonies, laws were made by the respective Legislative Councils
- In the French colonies Africans became citizens with full rights while those in the British colonies remained subjects
- The French used assimilated Africans in their administration while the British were not represented in the House of Commons as they had Legislative Council in their colonies
- French treated colonies as part and parcel of the French empire while the British treated them as separate entities

Similarities

- Both the French and the British maintained forced labour in public work
- They both abolished Slave Trade and slavery in their colonies
- They both paid low wages to the Africans and discriminated them
- Both imposed heavy taxation on the Africans

Questions on the French Policy of Assimilation in West Africa

(a) Name two communes in Senegal during the French Assimilation

(b) Give two reasons why the French policy of Assimilation was more successful in the four communes of Senegal

(c) State five ways though which the people of the four communes of Senegal enjoyed as a result of application of the Assimilation Policy

(d) Explain five factors which undermined the application of the French policy of Assimilation in West Africa

(e) Discuss the effect of French Policy Of Assimilation in Senegal

(f) Compare and contrast the British and the French system of administration.

14 EMERGENCE AND GROWTH OF NATIONALISM IN AFRICA

NATIONALISM IN GHANA

The educated Ghanaians like Dr. Aggrey, George Ferguson, and John Mensah Sarban spearheaded the nationalistic movement in the country. Others like Chief Osei Aggreman Prempeh also raised the political consciousness of their subjects. However, the real struggle for political freedom in Ghana started soon after World War II. This happened all of a sudden when people realized that colonialism was another form of oppression.

Causes of Nationalism in Ghana

- Rural health services and education policy in Ghana was not good enough. Upto 1950 government secondary schools in Ghana were only two and the rest were built by the missionaries.
- Ex-service men were radicalized by the shattered myth of white supremacy and they began demanding for self determination.
- Rulers were regarded as economic swindlers and their self-importance was repugnant.
- Some young District Commissioners had the ruling class mentality and delt with the old chiefs as if they were their subjects.
- There was wide spread redundancy amongst the educated elite and when employed, the local pay was awful
- African culture was rejected to some extent.
- Forced cutting down of African cocoa trees to curb the spread of cocoa disease annoyed some people
- Africans who were willing to practice import and export trade were denial trade license

- After the war, the prices of commodities hiked and this led to widespread inflation in Ghana
- The educate elite sensitized the masses about their political rights

Some external forces also contributed to the nationalist feelings. African Americans like Marcus Garvey and W.E. Du Bois raised strong Pan African conscience. In 1945 a conference was held in Manchester to promote Pan African ideas. This was attended by Kwame Nkrumah of Ghana, Azikwe of Nigeria and Wallace Johnson of Sierra Leone. The Ghanaian nationalists were also inspired to struggle for their independence by Indian and Pakistan which became independent in 1947 and 1948 respectively.

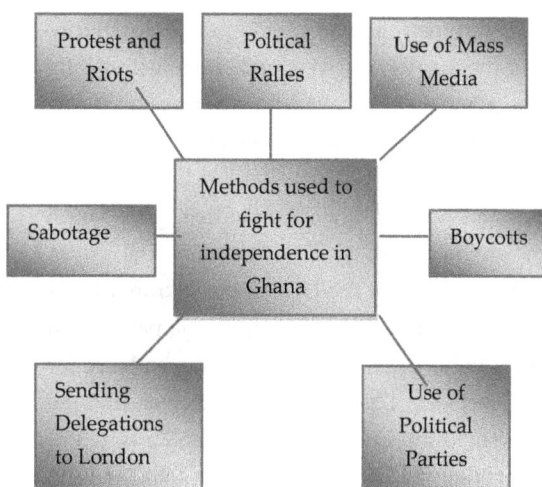

Sir Alan Burns' Constitution of 1946 provided for a new Legislative Council that was made up of the governor as the president, six government officials, six nominated members and 18 elected members. As a result of this new development, Dr. J. B. Danquah formed the United Gold Coast Convention (UGCC). Other officials were George Grant, Akuffo Addo, William Ofori, Atta, Obetseb Lamptey, Ako Aggrei and J. Isiboe. Their aim was independence for Ghana

Kwame Nkrumah

Nkrumah was presented an opportunity to serve as the Organizing Secretary of UGCC in the late 1947 and he made the crucial decision to return to Gold Coast to lend a hand in the anti-colonial crusade which snowballed in the aftermath of the World War II. He was put behind bars together with other leaders of the UGCC purportedly for inciting the veterans, workers and farmers in the colony. This made Nkrumah to gain widespread popularity among the masses, who responded enthusiastically to his combative and sizzling approach to the burgeoning anti-imperialist movement.

Nkrumah formed the Committee on Youth Organization (CYO). This became the most organized section of the UGCC, but Nkrumah was isolated from the top leadership of the party, who objected to his call for immediate independence for Gold Coast. On 12th June 1949, Nkrumah and the CYO formed the Convention Peoples' Party (CPP) in a meeting, in Accra, which was attended by a mammoth crowd.

Meanwhile, Nkrumah forged closer relations with other anti-colonial and Pan Africanist organizations which were operating in other West African colonies. In 1950, Nkrumah was once more arrested by the colonial government and charged for sedition when CPP called for a positive action campaign which led to a massive walkout and revolt right through Gold Coast.

The executive members of the CPP continued with the struggle for independence while Nkrumah was in prison. In a popular election held in 1951 CPP won overwhelmingly. Nkrumah was released from confinement and appointed leader of government business in a transitional arrangement that eventually led to the independence of Ghana on 6th March 1957. Nkrumah became the first head of state of an independent post colonial nation in Africa south of Sahara.

Kwame Nkrumah contributed immensely to the liberation struggle in other parts of Africa. His contributions were:

- He inspired other African nations to continue fighting for their independence
- He funded the nationalists in other African countries, for instance Guinea and Algeria
- He supported other African leaders any time they had differences with their former colonial masters
- Nkrumah championed the development of Trade Unionism in the continent
- He attended the Manchester Pan African Congress where the plight of African countries were addressed
- He convened the first Pan African congress in Africa in Ghana where the idea of OAU was mooted
- Ghana under Kwame Nkrumah gave moral and material support to other African countries not yet independent
- Nkrumah allowed some African Nationalist to establish military bases in the Ghana

Roles of Kwame Nkrumah in the struggle for independence in Gold Coast

(a) Kwame Nkrumah participated in the Manchester Pan Africa Congress where the need for independence of African countries was discussed

(b) He became the Secretary General of UGCC

(c) Nkrumah left UGCC because they thought it was too conservatist and formed Conventional Peoples Party (CPP)

(d) He rallied together the farmers, the war veterans, the elites, students and businessmen against the colonialists

(e) He encouraged CPP to use positive action to address the plight of the masses

(f) CPP under him won elections and formed the first African government before independence

(g) In 1957 Nkrumah lead Ghana into independence and become the first president

Questions on Nationalism in Ghana

(a) Name two political parties that contributed to the struggle for independence in Ghana

(b) State five causes of nationalism in Ghana

(c) Identify two methods used to fight for independence in Ghana

(d) Mention two factors which made Ghana attain independence before most African states

(e) Give two ways in which the attainment of independence in Ghana contributed to the liberation of other African countries from colonial rule

(f) Explain five contributions of Kwame Nkrumah in the struggle for independence of Ghana

NATIONALISM IN SOUTH AFRICA

Among members of the African nationalist, an all inclusive (multi-racial) democratic society was the most ideal South Africa which was otherwise a heterogeneous and racially divided society. With equality and equity, it was anticipated that discrimination, inequality and barriers based on colour or race would come to an end. The nationalists sought to bring together all the natives of South Africa in the fight for freedom and against racism and discrimination which had evolved over time.

The original push which resulted in the formation of the African National Congress (ANC) was to bring all together the native people to fight for their freedom. A Freedom Charter which asserted that South Africa belonged to all who lived in it, "blacks or whites," was issued by the party. It also called for the universal suffrage and the individual freedoms based on the Universal Bill of Right.

Most of the political activists of the 1920's were greatly influenced by the teachings of Marcus Garvey. Preaching the unity of all blacks, he claimed that liberty would come about only through the return of all Afro-Americans to their ancestral home.

By 1925, adversaries of the racist regime, in the cities and rural districts had adapted the teachings of Garvey to fit in the black South African experience. Nowhere was agitation against government attempts to introduce administrative change more marked than in the Eastern Cape area of Herschel. Two changes in particular raised traditionalist tempers in the region – a proposal to establish local council, with an accompanying increase in taxation, and a demand that land ownership be registered.

Marcus Garvey

Segregation in public Transport	Segregation in Schools	Segregation in recreation facilities

Banning of inter racial marriage	Application of Apartheid Policy after 1948	Denial of Voting

Unequal wealth distribution	Banning of political parties	Job segregation

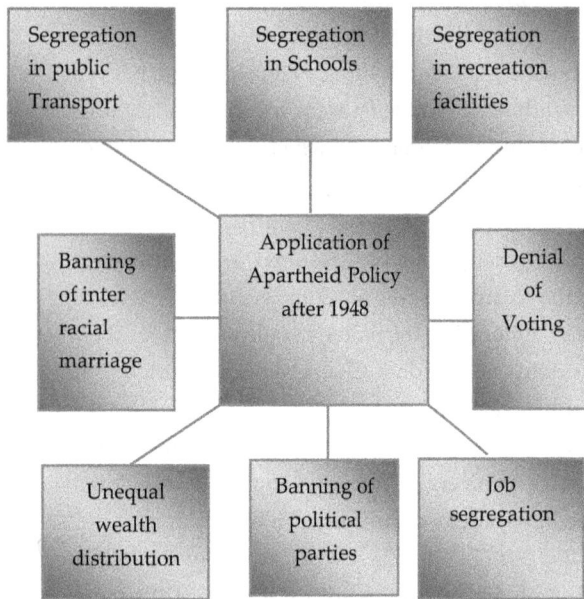

- Those no longer allowed in the cities including the old and no longer useful were forcefully removed to areas outside the cities designated as reserves for the blacks.

In 1956, the government prosecuted 156 opposition leaders, including Nelson Mandela, leader of ANC. In 1962, while posturing blamelessly against the communists and those responsible for the insurgence, government forces created what became known as the Sharpeville Massacre. In the black township of Sharpeville, south of Johannesburg police fired on a crowd of about 10,000 which had gathered in front of a police station to protest against pass laws. The police killed 67 and wounded 186 people, most of them shot in the back while trying to flee.

In 1948 the most conservatist of white political party, the Nationalist Party, won an all whites elections. This party, predominantly rural and consisting largely of the Dutch heritage, was the most adamant in maintaining a separation between whites and the other races. They applied the old apartheid dogma that blacks were "temporary sojourners" in the cities.

- New laws and a new segregation wiped out the so called "urban black spots" and all areas where people of different races had co-existed peacefully.
- Other non whites were regarded as migrant workers who had to have special work permits, which were to be renewed every year.
- Blacks were now obliged to carry pass books, open to inspection by any policeman or agent of the government whenever asked.
- Every square inch of South Africa was designated as belonging to a racial grouping, and blacks where removed from villages and land where for generations they had regarded as their own.

Response to white Repression in South Africa

There were mixed reactions to the racist policies by different groups of people. These reactions included:

- ANC turned to boycotts, strikes and civil disobedience. In the early 1950's they began their defiance campaign, together with some of the South African Indians.
- Though committed to non violence, ANC top leadership realized that peaceful protests were too dangerous and not practical enough to counter the brutish white minority rule. The leadership of ANC led by Nelson Mandela and Walter Sisulu, adopted a more confrontational stance and allied their movement with the Communist Party to form the "Spear of the Nation" (Umkhonto we Sizwe). In 1963, Mandela was found in the Umkhonto's hideout. Together with others, he was imprisoned for life in Robbin Islands as a consequence.

- Africans decamped from the established mission churches to the newly established independent churches in South Africa
- Women organized pickets near shops and molested all natives coming away with purchases from white shopkeepers until prices were cut.
- The Communist Party of South Africa, originally all white joined ranks with blacks and Asians against the repressive regime. The Communist Party worked "underground" and the government and police had another charge against its non–white opponent.
- Criticism from Britain and other Commonwealth nations made the racist regime in South Africa to approve a new constitution which in 1961 withdrew the country from the Commonwealth and made South Africa a Republic.
- In 1962, UN General Assembly passed a resolution which condemned apartheid policies.
- In 1963 UN Security Council passed a resolution which called for a voluntary arms embargo against South Africa, and that year a Special Committee against apartheid was established to encourage and oversee plans of action against the regime.

By 1960 South Africa's growth was second only to that of Japan. Trade with Western countries grew, and investors from USA, France and Britain rushed to get a piece of action. South Africa's security forces appeared to be in control. But in 1970, this rosy picture began to fade.

- In 1974, resistance to apartheid was encouraged by the withdrawal of Portuguese from Mozambique and Angola. The Portuguese could no longer afford to continue fighting the liberation movement in its colonies, which were being fueled by the Soviet Union and China.

- South African troops withdrew from Angola in early 1976, having failed to prevent the liberation forces from gaining power in that country. Black students in South Africa celebrated that victory.
- In 1976, a law limiting instructions in schools to Afrikaaner and English only sparked off a student demonstration which the police fired upon and a 13 year old student was killed. This provoked a violent outrage which lasted for three days in Soweto, and later to other black townships, between the public and police. Two white men died and at least 150 blacks, mostly school children. The liberation movement spread to teachers, churchmen and other black men throughout South Africa.

Peaceful methods used to fight for independence
(a) Mass Media
(b) Hunger Strike
(c) Boycotts
(d) Negotiations
(e) Diplomacy
(f) The Church
(g) Peaceful Demotrations
(h) Formation of political parties

In 1978 the Defense Minister of Nationalist Party P. W. Botha became the Prime Minister. Botha's entire white regime was worried about:

- The Soviet Union who were helping the insurrectionist in South Africa
- The economy of South Africa was slowly beginning to take a nose dive.
- Too much money spent to maintain the segregated homelands created for blacks were becoming uneconomical to govern.
- Maintaining blacks as third class citizens was not working well.

- The black labour remained pivotal to the economy and illegal black labour unions were thriving.
- Many blacks remained too poor to make meaningful contribution to the economy yet they were more than 70 percent of the population.
- Capitalism functioned on goodwill, and it was good will with which Botha's regime was most concerned, not for the sake of it, but also because of the need to prevent the blacks from being attracted to communism.
- He was concerned over the popularity of Nelson Mandela whom he denounced as an arch Marxist committed to violent revolution. However, to quiet down black opinion and nurture Mandale as a benevolent leader of the blacks, the government removed him from Robben Island to a more pleasant prison in a rural area just outside Cape Town. There the government allowed Mandela more visitors, including visits and interviews by foreigners – to let the world know that he was receiving good treatment.

P. W. Botha

Reforms Intitiated by P. W. Botha included:
- Botha created a new constitution to win the hearts and minds of blacks and to fend off anti apartheid campaign in USA and European.
- He declared Black homelands (Bantustans) national states and abolished pass laws.
- He legitimized black labour unions.

- His government recognized the rights of blacks to lastingly have their home in urban centres and own property.
- Botha's government committed itself to "separate, but equal" education and increased the spending on black schools in 1968.
- The government enhanced the effectiveness of the South African police.

Botha was forced to initiate these reforms because:
- The anti-apartheid movements in the USA and Europe were gaining grounds for the stay away from South Africa crusade
- US firms were beginning to withdraw from South Africa. By 1987 the growth of South Africa's economy had dropped to among the lowest rate in the world.
- There was mounting pressure to let go Mandela whose incarceration had turned into national hero. Botha's efforts to win over the hearts and minds of Blacks in South Africa failed when Mandela turned down the offer to be released from jail on condition that he denounced violence in 1985.
- South Africa was becoming an outlawed state among the nations of the world and the isolation was beginning to pinch. For instance, the ban in taking part in international events like the World Cup and Olympics was frustrating to many whites in South Africa
- Investing in South Africa by America and other western nations which had upheld the apartheid regime during the Cold War era, was coming to an end.
- The crusade to overthrow the apartheid regime spread like bushfire.

ANC leaders, in exile, call for consumer boycotts, rent strikes and war to make the townships uncontrollable escalated. Rage was vented on black policemen and township officials regarded as government stooges. Violence also erupted between the followers of the opportunistic Zulu chieftain, Buthelezi and supporters of the ANC.

Botha declared a state of emergency. Police was ordered to move in against the troublemakers and special attention was given to student leaders. Many were rounded up, and out of sight of the public, they were tortured and sometimes killed slowly with rat poison in their food. In 1989, 4000 death were reported, mostly of blacks. In August 1989, Botha retired and was replaced by Fredrick de Klerk.

For the sake of making South Africa a working nation, Fredrick de Klerk opted to diffuse tension in the country by developing a strategy which would promote peace with the black community, who were the majority. He began by giving them a voice in the politics of the nation. In 1991, Fredrick de Klerk's government repealed the Apartheid Laws and in March 1992, held a referendum on his policy which received an overwhelming support. The way was opened for South Africa's first non racial democratic elections, which was held in April 27th 1994.

Fredrick de Klerk

ANC won 63 percent of the nearly 20 million votes which were cast in that election. The Nationalist Party received 20 percent. Buthelezi's party, the Inkatha Freedom party won 10 percent and white rights party, Freedom Front won 2 percent. In the new parliament, 252 of its 400 seats went to ANC. On May 10th 1994, Mandela was sworn in as South Africa's first black president and his cabinet was diverse: with 17 of its members form ANC; 10 from Nationalist Party and 10 from Buthelez's party. A commission was established for reconciliation. The aim of this commission was to give amnesty for crimes committed if people accepted their wrongs.

Nelson Mandela

Political developments in South Africa between 1990 and 1994

(a) The ban on the political parties was lifted, for example ANC in 1990
(b) Registration of political parties was done
(c) Political detainee were released, for example Nelson Mandela and Walter Sisulu were set free on February 1990
(d) There was relaxation of the apartheid laws, for example Lands Act of 1913 and Group Area Act of 1950 were repealed and this allowed Africans to own land
(e) The first multi-racial elections in South Africa was held on April 1994

African countries took an active part to assist South Africans to fight the Apartheid Regime. These contributions included:

- South African guerilla fighters were trained in African countries like Algeria
- African countries gave political asylum to political refugees and offered them material help, education and health services
- Some countries in Africa contributed fighters to South African liberation movement

261

- They applied pressure to South Africa through the OAU and UNO to embrace an all inclusive government
- South Africa was isolated and economic sanctions were successfully applied to her.
- South African got a lot of sympathy and support from independent African states in her liberation struggle.

Role of Nelson Mandela in the struggle against Apartheid

(a) Mandela assisted to form the youth league of ANC

(b) He served as the Deputy President of the ANC

(c) As a lawyer he represented other African nationalists in cases against Apartheid regime

(d) He was involved in the defiance campaign organized by ANC

(e) He was amongst the nationalists who formulated and issued the freedom charter in 1955

(f) Together with others he formed the military wing of ANC (Umkhonto We Sizwe) Spear of the Nation

(g) He visited other countries to drum up support for ANC

(h) Addressed Pan African Congress in Ethiopia to highlight the evils of Apartheid

(i) He underwent the guerilla training in Algeria in order to effectively fight Apartheid

(j) He used the press to motivate African Nationalism

(k) His imprisonment inspired other African nationalists in South Africa

---

The roles played by the church in promoting African Nationalism in South Africa included:

- The church often spoke against the injustice carried out to the indigenous people
- Churches were involved in mass mobilization of their Christian followers to fight apartheid polices
- The church carried out civic education to Africans who became aware of their political rights
- The church appealed to other churches and governments abroad to come to the rescue of the suffering blacks
- Churches provided welfare services to the displace people during the period of struggle
- Church owned press media joined in condemning apartheid and highlighting the plight of the people.

The problems encountered by the nationalists in South Africa in their struggle for independence include:

- Many nationalist like Steve Biko were killed by the adamant regime
- The nationalists were harassed, arrested and jailed or detained, for instance. Mandela and Walter Sisulu
- Many nationalists were forced to flee the country to settle in other countries like Kenya, Zimbabwe, Angola and Tanzania as refugees
- Political parties in South Africa were outlawed and the nationalists were forced to operate in secret.
- Trade Unions were frequently intimidated by the security agents
- The South African government employed a divide and rule technique. Bantustans were created to give some Africans a mistaken belief that they were free
- Pass laws were used to bring under control the freedom of movement of the South African nationalists

Results of the South African nationalism

• Many lives were lost during the armed struggle in South Africa

• There was mass destruction of property in the country

• Protests and riots slowed down the pace of economic development in the country

• A Multi racial election was held in 1994 which was won by Nelson Mandela. He became the first black African president in the country

• South Africa was re-admitted to major regional and international organizations

• The lifting of sanctions enhanced rapid economic development in South Africa

• Nationalist leaders went back to South Africa

NATIONALISM IN MOZAMBIQUE

The Portuguese coupled heartlessness and racist exploitative tendencies in Mozambique. Anything taken to mean dissent was cold-bloodedly kept in check. This was made public in 1959 and 1960 when a co-operative movement among the peasants in Capo Delgado Province was ruthlessly suppressed and the leaders taken into custody.

In the same way, a peaceful protest in the same province on 16th June 1960 was gunned down and more than 500 were people put to death. The Portuguese security forces harassed the leaders of any organization which made any slight attempt to challenge the harsh conditions they imposed on Africans. The leaders were either arrested or forced to run away to exile

The Portuguese were not for independence, but the degree of unrest which the nationalist unleashed, in spite of the extreme suppression, forced them to initiate some few reforms. They passed a series of laws between 1961 and 1963, but this proved to be too little to late

Dr. Eduardo Mondlane

Factors which favoured the growth of nationalism in Mozambique

(a) Portuguese administrators replaced the traditional leaders arbitrarily
(b) Portuguese settlers pushed many Africans out of their land
(c) Africans were forced to pay heavy taxes
(d) Portuguese forced the Africans to work on their farms
(e) Racial discrimination was rampant in Mozambique, for example the poor Portuguese immigrants treated Africans with contempt and competed with them for similar job opportunities
(f) Many restrictions were imposed on Africans, for example the press was highly censored
(g) Portuguese security police brutally treated the Africans

The Mozambique Liberation Front (FRELIMO) was a merger of three political movements:

- Mozambique African National Union (MANU)
- National Democratic Union of Independent Mozambique (UDENAMO) and
- Union of Independent Mozambique (UNAMI)

Leaders of the three political parties came together in Dar es Salaam (Tanzania) under the auspices of President Julius Nyerere on on 25th June 1962 and decided to form a single party. Dr. Eduardo Mondlane was chosen as the president of FRELIMO which embanked on an armed struggle course.

Dr. Mondlane fruitlessly attempted to obtain funds from the USA. However, he succeeded in securing funds from private donors for social welfare projects and got military support from Algeria, Russia and China. FRELIMO also won moral and material support from the World Council of Churches and the Vatican. In September 1962, the first foray of the FRELIMO guerrillas infiltrated across the northern border of Mozambique from Tanzania and launched attacks on administrative posts. The northern provinces of Capo Delgado and Niassa remained the prime target of FRELIMO for a long time because of there proximity to FRELIMO bases in Tanzania. A large part of this territory was liberated by the FRELIMO who won the support of the local population and drew the bulk of their fighters from them.

Factors which favoured the FRELIMO Movement

(a) The Portuguese soldiers could not withstand the FRELIMO guerillas who attacked isolated administrative posts

(b) Most Africans in Mozambique gave the FRELIMO moral support

(c) Heavy forests, for example Tete and Cabo Delgodo, were ideal for the guerila warfare

(d) The FRELIMO strategy of attacking the Portuguese targets simultaneously overwhelmed the colonial government

(e) The FRELIMO fighters had the geographical advantage of their terrain

(f) The FRELIMO fighters were friendly to the local people, cultivated their own crops and avoided to tyrannize the general population

(g) Unity was boost up when people came together from different groups to fight in the same units

(h) African countries gave the nationalists a base to operate from and financial assistance to prop them up.

(i) The FRELIMO collaborated with African liberation movements in Southern Rhodesia and South Africa.

(j) FRELIMO system of administration in liberated areas attracted many people

Samora Machel

FRELIMO employed the classic guerrilla strategy of hit and run tactics such as sabotage and ambush. They targeted areas where control was weakest or confused such as the borders or inaccessible rural areas as a basis of operation and retreat. The objective was not to vanquish the Portuguese militarily, but cripple them economically and destroy their morale. Through the process of attrition, the FRELIMO would coerce the Portugues to a negotiating table.

The Portuguese responded to the FRELIMO menace with an awesome force of more than 70,000 troops. Their undertakings were buttressed by arms from the NATO, loans from USA and West Germany and aid from South Africa. The suppressive measures unleashed by the state gave little room for subversive activities. Foreign catholic priests were forced to flee from the territory, while Protestants were persecuted, with some clergy being jailed or killed. The clerics had tried to intercede to some limited extent. A massive counter–insurgency coded the Operation Gordian Knot in the 1970's forcefully moved many villages to camps, used scorched earth tactics and sent the local population into panic. Hundreds of civilians were massacred in a village in Tete.

The FRELIMO was not a homogenous group. Its leadership and the majority of FRELIMO's central committee were committed to socialism while a substantial faction was opposed to this line of thought. Besides, there was considerable infighting and purges within the group. The movement was dented a further blow when Dr. Mondlane was assassinated in Dar es Salaam in 1969. The brief factional struggle was resolved in 1970 when Samora Machel emerged as the leader of FRELIMO and consolidated his position.

By early 1970's, a force of 7,000 was under the command of the FRELIMO and she effectively controlled much of Northern and Central Mozambique. A force of about 60,000 troops deployed by the Portuguese to meet the challenge drained the resources of the FRELIMO and the level of causalities mounted.

Apart from Mozambique, the Portuguese were engaged in counter insurgence struggles against the nationalists in Angola and Guinea Bissau. Discontent amounted within the Portuguese army. This culminated in a left wing military takeover on 25th April 1974. The new government was determined to end all colonial discord and disengage from the colonial territories as rapidly as possible. Moreover, because it shared common ideologies with the FRELIMO, the new government empathized with it.

On 7th September 1974 the Lusaka Accord was signed between the two parties that provided for a ceasefire, Mozambique's independence and for the installation of a FRELIMO led transitional government. The agreement made no provision for elections prior to independence; FRELIMO would not hear of it and the government did not insist: Joaquim Chissano was installed as Prime Minister under a Portuguese governor to head the government that would take Mozambique to independence.

Joaquim Chissano

A coup attempt was launched by white settlers to forestall back rule, but this was quickly suppressed. On 25th July 1975 the People's Republic of Mozambique attained independence under a FRELIMO government with Samora Machel as the first president and the name of the capital Laurenco Marques, was changed to Maputo

---

Questions on Nationalism in Mozambique
(a) Name the founder leader of the FRELIMO
(b) Name two nationalist parties that fought for independence in Mozambique
(c) State five factors which favoured the growth of nationalism in Mozambique
(d) Which factors favoured the FRELIMO Movement?
(e) State two problems that Mozambique nationalists faced in the struggle against the Portuguese rule

15 PAN AFRICANISM

Pan-Africanism is a movement that aims at making all people of African descent to come together. It was pioneered by black Americans in the diaspora like Booker T. Washington, Henry Sylvester Williams, William Du Bois, George Padmore and Marcus Garvey.

Factors which led to the rise of Pan – Africanism include:

- Slavery and Slave Trade made Africans to put up with demeaning experience.
- Colonialism in Africa subjected the Africans to many forms of ills like forced labour, land alienation, rape among others
- Racist treatment reinforced a sense of solidarity within the diaspora.

Aims of Pan-Africanism
(a) To unit all the people of African origin
(b) To challenge the ideology of European superiority
(c) To improve the African conditions in the diaspora and within the continent
(d) To fight neo-colonialism
(e) To restore the dignity of the black people
(f) To create a forum for Africans to protest against European colonization and discrimination

The Pan African Conference of 1900
The conference was held in London from 23rd to 25th July 1900 (just prior to the Paris Exhibition) in order to allow tourists of African descent to attend both events. It took place in the Westminster Hall and was organized by a Trinidad barrister, Sylvester Williams. The conference was attended by Thirty seven delegates and about 10 other participants and observers from Africa, UK, the West Indies and USA. It was chaired by Bishop Alexander Walters of the Zion Church.

Du Bois played a leading role in the conference. He drafted a letter addressed to European leaders. This was a plea to them to end racism, to grant colonies in Africa and West Indies independence and recognise political and other rights of the black Americans.

Du Bois

Bishop Alexander Walters in his opening address, "The Trials and Tribulations of the Coloured Race in America," noted that for the first time in history black people had gathered from all parts of the globe to discuss and improve the conditions of their race, to assert their rights and recognition so that they might take an equal place among nations.

In September, the delegates petitioned Queen Victoria through the British government to look into the treatment of Africans in South Africa and Rhodesia. Specifically the delegates addressed:

- The degrading labour conditions in Kimberley and Rhodesia
- The legalized bondage of African men, women and children to white colonists
- The system of compulsory labour in public works
- The "pass" system used for people of colour
- The local by-laws tending to segregate and degrade Africans such as curfew and use of separate public transport.
- Difficulty of owning legal property
- Difficulty of obtaining franchise

The conference marked an early stage in the development of the anti-colonist movement, and was established to encourage the unity of Africans and the people of African descent, particularly in territories controlled by British.

First Pan African Congress (1919)

In 1919 the first of the series of five Pan African Congresses was held in Paris. It was organized by an American thinker and Journalist, W.E.B. Dubios. Fifty seven delegates representing 15 countries attended the meeting. The Most important mission of this conferene was to make an appeal to the Versailles Peace Conference. Among its petitions were:

- The allies to administer the former German territories in Africa as a consortium on behalf of the Africans who inhabited the region
- Africans should take part in governing their colonies "as fast as their development permitted" until some unspecified time in future Africa when they would be granted self rule.

The Second Pan African Congress (1921)

The congress, which met in a number of sessions in London, Paris and Brussels, is reckoned to be the most radical of all the meetings. The London session resulted in the declaration of the London Manifesto. According to this Manifesto, it declared that:

England systematically enslaved the natives (and was still enslaving them) and declined to train the black or brown men in real self government. But it freely gave the same privilege to the whites.

The only dissenting voice was that of Blasé Diane who although African, was effectively a French politician, representing Senegal in the French chamber of Deputies.

The Third Pan African Congress (1923)

This was a shoddily organized and disappointingly attended congress which was held in London and Lisbon. This congress repeated the demands for some form of self rule and spelt out the relationship between Africa and Europe. It also mentioned the problems of Africans in the diaspora. Specifically, the congress addressed issues like:

- The development of Africa for the benefit of Africans and not merely to benefit Europeans
- Home rule and responsible government for the British West Africa and the British West Indies
- Abolition of the posturing of a White minority rule to dominate a black majority in Kenya, Rhodesia and South Africa.
- The suppression of lynching and mob law in USA

Fourth Pan African Congress (1927)

The congress was held in New York. It adopted similar resolutions to those of the third Pan African Congress.

Why Pan Africanism was not well developed in Africa prior to 1945

- The movement was outlawed by the colonial governments which could not allow Africans to engage in activities regarded as contrary to their policies.
- Africans in the colonies were preoccupied with internal problems like land alienation, forced labour and taxation
- There was lack of effective machinery to communicate Pan Africanist ideas
- There was lack of contact between Africans in different colonies

- There was lack of adequate African representation in the movement before 1945. Africans in the movement were the few who were staying outside Africa as either persons in exile or students.
- The 'divide and rule' policy used by the Europeans made it impossible for Africans to communicate and cooperate.
- The only Countries that were independent (Liberia and Ethiopia) could not champion Pan-Africanism since they had their own internal problems and paid little attention to external affairs.
- There was lack of venue to hold the meetings on the African soil since the colonial government would not have given their backing to such a meeting.
- Few people were educated and only a minority in Africa had higher education hence there was widespread illiteracy and ignorance.
- Africans were too poor to make meaningful contribution to the movement

Manchester Pan – African Congress of 1945
The fifth Congress was held in Manchester in the North Western of England in 1945. Ninety delegates, out of whom twenty six were from all over Africa, attended the Congress. These included Peter Abraham of ANC, and a number of men who were to become political leaders in their countries soon after, like Hasting Banda, Kwame Nkrumah, Obafemi Awolowo and Jomo Kenyatta. Marcus Garvey's wife and the radical Trinidadian, George Padmore, were also in attendance. W.E.B Du Bois, the convener of the first congress in 1919 also attended at 77 years of age.

It was agreed upon in the congress that racial discrimination be made a criminal offence. The Congress also decried imperialism and capitalism.
Why the Pan-African movement became active in Africa after 1945

- The 2nd World War strengthened nationalism in the African continent because Africans were given a boost to make an effort by UNO, USA and USSR which were not for the idea of having colonies.
- The 1945 Pan-African Conference in Manchester, brought many African elites together. They later inspired their colleagues back home to join the movement.
- The attainment of political independence in India in 1947 and Burma (now Myanmar) in 1948 raise the spirits of scores of nationalists in Africa.
- The slowing down of the Pan Africanism activities in America during the Cold War period activated the same in Africa. The USA government made an effort to control the activities of people like Padmore who had linkages with USSR.
- The achievement of independence by Ghana in 1957 stimulated other African nations to center their attention to the liberation of their respective countries rather than to fight for the common good of fellow Africans outside the continent.

The Manchester Pan–African Congress is regarded as the turning point in the history of the movement because:
- The congress was dominated by African representatives, for example Jomo Kenyatta of Kenya, Kwame Nkruma of Ghana, Leopold Senghor of Senegal among others.
- The African representatives made great contributions and discussed issues related to political and economic status of the Africans in Africa
- The African representatives agreed that they would go back to Africa and lead their countries to independence
- It was suggested for the first time that if the colonial powers were not ready to give

independence willingly then force would be used
- The conference made demands for universal suffrage and condemned capitalism
- During the conference, the solidarity and unity among Africans began to develop and it paved way to the formation of OAU.

Challenges encountered by the Pan African movement

- Many European groups fought the activities of the Pan Africanists. Marcus Garvey, for example was arrested, tried and convicted of fraud (collecting funds unlawfully) and imprisoned for five years.
- It was difficult for the Pan Africanists to involve themselves in African affairs since majority of the Africans were still under colonial bondage.
- Illiteracy and ignorance amongst some people of African origin frustrated their effort to offer meaningful support.
- The movement was restricted to the African continent after independence in 1960's because of the absence of African-Americans in the continents.
- After independence Africa was divided into radical and the conservative leaders and between the francophone and the Anglophone countries.
- European powers dominated the international media which they used to discredit the Pan-Africanists and spread negative propaganda about their activities.
- The deep rooted economic ties between the colonies and their former colonial masters frustrated any meaningful cooperation among the group members.
- Lack of venues to hold conferences in Africa especially before 1957 meant that the movement could not take root in Africa quickly. The far-away venues were inconveniencing.

Achievements of Pan African Movement

- Pan African Movement was the fore-runner of OAU
- It created a sense of togetherness among the people of African origin
- The movement gave rise to political awareness among people of African origin and a sense of deep concern for the blacks who were going through difficulties all over the world.
- Encouraged nationalism and attainment of independence among African states
- The movement enabled African leaders to be more committed to African problems. For example, the black caucus in the USA played an important role in pressurizing the US congress to take drastic measures against the apartheid regime in South Africa.
- The movement led to the development of the spirit of solidarity among African people when dealing with issues which affected the continent.
- It provided a forum for African people to discuss their common problem with one voice
- The movement laid the foundation for the interest in research on African culture, history, literature, music, religion, medicine and art
- It put in place steps towards the restoration of status and dignity to the African people, which had been eroded by Slave Trade, colonialism and racism.

Questions on Pan Africanism
(a) Define the term Pan-AfricanismGive two founder members of Pan Africanism Movement
(b) State three factors which led to the rise of Pan Africanism
(c) What were the aims of Pan-Africanism?
(d) State two reasons why Pan Africanism was not active in Africa before 1945
(e) Why is the Manchester Pan – African Congress of 1945 regarded as the turning point in the history of the movement?
(f) State six achievements of Pan African Movement

16 INTERNATIONAL RELATIONS

INTERNATIONAL RELATIONS refer to the co-operation or interaction between individuals or groups of nations of the world. They interact socially, economically and politically in many ways. Interactions between nations are important because:

- Countries are closely knit like families and there is a lot of socio-economic inter dependence among them.
- No country is self reliant to the extent that it does not need others
- Countries are able to collectively solve problems of global concern, for example desertification, pollution, HIV/AIDS and terrorism
- International relations enhances peace and security in the world through diplomatic means
- The relations promote international understanding and unity. This is done through encouraging cultural exchange between nations.
- It promotes economic growth through trade. Due to good relations, there is expanded international trade which enables countries to acquire goods they don't produce
- Developing countries get financial and technical assistance from developed nations.

Levels of Relations between Nations include:

- Economic relations, for example through trade and commercial activities among nations. Rich countries give grants to less developed countries.
- Diplomatic relations, for example high commissioners and ambassadors encourage cordial relations among nations
- Political relations, for example co-operation among countries with similar political ideology

or similar political systems – Tanganyika united with Zanzibar to form Tanzania.

- Socio-cultural relations, for example exchange programmes like education and competitions like Commonwealth Games

Bilateral relations involve interactions between two countries while multi lateral relations involve relations between more than two countries. International relations can also either involve governmental organizations like UNO, Commonwealth, NAM, COMESA and AU or non governmental organizations like the Red Cross, Amnesty International and Transparency International.

International Governmental Organizations:

- Provide member states with a forum to consult and tackle problems of common concern.
- Act as regulators in their fields to ensure the welfare of mankind, for example World Health Organization (WHO) regulates health sector through immunization, vaccination and other prevention campaigns.
- Enhance peace and security through peace-keeping missions and quick response to disasters.
- Contribute to charity and facilitate equitable distribution of resources in the world. For example, the International Monetary Fund (IMF) and World Bank give fiscal advice or advance loans to developing countries repectively.

Questions on International Relations
(a) Distinguish Bi-lateral from Multi-lateral Relations
(b) What is the importance of international relations?
(c) Name two types of international organizations
(d) State five benefits of international relations

FIRST WORLD WAR 1914 – 1918

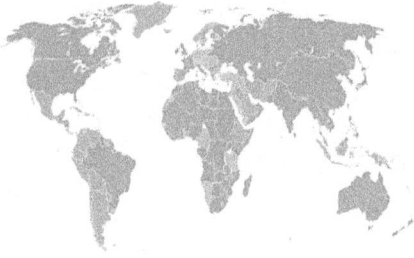

Map of the world with the participants in World War I. The Allies are depicted in green, the Central Powers in orange, and neutral countries in grey.

The World War I was unique because:

- The war involved a large number of warring nations
- The size of the armies involved in it was very large
- The weapons which were used were quite deadly

Trench War

- Colossal amount of money was spent to finance it
- Very many people lost their lives fighting or as casualties
- There was widespread human agony

Armored tanks

Causes of the World War 1

- Imperialism: this is when countries increased their power and wealth by bringing additional territories under their control. Before the World War I, Africa and parts of Asia were points of contention among European countries. This was especially true because of the raw materials these areas could provide. The increasing competition and desire for greater empires led to an increase in confrontation that assisted to push the world into World War I.
- Militarism: as the world entered the 20th century, an arms race began. By 1914 Germany had the greatest increase in military buildup. Great Britain and Germany both greatly increased their navies in this time period. Further, in Germany and Russia particularly, the military establishment began to have a greater influence on public policy.
- Alliance system – the world was polarized into antagonistic camps, for example the Triple Alliance made up of Germany, Italy and Austria-Hungary on one hand and Triple Entente made up of Britain, France and Russia on the other. If one country was attacked her allies were bound to be drawn into the conflict.
- Need for revenge: the French wanted to regain Alsace-Lorain from the Germans and avenge its defeat by Germany during the Prussian War
- Growth of nationalism: Much of the origin of the war was based on the desire of the Slavic peoples in Bosnia and Herzegovina to secede from Austria-Hungary and join Serbia. But in a more general way, nationalism of the various countries throughout Europe contributed to not only the beginning, but also the extension of the war in Europe. Each country thirsted to showcase their dominance and power.

- The Balkan wars – the disintegration of the Ottoman Empire created instability in the Balkan region especially in Serbia where the leaders were sharply in collision with Austria - Hungary

- Kaiser Wilhelm was young and inexperienced to lead a powerful country like Germany. Unlike his predecessor (Otto Von Bismark), he created many enemies and drove them into allies against a possible German attack.

Kaiser Wilhelm

- The assassination of Frank Ferdinand (Archduke of Austria) and his wife in June 1914 at Sarajevo in Bosnia which sparked off the war between Serbia and Austria was the immediate cause of the World War I

Arch Duke Franc Ferdinand & his wife

Schlieffen Plan

Count Alfred Von Schlieffen, who masterminded the Schlieffen Plan, served as Germany's Chief of General Staff from 1891 to 1905. It was this plan which the Germans used against the French in August 1914, long after Schlieffen had retired from the army in 1906. According to this plan: -

- Germany would attack France and then Russia. German's military might would be put on one frontier and then moved to another.

- A devastating attack on France via a neutral Belgium would be done as soon as Russia announced its intentions to mobilize. This would take six weeks.

- A holding operation on the Russian/German border would be carried out if necessary

- A massive and successful surprise attack against France would be enough to put off Britain.

- Germany would use her modernized rail system to fast track the movement of his troops from the French frontier to the Russian front. Russia would then be attacked and defeated.

The Schlieffen Plan failed during the actual war because:

- Russians mobilized her troops faster than expected and this meant that German forces had to be deployed to the Eastern front faster than it had been anticipated.

- The French stood their ground and this enabled the allied powers to mobilize faster than the Germans had projected.

- The Germans did not expect both sides to be evenly marched.

- The German did not think likely that Britain would join the war, when it invaded Belgium.

The events which led to the outbreak of the World War I in 1914 included:

- The Serbian's refusal to accept all terms of the ultimatum issued to them by Austria-

Hungary, made the latter to declare war on her. The terms of the ultimatum which Serbia was expected to respond positively to within 48 hours were: -

- ✓ An apology from Serbia for the murder of Franc Ferdinand and his wife.
- ✓ Serbia to suppress all anti-Austrian publications and organizations in the country
- ✓ Serbia to dismiss all officials to whom Austria-Hungary objected to
- ✓ Austrian police to enter Serbia to investigate the Serbian complicity in the murder
- ✓ Austria to supervise the suppression of the anti-Austrian societies
- ✓ Austrian police to enter Serbian territory to ensure that the demands were met.

- When Austria-Hungary declared war on Serbia, Germany warned other European nations (France, Britain and Russia) to keep off the war between the two nations, but Russia refused and supported the Serbians who were fellow Slavs. Germany declared war on Russia when she refused to demobilize her forces. The Russians were determined to support the Serbians against the Austro-Hungarian onslaught because:

- ✓ She was not willing to see a fellow Slav country crushed by a vastly stronger opponent
- ✓ Russia had ambitions in the Balkans and wanted to take advantage to pursue them

- When France failed to give clear guarantees of remaining neutral in the conflict, Germany declared war on France as well.
- Germany attacked Belgium which appealed to others countries for assistance.

- When Germany refused to accept the British ultimatum demanding for the respect of Belgian's neutrality, she declared war on Germany. Britain supported Belguim because she did not want a great and hostile naval power within her proximity.
- The unrestricted submarine warfare by Germany made USA to join the allied forces when a ship carrying her nationals was sunk by the German U-boat. This act provoked USA which for along time kept away from the European conflicts to join the allied forces. America was also motivated by other reasons like:

- ✓ The American citizens mounted pressure on the government to join the war
- ✓ The American nationals funded the allied forces
- ✓ A secret telegram to Mexico urging them to join Germany against USA caused outrage
- ✓ America invested heavily in Europe and the fear of heavy loses in case the allied forces lost the war motivated USA to join them
- ✓ Industrial unrest in USA was blamed on Germany

Importance of British Supremacy at sea

- The British naval forces assisted in blockading the central powers particularly the Germans from accessing food and raw materials from other parts of the world. This derailed their war plans.
- Her naval supremacy enabled the allied forces to capture most colonies of the central powers.
- The sea barricade enabled the allied forces to maintain uninterrupted communication with each other, as well as safeguard the British food and raw material supplies from other parts of the world.

USA was hesitant to join the World War I. This was because:

- The Monroe Doctrine of 1828 forbade USA from interfering in European affairs
- The war had not interfered with the economic interest of USA
- To avoid civil war in USA because there were nationalilties of Germany, France and Britain in USA
- She did not want to interfere with her trade partners
- European states, for example Germany had huge USA debts

The Central Powers lost the World War I because:

- The Allied Forces had more resources in terms of food, raw materials and equipment at their disposal.
- The allies had manpower from twenty seven countries compared to the four members of the central powers
- The sea lanes also assisted in the transportation of troops and goods
- Mutinies in the German army led to the defeat of Germany. Her allies also quickly surrendered.
- The geographical position of the Central Powers. They were surrounded by their enemies.
- The entry of USA into the war tilted the scale to the favour of the allied forces
- Germany lost most of her troops in 1918 and was forced to use inexperienced soldiers
- The allied forces used their naval superiority to prevent any ship from entering and leaving Germany. This cordon disadvantaged the central powers in that: -
  - ✓ It denied the central powers essential supplies like food, equipment, raw materials and troops.
  - ✓ The central powers could not utilize the navy.

- Invasion of Belgium which for along time had remained a neutral country, made Britain to join the allied forces against Germany.
- German's tactical blunders cost her war. Her Schiliffen Plan was disastrous.

Results of the First World War
Political Effects

- New nations like Hungary and Yugoslavia were created after the war
- The war led to the rise of USA and Russia as super powers
- German size was reduced by $1/8$ and she lost her territories abroad
- The League of Nations was formed to maintain world peace and security
- It created the spirit of nationalism in Africa
- The war created a revolution in Russia and the rise of communism
- It led to the rise of dictators because of the difficult economic times

Economic Effects

- A lot of money was spent on funding the war
- The war led to economic strain in Europe which weakened their hold on the rest of the world
- A lot of property was destroyed
- Use of vehicles and aircraft became widespread

Social Effects

- Many lives were lost
- Many people were displaced
- The war led to separation of families
- It led to the spread of diseases like influenza
- The war led to starvation and death
- Many women took up jobs which were otherwise left for men

"The Big Four" made all the major decisions at the Paris Peace Conference (from left to right, David Lloyd George of Britain, Vittorio Orlando of Italy, Georges Clemenceau of France, Woodrow Wilson of the U.S.)

PEACE SETTLEMENT (1919–1920)

The Paris Peace Conference was a meeting of the allied victors, following the end of the World War I to set the peace terms for the defeated Central Powers following the armistice of 1918. It took place in Paris (1919) and involved diplomats from more than 52 countries and nationalities. The five major powers (France, Britain, Italy, USA and Japan) controlled the conference. In practice, Japan played a negligible role and the "big four" leaders were the dominant figures at the conference. These were represented by the USA President Woodrow Wilson, the Prime Minister of Britain, David Lloyd George; the Prime Minster of France, Clemenceau; and the Prime Minister of Italy, Vittorio Orlando.

The "big four" met together informally 145 times and made all major decisions, which were in turn ratified by others. The conference came to a close on 21 January 1920 with the inauguration of the General Assembly of the League of Nations. Five major peace treaties were concluded at the Paris Peace Conference:-

(a) The Treaty of Versailles on 28 June 1919 (Germany).

(b) The Treaty of Saint-Germaine on 10 September 1919 (Austria).

(c) The Treaty of Neuilly on 27 November 1919 (Bulgaria)

(d) The Treaty of Sévres on 10 August 1920

(e) The Treaty of Lausanne on 24 July 1923 (Ottoman Empire)

The decisions enacted unilaterally by the conference, largely on the whims of the "Big Four," did not favour minor powers which attended the conference and the vanquished, especially Germany. The Treaty of Versailles in particular crippled Germany's military strength and placed full blame for the war and costly reparations on her shoulders. This public humiliation brought about resentment in Germany and is sometimes construed as one of the causes of Nazi success and in some way led to the World War II.

The League of Nations proved contentious in the United States of America as critics said it subverted the powers of the Congress to declare war. The USA Senate therefore failed to ratify any of its Peace Treaties and refused to join the League. Neither the Republican Germany nor the Communist Russians were invited to attend the Peace Conference. Numerous other nations send delegates which appealed for additions to the treaties, but without making any headway.

The Treaty of Versailles

The results of the peace settlement (Versailles Treaty) were:

- Germany lost all her processions abroad which were put under the supervision of the League of Nations
- Germany was forced to pay $ 6.5 billion for damages caused to other countries during the war
- Germany was totally disarmed and only allowed to retain a force of 100,000 men and officers. Her air force was also disbanded
- Austria was allowed to remain independent despite having many Germans in it
- Poland got ⅓ of its land which had been taken by Germany and the Port of Danzig was declared a free port
- The Saar region was put under the League of Nations for 15 years
- Alsace - Loraine was given back to France
- The Rhine region was demilitarized
- New states, for example Yugoslavia and Czechoslovakia were created
- Finland became totally independent from Russia

Weaknesses of the Versailles Treaty

- Germany was heavily punished and they felt that the treaty was unfair to them
- The interest of colonial people were ignored by the European powers
- The interests of minority powers were ignored
- Japan gained very little from the treaty and felt let down
- USA failed to ratify the treaty

Questions on the Peace Settlement of 1919 -1920
(a) Mention two major peace treaties which were concluded at the Paris Peace Conference
(b) Name two countries which took the major part in the peace settlement after the World War 1
(c) What were the weaknesses of the Versailles Treaty?
(d) What were the results of the Peace Settlement?
(e) Mention two ways how the Peace Settlement led to the World War II

THE LEAGUE OF NATION

was established by the victors of the World War I in 1920 with the solitary purpose of preventing the occurrence of another war. It was the brain child of Woodrow Wilson, the US president who was supported by Lord Robert Cecil of Britain, Jan Smuts of South Africa and Leon Bourgeois of France. The League of Nations came into force during the first meeting in London (Britain) on 10th January 1920.

The reasons for the formation of the League of Nations were to:

- Prevent the outbreak of another world war.
- Foster international co-operation in solving problems as they arose.

- Jointly take instantaneous action against an established aggressor through economic sanctions or military means.
- Secure and maintain fair and humane conditions of labour as one way of maintaining world peace.
- Oversee the development of territories lost by the Central Powers during the First World War like Tanganyika, Togo and South West Africa

Organs of the League of Nations

The Assembly was one of the organs of the League of Nations. It met once a year in Geneva and was made up of three delegates from each member state. It elected non-permanent members to the council. The functions of the Assembly included:

- Controlling the budget of the organization
- Admitting new members with the approval of a two-thirds majority.
- Appointing non-permanent members of the League of Nations Council.
- Considering treaties.
- Supervising the work of the League of Nations council.
- Appointing the 15 judges of the permanent Court of International Justice.
- Giving approval to the appointment of Secretary-General.

Secretariat was based in Geneva (Switzerland) and consisted of the Secretary General and his staff. This was the administrative wing of the League. The functions of the Secretariat included to:

- Prepare agenda for discussion
- Collect materials required for meetings
- Carry out all correspondence
- Publish relevant reports
- Implement decisions of the League of Nations

- Provide continuity

The Council was made up of permanent and non-permanent members. The permanent members were France, Britain, Italy and Japan. There were four non permanent members, elected by the General Assembly. The main role of the council which sat in Geneva was to appoint committees and Secretary General with the approval of the majority of the Assembly. It also dealt with disputes amongst member states, reduction of armament, and admittance or expulsion of members.

The International Court of Justice (ICJ) was set up between 1920 and 1922. The court, based in Hague (Holland), was made up of eleven judges and four deputy judges who were elected to serve for a period of nine years by the Assembly and the Council. The decisions made by the court were binding to all parties involved in the dispute. The aim of the court was to adjudicate in disputes between nations.

International Labour Organization (ILO) consisted of four delegates - two for member states and two for workers from each member state. Its main aim was to maintain good working conditions for men, women and children.

Mandate (Trust) Commission The responsibility of the Mandate Commission was to supervise the administration of the trustee (Mandate) colonies. These were colonies which were taken over from Germany and her allies after the World War I.

Specialised Agencies
- International Labour Committee
- The Health Committee

- Economic and Finance Committee
- Child Welfare Committee
- Drug related problems Committee

Weakness of the League of Nations

- The League was perceived as being dominated by the "big five" which included Britain, France, Italy, USA and Japan.
- Many countries were out of the League of Nations and were not bonded by its covenant
- Withdrawal of some members states like Japan, Italy and Germany complicated matters to the League
- Individual nations were more pre-occupied with their national interests and pride, at the expense of the organization's interests.
- The Appeasement Policy of Britain and France forced them to stand aside and avoid taking a firm action against Germany any time she violated the covenant of the League.
- Member countries were not willing to take disputes to the International Court of Justice and made many secret treaties contrary to the covenant of the League.
- The League of Nations did not have a military wing to reinforce its decisions
- The league did not have enough funds to implement its decisions
- Rise of dictators, for example Hitler and Mussolini made it not easy for the League to operate
- The USA Congress refused to ratify the treaty of the League of Nations. This denied the organization diplomatic and economic strength.
- The Treaty of Versailles was vindictive - Germany was severely punished and she did not feel duty-bound to honour it.
- Nationalist ambition of member countries - some continued to pursue re-armament policy which was against the treaty

Failures of the League of Nations

The League of Nations failed to maintain world peace in the following ways:

- It failed to solve the Sino-Japanese dispute after Japan invaded Manchuria (China) in 1931. Japan refused to abide by the League's demands that it withdraws from the Chinese territory and pulled out of the League in 1933.
- The Italians invaded Ethiopia in 1935 and instead of accepting the League's verdict that he withdraws his troops from Ethiopia, Benito Mussolini pulled out of the League.

Benito Mussolini

- The League failed to halt the German's breach of the terms of the Versailles Treaty. She embarked on a remilitarization programme and established a navy and an airforce.
- Many nations continued to make many defensive pacts in total disregard of the Treaty of Versailles.
- Germany invaded other regions such as Poland and Austria between 1936 and 1939, while Russia invaded Finland in 1939. These attacks were a total contravention of the League's covenant.

Achievements of the League of Nations

- The League of Nations achieved its objective of treating the minority groups humanely. The International Office for Refugees, for example, assisted refugees.
- The League ensured that peace treaties were signed to promote security in the world.

279

For example, the Locarno Treaties of 1925, settled boundary disputes between Germany and France.

- The League of Nations took good care of Trust territories like Togo, Tanganyika, Cameroon and Rwanda-Burundi.
- The League successfully restored financial stability in Austria following the economic slump in the country after the World War 1.
- The League assisted to regulate, manufacture and sell arms. It also held disarmament meetings.
- The League was able to bring to an end several inter-state disputes in a nonviolent manner. It solved the frontier dispute between Turkey and Iraq over the Mosul province (1924-1926), the dispute between Poland and Germany over Northern Silesia.
- The League maintained peace in the world for about 20 years
- The League of Nations kept up peace and security in the city of Danzig in spite of the hostility between the Poles and the Germans.

Questions on the League of Nations

(a) What was the main aim of the League of Nations?

(b) Give two objectives of the League of Nations

(c) Give two functions of the Secretariat

(d) Give two functions of the Assembly

(e) Give two functions of the Council

(f) Mention two incidents when the League failed to fulfill its mandate

(g) Explain the problems which faced the League of Nations

(h) What was the weakness of the League of Nations?

(i) Explain six achievements of the League of Nations

THE SECOND WORLD WAR 1939-1945

The causes of the World War II can be divided into long term and short term. There is little doubt that one of the long term causes of the World War II was the infuriation felt in Weimar Germany, caused by the Treaty of Versailles. The unfavorable conditions imposed on Germany by the Treaty of Versailles made her nurse a grudge against the allied powers. Hitler violated the Versailles Treaty and this increased his popularity at home.

Weaknesses of the League of Nations

Another long term cause was the obvious inability of the League of Nations to deal with major international issues in the 1930's in Manchuria and Abyssinia. In both conflicts the League showed that it was unable to control those powers which acted outside the acceptable international norms.

Hitler's Ambitions

With the apparent weakness of the the League of Nations, Hitler must have known that at the very least he could push the boundaries and see what he could get away with. His first major transgression was his defiance of the Versailles Treaty when he introduced re-armament into Nazi Germany. The expansion of all the three arms of the military was forbidden by the treaty. Hitler, however, ignored these restrictions. The world powers did nothing. The same occurred in 1936 when Nazi Germany re-occupied the Rhine region, forbidden by the Versailles Treaty. Hitler felt confident enough to ignore it.

Adolph Hitler

Appeasement Policy

By 1938 very many in UK had supported Neville Chamberlain's attempt of avoiding war and public opinion was on his side. This, however, changed when it became clear that appeasement policy had failed and the public rallied behind Winston Churchill, the man who had insisted that Chamberlain had taken the wrong course of action. The policy of appeasement practiced by Britain and France only encouraged the fascist and Nazist dictators to carry on with acts of aggression.

Militarization

Rearmament and rise of dictators like Adolph Hitler, of Germany, Benito Mussolini of Italy, Emperor Hirohito of Japan and General Franco of Spain created uncertainty in the world.

The allied powers were unable to stop Germany's remilitarization programme after First World War because:

- France was too weak to resist German's re-armament - World War I was fought in her soil
- USA had reverted back to her isolationist policy
- Belgium and Poland were afraid of the consequences of antagonizing Germany.

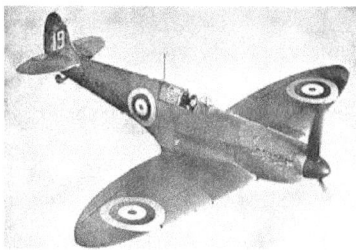

Alliance System

Establishment of alliances between major powers encourages acts of aggression because of the feelings of mutual support. For example, the rise of Berlin–Rome–Tokyo axis threatened peace and increased mistrust.

Economic Depression

The great depression of the 1930's caused much economic hardships in Europe and forced some countries to have a strong desire to expand and jealously guard their markets. Germany, in particular was hard hit by the forced reparations and her territories like the mineral rich Saar region which were put under foreign domination.

Growth of Nationalism

The growth of nationalism in Germany, Italy and Japan gave them the desire to acquire more territories and this escalated tension.

Impact of the First World War on the Second

- The size of Germany was reduced and she lost her colonies abroad. This made Germany bitter and she started a mission of revenge
- After World War I there was anarchy which led to the rise of dictatorship, for example Hitler of Germany and Mussolini of Italy
- Treaty of Versailles: Germany was forced to pay for the war damages. This affected her economy as she was faced with unemployment, food shortage and inflation. Germany blamed the Versailles Treaty for all her misfortunes.
- Decline of Trade: Germany could not compete favourably with other nations for raw materials and markets. Britain, France and USA unfairly controlled most of the resources and people
- Economic depression: It was brought by the First World War between 1929 - 1931. Each country had to protect her markets and resources. This caused bitterness.
- League of Nations: The League of Nations was formed after the First World War to prevent the outbreak of another war. It was weak and failed to prevent the aggression of Germany, Italy and Japan

- Appeasement policy: Britain and France gave in to the demands of Hitler because the two countries under estimated Hitler's political demands and assumed that any time he made one it was the last one. They did not want to provoke him to start another war in Europe. At the same time, they had colonies in the Far East and feared the Japanese's growing imperialism and inclination towards Germany and Italy.

USA joined the World War II much later mainly because she wanted to safeguard her national interest and once more wanted to avoid being entangled in European affairs. The Japanese attack on her naval base at Pearl Harbour, however, forced her to reconsider her neutrality in the warfare.

The Central Powers lost to the allied forces during the World War II because:
- The Germans were fighting in many fronts - Hitler versus Britain and her allies on the western front and the Russian on eastern front
- The combined resources of the British empire, USA and USSR out numbered and gunned the Central Powers

- The late entry of USA into the war on the side of the allies in 1941 tilted the scale to their favour
- Some German territories turned against her

- The allies used their naval superiority to starve their enemies off supplies
- The use of atomic bomb by the Americans made the Japanese to withdraw from the conflict.
- The axis powers made tactical blunders and miscalculations, for example the German offensive on USSR – It was a disaster for the Germans who were ill – equipped for the Russian winter.

Hitler was interested in occupying Russia during the World War II because: -
- Russia was rich in natural resources like oil and coal
- She wanted to provide space for German expansion
- They were mainly Slavs – an "inferior" races which he craved to get rid of like the Jews

Result of the Second World War
Social Effects
- It is estimated that about 30 million people died either directly in the battle field as combatants or civilians through bombing. The atomic bombs which were used against Japan (Hiroshima and Nagasaki) released radio-active elements which affected many people long after the war.
- The war led to lasting ill-health and shortening of life span for millions of people as an upshot of years under incarceration or poor nourishment.
- It led to psychological and emotional problems to families, individuals and nations as a result of the trauma of war.
- Large numbers of people were displaced and they suffered greatly as refugees
- The myth of European military superiority was shattered due to the defeat of the British

and American forces in the Far East by the Japanese forces.

Economic Effects

- The war led to the destruction of property, buildings, industries and bridges.
- Agriculture and Industry were upset due to lack of equipment, raw materials and human resources.
- Economics of the countries that were involved in the war were destroyed leading to economic slump.
- External trade almost came to stand still due to apprehension and insecurity.
- There was a high inflation rate which led to high cost of living.

Political Effects

- The prior balance of power was destroyed and the power vacuum was filled by two new super powers, USA and USSR.
- The communist zone extended to cover half of the continent of Europe.
- The division of European into two antagonistic blocs led to the development of Cold War. This was preceded by arms race between USA and USSR.
- The failure of the League of the Nations to maintain world peace led to the foundation of the United Nation Organization.
- Dictators like Adolph Hitler were defeated during the war
- Germany was divided into two, capitalist West Germany and Communist East Germany. The city of Berlin was also divided between the East and the West.
- Participation of Africans in the war strengthened African nationalism.

Effects of the Second World War in Europe were:

- The war led to the loss of many human lives. Many of the survivors were maimed.

- The war was costly and this slowed down the rate of economic development.
- It led to the destruction of property such as industries and building through bombing.
- Germany was occupied and torn apart by the Allied Force.
- The balance of power in Europe was changed with the coming out of USSR and USA as new powers.
- Communist governments were established in many parts of Eastern Europe through the influence of the USSR.
- The war increased USA's participation in European affairs though North Atlantic Treaty Organization (NATO) and the Marshall plan.
- The war stimulated the development of sophisticated weapons and industry.
- It led to displacement of people who became refugees.
- European countries became more committed to the idea of maintaining peace in the world through the formation of the UNO.
- The war left bitter feelings and mistrust among the countries which fought.
- The expansion of the USSR in Eastern Europe and USA's determination to keep her growth in check led to the Cold War.

Questions on World War II 1939 - 1945

(a) Mention one reason why Hitler was interested in occupying Russia during the Second World War

(b) Give two reasons why the allied powers did not stop Germany's remilitarization after World War I

(c) State five causes of the World War II

(d) State five factors that enabled the allied forces to defeat the Central Powers

(e) Mention two ways why Britain and France adopted appeasement policy against Germany

(f) Explain five political results of the World War II

(g) Explain how the effects of the First World War led to the outbreak of the Second World War

(h) What was the fundamental objective of the Marshall Plan after the World War II

THE COLD WAR

This is the name given to the icy relationship that developed predominantly between USA and the USSR after the World War II. The Cold War dictated international affairs for decades and major impasses like the Cuban Missiles Crisis, the Vietnam War, the Israeli-Arab conflict and the Berlin Wall were all attributed to it.

Weapons Used during Cold War

(a) Propaganda
(b) Economic sanctions
(c) Giving financial and military support to the allies of the enemy
(d) Arms race
(e) Severance of diplomatic relations
(f) Denial of aids to allies from opposing blocs
(g) Spying on opponents

Features of Cold War

- Mutual suspicion
- Economic alliances
- Military conflicts between communists and non communists
- Arms race and
- Ideological competition

A clash in viewpoint held dogmatically (capitalism versus communism), formed the basis of the international power struggle between USSR and USA with both sides vying for supremacy and exploiting every opportunity to expand. Logic would dictate that since USA and USSR fought together during World War II, their relationship thereafter would be firm and friendly. But this never happened and any appearance that these two powers were friendly during the war was illusory.

Prior to the war, America depicted the Soviet Union as the devil-incarnate. The Soviet Union also gave America the same thought, so their "friendship" during the war was simply the result of having the Nazi Germany as their mutual enemy. As a matter of fact, one of the America's leading generals (Patton) stated that he felt that the allied army would come together with what was left of the Wehrmacht in 1945, utilize the military genius that existed within it and fight the oncoming Soviet's Red Army.

Winston Churchill

Churchill himself was furious that Eisenhower, who was the supreme head of the allied command, agreed that the Red Army should be allowed to get to Berlin first ahead of the allied forces. His fury was shared by Montgomery who was a senior British military figure. So the extreme distrust that existed during the war was certainly present before the end of the war.

Eisenhower

Josef Stalin of USSR and Truman of USA were distrustful of each other. The Soviet Union had a vast army in the field (Red Army) supremely lead by Zhukov while the Americans had the most powerful weapon in the world, the atomic bomb.

Josef Stalin

For many, the growth in the weapons of mass destruction was the most worrying issue. Both USSR and USA massively built up their stockpiles of nuclear arsenal. However, it's possible that the sheer power of these weapons and the fear that they evoked, may have stopped a nuclear war. Confronted by awesome statistics, world leaders had to move to a position where they trusted each other more. Throughout the 1960's and 1970's "détente" had been used to ease bad relations between the super powers. This culminated in the Reyk Javic meeting between President Gorbachev and Reagan that started real progress in the cut in nuclear weaponry in future meetings.

Factors which led to Cold War

- Ideological differences between the capitalist USA and the communist USSR– each wanted to control the spread of another.
- Disagreement between USA and USSR over disarmament led to arms race and suspicion
- The "Iron Curtain" policy adopted by Russia, for example sealing off Eastern Germany from the West intensified the bad relationship between the two blocs
- Economic rivalry, for example USA came up with the Marshal Plan while USSR came up with COMECON to woo other countries to join

their camp. The fundamental objective of the Marshall Plan was to assist in the reconstruction of destroyed states in liberated areas

- Formation of military alliances, for example NATO by the West and Warsaw Pact by Russia to assist others militarily
- Difference over Germany after the war, for example Russia wanted a politically weak Germany while the West wanted a stable and prosperous Germany
- Misuse of veto power by Russia to suppress the American interests in the United Nations Organization threaten the latter
- Giving military support to the opponents of the enemy, for example in Vietnam posed a threat to the two blocs

The Decline of Cold War

The main reason which led to the collapse of the Cold War was the fall of Soviet Union and the collapse of communism in Eastern Europe. Russia officially became an aid recipient rather than donor. This failure made many countries like Bulgaria, Romania and Poland which were inclined to the East to embrace democracy. The collapse of communist rule in Eastern Europe was attributed to:

- Communism was a complete failed economic policy, for example communist countries remained backward
- Soviet Republics started to demand for independence
- Communist satellite states, for example Poland, began demanding for more democratic space
- There was widespread violation of human rights in the communist states

Other factors which contributed to the decline of Cold War were:

- The successor of Josef Stalin, after his death in 1953, Nikita Khrushchev, was more flexible and willing to relax both Cold War abroad and authoritarianism at home. He announced the policy of peaceful co-existence in 1956 and defused the Cuban Crisis by withdrawing the Soviet Missiles in Cuba

Nikita Khrushchev

- Truman was succeeded by David Eisenhower who compromised with the Soviet Union over a number of issues. For example, he convened the Camp David Summit in 1959 with Khrushchev in which a co-operative spirit emerged between the East and the West.
- The signing of the Strategic Arms Limitation Treaty (The SALT Treaty) in 1972 between USA and Russia limited strategic arms to certain quantities. This was followed by the improvement of the Chinese – American relations in 1972 and American relations with Russia when US President, Nixon visited Beijing and Moscow
- Reagan longed for peace and asked the Russian leaders to consider easing of tension between the East and the West. He was also involved in the *Strategic Defense Initiative (SDI)* - Star Ways - (1983) whereby space stations were created that would destroy every missile in the sky

Ronald Reagan

- In 1985, Mikhail Gorbachev introduced the *Glasnost* (openness policy) and the *perestroika* reforms (economic restructuring that appealed favourably to the west) which won him the Nobel peace Prize in 1990.

Mikhail Gorbachev

- The signing of the Strategic Arms Reduction Talks (START) Treaty in 1991 by Gorbachev and George Bush officially ended the Cold War. Destruction of weapons of mass destruction commenced.

George Bush

- Successful re-unification of Germany under Helmut Kohl in 1990 and the collapse of the Berlin Wall created a peaceful atmosphere in Europe.

• In 1991 Warsaw, a military pact for communist blocs was dissolved and some Soviet States joined North Atlantic Treaty Organization (NATO)

Effects of Cold War on International Relations

• Cold War led to break up of certain states, for example Germany was split into Communist East and Capitalist West

• It led to arms race leading to production of dangerous weapons

• Activities of the super powers intensified real wars in areas where they had interest, for example in Korea and Vietnam

• Cold War caused insecurity as each power tried to spread its own ideologies

• Mistrust and accusations of the two powers resulted into international insecurity and disruption of world peace

• Competition of world dominance caused various crisis, for example Cuban Crisis and Hungarian Revolution of 1956

• Oppressive regimes found their way to power because they were supported by either the West or the East.

• A lot of money was spent on military hardware at the expense of social services

• Cold War undermined efforts of UNO to achieve international co-operation

• The Cold War led to competition for world dominance between the two super powers

• Cold War brought immense divisions and conflict to people of the same continent, region and countries based on pro-west or pro-east ideologies, for instance in Angola

• Some member countries adopted a neutral policy to save them from joining either of the blocs, hence the rise of Non Aligned Movement (NAM).

• Cold War led to the formation of economic and military alliances like NATO (1949), the Warsaw Pact (1955) and the European Economic Union (1957).

• The Cold War led to development in science and technology.

Effects of the end of Cold War on Africa

• Some African countries, that were formerly socialist, got into problems following the collapse of USSR in 1990. These countries included. Somalia, Ethiopia, Angola and Mozambique.

• The end of the Cold War has led to the removal of financial aid and military support for African countries. Military or food aid is no longer rushed to countries experiencing problems to woo them. The failure to prevent the Rwanda genocide or Somali crisis and ending the current Al-shabaab crisis, is partly attributed to the aloofness of USA and Russia in African affairs.

• The end of war has led to emergence of USA as a "world policeman" over developing nations. These countries must toe the USA line or face the consequence of being denied financial assistance.

• The end of the Cold War has led to marginalization of Africa in international affairs.

• Africa no longer has a choice of donors and must depend primarily on the west.

287

Questions on the Cold War

(a) What was the main cause of the cold war

(b) State the main reason for the collapse of the cold war

(c) State two factors that led to the collapse of communist rule in Eastern Europe

(d) Give three characteristics of the Cold War

(e) Explain six factors which led to the rise of Cold War

(f) Identify two weapons used in the cold war

(g) Explain five factors which led to the decline of Cold War

(h) Give six effects of Cold War on international relations

UNITED NATIONS ORGANIZATION

Membership to the United Nations Organization (UNO) is open to all peace-loving nations that accept the obligations of its charter. By 1945, only 51 states had signed the charter. Kenya Joined on 16th December 1963 after attaining its independence. By April 2003 the membership of the organization had grown to 191 states.

The United Nations Organisation charter was based on the following principles: -

(a) Sovereign equality of all its members.

(b) Member states fulfill, in good faith, their charter obligations.

(c) Member states settle international disputes amicably

(d) Member states refrain, in their international relations, from threat or use of force against others.

(e) Member states assist the UNO in any action it takes in accordance with the charter, and does not assist states against which the UNO is taking preventive or enforcement action.

(f) The UNO ensures that states which are not members act in accordance with these principles in so far as necessary for maintenance of international peace and security.

United Nations Organization was established in order:

- To maintain world peace and security
- To develop friendly relations among nations
- To promote respect for fundamental human rights and freedom
- To promote progress and better living
- To co-operate and promote cultural interactions between member nations
- To protect the interests of the minority groups such as women and children
- To promote economic development among member states as it worked towards reconstructing the world economy, which was destroyed during the World War II
- To replace the League of Nations which had collapsed and continue to maintain peace and security
- To promote international understanding and co-operation among nations

Organs of the United Nations Organization

General Assembly
Functions of the General Assembly include:

- Admit and suspend members from the organization
- Discuss matters affecting the world peace and security
- Make recommendations on matters of peace and security
- Consider and approve the UNO budget
- Receive and consider reports from Security Council
- Elect jointly with Security Council the judges of the ICJ
- Appoint Secretary General
- Promote high standards of living

Security Council
has 15 members. Ten of these serve on temporary membership while five are permanent members. The permanent members are China, Russia, USA, France and Britain. The permanent members have veto powers.

Functions of the Security Council include:

- Maintain world peace and security
- Call upon states to settle their disputes peacefully
- Investigate any causes of disputes

- Approve admission, suspension or expansion from UN membership
- Facilitate military action against aggressors

The Secretariat

Functions of the Secretariat include:

- Survey economic and social trends and problems
- Bring to the attention of Security Council any problem that threatens international peace
- Administer peace keeping operations
- Carry out research on issues like human rights and sustainable development
- Organize international UN conferences on issues of world concern
- Monitor implementation of United Nations programmes by other organs
- Interpret speeches and translate documents into UN official languages
- Register treaties
- Carry out correspondence and publications

International Court of Justice

Functions of the International Court of Justice (ICJ) include:

- Ensure that treaties made between countries after the World War II are maintained
- Arbitrate international disputes
- Interpret international laws

Attempts to Promote World Peace

- Peaceful settlements of disputes - The UNO has tried to promote world peace by encouraging peaceful settlements of disputes in the world.
- Application of sanctions - the UNO has attempted to promote world peace by imposing mandatory sanctions against countries that are seen as threat to world peace in an effort to bring them back into fold.
- Peacekeeping operations - The UNO has attempted to promote world peace by encouraging the development and application of international law.
- Promoting of international law - The UNO has attempted to promote world peace by encouraging the development and application of international law.
- Disarmament - The UNO has attempted to promote world peace by encouraging disarmament through its disarmament commission and numerous conferences on disarmament that it has sponsored.
- Decolonization- the UNO has attempted to promote world peace by encouraging the process of decolonization and thus removing one of the major sources of world conflicts.
- Development - The UNO has attempted to promote world peace by encouraging the social and economic development of third world countries through the work of its numerous specialized agencies, for example United Nations Development Programme (UNDP).
- Creation of general awareness - The UNO has encouraged awareness in the world about peace.
- Promotion of regional co-operation - The UNO has prompted regional co-operation in different areas between different countries.
- Protection of human rights especially that of refugees or people in war ravaged countries.
- Authorizing the use of force to restore peace.

Achievements of the United Nations Organization include:

- The organization has succeeded in keeping peace in the midst of threats of nuclear war and seemingly endless regional conflicts in the world. UNO has developed more than 35 peacekeeping missions and observer nations.

- The organization has brought about independence of 80 countries which are now among its member states. Its Trusteeship Council assisted Tanzania, Togo and Cameroon to become independent
- The organization has Initiated development programmes in developing countries by giving them financial and technical aid
- It has encouraged reduction of arms race by signing treaties
- UNO has assisted in promoting human right, for example adopting universal rights spelling out the freedom and rights of people
- UNO has encouraged the rights of women to vote and children to receive education
- The organization helps to promote democracy around the world. It has enabled people in more than 45 countries to participate in free and fair elections, e.g. in Namibia, Cambodia, El Salvador, Eritrea, Mozambique and South Africa.
- United Nations provide humanitarian aid to victims of conflicts. More than 30 million refugees fleeing war torn areas, facing famine or persecution have received aid from the UN High Commission for Refugees (UNHCR) since 1951.
- UNO has encouraged co-operation in solving global problems, for example pollution
- UNO has gotten rid of dangerous weapons in the world, for example land mines
- UNO has encouraged health care, for example fighting AIDS/HIV
- It has assisted in setting up safety standards for sea and air travel
- UNO has encouraged scholarly work and academic co-operation

Problems UNO faced in its efforts to achieve world peace include

- Insufficient funds - The UNO lacks sufficient funds with which to carry out its work effectively. For example, it has often not been able to send enough peacekeeping forces due to lack of sufficient funds.
- Veto power - The permanent members with veto powers often adopt policies that promote their own national interests at the expense of the collective interests of most countries in the world.
- Ideological disputes - The work of the UNO in promoting world peace is often hampered by ideological disputes among member states. This was manifested in the Cold War period.
- The arms race - The UNO has found it difficult to achieve world peace because of the arms race in different parts of the world. The arms race generates and sustains conflict rather than peace.
- Differences in economic development levels of member states militate against co-operation.
- National sovereignty - The member states of the UNO are sovereign states that jealously guard their national sovereignty.
- Lack of machinery - It lacks a standing army to implement and effect its resolutions.
- Regional conflicts- The UNO attempts to promote world peace have been frustrated by deep-rooted regional conflicts. For example, the Palestin-Israeli conflict.
- Voting as a block has frustrated the UNO efforts to promote peace.
- Loyalty to other organizations - the interests of these organizations are not in accord with those of the UNO.

- It is unable to stop aggressions and conflicts between individual countries when super powers are involved.
- The increased occurrence of natural disasters such as famine, floods and epidemics has created an unexpected demand for economic resources.
- Some decisions of UNO are ignored and members take action without reference to it, for example America and Britain invaded Iraq without its consent
- The threat of terrorism undermines efforts to maintain peace and security

International terrorism and increasing cases of HIV/AIDS especially in third world countries has remained a major bone of contention in the world today. The Middle East has also remained a hotbed due to the USA imperialism in the area.

Questions on United Nations Organization

(a) Give the main function of the international court of justice (ICJ)

(b) Identify two major threats to world peace today

(c) State two reasons why United Nations was established

(d) Give two functions of the General Assembly

(e) Name two countries with veto powers

(f) Give three functions of the secretariat of the United Nations organization

(g) Give two functions of the security council of the United Nations

(h) What are the achievements of the United Nations Organization?

(i) What problems has the UNO faced in its efforts to achieve world peace?

(j) Outline the challenges facing the United Nations Organization

(k) State five ways in which the United Nations Organization has attempted to promote world peace

---

NON-ALIGNED MOVEMENT

is a group of states which are not formally aligned with or against any major power bloc. As at 2012, the movement had 120 members and 17 observer countries. The organization was founded in Belgrade in 1961 and was largely conceived by India's Prime Minister, Jawaharlal Nehru; Burma's first Prime Minister U Nu; Indonesian first President Sukarno; Egypt's second President Gamal Abdel Nasser; Ghana's first President Kwame Nkrumah; and Yugoslavia's first President Josip Broz Tito. All six leaders were prominent advocates of a middle course for states in the Developing World between the Western and Eastern blocs in the Cold War.

Jawaharlal Nehru of India

The Non Alignment Movement (NAM) was never established as a formal organization, but became the name to refer to the participants of the Conference of Heads of States or Government on Non Aligned Countries first held in 1961. The term "Non Aligned Movement" itself was coined by an Indian diplomat V. K. Krishna Menon in his 1953 remarks at the United Nations.

In a speech given during the Havan Declaration of 1979, Fidel Castro said the purpose of the organization was to ensure the national independence, sovereignty, integrity and security of non aligned countries in their struggle against imperialism, colonialism, neocolonialism, racism and all forms of foreign aggression, occupation, domination, interference or hegemony as well as against great power and bloc politics.

Fidel Castro of Cuba

The countries of NAM recently represent nearly two thirds of the United Nations membership and contain 55 % of the world population. Membership is particularly concentrated in countries considered to be developing or part of the third world. The movement was formed because: -

- Non-aligned countries needed co-operation among themselves to ensure peace in the world
- The foreign policy would enable them to get aid from both blocs for economic development
- Members wanted to establish their own identity in world politics
- Developing countries wanted to safeguard their independence
- Newly independent states did not want to join bloc rivalry between USA and USSR
- Members wanted to discourage arms race between the super power

---

Objectives of Non Alignment Movement
- To safeguard the sovereign of member states
- To push for independence of 3rd world countries
- To work towards disarmament of super powers
- To discourage military alliances.
- To promote economic independence and discourage neo-colonialism
- To fight racism

Achievements of the Non-Alignment Movement

- NAM has assisted to manage international crisis since it members were not committed to any course of military action. For example during the 1961 Berlin crisis, Nehru of India and Kwame Nkrumah of Ghana went to Moscow for a peace mission, while Achmad Sukarno of Indonesia and Modibo Keita of Mali went to Washington DC to try and create a conducive atmosphere for managing the crisis.
- NAM has speeded up decolonization process in most of the third world countries
- NAM has assisted its members to safeguard their national security and territorial integrity
- NAM has assisted in solving international conflicts. For example, India (one of the leading NAM member) played a key role in solving the Korean War, the Suez Crisis and Indo-Chinese conflict.
- NAM has contributed to the relaxation of international tension by distancing itself from the two military blocs, USA and USSR.
- NAM has enabled members to speak with one voice in international forum and they were able to exert their voting power as Afro-Asian bloc to influence world affairs. NAM was able to dismantle Apartheid because of its numerical strength in UNO despite the Reagan (former USA president) administration's opposition to sanctions against South Africa.
- Neutrality of NAM members has been maintained. The movement has given members freedom to put their national interests before those of the greater power blocs.
- NAM has worked towards the creation of a new economic world order. The non-aligned nations received economic aid from both blocs and also readily expanded their trade with both sides of the ideological divide.

- The NAM through the Cairo and Colombo Summits termed as World Disarmament Conferences played a key role in the disarmament process. The 1967 Treaty of Tlatelolco, signed by 22 states, set up a weapon Free Zone in Latin America.
- The Solidarity fund established during the Harare Summit of 1986 cushioned the frontline states against the economic sanctions imposed on them by the apartheid regime of South Africa.

Relevance of Non-Aligned Movement Today
- There is still need to articulate the voice for justice and sanity in arms production
- There is still need to come up with a new and just economic world order
- NAM has the task of addressing emerging issues, for example HIV/AIDS, pollution and growing international terrorism
- NAM needs to fight neocolonialism and safe guard the independence of third world nations
- Members still need to speak with one voice in international forums
- There is still need to promote world peace and security

Factors undermining the activities of the Non-Aligned Movements (NAM) since 1947 include

- Political instability - Civil wars and military coups in DRC, Sudan, Rwanda and Burundi; and the interstate wars between Iran and Iraq has undermined the contributions of the countries in the movement.
- Close ties with former colonial masters has made it hard for the members to pursue an independent policy.
- Border disputes between neighbouring member countries has weakened co-operation, for example between North and South Korea;

Morocco and Algeria; Vietnam and Cambodia; and Ethiopia and Somalia.

- National interest is placed before those of the movement.
- NAM Lacks enough funds to meet its financial obligations since most of its members are drawn from third world nations
- Ideological differences exist between members state. For example, some countries were inclined towards the West and other towards the East.
- Personality differences between leaders of member states limited fruitful discussions. For example, several leaders rejected the radical approach of Fidel Castro of Cuba to major issues.
- Most members belong to different organizations like AU, the Arab League, Commonwealth and Francophone nations. This has created divided loyalty.
- The break up of the Soviet Union undermined the movement. Once the power bloc rivalries quieten down, NAM appeared to become irrelevant.
- NAM lacks a permanent Army or a permanent institutional framework that can enable it to effectively carry out its mandate. For example, it failed to persuade Iraq and Iran to end the 8 year long war from 1980.
- Because the NAM was formed as an attempt to thwart the Cold War, it has struggled to find relevance since the end of Cold War.
- The movement fell apart when the Soviet Union invaded Afghanistan in 1979. While Soviet allies supported the invasion, other members of the movement (particularly Muslim states) condemned it.

While many of the NAM members were quite closely aligned with one of the super powers, the movement still maintained cohesion throughout the Cold War. After the breakup of Yugoslavia, a founding member, its membership was suspended. In 2004, Malta and Cyprus pulled out of the movement and joined the European Union. Belarus remains the sole member of the movement in Europe up till now.

> **Questions on Non Aligned Movement**
> (a) Name three founder members of Non Aligned Movement
> (b) Give five factors that led to the formation of the Non-aligned Movement
> (c) State five objectives at the Non-Aligned movement
> (d) Explain six achievements of the Non-Alignment Movement
> (e) Explain six factors which undermine the activities of the non-aligned movements since 1947
> (f) Explain the relevance of non-aligned movements today

COMMON WEALTH NATIONS

is a voluntary association of 53 independent and sovereign states. Most of the countries are former British colonies or dependencies. No one government in the Commonwealth exercises power over other states as is the case in a political union. Rather, the relationship is one of an international organization through which countries with diverse socio-political and economic background are regarded as equal in status and co-operate within a framework of common values and goals as outlined in the Singapore Declaration issued in 1971.

Such common values and goals include the promotion of: -
- Democracy
- Human rights
- Good governance
- The rule of law
- Individual liberty
- Free trade
- World peace

The symbol of this free association is Queen Elizabeth II who serves as the head of the Commonwealth. This position, however, does not empower her with any political or executive power over any Commonwealth member state. The position is purely symbolic, and it's the Commonwealth Secretary General who is the chief executive of the Commonwealth.

The Commonwealth was officially formed in 1931 when the statute of Westminster gave legal recognition to the sovereignty of dominions. Known as the "British Commonwealth, the original members were the United Kingdom, Canada, Australia, New Zealand, South Africa, Ireland and Newfoundland, although Australia and New Zealand did not adopt the statute until 1942 and 1947 respectively. In 1949, the London Declaration was signed and marked the birth of the modern day Commonwealth.

Commonwealth members in Africa include Kenya, Uganda, Ghana, Nigeria, Zambia, among others. The newest member of Commonwealth is Rwanda which joined on 29th November 2009. The most recent departure was Gambia, which severed its connection with Commonwealth on 3rd October 2003.

> **Organs of Commonwealth**
> (a) The Commonwealth Parliamentary Association
> (b) The Commonwealth Fund for Technical Co-operation
> (c) The Commonwealth Secretariat
> (d) The Commonwealth Development Corporation
> (e) The Commonwealth Speaker's Committee

Common Features of Commonwealth Countries

- The member countries accept the queen as the head of the commonwealth
- They maintain close cultural ties, for example they all participate in Commonwealth Games
- Members share common democratic institutions, for example parliamentary system of government
- Member states use English as the official language
- Members have close economic ties, for example rich nations like Britain and Canada provide the poorer members with economic and technical assistance.
- Member states hold regular meetings to discuss matters of mutual interest
- They form a power bloc and have set standards and influence
- Members have similar backgrounds to their educational system

Organization of the Commonwealth

The Head of State Summit - meets once in every two years for a week for extensive decisions and consultations. Decisions are reached by consensus.

Ministerial Meetings - The Commonwealth Ministers of Finance, Foreign Affairs and Defense hold regular meetings once every year while Ministers of Health, Education and Law holds theirs once every three years

The Commonwealth Secretariat - headed by the Secretary General and has a staff of 350 officers drawn from member countries. Activities of the Commonwealth are co-ordinated by the secretariat. The first Secretary General of the Commonwealth was Arnold Smith of Canada. In 1990, Chief Emeka Anyaoku of Nigeria became the first African Secretary General.

Specialized Agencies: -

(a) The Commonwealth Fund for Technical Co-operation supplies funds, finance, experts and advisers for projects carried out in member states.

(b) The Commonwealth Agricultural Bureau provides co-operation in the field of agriculture.

(c) The Commonwealth Parliamentary Association helps to improve relations between parliamentarians of member states.

Functions of the Commonwealth

- Commonwealth provides a forum for consultation by member states on issues affecting them
- It assists the economically poor member states meet some of their economic needs though financial and technical assistance.
- It provides consultancy services in all areas
- Education is encouraged through exchange programmes. Students from member states also get scholarship from other states to pursue further studies.
- It helps in the development of the legal systems of the members states
- Encourage cultural exchange programmes among member states.
- It encourages co-operation between member states in the field of medicine
- Members co-operates in matters relating to parliamentary practice and development among member states
- The Commonwealth Press Union fosters close co-operation between broadcasting stations of member states

Benefits Accruing to Member Countries

- Member states receive technical know-how through the provision of experts and advisers in various fields, for example Agriculture.

- The developing member states of the organization have acquired skilled manpower through the provision of scholarships and setting up training programmes by the developed member states of the organization, for example Britain and Canada,

- Member states have been able to interact with one another through activities such as commonwealth games and exchange progammes.

- Member states conduct trade among themselves with relative ease and it has assisted them to develop their economics.

- The developed member states provide financial aid to the developing member states of the organization and this has encouraged economic development among the latter.

- The organization has provided a forum for member states to air their views with one voice on international issues.

- The organization has encouraged friendship and understanding among member, for example the Commonwealth peace keeping force was sent to Zimbabwe.

- The organization has encouraged friendship and understanding among member states through conferences such as the commonwealth heads of government meeting.

- It has enhanced the democratization process in developing member states of the organization through sending observers to monitor elections, for example in Kenya and Uganda.

Challenges facing the Commonwealth nations include:

- Domination by developed nations undermines its decisions and policy matters.

- Some member countries are faced with civil wars because of poor governance hence enjoy less peace

- Most member states are poor, remits less funds to the organization, and this limits its funds for operation

- Being a voluntary organization withdrawal of members, for example South Africa and Pakistan greatly affects it.

- Perpetuation of colonial tendencies, for example Britain against Zimbabwe cause disunity

- Members are drawn from different organizations and this affect their allegiance

- National interests supersede the group's interest

- Racial discrimination, for example denial of visa limits movement of its members within the group

- Ideological differences, for example capitalism and communism affect the group

- Personality difference of the leaders prevent meaningful discussions

---

Questions on the Commonwealth

(a) Name three dominions of the Commonwealth
(b) Name any two Commonwealth Organs
(c) Identify the common features of the British Commonwealth countries
(d) Describe the functions of the commonwealth
(e) Explain six ways the Commonwealth member countries have benefited from the organization
(f) Explain the challenges facing the commonwealth

17 SOCIAL, ECONOMIC AND POLITICAL DEVELOPMENTS IN AFRICA SINCE INDEPENDENCE

TANZANIA

Political Developments in Tanzania since Independence

- Tanganyika became a Republic with an executive president (Mwalimu Julius Nyerere) in 1962.
- In April 1964 Zanzibar and Tanganyika emerged to form a union of Tanganyika and Zanzibar. The union became known as Tanzania. Nyerere became the president of the United Republic of Tanzania and Abeid Karume of Zanzibar became the vice president
- In 1967 Nyerere launched the Ujamaa (socialism) policy through the Arusha Declaration to guide the socio-political and economic activities of the country
- In 1973 Chama Cha Mapinduzi (CCM) initiated plans to have the Capital City (Dar es Salaam) transferred to Dodoma
- In 1977 the Tanganyika African Union (TANU) and the Afro-Shirazi party merged to form Chama Cha Mapinduzi (CCM). This became the ruling party
- In 1977 the East African Community (EAC) collapsed because of the difference between the three leaders in East Africa – Iddi Amin of Uganda, Jomo Kenyatta of Kenya and Nyerere of Tanzania

Iddi Amin Dada

- In 1979 Tanzania went to war with Uganda after Amin invaded the country and occupied Kagera region. Nyerere overthrew Amin and reinstalled Milton Obote as president

Milton Obote – First President of Uganda

- Nyerere retired from active politics in 1985 and was succeeded by Ali Hassan Mwinyi from Zanzibar
- Tanzania adopted multi-party democracy which was won by Benjamin Mkapa of CCM in 1995
- In 2006 Tanzania witnessed another peaceful transmission of power after a general election which was won by Jakaya Kikwete of CCM

President Julius Nyerere contributed a lot towards the struggle against colonialism in Africa especially in Mozambique. His contributions included:

- Nyerere allowed the liberation group in Mozambique to operate from Tanzania
- He encouraged different liberation groups to merge and form one strong movement
- He gave the freedom fighters logistical and financial assistance

Julius Kabarage Nyerere

Nyerere came up with the Ujamaa (brotherhood) policy as one of his strategies for development. This policy was coined up in a meeting held in Arusha. The declaration was based on social justice, economic equality and national brotherhood.

The aims of the Arusha Declaration were:
- To promote self reliance
- To build a socialist state based on African principles
- To nationalize means of production
- To ensure equal distribution of resources

Challenges Faced by Julius Nyerere as President
- The failure of the *Ujamaa* policy due to poor planning
- Prolonged drought that resulted in reduction of crop production and food
- Inadequate resources, capital and skilled manpower
- Poor state of basic infrastructure such as transport, communication and energy.
- Nationalization policy led to the economic decline because foreign investors kept away from the country
- The country was heavily indebted and Tanzania had a big problem of servicing the foreign debt
- He faced persistent budget deficits due to high inflation
- Collapse of EAC in 1977 left Tanzania in a bad economic state
- Tanzania's economy was hurt by its involvement in the liberation struggle and history of many refugees.

Besides these problems, Nyerere also faced a number of political problems like:
- Army mutiny immediately after independence
- Ideological differences between Tanganyika and Zanzibar
- Political difference between East African leaders, for example his difference with Amin led to war with Uganda.
- Karume's assassination threatened the existing stability in the country
- Africanisation of political institutions led to bad relations between Nyerere and the West

Social challenges which Tanzania has faced since independence include:
- An influx of refugees from Rwanda and Burundi due to ethnic and political turmoil in those countries stretched her resources and amenities
- Tanzania faced high illiteracy levels due to over emphasis on adult education
- There were inadequate housing especially in the urban areas
- The policy of one man one job as per the Arusha Declaration policy created unemployment among the youth
- There was high rate of crime due to the mass exodus of people from rural area to urban centres
- HIV/AIDS and other ailments increased mortality rate. This was partly due to the inadequate health facilities in the country.
- There was increased threat of terrorism, for example the bombing of American Embassy in Dar es Salaam which coincided with that of Nairobi.
- Increased population strains the existing few amenities
- There is high level of poverty among the people in the country
- Peddling of drugs is an increasing problem

Economic problems which Tanzania has been facing since 1964 include: -

- Price fluctuation of agricultural produce has adversely affected the farmers
- Repatriation of huge profits by foreign owned companies reduced her income
- Dilapidated transport network affected her industrialization programme
- Nationalism of key sectors of economy discouraged foreign investment and donor support
- Black marketeering across borders limit her income
- Weaker currency affects her balance of payment
- Adverse weather conditions curtailed farming activities
- She experienced rampant corruption

DEMOCRATIC REPUBLIC OF CONGO (DRC)

In May 1960, elections were held in Congo. Patrice Lumumba's party, Congolese National Movement Party (MNC) emerged the winner. It was followed by Joseph Kasavubu's Abako (Alliance des Ba-Kongo) party. As a compromise, in June Kasavubu became the president and head of state while Lumumba became the Prime Minister and head of coalition government which included dozen other minor parties. Moise Tshombe's party won control of the provincial assembly in Katanga.

Moise Ishombe

Just four days after independence, signs of army mutiny began to emerge. The reason was the fury of the African soldiers who were dissatisfied with the continued domination of the Belgian officers in the military. Little had been done by the Belgians to prepare the Congolese for independence. The level of education was low and most African soldiers were still of low rank.

Lumumba gave in as tension mounted during the first week of independence and dismissed the Belgians officers and appointed Congolese men in their place. Without effective command, the army went berserk in riots against the Belgian population and before mid July 25,000 Belgians had fled the country. Belgium brought in 10,000 soldiers to evacuate Europeans and protect their property, especially in the rich Katanga region.

Congo crisis

In July 1960 Moise Tshombe took advantage of the collapsed government. He declared Katanga region independent and with the help of the Belgian troops, expelled all units of the Congolese army from the region. With the West showing signs of support for Tshombe, Lumumba raised the stake by asking for Soviet help in recovering Katanga. Within two months of independence, Congo became a potential flashpoint of the Cold War.

In September 1960 Kasavubu announced that he had dismissed Lumumba who equally claimed the same. Mobutu, Minister for defense, temporarily took over leadership to "neutralize" the politicians.

In 1961 he closed the Russian Embassy in Congo and handed over power to Kasavubu. Lumumba was meanwhile arrested and assassinated. This led to widespread unrest in Congo and Gizenga, Lumumba's supporter declared Kasai region independent.

In August, UN troops began to disarm Katanga soldiers. The UN Secretary General, Dag Hammarskjöld died in a plane crash in Congo while flying in to negotiate with Tshombe. In 1963 Tshombe fled into exile in Spain, but was invited back in 1964 by Kasavubu as Prime Minister.

Mobutu Sese Seko

In 1965 Mobutu staged a bloodless military coup and dismissed both Kasavubu and Tshombe. He took control as president.

Reforms initiated by Mobutu Sese Seko

During his tenure as president, Mobutu introduced the following reforms: -

- Centralized power and became the head of state
- Banned all political parties and made Mourvement Populaire de la Revolution (MPR) the only party.
- Nationalized all industries in 1973 and forced out foreign owned firms and investors from the country.
- Reduced administrative regions
- Declared himself the president for life

- Encouraged Congolese culture and ordered all Africans to adopt African names. He changed his name from Jospeh Mobutu to Mobutu Sese Seko Ngbendu wa Za Banga (authenticity programme).
- Changed the name of Congo to Zaire
- Renamed major towns using African names, for example the capital, Leopoldville to Kinshasa.
- In 1990 Mobutu ended the ban of multiparty politics and appointed a transitional government, but retained substantial powers.
- He expanded primary and secondary education
- He improved medical services, building some hospitals and dispensaries

Economic Challenges Faced by Mobutu Sese Seko

- In 1989 Ziare defaulted on loans from Belgium resulting in a cancellation of development programmes in the country. This increased deterioration of the economy
- In 1994 the World Bank closed its office in Kinshasa and declared the country bankrupt.
- Mobutu and his officials looted a lot from the public coffers
- There was over exploitation by foreign based mining companies which siphoned back all profits
- Poor means of transport and communication slackened the pace of development in the country
- Fluctuating prices of mines and farm produce reduced revenue for the country
- The country lacked skilled manpower due to high levels of illiteracy.

In 1991 following riots in Kinshasa by unpaid soldiers, Mobutu agreed to a coalition government with opposition leaders, but retained control of the security apparatus and important ministries. In 1994, Mobutu accepted the appointment of Kengo wa Dondo, an advocate of austerity and free market reforms as Prime Minister.

In 1995 Mobutu accepted the main opposition leader, Etienne Tshesekedi as Prime Minister. The four years witnessed a struggle between the two leaders for supremacy and executive control.

In 1995 a million Hutu refugees fled into Zaire from Rwanda. The sympathy of Mobutu's government was with the Hutu. A decree was passed by Mobutu which expelled all ethnic Tutsi from the army and civil service. Tutsi property was looted in Kinshasa. In 1996 - 1997 Tutsi rebels captured much of Eastern Zaire while Mobutu was abroad for treatment. In May 1997 the Tutsi and other anti Mobutu rebels assisted with Rwanda captured the capital Kinshasa and installed Laurent Desire Kabila as president. Mobutu fled to Morocco where he died in exile.

In August 1998 rebels backed by Uganda and Rwanda rose up against Kabila and advanced to Kinshasa. Zimbabwe and Namibia sent troops to repulse them. Kabila was also assisted with Angolan forces. The rebels took control of much of Eastern DRC. In July 1999 the six African countries involved in the war in DRC met in Lusaka (Zambia). They agreed on a ceasefire. In 2000 a strong force of 5,500 UN troops was sent to DRC to monitor the ceasefire. In January 2001 President Laurent Kabila was shot dead by his bodyguard. Joseph Kabila, his son took over presidency.

Laurent Desire Kabila

Political Challenges Faced By DRC since Independence

- Political upheaval due to ideological differences, tribalism and colonial hangovers.
- Ethnicity made it difficult for the government to achieve national unity due to tribal groupings.
- Belgian administration retained high ranks in the army and civil service which made it impossible for Africans to be independent under African administration.
- Secession of Katanga and Kasai regions weakened the country.
- The foreign troops in Congo undermined Congo's sovereignty.
- Lumumba's assassination made the country to almost break up.
- Around 1960 to 1964 the UN and Belgian interfered a lot with the country's internal affairs.
- When Mobutu took over there was a shift from democracy to dictatorship.
- Congo rebels put up a rebellion to end Mobutu's rule in 1997. These rebellions greatly destabilized the country
- Kabila was assassinated in 2001. His successor found it difficult to bring peace into DRC
- The relationship between DRC and her neighbours has remained tense with accusation and counter accusation by rebel groups approved by each other.

The Barons

Economic challenges faced by African states since independence include:

- Debt crisis due to over borrowing and slow repayment
- Mismanagement and corruption in most African countries
- Unemployment of the ever increasing population
- High population and the great pressure on the existing resources
- Climatic fluctuations which has led to low food production.
- Inadequate industrial input leading to slow growth

Questions on Social, Economic and Political Developments in Africa

(a) Mention three principles upon which Ujamaa ideology of Tanzania was based?

(b) State five political developments in Tanzania since independence

(c) State five political challenges that Tanzania faced during the rule of President Julius Nyerere

(d) In what way did Mwalimu Julius Nyerere contribute towards the struggle against colonialism in Mozambique

(e) Outline six social challenges faced by Tanzania since independence

(f) Sate two social developments during the reign of Mobutu Sese Seko

(g) State three economic challenges faced by Mobutu Sese Seko as president of Democratic Republic of Congo

(h) Describe six political challenges which DRC has faced since independence

18 REGIONAL CO-OPERATIONS IN AFRICA

ORGANIZATION OF AFRICAN UNITY (OAU) was formed in 1963 in Ethiopia where the 32 Foreign Affairs' Ministers of African countries met to prepare an agenda for the heads of state meeting. The membership grew from 32 to 54 in 1984, when a government in exile – Saharawi Arab Democratic Republic was admitted into it. This led to the withdrawal of Morocco from the organization in the same year.

> **Objectives of the OAU**
> - To promote continental unity
> - To co-ordinate efforts towards the uplift of African people
> - To defend African sovereignty
> - To eradicate colonialism
> - To promote international co-operation

Principles of OAU
- Adherence to the principle of non alignment
- Peaceful settlement of disputes
- Respect for the sovereignty and territorial integrity of each country and its legitimate right to independent existence
- Non interference in the internal affairs of member states
- Condemnation of political assassinations or any form of subversion by one country in another member country
- Recognition of sovereign equality of member states

THE STRUCTURE OF OAU
Assembly of the Heads of States and Government
This was the supreme policy making body and met once a year or any other time when there was emergency. Its main responsibility was to co-ordinate the policies and the review the structures of the organization. Resolutions were passed by a two-third majority.

The council of Ministers
This organ was made up of Foreign Affairs Ministers of member countries. It met twice a year and had the following functions:
- Prepared agenda for discussion by the heads of states and government
- Prepared the budget of OAU which was approved by the heads of states and governments.
- Implemented decisions made by the Assembly of Heads of States and Government

The Secretariat
This organ was headed by the Secretary General and was based in Addis Ababa, Ethiopia. The Secretary General was elected by the Assembly of Heads of States and Governments. Its main function was to provide administrative services to the organization. In the secretariat there were many departments. These included political, Finance, Education, economic development and cooperation and science among others.

The Commission for Mediation, Conciliation and Arbitration
This was one of the key organs and it settled disputes between the states – boundary and refugee related disputes were some of the disputes settled by this organ. The organization also had other specialized agencies. These included:
- The OAU Liberation Committee based in Dar es Salaam, Tanzania – co-ordinated the activities of liberation movement in Africa.
- Economic and Social Commission handled all issues related to economic development in Africa. The African Development Bank based in Cote 'dIvoire which was established to

provide capital and technical advice to members operated under this commission.

- The commission on education, science and culture
- Conference on African Trade Ministers
- The Pan African News Agency (PANA)
- Union of African Railway
- Organization of African Trade Union Unity (OATUU)
- Union of African National Television and Radio Organization
- Union of African Journalists (UAJ)

Achievements of OAU

- Organization of African Unity provided a forum where independent African nations discussed their common problems like desertification, foreign interference, and dependency and at the same time sought for solutions to the problems
- The OAU achieved total liberation of African countries by offering military support to the nationalistic struggles in Mozambique, Angola, Rhodesia, Namibia and South Africa.
- Assisted African people to speak collectively in one voice on matters affecting Africa and they even attempted to formulate a common foreign policy.
- The organization embarked on common economic ventures for Africa. For example, creation of the African Development Bank (ADB) which represented the collective contribution by all Africans towards emancipation of Africans from economic backwardness
- It was instrumental in the formation of regional organizations like ECOWAS, SADDC and COMESA
- Solved disputes among African countries amicably

- Provided economic and technical co-operation in Africa
- Encouraged social and cultural heritage of African, for example through games like All African Games
- Developed postal telecommunication, Radio and Television network, for example UNTNA
- It condemned human rights violation in countries like Namibia and South Africa. It encouraged economic sanctions against the Apartheid Regime of South Africa.
- It offered solution to border disputes between member states like Kenya vs. Somalia, Ethiopia vs. Somalia, Libya vs. Chad, Morocco vs. Algeria, Chad vs. Nigeria and the Rwanda–Burundi conflict.

Organizations which were formed by the Organization of Africa Unity (OAU) member countries to promote economic co-operation among Africa countries, included:

- Preferential Trade Area (PTA)
- Common Market for Eastern and Southern Africa (COMESA)
- Southern Africa Development Co-ordination Conference (SADEC).
- Economic Community of West African States (ECOWAS)

Factors Which Undermined the Activities of the OAU

- National interest of member states sometimes took precedence over continental commitment.
- Personality differences among leaders made it difficult for some of them to come together.
- The organization lacked sufficient funds to implement its activities because some member failed to remit their subscription regularly.

- Lack of an army to enforce decisions of the organizations especially on critical and urgent issues.
- Some foreign governments interfered with the activities of the organization.
- Divided loyalty - members belonged to different organizations which had different agenda from that of OAU
- Political instability and the resulting refugee problem made it difficult for the organization to operate effectively.
- Close attachment to former colonial masters by some member states undermined their independence
- Member states were preoccupied by their individual problems like famine, drought and diseases and gave little attention to OAU
- OAU lacked an effective machinery to effect its decisions. It also lacked a standing army to implement and effect its resolutions.
- Different political ideologies among member states brought disunity among them.
- Disputes among member states, for example border disputes between Ethiopia and Somalia led to conflicts among members.
- OAU lacked executive authority to enforce decisions.
- Emergence of dictators like Amin Dada of Uganda, Jean Bedel Bukassa of Central African Republic, and Mobutu of Congo crippled activities of OAU.

AFRICAN UNION

The idea of African Union was mooted in Sirte, Libya in 1999 in a heads of states and government meeting hosted by the Libyan leader, Mauammer Gadaffi. The "Sirte declaration" called for the establishment of the African Union (AU). The union would accelerate the process of integration in Africa and enable the continent to play its rightful role in the world economic globalization.

Mauammer Gadaffi

It would also address the social, economic and political problems which faced the continent. African Union (AU) officially came into being in 2002 at the summit held in Durban, South Africa.

African Union was different from the OAU in a number of ways. These included:
- AU challenges the principle of non-interference which was emphasized by OAU. It allows for intervention in individual member states experiencing conflicts like Somalia and human rights abuses.
- AU envisages a union of African people which was formally seen as an association of African heads of states – people participates in Pan African parliament and economic and social councils.
- AU has an ambitious development agenda for Africa – provided for New Partnership for African development (NEPAD) whose goals were to: -
  - ✓ Promote accelerated growth and sustainable development
  - ✓ Eradicate the widespread poverty in the continent
  - ✓ Halt the marginalization of Africa in the globalization process
- AU has accountability mechanism which provides for a conference on security, stability, development and co-operation in Africa. It established an African Peer Review Mechanism (APRM) and a panel of eminent persons appointed to oversee its activities.

- AU proposes to establish a peace and Security Council with law enforcement powers through the creation of a standing African military force. The military is to be overseen by the proposed African Court of Justice.

Objectives of the African Union
- To achieve greater unity and solidarity
- To accelerate political, social and economical integration of Africa
- To defend the sovereignty, integrity and independence of member states
- To encourage international co-operation
- To promote African common position on issues which affect them
- To promote democratic principles and bring about popular participation in good governance
- To promote and protect human rights
- To establish necessary conditions which would enable the continent to play a more consequencial role in world affairs
- To work closely with relevant international partners in eradicating preventable diseases and promotion of good health in the continent

---

THE STRUCTURE OF THE AU

The Assembly

Comprise of the heads of states and governments and is the supreme organ of the Union. It is the most important decision making body of the union. The Assembly has the following functions: -

- Determine the common policies of the union
- Revive, consider and take decisions on reports and recommendations from other organs of the union.
- Consider requests for admissions of new members
- Establish new organs of the union.
- Adopt the budget of the union

- Give directions to the Executive Council on the management of conflicts, war and other emergency situations and restoration of peace
- Appoint and terminate the judges of the Court of Justice

Executive Council

This organ is made up of foreign affairs ministers and is responsible to the Assembly. The function of the organ is to co-ordinate the policies in areas of common interest to members. Areas of common interest include foreign trade, water resources and irrigation, environmental protection and humanitarian action, transport and communication, science and technology among others.

The Commission

This is the Secretariat of the union and is made up of the Chairperson, Deputy Chairperson and eight Commissioners. It deals with administrative matters and implements the decisions of the union. It coordinates the activities of the union and meetings. The commission also considers application for membership.

Permanent Representatives Committee

It is made up of ambassadors to the African Union who are permanent and it is based in Ethiopia.

Peace and Security Council

The proposed council is to comprise of 15 members whose responsibility will be to monitor and intervene in conflicts among member states. A Peace Fund is proposed to enhance its work and a Council of Elders to advise it. The proposed army is to be at its disposal.

Pan African Parliament

Consist of elected representatives from five regions in Africa. The aim is to involve the civil society in its participation.

Economic, Social and Cultural Council

The organ offers advisory function. It is made up of professionals and civil representatives from member states.

The Court of Justice

The court will deal with human rights abuse in Africa.

Financial Institutions

Three financial institutes will be set up to provide funds for projects and programmes in member states. They will include the African Central Bank, the African Monetary Fund and the African Investment Bank.

Specialized Committees

Different technical committees will be set up and there duties will include:

- Prepare projects and programmes of the union and submit them to the Executive Council
- Supervise, follow up and evaluate the implementation of decisions taken by the organs of the union
- Coordinate and harmonize projects and programmes of the union
- Make reports and recommendations on the implementation of the provisions of the Act.

Africa has been unable to achieve full economic integration because:

- The economies of African countries were designed to be providers of raw materials to the colonial governments. This colonial legacy still persists and many African countries still depend heavily on the West for manufactured goods, machinery and technology.
- Member states are unable or not enthusiastic to interfere in the internal affairs of other states even where there is an urgent need. This was evident in Rwanda and Somalia where the neighbours took too long to react to the genocide and the state failure respectively
- Poor transport and communication network has impeded trading activities in the continent. This has affected both the former and the current regional blocs.
- Rivalries among member states of trading co-operations hinder their operations.
- There is uneven distribution of resources in Africa. Some countries are endowed with strategic natural resources such as oil and minerals while others are impoverished. Integrating countries with wide economic disparity is difficult.
- Prices in the world market are dictated by the industrialized countries and do not favour African countries.
- Many countries in African are poor and are unable to make full contributions to the organizations. Most organizations cannot therefore meet their targets because of financial constrains
- Most of the African countries suffer from budgetary deficit and balance of payment problems hence lack adequate foreign exchange required for international trade.

THE EAST AFRICAN COMMUNITY (EAC)

The organization was formed in 1967 in Arusha, Tanzania by the three heads of East African states. These were Julius Kabarage Nyerere, Mzee Jomo Kenyatta and Milton Obote of Tanzania, Kenya and Uganda respectively.

The objectives of the community were:

- To run essential services within the East African region like Railways, Post and Telecommunication, Airways, and Research in Agricultural and Medical Services.

- To maintain a common market for the member states.
- To provide a forum for discussing economic and political issues of concern
- To promote political co-operation between the three countries.
- Facilitate free movement of the people of the regions to foster greater co-operation and understanding among them.

Organs of the East African Community

(i) East African Authority

This was the supreme organ of the community and was made up of the three head of states. The first chairman was Julius Nyerere and this chairmanship was on a rotational basis.

(ii) East African Legislative Assembly

This assembly was made up of 27 members – nine from each state. There were also 3 ministers and three deputies – one from each country. Kenya was represented by the late Robert Ouko as the minister of East African Community. Other members included the Secretary General, the Chairman and Counsel to the community. The Assembly enacted laws to govern the common services offered by the community.

(iii) The Secretariat

The secretariat was based in Arusha and its role was to co-ordinate the activities of the community.

(iv) Common Market Council

The organ ensured that the functions and development of the common market were run in accordance with the treaty

(v) Common Market Tribunal

(vi) Special Councils

Communication Council: Provided a forum for consultations under review

- Financial Council: - Considered and approved major financial decisions relating to the services offered by the community.
- Economic Consultative and Planning Council: - Advised the Authority on the long term planning of the common services.
- Research and Social Services Council: - Coordinated the policies of each of the partner states on research and social matters.

The community provided the following services within the region:
- Post and telecommunication.
- Research services – forestry, veterinary, agriculture, fisheries, and desert locust control.
- Railways and harbour
- Meteorological services
- Income tax assessment and collection
- Publishing services, East African Literature Bureau

Challenges that faced the East African Community up to 1977

- Unequal distribution of services and accrued benefits from the organization by the member countries made Tanzania and Uganda develop hard feelings about Kenya's economic dominance of the organization.
- Individual differences between leaders made it more difficult for them to hold meetings that would promote dialogue and unity.
- Ideological differences - Each of the three countries pursued different economies policies.

Kenya followed capitalism, Tanzania followed socialism and Uganda had a mixed economy.

- The coup d'etat which over threw Milton Obote undermined the unity that was desired for the survival of the organization. Nyerere refused to recognize Amin as the President of Uganda. Political instability in Uganda also undermined unity in the region.

- National pride and interests - National interests were given more priority than the regional interests. Tanzania, for example favoured railway transport while Kenya favoured road transport.

- Boundary closures - Tanzania closed its common border with Kenya in 1977, thereby bringing to a standstill the community activities. There was also boundary closure between Tanzania and Uganda during the war between the two countries in 1978.

- Animosity towards nationals from member states made them co-operate without having an important effect.

- Financial constraints ensued from the failure by member states to subscribe to the organization.

- The use of different currencies by the three nations made monetary transactions within the region problematic.

THE NEW EAST AFRICAN COMMUNITY-2001

The New East African Community was rekindled by the three heads of states of East Africa who once again met in Arusha in 1999. They were Benjamin Mkapa, Daniel Arap Moi and Yoweri Kaguta Museveni of Tanzania, Kenya and Uganda respectively. The treaty came into force in 2000 and was officially inaugurated in January 2001.

Aims of the East African Community

- To harmonize trade policies and relations with other regional and international organizations

- To encourage free movement of people within the region by easing border crossing

- To attain peace and security in the area by strengthening political co-operation among member states

- To harmonize fiscal and monetary policies in the area

- To promote co-operation in legal and judicial matters

- To improve infrastructure in the area, for example developing roads linking the countries in the region

- To promote development in areas of common interest, for example Lake Victoria and its basin

- To liberalize trading activities by adopting a common tax system

Organs of the Community

The treaty that established the East African Community (EAC) in 1999 outlined the main organs as:

(i) The Summit of the Heads of State

The summit is made up of the heads of states of the East Africa. It is responsible for giving direction and carrying out the goals and objectives of the community

(ii) The Sectorial Committee

The Sectorial Committee comes up with the programmes of the East African Community and monitors their implementation

(iii) Secretariat

The secretariat is based in Arusha and carries out on daily basis administrative duties of the community.

(iv) The Council of Ministers

The Council of Ministers is the main decision making organ of the community and it is made up of the designated ministers from member states

(v) The East African Court of Justice

The Court of Justice ensures that the community laws are properly interpreted and implemented.

(vi) The Co-ordinating Committee

The committee is made up of permanent secretaries of the three states and is held responsible by the Council of Ministers. It is in charge of regional co-operation and co-ordination of the activities of the Sectoral Committee.

(vii) The East African Legislative Assembly

It provides a democratic conclave for deliberations. It also acts as a watchdog of the activities of the community. It is a 30 - member assembly whose members are drawn from the member state.

(viii) The Court of justice of East Africa

This is the highest Court of Appeal in the region.

Other autonomous institutions established by the Council include:

- The East African Development Bank (EADB).
- Lake Victoria Fisheries Organization (LVFO)
- Inter-University Council for East Africa (IUCEA)

In 2005 the member countries signed up a protocol which addressed the following: -

- Elimination of internal tariffs and other charges of equivalent effect
- Elimination of non tariff barriers
- Establishment of a Common Market
- Cooperation in customs duties
- simplifying and harmonizing trade documents and procedures
- Deterrence of dumping of goods

Benefits which have accrued to member states of the East African states include:

- The community has provided a wider market and stronger bargaining power for member states
- It has given member advantage of economies of scale
- There has been a relatively balanced economic growth within the region
- It has enhanced regional co-operation through common services
- It has encouraged industrial projects, for example bicycle manufacture in Uganda, tyres and tube production in Tanzania
- It has strengthened currencies of member states
- Professionals, famous artists and businessmen are now able to interact more easily within the region
- EAC promotes trading activities in the area
- Civil societies within the area are now united, for example the law society of East African.

Achievements of the East African Community

- There is easy movement of indigenous people within the three states. An East African passport has been introduced to facilitate this movement.
- It has provided a forum where leaders of EAC meet to discuss their common problems
- It has facilitated the improvement and expansion of transport and communication networks between the three East African countries.
- Tariffs in trade among member states have been reduced and this has eased trading activities in the area

- Investment procedures have been simplified to enable all citizens to invest more easily within the community.
- It has enhanced co-operation of the civil society leading to formation of the Law Society of East Africa and the Business Council of East Africa.

Problems Faced by the East African Community

- Suspicion still exists over perceived dominance of Kenya in the community affairs.
- Livestock theft across the porous borders is common, especially among the Pokot and Karamajong' of Kenya and Uganda respectively.
- Some members states subject goods from other countries to many trade barriers
- Smuggling of goods (black marketeering) across borders deny member states revenue
- The recent wrangles between Kenya and Uganda over the ownership of Migingo Island created bad blood between the nationals of the two countries.
- Members produce similar goods and this thwarts regional trade
- Poor transport and communication network hinders free movement of people and goods within the region
- The use of different currencies by the three nations has made financial transaction problematic.
- Duplication of membership to other regional organizations like SADC and COMESA has led to divided attention
- Despite signing the treaty in 1999, Tanzania's customs department is still over taxing Kenyan products.

COMMON MARKET FOR EASTERN AND SOUTHERN AFRICA (COMESA)

The community is made up of 19 member states namely Angola, Comoros, Ethiopia, Burundi, Eritrea, Kenya, Seychelles, Egypt, Madagascar, Malawi, Mauritius, Mozambique, Rwanda, Sudan, Swaziland, Uganda, DRC, Zambia and Zimbabwe.

Objectives of COMESA
- To attain sustainable growth and development among member states
- To promote joint development in all fields of economic activities with a view to raising peoples' standard of living and fostering close relations.
- To create an ideal environment for foreign and domestic investment.
- To co-operate in the promotion of peace, security and stability in the region
- To strengthen Common Markets and a common position in international trade.

Yoweri Museveni, Mwai Kibaki and Jakaya Kikwete

Member countries within the Eastern and Southern African region are all free to join COMESA as long as they adhere to its treaty of 1991. The terms of this treaty were:
- Equality and interdependence of member states
- Solidarity and collective self reliance among members
- Inter-state co-operation and harmonization of policies
- Adoption of non- aggression policy

311

- Protection of human rights in accordance to the provisions of the African charter on human and peoples' rights.
- Promotion of accountability, tranparency and participation in leadership.
- Recognition of the rule of law
- Peaceful settlement of disputes among member states.

Organs of COMESA

The Authority

It comprises of the heads of states and government of the member states. The Authority is the supreme-policy making organ of COMESA. It meets once a year, but may hold an extra-ordinary meeting on request of any member of the authority.

Council of Ministers

It comprises the designated ministers from member states and meets once a year. The Council of Ministers makes policy decisions on the programmes and activities of COMESA. Specifically it deals with:

- Making staff rules and financial regulations of the Secretariat
- Choosing economically depressed areas of the common market
- Considering and approving the budgets of the Secretariat and court
- Giving out regulations, directives and recommendations based on the treaty
- Monitoring and ensuring proper functioning of the Common Market.

Committee of Governors of Central Banks

The governors of banks of member states form a committee to manage the COMESA's Clearing House. They also ensure that monetary policies are implemented and financial co-operation maintained.

Inter-Governmental Committee

This is a committee of Permanent Secretaries from member states which develops and manages programmes and action plans in all areas of co-operation except in the financial sector.

Technical Committee

This committee deals with administrative and budgetary matters

Secretariat

It is headed by the Secretary General and the current one is called Erastus Mwencha, a Kenyan who was appointed in 1997. The Secretariat is based in Lusaka (Zambia) and its roles are:

- Providing technical support and advisory services.
- Co-ordinating the activities of the group.
- Submitting reports on activities of the Common Market to the Council and Authority
- Responsibility for the administration and finances of the Common Market
- Submitting the budget of the Common Market to the Inter Governmental Committee
- Making certain that the Common Market continues to operate
- Submitting reference to court concerning any breach of the treaty
- Promoting a joint position by members in multinational negotiations with other countries.

Consultative Committee

It is composed of business community and other stakeholders. Consultative Committee provides linkage and facilitates dialogue between business communities and other stakeholders

The Technical Committees

Technical committees include:

- Committee on Natural Resources and Environment
- The Committee on Agricultural Matters
- The Committee on Trade, Customs and Immigrations Matters
- The Committee on Transport and Communication
- The Committee on Labour, Culture and Social Affairs.

Specialized independent institutions include:
- The Eastern and Southern African Trade and Development Bank (PTA Bank) based in Nairobi, Kenya.
- The PTA Reinsurance Company based in Nairobi, Kenya.
- The COMESA Clearing House based in Harare, Zimbabwe.
- COMESA Association of Commercial Banks based in Harare, Zimbabwe.
- COMESA leather Institute based in Addis Ababa, Ethiopia.

Court of Justice

The court ensures proper interpretation and application of the provisions of the treaty. It also adjudicates and settles disputes between members

Achievements of COMESA

- Members conduct trade easily because of the liberalized economies
- COMESA provides a wide, harmonized and a more competitive market both for internal and external trading.
- COMESA has established harmonized monetary, banking and financial policies in the region.
- It has improved the administration of transport and communication to ease movement of goods, services and people within the region.

- COMESA has created an enabling environment for investment
- The harmonization of macro-economic and monetary policies throughout the region has been achieved.
- COMESA offers a wide range of products to its members.
- Common Market provides room for industrial productivity and competitiveness
- It has ensured cooperation in the promotion of peace, security and stability among member states in order to enhance economic development in the region.
- COMESA has encouraged increased agricultural production and exploitation of natural resources.
- It has encouraged member states to practice good governance, accountability and respect for human rights. Burundi and Rwanda were subjected to these demands before they were admitted to COMESA.
- Contribute to employment of many people

Challenges Facing COMESA

- Double loyalty makes it difficult for some members to give due attention to COMESA
- Personality differences among the leaders affect its operations – Museveni of Uganda and El Bashir of Sudan were involved in disagreement over rebel activities in their two countries.
- Some countries are accused of undermining others, for example Uganda and Rwanda are often accused of meddling in affairs of DRC.
- Civil wars have undermined the success of COMESA – wars in Uganda, DRC, Rwanda and Burundi and Southern Sudan undermine the operations of a Common Market.
- Boundary conflicts between members, for example Eritrea and Ethiopia undermines its success

- Member states quarrel over trading rights. For example, Kenya and Egypt quarreled over duty-free cement dumped in Kenya by Egypt, on which Kenya wanted to charge duty.
- Competition from foreigners pose threat to COMESA
- Poor transport between member states hampers the movement of goods
- Some countries, for example Tanzania and Namibia pulled out of the organization. The two founder members have opted for the South African Development Co-operation (SADC).

ECONOMIC COMMUNITY OF WEST AFRICA STATES (ECOWAS)

As the name Economic Community of West Africa (ECOWAS) suggests, countries which form this trading bloc are from the West African region. These countries include:

- Guinea
- Mauritania
- Benin
- Niger
- Gambia
- Ghana
- Liberia
- Togo
- Coted'Ivoire
- Nigeria
- Senegal Mali and
- Burkina Faso

Objectives of ECOWAS

- To harmonize agricultural policies and carry out joint agricultural projects amongst the member states notably in research and food processing.
- To set up a fund to finance community projects mainly in poor states and to compensate members adversely affected by the liberalization of the trade.
- To set up technical and specialized commissions of mutual interest.
- To promote co-operation in transport, communication and cultural matters.
- To take up measures against foreign investment by setting up joint ventures thus reducing dependence on the outside world.

Achievements of ECOWAS

Since its inception, the group has had its successes and pitfalls. Some of the notable areas where it has done well include:

- In 1981 ECOWAS adopted the Defense Act. This meant that members agreed to join hands in a common defense pact in case of external aggression to a member state. The ECOWAS monitoring group ECOMOG was established as a multinational peacekeeping or peace enforcement force. This force has assisted foster peace in several member states like Liberia, Sierra Leone and Guinea-Bissau.
- The heads of state meet regularly to iron out problems facing the region – in 1999, they established a mechanism for conflict prevention, management, resolution, peacekeeping and security.
- Success in promoting industrial development in some countries through joint ventures has been realised
- Free movement of people within the region has been guaranteed through a set of rules.
- The member states are making efforts towards linking up their roads, railway and telephone connections with their neighbours.
- An agreement on development strategy has been reached by giving priority to agriculture and related industries
- A ten year forestation project in the *Sahel* region was commenced in 1982

- An exchange programme for students within the region began in 1982.

Problems Experienced by ECOWAS

- West Africa still controls only less than ten percent of the trading activities in the region and the rest is controlled by foreigners.
- Much of the on going trade is unofficial because of the rampant smuggling which takes place across the national frontiers.
- Some states still drag their feet in ratifying protocols, for instance only ten out of the sixteen states have ratified the protocol on free movement of people.
- Many ECOWAS states do not have convertible currencies and this set hurdles in regional transactions.
- Political problems have arisen from time to time.
- ECOWAS has failed to stop Nigeria from dominating trading activities in the region.

Challenges facing ECOWAS

- Co-ordinating the activities of ECOWAS is hard because of the vastness of the region.
- Poor state of communication and transport network within the region makes it hard for the business community to transact business in the area.
- Sharp division between the Francophone, Lusophone and Anglophone states, both in administrative approach and language, slow down activities and interactions between the member states.
- Member states still harbour strong attachment to their former colonial masters and transact businesses with them instead of the member states.
- Political instability in the region has interrupted the operations of the community – fighting in Sierra Leone, Liberia and Burkina Faso in the 1990's rendered economic and other forms of co-operation impossible.
- Foreign interference is another challenge that has faced ECOWAS for many years – presence of French soldiers in Cote d'Ivoire created a lot of tension and apprehension between Cote d'Ivoire and Guinea.
- Member states violate the regulations of the organization with impunity – Ghana closed her border with Togo and Nigeria extradited about 1 million Ghanaians who had flocked into Nigeria to benefit from the oil boom in the country.
- Suspicion still exist among members that Nigeria is a major beneficiary of the organization because of her wealth and huge population.

Questions on Regional Co-operation in Africa
(a) Mention three differences between the former organization of African Unity and the present African Union
(b) Explain the factors which undermined the activities of the OAU
(c) Why was the Economic Community of West Africa States (ECOWAS) formed?
(d) Explain the achievements of COMESA
(e) What are the challenges facing COMESA
(f) Why was the East African Community formed?
(g) Explain six factors that led to the collapse of the East African Community in 1977
(h) Give three objectives of the rebirth East African Community
(i) State five benefits member states obtained from East African Community
(j) Explain problems which have been facing the East African community since 2001

19 THE ELECTORAL PROCESSES AND FUNCTIONS OF GOVERNMENTS IN OTHER PARTS OF THE WORLD

INDIAN

India got Independence in 1947 and was led into it by Jawaharlal Nehru of Congress Party as the first Prime Minister.

> ### How the State Government in India is organized
> - Executive power is vested in the governor who is appointed by the president
> - The Governor appoints the Chief Minister who on his advice appoints other ministers
> - The Governor nominates – six to the Legislative Council
> - All decisions of the Council of Ministers in a state must be communicated to the Governor
> - The Governor has the power to dissolve the Legislative Assembly
> - His/her assent is necessary for a bill to become law

Central Government of India

The government of India known as the Union Government or Central Government is the governing authority of the union of 29 states and seven union territories. It is based in New Delhi, the capital of India. The Union and individual states all consist of Executive, Legislative and Judicial branches.

The legislative power in India is exercised by parliament, a bicameral legislature consisting of the President of India, the *Rajha Sabha* and the *Lok Sabha*. The former is considered to be the Upper House and consist of members appointed by the President and elected by the state and territorial legislatures. The latter is considered the Lower House or the House of the People.

Members of Cabinet include the Prime Minister and the Council of Ministers. The Cabinet as a whole is responsible to the *Lok Sabha*. The executive branch of the government is the one that has sole authority and responsibility for the daily administration of the state bureaucracy.

> ### Features of Central Government
> - India has an elected President and Vice President
> - The President appoints a Prime Minister who picks ministers to form a Cabinet
> - India has Supreme Courts
> - Chief justice heads the judiciary
> - There are two chambers of parliament in India: the Upper and Lower Houses.
> - India has Civil Servants

State governments of india

rule each state and the Chief Minister heads the Council of Ministers in them. While the Central Government handles the military and external affairs, the State Government deals with internal security. The State Government's legislatures are bicameral in seven states while the rest are unicameral. All the members of the Lower House are elected for a five years term and ⅓ of the members of Upper House, in bicameral states, are elected every 2 years for a six year term

In a state with a bicameral legislature the Lower House is called *Vidham Sabha* (Legislative Assembly) while the Upper House is called *Vidham Parishad* (Legislative Council). By law the Upper House cannot be more than ⅓ the total size of the Lower House, but must have more than 40 seats. The Lower House is composed of members directly elected from individual constituencies while the Upper House consists of members elected by the Lower House, members nominated by the State Government and members elected from specially designated teachers and graduate constituencies.

State executive branches are headed by governors appointed by the Central Government. The President and cabinet are also members.

State High Courts have jurisdiction over the whole state, but report to the Supreme Court of India which may override the high court's judgments and rulings.

THE PRESIDENT

The executive power is vested mainly in the President of India. The President enjoys all constitutional powers and exercises them directly or indirectly through officers subordinate to him. He/she acts in accordance with the aid and advice tendered by the Prime Minister, who leads the Council of Ministers. The Council of Ministers remains in power during the "pleasure" of the President. However, in practice, the Council of Ministers must retain the support of Lok Sabha.

The President is responsible for making a wide variety of appointments. These include:-

- Governors of states
- The Chief Justice and other judges of the Supreme Court and High Court
- The Attorney General
- The Controller and Auditor General
- The Chief Election Commissioner and other Election Commissioners
- The Cabinet Secretary

The President as head of state receives the credentials of ambassadors from other countries whilst the Prime Minister, as head of government receives credentials of high commissioners from other members of the commonwealth, in line with historical traditions.

The President is the commander- in- chief of the Indian armed forces. He/she can grant a pardon to or reduce the sentence of a convicted person for one time, particularly in cases involving punishment of death.

> ### Powers of the President of India
> - The president of India has powers to declare a state of emergency and rule by decree
> - He/she has power to assent or veto a bill. This can be overturned if both Houses re-pass the bill
> - In his/her capacity as the commander-in-chief, the president can declare war
> - The president has powers to appoint the Prime Minister, but the constitution dictates that this must be done with the consultation of parliament
> - He/she has powers to appoint governors and Supreme Court and High Court judges

Executive powers of the President

- Head of the Union: all executive powers are exercised in his name
- Appointments: The President appoints the governors of state, the judges of the Supreme Court and High Court
- The President appoints the Prime Minister and with his advice the other ministers of the Union of Council of Ministers
- In case the President has doubts about the level of confidence the Council of Ministers enjoys in the *Lok Sabha,* he can dissolve it and call for fresh elections.
- The President is the supreme commander of the armed forces of India and is entitled to declare war or conclude a treaty

Legislative powers and functions of the President

- The President can summon from time to time either separately or jointly, the House of Parliament. He/she can prorogue the Houses or dissolve the lower chamber of parliament,

Lok Sabha.

- The President may address either or both Houses of parliament. The president may also send messages to either Houses or both especially when he has a serious disagreement with the Council of Ministers
- The President nominates a number of members in both Houses. The purpose of the nomination is to ensure adequate representation in parliament of all sections of population which may not always be achieved through elections.
- A bill passed by both Houses requires the President's assent in order to become an act.
- A bill passed by a state legislature may also be reserved for consideration of the President by the governor of state

Financial powers and functions of the President
- No proposal for spending money or raising revenue for purposes of government can be introduced in parliament without previous permission of the President

PRIME MINISTER OF INDIA
The Prime Minister is by convention the leader of the victorious party. He/she is the chief advisor to the President and heads the Council of Ministers. The Prime Minister leads the executive branch of the government of India. The incumbent Prime Minister is Nerendra Modi of the Bharatiya Janata Party

Narendra Modi (Indian PM)

The Prime Minister is the senior most member of Cabinet in the executive branch of government in a parliamentary system. He/she selects and can dismiss other members of the Cabinet and allocates posts to members within the government. The Prime Minister is the chairman of the Cabinet and is responsible for bringing proposals of legislation. The resignation or death of a Prime Minister leads to dissolution of the Cabinet. He/she is appointed by the president to assist the latter in administration of the affairs of the executive.

Powers of the Prime Minister
- The Prime Minister is the head of the Council of Ministers which aid and advice the President of India.
- All ministers are appointed by the President on the advice of the Prime Minister.
- Inconvenient ministers are dismissed and ministerial portfolios are redistributed, as per the Prime Minister's desires
- The Prime Minister decides how many ministers should be there.
- The Prime Minister can make parliament pass whatever laws he wishes the parliament to pass because he enjoys majority support.

Union Council of Ministers
India has a three-tier ministry consisting of Cabinet Ministers, Ministers of State and Deputy Ministers. The Cabinet is the policy making body. It is an informal body and its members are chosen by the Prime Minister himself. The Council of Ministers is responsible to the House of the People. This obliges the President to appoint the leader of the majority party as the Prime Minister and to appoint other ministers on his advice. Thus the Prime Minister is not the President's nominee, but the peoples' choice.

The Council of Ministers is in charge of administering all the subjects entrusted to the National Government by the Union. Because the

Prime Minister has majority support in parliament, Cabinet can make the parliament pass whatever law the Prime Minister wants it to pass. The Prime Minister and the Cabinet have an absolute control over the nation's finances, the proposals for taxes and expenditures are really made by the Cabinet and only formally approved by the parliament. Judges of the Supreme Court and High Court are appointed and transferred by the President on Cabinet's advice.

Features of the Cabinet System in India

The Cabinet system of the government of India works on the basis of several broad principles. These include:

- There is a constitutional head of government, the President, whose position is one of dignity, but not power.
- The Prime Minister and the Council of Ministers are collectively responsible to the House of the People (*Lok Sabha*). If any action of the government is not supported by the House of the People, the government is obliged to vacate office.
- The inner ring in the Council of Ministers act as the policy making part of the ministry
- Ministers belong to the same party except in rare cases of coalition governments. They are important party leaders and hold same views and champion the same policy.
- The Prime Minister may dismiss any inconvenient minister at any time. He chairs the meetings of the Cabinet and in policy making his word is final.

Functions of the Cabinet in India
- The cabinet formulates policy issues that affect the management of the government in India
- The cabinet defends the government policies
- It ensures that government policies are implemented by the civil servants
- The cabinet advices the president
- The cabinet gives approval to the budget and estimates the expenditure
- The cabinet exercises general direction and control of government departments

---

Main Features of the Indian Parliament

- India has a bicameral parliamentary system made up of two Houses – *Lok Sabha* (Lower House / House of the People) and *Rajha Sabha* (Upper House / Council of States).
- The Prime Minister is chosen from the majority party or a combination of parties which have formed a coalition government
- The Upper House has 250 members. Out of these 12 are nominated by the President and it is not dissolved. A third of the members of this house retire every 2 years
- The State Legislature handles legislation on criminal and civil procedures, marriage and divorce

Lok Sabha

The Assembly of People is the Lower House of India's bicameral parliament. It is composed of representatives of the people from 543 constituencies chosen by direct election on the basis of adult suffrage, and meets in the *Lok Sabha* chambers of the *Sansad Bhavan* in New Delhi. *Lok Sabha*, unless dissolved continues to operate for five years from the date appointed for its first meeting and the expiration of the period of 5 years.

Rajha Sabha

This House is also known as Council of States or Upper House. *Rajha Sabha* is a permanent body and is not subject to dissolution. However, ⅓ of the members retire every second year, and are replaced by newly elected members. Each member is elected for a six year term. Its members are directly elected by members of legislative bodies of the states. *Rajha Sabha* has 250 members in all.

The Supreme Court

is the highest judicial forum and final court of appeal under the constitution of India. It comprises of Chief Justice and 30 other judges. It has original appellate and advisory jurisdiction. As the final court of appeal of the country, it takes up appeals primarily of various states of the Union and other courts and tribunals. The Supreme Court has extensive original jurisdiction for the protection. It also acts as the court to settle disputes between various governments in the country. As an advisory court, it hears matters which may specifically be referred to it under the constitution by the President of India. It may also take cognisance of matters on its own, without anyone drawing its attention. The laws declared by the Supreme Court become binding on all courts within India.

ELECTIONS IN INDIA

India has an asymmetric Federal Government with elected officials at the Federal, State and Local levels. It is committed to holding regular free and fair elections. These elections determine the composition of the government, the state and the Union territorial assemblies, the President and Vice Presidency. Elections to the House of the People (*Lok Sabha*) and the Legislative Assembly of every state are held on the basis of universal adult suffrage. These elections take place every 5 years.

Elections are conducted according to the constitutional provisions, supplemented by laws made by parliament. An election commission was set up for the supervision, direction and control of the preparation for, and conducts of the elections. Laws which govern elections include:

- Presidential and Vice Presidential Elections Act of 1952
- The Representation of the People's Act of 1950 and
- The Conduct of the Elections Rules Act of 1961

Presidential Elections

The constitution provides for the election of the President by an Electoral College consisting of the elected members of both the Houses of parliament and the State Legislative Assemblies. The election is by a system of proportional representation by means of the single transferrable vote. For the presidential election, the quota is set at 1 more than ½ total votes cast.

No person is eligible for elections as president unless he is a citizen of India, unless he has completed the age of 35 years and unless he is qualified for elections as a member of the House of the People and if he holds any office of profit under the government of India.

Elections of Vice President

A Vice President is also elected by members of an electoral college consisting of members of both Houses of parliament in accordance with proportional representation by means of the single transferrable vote. The Vice President should be qualified for elections as a member of the Council of States (Upper House).

Elections of members of *Rajha Sabha*

Members of the Upper House of parliament or the Council of States are elected directly. The Council of States consists of 12 members who are nominated by the president and not more than 238 representatives of the states and of the Union territories. A nominated member is not eligible to vote.

An elected member holds office for six years. A member chosen to fill a vacancy serves for the remainder of his predecessor's term of office. The Council of States is not subjected to dissolution, but as nearly as possible ⅓ of the members thereof retire as soon as may be on the expiration of every second year. Thus elections are staggered with ⅓ members being elected every 2 years.

Elections to the House of the People and State Assemblies

The country is divided into 543 parliamentary constituencies each of which returns one Member of Parliament to the *Lok Sabha*. The size of each constituency is determined by an independent delimitation commission. The electors cast one vote each for a candidate who gets the most votes. All the seats in the House of the People allotted to the state are seats to be filled by persons chosen by direct elections from parliamentary constituencies in the state.

The State Assemblies or *Vidhan Sabha* are directly elected bodies. The Legislative Assembly of each state consists of not more than 500, and not less than 60 members chosen directly by direct elections from territorial constituencies in the state. Elections of members of Legislative Councils (*Vidhan Parishad*) consist of representatives chosen by the members of *Vdhan Sabha* and local authorities, and also by graduates and teachers in the state having such *Parishads*. The governor also nominates some.

Qualifications of Candidates

A person is not qualified to be chosen to fill a seat in parliament unless he is a citizen of India and subscribes before some person authorized in that behalf by Election Commission of India an oath of affirmation according to the form set out for the purpose. To contest for that seat in the Council of States, he/she should not be less than 30 years of age and, for the *Lok Sabha* not less than 25 years of age.

A person is not qualified to be chosen as a representative of any state or Union territory in the Council of State unless:

- He is an elector for a parliamentary constituency in India.
- He is of sound mind and stands so declared by a competent court
- He is an undischarged solvent
- He is not a citizen of India or has voluntarily acquired the citizenship of a foreign state or under any acknowledgement of allegiance or adherence to a foreign government
- He is disqualified by a law made by parliament

Disqualification for members of parliament and state legislatures

- A person convicted of an offence punishable under:

Indian penal code e.g. promoting enmity between different groups on grounds of religion, race, place of birth

   ✓ Offence of bribery
   ✓ Offence of undue influence at an election
   ✓ Offence relating to rape
   ✓ Offence of cruelty towards a woman by husband or by a woman towards a relative of the husband

- Punishment for preaching and practice of "untouchable" and to enforcement of any disability arising thereof
- Offences of importing or exporting prohibited goods

- Offence of being a member of an association declared unlawful

Functions of the Electoral Commission of India
- The electoral commission appoints election officials, for example presiding officers
- Establishes the code of conduct to be maintained before and during the electioneering and election period
- Regulates the election expenditure for each party and candidates, for example monitor the money spent on elections
- Register voters and keeps updating the voters register from time to time
- Facilitates proper media coverage of the election process both at national and state levels
- Ensures that elections are free and fairly done, for example observes the casting and counting of votes
- Decides on the polling day for the various constituencies
- Prepares the polling stations, for example availing electronic voting machines, ballot boxes, ballot papers and polling booths
- Determines the status of the parties after registration and categorize them, for example into State parties, unrecognized parties and registered parties

Questions on Electoral Processes in India
(a) Give two names of houses or chamber in Indian parliamentary system
(b) Explain the features of the government in India
(c) How is the state government in India organized?
(d) What are the functions of the Electoral Commission of India?
(e) What are the constitutional powers of the President of India?
(f) What are the powers of the President of India?
(g) What are the functions of the Cabinet in India?
(h) Discuss the main features of the Indian parliament

BRITAIN is a constitutional monarchy. This means that, while the Sovereign is the head of state, the ability to make and pass legislation resides with the elected parliament. Sovereignty rests in parliament which consists of the House of Commons, the House of Lords and the Crown. Effective powers reside in the House of Commons whose members are elected from single member constituencies. The executive powers rest on the Prime Minister who is the head of the Cabinet. The Prime Minister is usually drawn from the party holding the most seats in the House of Commons: The Monarchy usually asks the leader of the majority party to be the Prime Minister.

Historically, the hereditary and life peers of the realm, high officials of the Church of England, and the Lords of Appeal (who exercised judicial functions until a Supreme Court was established in 2009) had rights to sit in the House of Lords, but in 1999 both Houses voted to strip most hereditary peers of their right to sit and vote in the chamber.

Most legislation originates in the House of Commons. The House of Lords may take part in shaping legislation, but it cannot permanently block a bill passed by the House of Commons, and it has no authority over money bills.

The two main parties are Conservative Party and Labour Party. The Liberal Democrats is another party which is a merger of the Liberal Party and Social Democratic Party.

The constitution of United Kingdom exists in no one document, but in centuries old accumulation of statutes, judicial decisions, conventions and traditions.

Monarchy

Although the British Sovereign no longer has a political or executive role, he/she continues to play an important part in the life of the nation. As the head of state, the monarch undertakes constitutional and representational duties which have developed over many years. The Sovereign acts as a focus for national identity, unity and pride; give a sense of stability and continuity; officially recognizes success and excellence and support the ideal of voluntary service. The hereditary monarch, who must belong to the Church of England, is almost entirely limited to exercising ceremonial functions as the head of state.

Queen Elizabeth

Functions of the Monarchy in Britain

- The monarchy advices the government
- Summons, prorogues and dissolves parliament
- The monarchy confers honours to men and women of distinguished service to the nation
- She gives royal assent to bills before they become law
- She approves all appointments to important state offices such as judges, senior members of the armed forces and civil service.
- The Monarchy consents to all Cabinet appointments
- The monarchy is the fountain of justice

- The monarch pardons and gives reprieve to people who have been accused of committing various offences.
- The Monarchy appoints Bishops and Archbishops of the Anglican Church.

At the beginning of each new session of parliament, the monarchy addresses both Houses together in the House of Lords to mark the formal opening of parliament. In the address, the monarch outlines government proposed legislations for the coming session.

Importance of the monarchy to the British people

- The presence of the monarchy helps to give some continuity to executive policy.
- It inspires the head of government with a sense of responsibility and dignity.
- It acts as a useful counselor to the head of government.
- It is the symbol of Commonwealth unity.
- It sets standards for social life. The presence of members of the royalty at the inauguration of scientific, artistic and charitable works ensures nationwide support.
- The royal family pays state visits to foreign government and undertakes tours in other countries of the Commonwealth, hence contributing to better understanding between Britain and other nations.

The Queen of England plays the following roles in relation to the British Government:

- At the end of election, the monarchy invites the leaders of the party with the majority votes in the House of Commons to form the next government.
- The Monarchy is the legal head of the state and the symbol of national unity.
- Before a bill becomes law the Monarchy gives the royal assent.

- The Monarchy has the powers to officially dissolved parliament at the end of its tenure of office.
- The Monarchy approves the appointment of the Cabinet.
- The Monarchy nominates members to the House of the Lord or makes peers
- She exercises the prerogative of mercy on convicts and criminals.
- She summons the parliament after General Election
- The Monarchy is the commander-in-chief of the armed forces.

LEGISLATURE

Parliament is the supreme legislative body in the United Kingdom. It alone possesses legislative supremacy and thereby ultimate power over all other political bodies in the United Kingdom and its territories. The parliament is a bicameral one consisting of an Upper House (the House of Lords) and the Lower House (the House of Commons).

Ways of becoming a Member of Parliament in Britain include:
- By election to the House of Commons.
- Nomination to the House of Lords by the Monarchy
- By virtue of holding certain offices, for example Bishop of the Church of England and some judges.
- By becoming a member of the House of Lords through inheritance.

The House of Lords includes two different types of members: the Lords Spiritual (Senior Bishops of the Church of England) and the Lords Temporal (members of the peerage) whose membership is not elected by the population at large, but is appointed by the Sovereign on the advice of the Prime Minister. Prior to the opening of the Supreme Court in October 2009, the House of Lords also performed judicial role.

Ways of Becoming a Member of the House of Lords in Britain
- Appointment by monarchy
- Through hereditary
- By virtue of position in society, for example distinguished jurists and head of Church of England

---

Roles of the House of Lords in Britain include:
- Facilitates Lower House (House of Commons) in process of law making
- Address non-controversial bills that the Lower House has no time to address
- Hold bills from the Lower House long enough in order to seek public opinion
- Question ministers about the activities of the government and stage debates on general issues of national policy
- The House of Lords sits as a court of appeal to hear criminal cases and is presided over by Lord Chancellor

The House of Commons is a democratically elected chamber with elections held at least every five years. The two Houses meet in separate chambers in the palace of Westminster (Commonly known as the House of Parliament) in London. By constitutional convention, all government ministers, including the Prime Minister are members of the House of Common.

Functions of the British Parliament (House of Commons)
- The British parliament discuses and makes laws. It also amends laws when need arise.
- Parliament approves the government budget and ways of raising money.
- It directs government's foreign policy and keeps development programs on tract.
- It checks the power of the executive to ensure that the rule of law is maintained (can pass a vote of no confidence on the Prime Minister).
- Debates issues of national interest.

The House of Lords in the British plays the following roles in parliamentary system:

- The House of Lords checks the powers of the House of Commons and therefore prevents nasty legislation being passed. Bills from the House of Common have to go the House of Lords for debate and approval.
- It provides a forum for the utilization of the talents of people who could not win a General Election. These people are created peers by the queen and become members of the House of Lords.
- It enhances unity in the country as commoners are created Lords by the queen and then become members of the House of Lord.
- It provides continuity in operations in parliament. Old and experienced peers retain their seats in the House of Lords until they die, so they provide guidance to new and young politicians.

Privilege Enjoyed by British Members of Parliament
- Enjoy freedom of speech while in the House
- Freedom from harassment within precincts of parliament, for example being arrested
- Protection against arrest for civil offences for a period of forty days before and forty day after parliament.

Parliamentary Sovereignty

This is a principal of the United Kingdom constitution. It makes parliament the supreme legal authority in the United Kingdom, which can create or end any law. Generally the courts cannot overrule its legislation and no parliament can pass laws that future parliaments cannot change.

Features of Parliamentary Supremacy in Britain

- Parliament is the supreme institution in Britain. All other institutions derive their power from it.
- Parliament is the only institution empowered to make, amend and abolish laws. No other institution has the right to invalidate the legislations of parliament.
- Parliament is the only institution empowered to approve government budget.
- Decisions of parliament are biding to all. They cannot be overruled or nullified by a court of law.
- Parliament has the powers to remove an unpopular government from office or the Prime Minister.

Factors limiting parliamentary supremacy in Britain

- Whatever decision is taken by members of the House of Commons, they must consider the moral values of the British society.
- Public opinion – parliamentarians are sensitive to public opinion. That is, unpopular government may not be re-elected.
- County governments are empowered to make by-laws without consulting parliament.
- The interests of the institutions are always taken into account before laws are passed in parliament, for example the church and universities
- A legislation passed by one parliament can be changed by a future one
- International laws are taken into account when laws are being made.

Over the years, parliament has passed laws that limit the application of parliamentary Sovereignty. These laws reflect political developments both within and outside the United Kingdom. They include:

- The devolution of powers of bodies like the Scottish parliament and Welsh Assembly.
- The Human Rights Act of 1998
- The United Kingdom's entry to the European Union in 1972
- The decisions to establish a United Kingdom Supreme Court in 2009 which ended the House of Lords function as the final Court of Appeal

EXECUTIVE

The executive is made up of the Prime Minister, the Cabinet and the Civil Service.

The British Prime Minister

is the chief executive officer and head of the government. He/she is called upon by the monarchy to form a government after a General Election. The Prime Minister is the leader of the party with majority seats in the House of Commons.

David Cameron – British Prime Minister

Powers and Functions of the Prime Minister

- The Prime Minister is the head of government and is invited by the monarchy to form the government when his or her party wins elections
- Appoints and dismisses ministers, but this is done with the consent of the monarchy
- The Prime Minister prepares the monarchial speech to be read during the opening of a parliamentary session
- He/she is in charge of the House of Commons (the Lower House made up of elected members of parliament)
- May request the monarchy to dissolve parliament before his/her five years in office expirers
- Prime Minister represents Britain in international fora
- The Prime Minister can change laws because she/he has the command of the majority members in parliament
- He/she recommends to the monarchy the names of candidates to be appointed to senior judicial office, royal commission and those to be conferred with civil honours and distinctions
- The Prime Minister presides over the meetings of the Cabinet
- He/she settles disputes between different ministries and ministers
- The Prime Minister is in charge of appointments, for example senior civil servants and Permanent Secretaries

The Cabinet

is made of ministers who are appointed by the Prime Minister with the approval of the monarchy. They are nominated from the party with the majority of seats. The cabinet performs the following functions:

- The Cabinet Ministers set up policies that guide the operations in the various departments of the ministry.
- Cabinet determines the policy to present to parliament for consideration.
- Cabinet is responsible for the co-ordination of government activity. For example, all ministers must implement Cabinet decisions with regard to their department.

Conventions that provide guidance on the operation of the cabinet in Britain include:

- Once a government is defeated, on a major issue or on a vote of no confidence, it is expected to resign. A government whose party is defeated in General Elections is expected to resign.
- The Cabinet is drawn from the House of Commons and the House of Lords.
- The entire Cabinet comes from the same political party of majority seats except during a crisis like war.
- The advice offered by the Cabinet must be accepted by the monarch, failure to which a crisis can occur.
- All members of the Cabinet take an oath and are bound to secrecy by this oath and the official Secrets Act.
- Members of the Cabinet are collectively responsible for all decisions and actions as well as individually responsible of the departments they head.

Questions on Electoral Processes in Britain

(a) Who is the head of government in Britain?

(b) List three ways through which a person may become a member of parliament in Britain

(c) State three roles of the House of Lords in Britain

(d) State three functions of the House of Commons in Britain

(e) State three privilege which members of the British Parliament enjoy

(f) Describe the functions of the British Parliament

(g) Explain six factors that limit parliamentary supremacy in Britain.

(h) Explain the powers and functions of the British Prime Minister

(i) Identify five functions of the monarchy in Britain

(j) What role does the Queen of England play in relation to the British government?

(k) What are the sources of the British Constitution?

(l) Highlight the features of the doctrine of the parliamentary sovereignty in Britain

---

Sources of the British Constitution

- Historical documents, for example the Magma Carta and the Parliamentary Acts, for example of 1911.
- The British conventions which have been used from generation to generations over a long period of time. For example, those which protect the British citizens against the excessiveness of the executive.
- Decisions made by the British law courts from time to time became part of the British constitution, for example in 1884 the supremacy of parliament was established by the courts of Britain.
- The Hansard - official verbatim report of proceeding in the parliament.
- Royal prerogatives / powers of king or queen to declare war or make treaties of peace.
- Legal publications by reputable authorities, for example scholars, lawyers, statements, political thinkers.

UNITED STATES OF AMERICA

One of the most widely held misconceptions about the American system of government is that it is a democracy. The form of government established by the American constitution was a Republic. This is a form of government which derives its powers directly or indirectly from a great body of the people, and is administered by persons holding their offices during their pleasure, for a limited period, or during good behaviour. The people elect representatives to make decisions on their behalf in the political process. The people do not voice their opinion directly in the policy making process, but rather their views are conveyed through their representatives.

The decisions made by the American political leaders are often different from the will of the majority of the people at any given point in time. Individual political leaders, however, are kept in check through frequent elections. Members of the House of Representatives must face re-elections every two years and senators every six. The president serves terms of 4 years. By staggering these elections so there is never a case in which congressional seats and the presidency are being contested at the same time, it's impossible for a majority to take control of the national government through one election.

How the Government of the USA is organized

- USA is a federal republic made up of about 50 states
- The head of state is a president who is elected every four years. He is the chief executive but he is not a member of the Legislative Council.
- There is separation of powers between the Executives, Legislature and Judiciary.
- America has a bicameral legislature (Congress). The Congress is made up of the House of Representatives and the Senate.
- Each state is divided into a number of electoral constituencies each of which elects representatives from each state.
- Each state has its own court system. The Federal Court (The Supreme Court) is the highest court in the country.
- Functions of the government are shared between the Federal Government and State Governments.
- The Federal Government tasks are of major concerns, foreign affairs, defense and making general laws for all Americans, regulating trade and commerce and issuing the currency.
- Each state has its own government to deal with matters pertaining to their territories.
- The Secretaries are appointed by the President and are not member of the Congress.
- State Government deal with matters pertaining to their territories, for example agriculture, education and health.
- There is a Vice President who is appointed by the president with the approval of the party.

The most significant feature of the USA constitution is the establishment of the Rule Of Law, the creation of a federal system with a supreme national government, the separation of powers into three branches that "check and balance" each other, and the establishment of a Republican form of government.

The Constitution and the Rule of Law

The constitution is considered the supreme law of the land both because of its content and because its authority is derived from the people. The government cannot create or destroy it. Among these concepts and ideas is the notion that the people are sovereign and the legislative government is based on the popular consent. No one is above the law, including the President.

Separation of Powers and Checks and Balances

Given the fear of consolidation of government's powers at the national levels, three branches of government (Legislature, Executive and Judiciary) were established. In case one or group of individuals could gain control or undue influence over these separate functions, there would be no assurance that the rights and liberties of citizens would be protected. For separation of powers to work in practice, each branch would "check and balance" the other. Each branch is independent from the other with regard to their appointments, tenure and compensation. Because each branch could not always be counted on to act in accordance with the public will, each branch had the means to check the actions of the other.

Federal System of Government

In practical terms, the single most important feature of the constitution is probably the federal system it created. The National Government has authority to enforce any of its enactments as it attempts to guide the states in their league of "friendship". Under this arrangement, the states would retain their unique powers and authority, pass laws and govern the people who live within their boundaries. The laws passed by the National Government would apply directly to the people of the nation and not to the states. The extent of the National Government's powers is limited.

The government of the United States of America is the Federal Government of the Republic of 50 states that constitute the United States, as well as one capital district and several other territories. The Federal Government is composed of three distinct branches (Legislature, Executive and Judicial) whose powers are vested by the US constitution in the Congress, the President and the Supreme Court and the Federal Courts. The powers and duties of these branches are further defined by acts of Congress, including the creation of Executive Departments and courts inferior to the Supreme Court.

The United States government is based on the principal of federalism, in which power is shared between the Federal Government and State Governments. "Checks and balances" among the powers and responsibilities of the three branches of the American government is one of its pillars. While the Legislative (Congress) has the powers to create law, the Executive (President) can veto any legislation – an act which, in turn, can be overridden by Congress. The president nominates judges to the nation's highest judicial authority (Supreme Court) but those nominees must be approved by the Congress. The Supreme Court in its turn has the power to invalidate as "unconstitutional" any law passed by the Congress.

The pros and cons of federalism have been subject of debate since the creation of the Republic.

Advantages of the Federal System of Government

- A federal system of government makes it possible for several states to work as one political unit.
- It ensures that the interests of smaller states and groups are protected.
- Federalism makes it possible for member states to solve common problem together.
- It makes available a large market of goods produced in the various states.
- Promotes trade within the federation by eliminating problems of customs duties and facilitates trade by establishing common currencies.
- It makes it possible for member states to be together without losing their identity.
- Facilitates interaction between people of different states and nationalities.
- It provides "checks and balances" in the systems between the Central Government and the states
- It ensures that the interest of smaller states and groups are protected
- It makes it possible for member states to benefit from the federal pool of resources
- Fosters state loyalties: many Americans feel close ties to their home state, and federalism maintains that connection by giving power to the states

Federalism's Disadvantages

Critics argue that federalism fall short in two ways:

- Prevents the creation of national policy: The United States does not have a single policy, which often leads to confusion
- Leads to lack of accountability: The overlap of the boundaries among national and state governments makes it tricky to assign blame for failed policies
- Most Americans know little about their state and local governments, and turn out in state and local elections is often less than 25 percent.

- Leaders need to be tolerant and flexible in order to accommodate varying states
- Where some states are endowed with more economic resources than others, there is always a temptation to secede.

Congress

The United States Congress is the Legislative branch of Federal Government. It is a bicameral composition of the House of Representatives and the Senate. The constitution grants numerous powers to the Congress. These include the powers to levy and collect taxes; to coin money and regulate its value; provide for punishment for counterfeiting; establish post offices and roads; issue patents; create Federal Courts inferior to the Supreme Court; combat piracies and felonies; declare war; raise and support the armies; provide and maintain the navy; exercise exclusive legislation in the district of Columbia, and make laws necessary to properly execute power since the United States was formed.

The House of Representatives consist of 435 voting members, each of whom represent congressional district. All 435 representatives serve a two-year term. Each state receives a minimum of one representative in the House of Representatives. In order to be elected as a representative, an individual must be at least 25 years of age, must have been a USA citizen for at least seven years, and must live in the state that he/she represents. There is no limit of terms a representative may serve. In addition to 435 voting members, there are six non-voting members, consisting of five delegates and one resident commissioner.

> **Function of Congress in the United States of America**
> - Monitoring the conduct of the President, Vice President and other high ranking government officials
> - Approves taxation measures and ensures that government expenditure is properly used
> - Makes and amends the laws
> - Appoints commissions of inquiry to investigate problems of national importance
> - Confirm Cabinet Secretaries and scrutinizes their appointments
> - The Congress is in charge of foreign relations, for example making treaties with foreign nations
> - Approves the appointment of senior civil servants like ambassadors
> - Reflects the collective aspirations and interests of the American people

In contrast, the Senate is made up of two Senators from each state, regardless of population. There are currently 100 Senators (two from each of the 50 states), who each serve for a six year term. Approximately ⅓ of the Senators stands for elections every two years.

The House of Representatives and Senate each have particular exclusive powers:

- The Senate, for instance, must approve many important presidential appointments, including Cabinet Officers, Federal Judges (including nominees to the Supreme Court), Departmental Secretaries, USA military and naval officers and Ambassadors to foreign countries.
- All legislative bills must originate in the House of Representatives. The approval of both chambers is required to pass any legislation, which then may only become law

by being signed by the President (or, if the President vetoes the bill, both Houses of Congress then re-pass the bill by a ⅔ majority of each chamber, in which case the bill becomes law without the President's signature)

• Congress has power to remove the President, Federal Judges and other Federal Officers from office. The House of Representatives and Senate have separate roles in this process. The House of Representatives must first vote to "impeach" the official then a trail is held in the Senate to decide whether the official should be removed from office or not.

• Congressional oversight is intended to prevent waste and fraud, protect civil liberties and individual rights, ensure executive compliance with the law, gather information for making laws and educating the public, and evaluate executive performance.

Barrack Obama – USA President

President

The executive powers in the Federal Government are vested in the President of the United States of America. The President and Vice President are elected as running mates by the Electoral College, for which each state, as well as the District of Columbia, is allocated a number of seats based on its representation. The President is limited to a maximum of two, four – year term.

Functions of the President of USA

• As the head of state – welcomes foreign dignitaries representing the states abroad and officiate in national ceremonies
• Chief executive – responsible for execution of laws and policies passed by the congress, appoints Cabinet Secretaries, top officials and agency director with the approval of the senate
• Chief legislator – initiates bills by building coalitions and using veto powers
• Chief diplomat – keeps the Congress informed of international developments.
• Commander-in-chief of the armed forces
• Protector of peace – intervenes in natural disasters, race riots and other emergencies
• He/she is the national voice of the people

The President is the head of state and government, as well as the military commander-in-chief and chief diplomat. The President, according to the constitution, must "take care that laws are faithfully executed," and preserved, protected and defend the constitution. The President may sign legislation passed by Congress into law or may veto it, preventing it from becoming law unless ⅔ of both Houses of Congress vote to override it. The President may unilaterally sign treaties with foreign nations. However, ratification of international treaties requires a ⅔ majority vote in the Senate.

The President may not dissolve the Congress or call for special elections, but have the power to pardon or release criminals convicted of offences against the Federal Government. The President enacts executive orders and (with the consent of the Senate) appoints Supreme Court justices and Federal Judges.

Factors limiting Presidential powers in the United States of America include:

- Congress controls the powers of the President, for example the people the President appointments to the executive must be approved by the Senate.
- Congress can refuse to approve funds for foreign policy with which it disagrees, for example war.
- Congress can impeach a President if his conduct while in office is not good.
- The Supreme Court may declare a President to have acted unconstitutionally or negate whatever decision he may have authorized. This can damage his/her image.
- The mass media monitors closely every action or speech by the President.
- The pressure groups also help to check presidential powers: where such groups disapprove something, the President is morally obliged to reconsider his decision.
- Public opinion in the USA reflects the wishes and feeling of the American's people.
- Elections – Since elections for the House of Representatives are held every two year and ⅓ of the Senate are elected every two years, a president's party may lose its majority in the congress.
- The President cannot dissolve congress and call for general elections as they are controlled and fixed for pre-determined periods
- The US President serves for a two, four–year term of office. This avoids absolutism in the presidency

Vice President

He/she is the second highest executive official in rank of the government. As first in the USA presidential line of succession, the Vice President becomes President upon death; resignation, or removal of the President, which has happened nine times in USA history. Under the constitution, the Vice President is the President of the Senate. By virtue of this role, he/she is the head of the Senators. In that capacity, the Vice President is allowed to vote in the Senate, but only when necessary to break a tie vote. The Vice President presides over the joint session of Congress when it convenes to count the votes of the Electoral College.

Cabinet, Executive Departments and Agencies

The day-to-day enforcement and administration of federation laws is in the hands of the various Federal Executive Departments created by the Congress to deal with specific areas of national and international affairs. The heads of the 15 departments, chosen by the President and approved with the "advice and consent" of the USA Senate, form a Council of Advisors generally known as the President's "Cabinet." In addition to departments, a number of staff organizations are grouped into the executive office of the President. These include:

- The White House staff
- The National Security Council
- The Office of Management and Budget
- The Council of Economic Advisors
- The Council on Environment Quality
- The Office of US Trade Representative and
- The Office of Science and technology.

Employees in these United States government agencies are called Federal Civil Servants. There are also independent agencies such as the United States Postal Services, the National Aeronautics and Space Administration (NASA), the Central Intelligence Agency (CIA) and the Environmental Protection Agency. In addition, there are government owned corporations such as the Federal Deposit Insurance Corporation and National Rail Road and Passenger Corporation

Judiciary explains and applies the laws. It does this by hearing and eventually making decisions on various legal cases. The constitution establishes the Supreme Court of the United States and authorizes the United States Congress to establish inferior courts as their need arise. The Federal Judges are appointed by the President and confirmed by the United States Senate. The Nation is subdivided into judicial districts and creates Federal Courts for each district.

The basic structure of the national judiciary is made up of the Supreme Court, 13 Courts of Appeals, 94 District Courts and 2 courts of special jurisdiction. The Congress retains the powers to re-organize or even abolish Federal Courts lower than the Supreme Court.

The Supreme Court adjudicates cases and controversies – matters pertaining to the Federal Government, disputes between states, and interpretation of the United States constitution, and in general, can declare legislation or executive action made at any level of government as unconstitutional, nullifying the law and creating precedent for future law and decisions.

Below the Supreme Court are the United States Courts of Appeals and below them in turn are the United States District Courts, which are the general trial courts for federal law, and for certain controversies between litigants who are not deemed citizens of the same state. There are three levels of federal courts with general jurisdiction meaning that these courts handle criminal cases and civil lawsuits between individuals. Bankruptcy Courts and Tax Courts are specialized courts handling only certain kind of cases. District Courts are trial courts wherein cases that are considered under the judicial code consistent with jurisdictional precepts of federal question jurisdiction and diversity jurisdiction and pendent jurisdiction can be filed and decided.

State Governments in USA

All State Governments are modeled after the Federal Government and consist of three branches: Executive, Legislative and Judiciary. The constitution upholds that all states have a Republican form of government.

Executive Branch

In every state, the executive branch is headed by a Governor who is directly elected by the people. In most states, the other leaders in the executive branch are also directly elected, including the Lieutenant Governor, the Attorney General, the Secretary of State and Auditor and Commissioners

Legislative Branch

All 50 states have legislatures made up of elected representatives, who consider matters brought forth by the Governor or introduced by its members to create legislation that becomes law. The legislature also approves state's budget and initiates tax legislation and articles of impeachment.

Except for one state (Nebraska) all states have a bicameral legislature made up of two chambers: a smaller Upper House and a larger Lower House. The two chambers make state laws and fulfill other governing responsibilities. The smaller chamber is called the Senate and its members generally serve longer terms (4 years). The larger Lower chamber is often called the House of Representatives, but some states call it the Assembly or the House of Delegates. Its members usually serve shorter terms (2 years).

Judicial Branch

State judicial branches are usually led by the state Supreme Court, which hears appeals from lower-level state courts. The court structures and judicial appointments are determined by legislation or the state constitution. The Supreme Court focuses on correcting errors made in lower courts and holds no trials. Rulings made in Supreme Courts are normally binding.

Local governments in USA generally include two tiers: counties and municipalities. They are generally organized around a population centre and in most cases correspond to the geographical destinations used in USA census. They vary in size. Municipalities generally take responsibility for Parks and Recreation Services, Police and Fire Departments, Housing Services, Emergency Medical Services, Municipal Courts, Transport Services and Public Works. In general Mayors, City Councils and other governing bodies are directly elected by the people.

Types of elections
- Presidential elections
- Elections of the senators and members of the House of representatives
- Elections of state governors

Elections in United States of America

The United States is a federation with elected officials at the Federal (national), State and Local Levels. On a national level, the head of state (President) is elected indirectly by the people through the Electoral College. All members of the Federal Legislature (the Congress) are directly elected. There are many elected officials at state level, each state having at least an elective governor and a legislator. There are also elected officials at the local level, in counties and cities.

Elections of the President and Vice President

An indirect vote in which citizens cast ballots for a slate of members of the US Electoral College is done. These electors in turn directly elect the President and Vice President. Each state is allocated a number of Electoral College electors equal to the number of US Congress. Once chosen, the electors can vote for any one. Nomination process includes the primary elections and nomination conventions. This too is also an indirect election process where voters can cast ballots for a state of delegates to a political party's nominating convention who then in turn elect their party's presidential nominee.

Questions on Electoral Processes in USA
(i) Explain the functions of the Congress in the federal system of government of USA
(ii) State five functions of political parties in the USA
(iii) Describe the functions of the federal government of USA
(iv) State advantages of a federal system of government
(v) Give five roles of the president in USA
(vi) Describe the limitations of presidential powers in the United States of America.

Functions of Political Parties in the United States of America (USA)

- Political parties are agencies of political education.
- Parties nominate candidates for elections to various political offices.
- Parties provide accountability: when party policies fail the votes can hold its candidates accountable at election time.
- Parties help to put the desire of the people on the government policy agenda.
- Parties provide outlets for citizens to express their sentiments about nominees.
- Different parties have different policies and principles this helps voters to sort out candidates.
- They make electoral politics coherent by working as agents of each candidate

Examination Techniques

To pass any History and Government examination, a student must have the knowledge of the subject and should also keep in view the following points: -

1. While preparing for examination, it is essential that: -
   (i) Students check through the syllabus to ensure that they have covered the topics laid down by Kenya National Examination Council (KNEC).
   (ii) Having covered the syllabus, they worked through a number of recent papers set by various bodies concerned.

2. When working through past papers, and in the examination itself:
   (i) Read the whole paper, including any special instructions carefully and do not let first impressions of the paper upset you.
   (ii) The questions may be divided as under:
      - The short questions which from your point of view are most easy for you. The first preference must be given to such questions. This is important since one question successfully completed in good time, gives the confidence to tackle the rest of the paper.
      - The questions which appear difficult should be tackled last, starting with the one which was done recently and scored well.
      - The questions which do not have clear answers, even if they appear easy, should be kept away from as much as possible.

3. Avoid spending too much time on one answer, thus leaving others questions incomplete or hurriedly done. Apportion the time allowed uniformly.

4. Before attempting a question, read it carefully, and be confident that you fully understand what is required. Don't display your ignorance on the answer sheet. Try to answer the question systematically and relevantly.

5. Pay attention to the proper presentation of your work. A carefully composed paper, written neatly, immediately creates a favourable impression to the marker.

6. Concentrate simply on maximizing your marks. Leave considerations of passing or failing until after the examination. It will help you avoid panic.

Sample Examination Papers

The sample questions given in this book are possible predictions, but not a perfect replica of the main exams. Learners are expected to use them for self evaluation.

311/1
HISTORY AND GOVERNMENT
PAPER 1
JULY / AUGUST 2015
TIME: 2½ HOURS

HISTORY SAMPLE PAPER 1
Kenya Certificate of Secondary Education

HISTORY AND GOVERNMENT
PAPER 1
TIME: 2½ HOURS

INSTRUCTIONS TO CANDIDATES:

(a) *This paper consists of THREE sections A, B and C.*

(b) *Answer ALL questions in Section A, THREE questions from section B and TWO questions from section C.*

(c) *Answers to all the questions must be written in the answer booklet provided*

SECTION A (25 MARKS)

Answer ALL Questions in this section.

1. Name any two archaeological sites in Kenya. (2mks)
2. Give two economic reasons why the Cushites migrated from their original homeland into Kenya. (2mks)
3. Identify one cultural practice which the highland Bantu acquired from the cushite (1mk)
4. Give one archaeological evidence of the contact between the East African Coast and the outside world. (2mks)
5. State two conditions that one has to meet in order to be naturalized as a Kenyan citizen. (2mks)
6. Name two components of human rights. (2mks)
7. Give two ways in which the Wanga benefited from collaboration with the British. (2mks)
8. State the main reason why Poll tax was introduced in Kenya during the colonial period. (1mk)
9. Give the main problem experienced by the white settlers in Kenya. (1mk)
10. Mention one political reform instituted in 1922 in Kenya. (1mk)
11. What were the features of missionary education in Kenya? (2mks)
12. Identify one demand that Kenyatta presented to the Hilton Young Commission on behalf of the Kikuyu Central Association. (1mk)
13. State one role that civilians played during the state of emergency in Kenya. (1mk)
14. Give two demands of African Elected Members Organization (AEMO) in 1958. (2mks)
15. Identify one specific group of people in Kenya recognized by the new constitution (1mk)
16. Give two examples of recurrent expenditure in Kenya. (2mks)
17. State one function of the senate as listed in the new constitution. (1mk)

SECTION B: (45 MARKS)

Answer any THREE questions in this question

18. (a) Outline the migration and settlements of the Eastern Bantu speaking communities in Kenya upto 1800. (5mks)
(b) Discuss the socio-political organization of the Mijikenda during the pre-colonial Period (10mks)
19. (a) Give five reasons why Imperial British East African Company rule failed in the British Protectorate of Kenya. (5mks)
   (b) Explain the achievements met by Imperial British East African Company during the period between 1888 – 1895. (10mks)
20. (a) Identify five grievances which the Africans in Kenya had against the colonial government between 1920 and 1930. (5mks)
   (b) Explain five external factors that hastened African nationalism in Kenya between 1945 and 1963. (10mks)
21. (a) State five ways through which the colonial government encouraged settler farming in Kenya. (5mks)
   (b) Explain five consequences of colonial land policies. (10mks)

SECTION C: (30 MARKS)

Answer any TWO questions in this question

22. (a) Identify five factors that led to the re-introduction of multi-party democracy in Kenya. (5mks)

(b) Explain five measures that have been taken to improve health care in Kenya since independence. (10mks)

23. (a) Why is national integration encouraged in Kenya? (3mks)

    (b) Explain the methods of conflict resolution applied by the Kenyan society today (12mks)

24. (a) State three principles of devolved government as contained in the new constitution. (3mks)

    (b) Discuss the challenges that may face a county government. (12mks)

311/1
HISTORY AND GOVERNMENT
PAPER 1
JULY / AUGUST 2015
TIME: 2½ HOURS

HISTORY SAMPLE PAPER (2)
Kenya Certificate of Secondary Education

HISTORY AND GOVERNMENT
PAPER 1
TIME: 2½ HOURS

INSTRUCTIONS TO CANDIDATES:

(a) *This paper consists of THREE sections A, B and C.*

(b) *Answer ALL questions in Section A, THREE questions from section B and TWO questions from section C.*

(c) *Answers to all the questions must be written in the answer booklet provided.*

SECTION A (25 MARKS)

Answer ALL Questions in this section

1. Give the main method used by anthropologists to gather their historical data. (1mk)
2. Mention **two** economic practices the Bantu's adopted from the Southern Cushites. (2mks)
3. State any **two** factors that strengthened unity among the Cushites. (2mks)
4. What were the reasons for the conflict between the Busaidi Sultan of Oman and the Mazrui governors of Mombasa? (2mks)
5. List **one** right of a person under arrest according to the Bill of Rights. (2mks)
6. Mention **one** way in which Disaster Management promotes National Unity. (2mks)
7. Identify any **two** roles of the Commissioner according to the East Africa order in Council of 1897. (2mks)
8. Give the main reason why the British were unable to completely crush the Nandi during their 1897 expedition. (1mk)
9. State **two** reasons why the Bukusu resisted colonial rule. (2mks)
10. Apart from the legislative council, mention **two** other bodies that assisted the central government in administering the protectorate during the colonial period. (2mks)
11. Name **one** commission that was established to look into African Education in colonial Kenya. (1mk)
12. State the political paper that was published by the Kenya African Union (KAU) periodically. (1mk)
13. Mention **two** principles of the concept of natural justice. (2mks)
14. State **two** major challenges facing the health sector in Kenya. (2mks)
15. Give **two** values and principles of the public service according to the new constitution. (2mks)
16. Name the head of the county government in the new constitution. (1mk)

SECTION B: (45 MARKS)

Answer any THREE questions in this question

17. (a) State **five** factors that contributed to the growth and development of towns along the Kenyan coast by 1500AD. (5mks)

(b) Explain **five** effects of Seyyid Said's transfer of his capital from Muscat to Zanzibar on the Kenyan Coast. (10mks)

18. (a) Identify **three** challenges encountered by Trade Unions in Kenya during the colonial period (3mks)

(b) Explain **six** effects of the development of urban centres during the colonial rule. (12mks)

19. (a) State **three** contributions of African women towards the development of political parties in Kenya before 1939. (3mks)

(b) Explain **six** effects of colonial rule on Africans in Kenya. (12mks)

20. (a) Identify the role of national philosophies in Kenya's development. (5mks)

(b) Explain the problems that have undermined the performance of national philosophies in Kenya. (10mks)

SECTION C: (30 MARKS)

Answer any TWO questions in this question

21. (a) State **three** principles of Devolved government according to the constitution of Kenya. (3mks)

    (b) Discuss **six** functions and powers of the county government. (12mks)

22. (a) Give **five** sources of the Kenyan law. (3mks)

    (b) Describe the structure of the judicial system in Kenya. (12mks)

23. (a) State the composition of the defense council in Kenya. (3mks)

    (b) Describe the challenges facing the Kenya Defense Force. (12mks)

311/2
HISTORY AND GOVERNMENT
PAPER 2
JULY / AUGUST 2015
TIME: 2 ½ HOURS

HISTORY SAMPLE PAPER 2 (1)
(Kenya Certificate of Secondary Education)

311/2
HISTORY AND GOVERNMENT
PAPER 2
TIME: 2½ HOURS

INSTRUCTIONS TO CANDIDATES:

(a) *This paper consists of THREE sections A, B and C.*

(b) *Answer ALL questions in Section A, THREE questions from section B and TWO questions from section C.*

(c) *Answers to all the questions must be written in the answer booklet provided.*

SECTION A (25 MARKS)
Answer ALL Questions in this section

1. Give **one** aspect of human activities studied in economic history. (1mk)
2. Give **two** shortcomings of oral tradition as a source of History. (2mks)
3. Name **two** species belonging to the Australopithecus. (2mks)
4. State **two** reasons why the camel replaced the horse as the beast of burden in the trade across the Sahara desert. (2mks)
5. State **one** result of the invention of the wheel in Mesopotamia. (1mk)
6. In what ways has brain drain undermined scientific revolution in Africa? (1mk)
7. State **two** factors that facilitated the growth of Asante Kingdom. (2mks)
8. State the main contribution of the discovery of chloroform in the field of medicine. (1mk)
9. Name **two** materials where messages were written before invention of papers. (2mks)
10. Mention **two** ways in which the railway facilitated industrial development in Europe. (2mks)
11. State **one** way in which European nationality contributed to the colonization of Africa (1mk)
12. Name **two** leaders of West Africa who collaborated with the French against Samori Toure in 1896. (2mks)
13. State **one** method used in the direct rule in Zimbabwe to maintain law and order. (1mk)
14. State **one** problem faced by African nationalists in Ghana. (1mk)
15. Why was the Economic Community of West African States (ECOWAS) formed? (1mk)
16. Identify **one** main political challenge which Zaire has faced since independence. (1mk)
17. State the Composition of the Congress in the United States of America (USA) (2mks)

SECTION B: (45 MARKS)
Answer any THREE questions in this question

18. (a) Identify the culture of man during the Old Stone Age period (5 mks)

    (b) Explain **five** ways through which early man adapted to the environment during Old Stone Age. (10mks)
19. (a) Give **three** limitations of using fire and smoke to convey messages during pre-colonial period. (3mks)

    (b) Explain **six** negative effects of modern telecommunication in the society today. (12mks)
20. (a) Give **three** pull factors for the scramble for Africa. (3mks)

    (b) Explain **six** results of the Chimurenga War of 1896 – 1897. (12mks)
21. (a) State **five** methods used by nationalists in Mozambique to struggle for independence. (5mks)

    (b) What were the differences between the British policy of indirect rule and French policy of Assimilation? (10mks)

SECTION C: (30 MARKS)
Answer any TWO questions from this question

22. (a) Give the names of **three** founders of Pan-Africanism. (3mks)

    (b) Explain why Pan-Africanism Movement was not active in Africa before 1945. (12mks)
23. (a) State **five** causes of the Cold War. (5mks)

    (b) Describe **five** political results of the Second World War. (10mks)
24. (a) Give **five** sources of the British Constitution. (5mks)

(b) Explain the importance of the monarchy to the British people. (10mks)

311/2
HISTORY AND GOVERNMENT
PAPER 2
JULY / AUGUST 2015
TIME: 2 ½ HOURS

HISTORY SAMPLE PAPER 2 (2)
(Kenya Certificate of Secondary Education)

311/2
HISTORY AND GOVERNMENT
PAPER 2
TIME: 2½ HOURS

INSTRUCTIONS TO CANDIDATES:

(a) *This paper consists of THREE sections A, B and C.*

(b) *Answer ALL questions in Section A, THREE questions from section B and TWO questions from section C.*

(c) *Answers to all the questions must be written in the answer booklet provided.*

SECTION A (25 MARKS)
Answer ALL Questions in this section

1. Give **two** types of sources of information on History and Government. (2mks)
2. State **two** characteristics of Kenyapithecus. (2mks)
3. State **two** contributions of William Harvey to the scientific revolution. (2mks)
4. Mention the main policy making body of the organization of the common wealth. (1mk)
5. Mention **one** social condition put forward as a criteria for membership into the non-aligned movement in the 1950s. (1mk)
6. State the main reason why nationalism developed in Ghana during the colonial period. (1mk)
7. Mention **two** places in Africa where the Cold War was witnessed. (2mks)
8. Name the first president of FRELIMO Movement in Mozambique. (1mk)
9. Which are the **two** major events which made 1917 the decisive year for the end of the First World War.? (2mks)
10. Identify **two** social classes that made up the Buganda society in Pre-colonial period. (2mks)
11. State the main role of ECOMOG in West Africa. (1mk)
12. Mention any **two** political parties in India. (2mks)
13. Mention **two** regions that were declared as mandated territories after the Versailles treaty of 1919. (2mks)
14. Mention **two** ways in which Mobutu Sese Seko displayed dictatorship in Zaire. (2mks)
15. State how Bismarck and the rise of Germany led to the scramble for colonies in Africa. (1mk)
16. State the reason why the Soviet Union Russian rejected the Marshall plan. (1mk)

SECTION B: (45 MARKS)
Answer any THREE questions in this question

17. (a) Mention **three** factors which influenced the evolution of man. (3mks)

    (b) Explain **six** reasons why studying History and Government is important for students in school. (12mks)

18. (a) Mention **five** traditional forms of water transport. (5mks)

    (b) Describe **five** contributions of television on economic development. (10mks)

19. (a) Give **five** reasons why Samori Toure resisted the French for a long time. (5mks)

    (b) Explain **five** results of Samori Toure's resistance against the French. (10mks)

20. (a) Why did the British use direct rule in Zimbabwe? (3mks)

    (b) Explain **six** effects of the British rule in Zimbabwe (12mks)

SECTION C: (30 MARKS)
Answer any TWO questions from this question

21. (a) State any **three** provisions of the Arusha declaration of 1967 in Tanzania. (3mks)

    (b) Describe **six** economic reforms introduced in Tanzania since 1985. (12mks)

22. (a) State **five** aims of the Pan-African movements. (5mks)

    (b) Explain **five** achievements of the Pan-African movement by 1960's. (10mks)

23. (a) State **five** objectives of the League of Nations. (5mks)

    (b) Explain the failures of the League of Nations. (10mks)

Sample Marking Scheme

The questions set in sample papers, both for paper 1 & 2 are standard KCSE examinations questions. The answers contained herein are also standard expected responses from the learners. In actual situation, the learner is expected to read the questions carefully and do a wise selection before making any attempt at answering any questions. The learner is also expected to follow instructions strictly and give only the required response. There are open and close ended questions. In close ended questions only the first responses are marked. Giving more than the required response does not therefore add any value to the student. Learners normally make assumption that in open ended questions, their answers are multiplied by two. They should be guided by the allotted marks because some of the questions are simple and have many responses.

Sample Marking Scheme for Paper 1(1)

311/1 – HISTORY PAPER 1 (1)

1. Name any **two** archaeological sites in Kenya. (2mks)
   - Rusinga Island
   - Fort Ternan
   - Kariandusi
   - Koobi Fora
   - Njoro River Cave
   - Gamble Cave
   - - Gedi (any 2x1 = 1mk)

2. Give **two** economic reasons why the Cushites migrated from their original homeland into Kenya. (2mks)
   - Search for water and pasture. (2x 1 = 2mks)
   - Search for land for Agriculture.

3. Identify **one** cultural practice which the highland Bantu acquired from the cushites. (1mk)
   - The age-set system.
   - Circumcision of males and female (2x1 = 2mk)

4. Give **one** archaeological evidence of the contact between the East African Coast and the outside world. (2mks)
   - Remnants of Chinese coins.
   - Remnants of Pottery. (any 1x1 = 1mk)

5. State **two** conditions that one has to meet in order to be naturalized as a Kenyan citizen. (2mks)
   - One must be over 21 years and above.
   - Must have lived in Kenya for at least seven years.
   - Must prove that he will continue living in Kenya after naturalization.
   - Must satisfy the minister in charge of Good Conduct.
   - Must satisfy the minister in charge that he/she has a green knowledge of Kiswahili language.
   (any 2 x 1 = 2mks)

6. Name **two** components of human rights.   (2mks)
    -   Condition of life.
    -   Social character / existence of the member.
    -   Must be enjoyed equally.   (any 2x1 = 2mks)

7. Give **two** ways in which the Wanga benefited from collaboration with the British.   (2mks)
    -   Mumias was made paramount Chief.
    -   Mumias warriors became agents of British colonialism.
    -   Mumias served as a terminus for trade caravans to Uganda.
    -   Mumia and his people acquired some material benefits through trade, western education and
        religion.   (any 2x1 = 2mks)

8. State the main reason why Poll tax was introduced in Kenya during the colonial period.   (1mk)
    -   To force the Africans to act on European settler farms / forced labour.   (1 x 1 = 1mk)

9. Name the main problem experienced by the white settlers in Kenya.   (1mk)
    -   Constant raids.   (1 x 1 = 1mk)

10. Name **one** political reform instituted in 1922 in Kenya.   (1mk)
    -   Removal of Governor Mortley and replaced by Sir Robert Coryndon.
    -   Abandonment of racial segregation.
    -   Allowing Asians to elect four members to the Legco   (1x1 = 1mk)

11. What were the features of missionary education in Kenya?   (2mks)
    -   It was elementary
    -   It was industrial and technical in approach.
    -   It was denominational aimed at inculcating doctrines.   (any 2x1 = 2mks)

12. Identify **one** demand that Kenyatta presented to the Hilton Young Commission on behalf of the
    Kikuyu Central Association.   (1mk)
    -   Introduction of free primary education.
    -   Provision of secondary and higher education.
    -   Abolition of Kipande system.
    -   Appointment of Africans to the Legco.
    -   Release of Harry Thuku.
    -   Giving of title deeds to Africans.
    -   Rejection of the proposed African federation.   (1 x 1 = 1mk)

13. State **one** role that civilians played during the state of emergency in Kenya.   (1mk)
    -   Supplying the freedom fighters with intelligence information.
    -   To supply food to the freedom fighters.
    -   To mobilize material of financial resources for the nationalities.   (any 1x1 = 1mk)

14. Give **two** demands of African Elected Members Organization (AEMO) in 1958. (2mks)
   - Increase of African representation in the Legco.
   - They demanded that every African of 21 years to be allowed to vote.
   - Registration of voters to be done on a common roll.
   - An end to the state of emergency. (2 x 1 = 2mk)

15. Identify **one** specific group of people in Kenya recognized by the new constitution (1mk)
   - The old
   - The youth.
   - Children
   - Persons with disabilities.
   - Minorities and marginalized groups. (1 x 1 = 1mk)

16. Give **two** examples of recurrent expenditure in Kenya. (2mks)
   - Provision of medical supplies for government hospitals.
   - Payment of salaries.
   - Maintenance of government infrastructures like buildings and equipment (1 x 1 = 1mk)

17. State **one** function of the senate as listed in the new constitution. (1mk)
It represents the countries and serves to protect the interests of the countries and their governments.
   - To participate in the law making function of parliaments by considering debating and approving bills concerning countries.
   - To determine the allocation of national revenue among countries and exercise oversight over national revenue allocated to the county government.,
   - To participate in the oversight of state officers by considering and determining any resolution to remove the president or deputy president from office in accordance with the law.
(any 1x1 = 1mk)

SECTION B

18. (a) Outline the migration and settlements of the Eastern Bantu speaking communities in Kenya upto 1800. (5mks)
   - They migrated from their Original homeland in the Congo Basin and settled in the Taita Hills area around Mt. Kilimanjaro by 2nd century AD.
   - Some of them later migrated northwards along the coast to Shungwaya. These were the ancestors of the Mijikenda, Pokomo and Taita.
   - The ancestors of the Mount Kenya group moved into the interior along the river Tana.
   - From about 1459, the communities which settled in Shungwaya were forced to disperse from the area due to external pressure from the Cushite.
   - The ancestors of the Mijikenda and Taita moved south and established their settlement along the coast while those of the Pokomo migrated into the interior and settled along River Tana while the Ameru migrated to the slopes of Mt. Kenya. (1 x 5 = 5 mks)

(b) Discuss the socio-political organization of the Mijikenda during the pre-colonial Period   (10mks)
- The Mijikenda were organized into between 4-6 clans with many sub-clans.
- Each village lived in protected villages known as Kaya.
- Young men became members of age-sets after going through circumcision.
- Senior age-set members made up the governing council Kambi (council of elders) who maintained law and order.
- The council was responsible for the administration of the clan.
- Council meetings were shared by headmen.
- The junior age-set members made up the warrior group which was charged with defending the community.
- The Mijikenda believed in the existence of one supreme God called Mulungu.
- Prayers were made directly to Mulungu.
- Sacrifices were offered to appease Mulungu.
- Priests presided over religious ceremonies and rituals.
- Other people like medicine-men and diviners played an important role.
- They believed in the ancestral spirits who gave guidance to families and also mediated between them and God.
- The elderly members of the society imparted societal values and norms to the youth.

(any 5x2 = 10mks)

19. (a) Give **five** reasons why Imperial British East African Company rule failed in the British Protectorate of Kenya.   (5mks)
- The region was vast and lacked natural resources for export.
- Inadequate capital to penetrate the interior.
- Competition from other companies e.g. GEAC.
- The region had no navigable rivers.
- Poor co-ordination.
- Fraudulent company officials.
- Hostility from African communities.
- Inexperienced company personnel.
- Attack by tropical diseases.
- Company directors lacked the drive and initiative   (any 5x1 = 5mks)

(b) Explain the achievements met by Imperial British East African Company during the period from 1888 – 1895.   (10mks)
- It managed to quell local aggression from Nandi, Maasai and Akamba.
- It laid the basis for colonial administration by establishing ports.
- It developed a rubber industry along the coast and the interior.
- It secured freedom of several slaves.
- It pioneered the building of roads e.g. escalators road between Kibwezi and Busia.

(any 5x2 = 10mks)

20. (a) Identify **five** grievances which the Africans in Kenya had against the colonial government between 1920 and 1930.   (5mks)

-   They demanded for land title deeds for the Africans.
-   African wages to be increased.
-   They demanded for equal pay for equal work done.
-   They hated the Kipande system.
-   Heavy taxation imposed on the Africans was opposed.
-   They resented forced labour.
-   Demand for better education for the Africans.
-   They called for the revocation of crown colony status.
-   African detainees like Harry Thuku to be released.
-   The Africans to be allowed to grow cash crops.
-   Some like the Akamba opposed destocking policy.
-   They opposed racial discrimination.
-   Demanded for the establishment of African co-operatives.
-   Demand for equal employment opportunities.   (any 5x1 = 5mks)

(b) Explain **five** external factors that hastened African nationalism in Kenya between 1945 and 1963.   (10mks)

-   The experience of the World War II ex-soldiers where they gained experience and the Whiteman's superiority was broken.
-   Granting of independence to India and Pakistan in 1947 motivated the Kenyan fighters.
-   The Atlantic charter signed by prime minister of Britain Churchill and Roosevelt of USA – declared their all subject people should enjoy right to self determination.
-   Pan Africanism insisted that Africans should enjoy political freedom in their continent.
-   The labour party in Britain which came into power after World War II favoured decolonization.   (any 5x2 = 10mks)

21. (a) State **five** ways through which the colonial government encouraged settler farming in Kenya.   (5mks)

-   They were given land – African land was alienated.
-   Provision of labour where Africans were forced to provide cheap labour.
-   Africans were denied to grow cash crops to avoid competition.
-   The colonial government provided them with loans.
-   The colonial government built roads, railways.
-   The colonial government encouraged the formation of co-operatives to help in processing and marketing of goods.
-   The colonial government provided extension services for crops and animal farming.

(any 5x1 = 5mks)

(b) Explain **five** consequences of colonial hard policies.   (10mks)

-   African land was alienated.

- Africans were pushed to reserves.
- Led to emergence of squatters.
- Disruption of traditional structures like migration and women became head of families.
- Indians were denied access to agricultural land compelling them to establish residences and businesses in urban centres.
- Africans were forced to look for wage employment in order to pay for taxes – it saw the seeds for African nationalist activities e.g. Mau Mau
- Land was curved for construction of railway.   (any 5x2 = 10mks)
-

Section C

22. (a) Identify **five** factors that led to the re-introduction of multi-party democracy in Kenya.   (5mks)
   - Western aid conditions: Donor countries refused to give aid to Kenya unless she embraced democratic and pluralistic policies.
   - Multi-party success in other countries like Zambia.
   - Pressure from the church e.g. Rev. Njoya, Bishop Muge and Bishop Henry Okul.
   - Massive rigging of 1988 general elections.
   - KANU's response to criticism: Those who criticized the government were expelled from the party or arrested.
   - Pressure from lawyers and journalists.
   - Murder of Robert Ouko in 1990 caused bitterness and anger because people believed the government was involved.
   - Saitoti review committee of 1990 where Kenyans were positive about many parties.
   - Repeal of Section 2A of the constitution in December 1991.
   - Unification of Germany led to collapse of communism and spread of democracy and liberty.
   - Political changes in U.S.S.R.   (any 5x1 = 5mks)

(b) Explain **five** measures that have been taken to improve health care in Kenya since independence.

(10mks)

   - Establishment of the Ministry of Health which is responsible for the National Policy and training of health personnel.
   - Establishment of National Hospital Insurance Fund.
   - Establishment of research institutions such as KEMRI.
   - Establishment of private hospitals like Nairobi and Aga Khan.
   - Provision of health education to masses.
   - Expansion of some hospital facilities e.g. Nyayo wards.
   - Conducting immunization programmes all over the country.
   - Training Medical Personnel.
   - Cost sharing policy in hospitals.   (any 5x2 = 10mks)

23 (a) Why is national integration encouraged in Kenya?   (3mks)
   - For promotion of peaceful co-existences.
   - It enhances the achievement of national goals.
   - It reduces ethnic tension and suspicion.

- To facilitate national development socially and economically.
- It enhances easier and efficient communication in the country.
- It facilitates equitable distribution of resources in the country.
- It enhances nationalism and patriotism.
- To create favourable investment conditions that attracts foreign investment.   (5 x 1 = 5mks)

(b) Explain the methods of conflict resolution applied by the Kenyan society today   (12mks)
- Arbitration: A neutral person is chosen to solve the conflict. It helps reach an acceptable decision.
- Diplomacy: It is the art of negotiation between individuals of countries to resolve conflicts and may involve creating understanding and room for reconciliation e.g. use of the UN.
- Legislation: This is legislation by Parliament. It involves passing of legislation that controls conflicts. It can be used to criminalize activities that lead to conflicts.
- Use of elders: Usually used to solve conflict between communities, parties in conflict appear before the elders who listen to them and come up with a solution.
- Religious action: It can be used among parties themselves and their followers involved in conflicts. Religious leaders are used to solve the conflict.
- Court action: It is where parties take other parties to court for arbitration.
- Policing: It is an act of conflict resolution used to maintain law and order or in situations of serious conflicts such as land and ethnic related clashes. The presence of police helps to control crime that brings about conflicts.
- Policing may also be done by local communities and peace keeping forces.
- International: Often used on border security and utilization of national
- Agreement: resources between countries.   (any 5x2 = 10mks)

24. (a) State **three** principles of devolved government as contained in the new constitution.   (3mks)
- They are to be based on democratic principles and the separation of powers.
- They are to have reliable sources of revenue to enable them to govern and deliver services effectively.
- No more than two thirds of the members of representative bodies in each county government shall be of the same gender.   (any 3x1 = 3mks)

(b) Discuss the challenges that may face a county government.   (12mks)
- High population.
- Inadequate financial base or inefficient revenue collection system.
- Tax evasion by individuals and organizations.
- Corruption and misappropriation of funds.
- Political interference on county affairs.
- Control by the national government may interfere with free decision making.
- Lack of qualified personnel.
- Elections of illiterate county representatives.
- Poor transport and communications.   (any 5x2 = 10mks)

Sample Marking Scheme for Paper 1(2)

311/1 – HISTORY PAPER 1 (2)

1. The main method used by anthropologists to gather information.
   - Observation.   (1 x 1 = 1mk)

2. Two economic practices adopted by the Bantu from Southern Cushites.
   - Cattle breeding
   - Iron-arrow head making.   (2x 1 = 2mks)

3. Two factors that strengthened unity among the Cushites.
   - The social celebrations.
   - The strong belief in a common ancestor.   (2x1 = 2mks)

4. Reasons for the conflict between the Busaidi and Mazrui governors of Mombasa.
   - Wish to increase there control over coastal towns including Mombasa to control trade.
   - Mazrui governors craved to be independent.
   - Mombasa rebels were encouraged by the fact that the Sultan of Oman was dealing with enemies at home.
   - Mombasa had fought hard against the Portuguese and didn't wish to be controlled by another foreigner.
   - In the course of the 18th century, trade prospered again between Kilwa and the French islands of re-union hence the Sultan was more determined than ever to maintain close control over the trade at the coast.
   - Open conflict began when Mohammed Ibn Uthman al Mazrui refused allegiance to the new Sultan in 1741.   (any 2x1 = 2mks)

5. One right for an arrested person according to the Bill of Rights.
   - The right to be informed immediately of the reason for the arrest.
   - The right to communicate with an advocate.
   - The right to be held separately from convicted persons since he / she is presumed innocent until proven guilty.
   - They should be taken to court as soon as possible or be informed for the reason of extended detention or released on bond or bail on reasonable conditions pending change or trial.
         (1 x 1 = 1mk)

6. One way in which disaster management promotes national unity.
   - People have used their personal wealth to assist fellow Kenyans who has been a victim of bomb-blast, drought, disease etc irrespective of their race.   (1 x 1 = 1mk)

7. Two roles of the commissioner according to the East Africa Order in Council of 1897.
   - The authority to set up the necessary administration bodies in the protectorate.
   - Had the authority to make laws.
   - Had the authority to establish courts of law.

- He was directly answerable to the secretary of states in London but nobody else.
- Powers to appoint headmen.
- Sent expeditions against resisting African communities. (any 2x1 = 2mks)

8. The main reason why the British were unable to crush the Nandi during the 1897 expedition.
   - British troops were recalled to deal with Mwanga's rebellion. (1 x 1 = 1mk)

9. Two reasons why the Bukusu resisted the British independence.
   - Their pride made them determined to preserve their community.
   - The British wanted to force them to recognize the Nabongo Mumia of the Wanga are the overall leader of the Abaluyia.
   - They hated the idea of strangers passing through their land as their land lay on the major route to Uganda.
   - The British demand that the warriors surrender all the guns they possessed.
   - The Bukusu hated the Waswahili whom the British had employed in their forces.
   - They resented the hut tax.
   - Had strong military organization and army which made them succeed in keeping Abawanga from their land. (any 2x1 = 2mks)

10. Apart from the legislative council, the other two bodies that assisted the central government in administration during the colonial period included?
    - The Advisory Council.
    - The Executive Council. (any 2x1 = 2mks)

11. One commission appointed to look into African education in colonial Kenya.
    - Phelps Stoke commission.
    - The Beecher Committee report. (1 x 1 = 1mk)

12. The political paper published by KANU periodically.
    - Sauti ya Mwafrika. (1 x 1 = 1mk)

13. Two principles of the concept of National Justice.
    - The law applies equally to all Kenyans
    - One is innocent until proven guilty by a reasonable court of law. (2 x 1 = 2mks)

14. Two major challenges facing the Health centre in Kenya.
    - Inadequate personnel.
    - Inadequate funds.
    - Increase of population. (2 x 1 = 2mk)

15. Two values and principles of Public service according to the new constitution.
    - Efficient, effective and economic use of resources.

- Involvement of the people in the process of policy making.
- Accountability for administrative works.
- Transparency and provision to the public of timely accurate information.   (1 x 1 = 1mk)

16. The head of the county government.
    - The Governor.   (1 x 1 = 1mk)

SECTION B

17. (a) Five factors that contributed to the growth and development of towns along the Kenyan Coast by 1500.
    - Development of the Indian Ocean trade.
    - Islamic religion enhanced unity.
    - Fertile soils that encouraged Agriculture.
    - Security as most towns were islands.
    - Settlement of Arabs and Persians at the Coast.
    - Deep natural harbours that allowed anchoring of ships.   (any 5x1 = 5mks)

(b) Effects of Seyyid Said's transfer of his capital from Muscat to Zanzibar.
    - Expansion of Coastal towns.
    - Development of clove plantations.
    - Expansion of slave trade – Zanzibar became a leading town in slave trade.
    - Exposed the interior of East Africa to the outside world.
    - Expanded the spread of Islam to the interior.
    - Led to more Arab settlement at the Kenya Coast / Coast was effectively controlled by Arabs.
    - He encouraged Indian merchants (Banyans to Zanzibar)   (any 5x2 = 10mks)

18. (a) Three challenges faced by Trade Unions.
    - Wrangles among leaders of Trade Unions.
    - Shortage or inadequate funds.
    - Ignorance of people on the role of Trade Unions.
    - Fear of victimization of the unionists.
    - Migration nature of the African workforce.
    - Poor leadership due to lack of trained personnel.
    - Leadership was ethnically based which undermine the unions.   (any 3x1=3mks)

(c) Six effects of the development of urban centres during colonial period.
    - There was influx of migrant African workers.
    - There was overcrowding in towns which led to development of slums.
    - Overcrowding led to pollution and epidemics.
    - It brought together different communities. This formed the basis of national unity.
    - Africans who failed to get jobs in towns resorted to crime.
    - It led to racial discrimination.
    - It led to development of welfare organization which catered for ethnic interests.

- The Kipande system was introduced to restrict movement of Africans into towns.
- It led to rural-urban migration. (any 6x2 = 12mks)

19. (a) The contributions of women towards the development of political parties in Kenya before 1939.
   - Women raised money for political parties.
   - They participated in public rallies.
   - They composed songs in praise of political parties or leaders.
   - They pressurized their husbands and other relatives to support the national cause.
   - Muthoni Nyanjiru lost her life demanding for the release of Harry Thuku. (any 3x1 = 3mks)

(b) Six effects of colonial rule on Africans in Kenya.
   - The colonial government introduced western education which undermined indigenous form of education.
   - Hospitals were built and modern medicine introduced which undermined traditional medical practices.
   - The introduction of western health care improved health standards of Africans in Kenya.
   - The introduction of Christianity created new alliance and divisions among Africans.
   - Colonial rule influenced Africans to adopt western values and practices e.g. new ways of dressing.
   - Colonial rule encouraged buildings of permanent and improved buildings.
   - Colonial rule led to the expansion and improvement of transport and communication systems which encouraged interaction between different African communities.
   - Africans suffered as their economies were upset by the Europeans by acquiring labour, raw materials etc.
   - Colonial boundaries were drawn placing some ethnic groups in two or more countries which led to border disputes.
   - It led to introduction of European administrative system of indirect rule in Kenya.
   - It led to fall of some Kingdoms e.g. the Wanga.
   - The Europeans introduced the monetary economy as they developed agriculture, transport, trade, industry.
   - Because of colonization Kenya continues to maintain closer ties with her former colonial master-neocolonialism. (any 6x2 = 12mks)

20. (a) The role of National philosophies.
   - Promotion of education through building of schools, labs and libraries.
   - Enhancing unity and understanding among people.
   - Improvement of medical services as hospitals and dispensaries are built.
   - Promotion of the welfare of people with special needs.
   - Improving the living standards of people as services and other social needs are catered for.
   - Encouraging nationalism and patriotism. (any 5x1 = 5mks)

(b) The problems that have undermined the performance of the National philosophies in Kenya.

- Corruption.
- Negative attitude from people.
- Misappropriation and embezzlement of public funds.
- Poverty.
- Tribal clashes and conflicts.
- Unemployment.
- Lack of commitment by political parties.
- Wrangles among leaders.   (any 5x2 = 10mks)

SECTION C

21. (a) Three principles of devolved government according to the 2010 Constitution.
    - County governments are based on democratic principles and separation of powers.
    - County governments shall have reliable sources of revenue to enable them govern and deliver services effectively.
    - Not more than two thirds of the members of a representative body in each county government shall be of the same gender.   (any 3x1 = 3mks)

(b) Six functions and powers of the county government.
    - Promotion of Agriculture – This is through promoting crop and animal husbandry, providing livestock selling yards and development of fisheries.
    - Provision and supervision of county health services. This is through licensing and control of undertakings that sell food to the public, veterinary services, cemeteries and refuse removal.
    - Putting in place legislation to regulate and control air pollution, noise pollution and other public nuisance and outdoor advertising.
    - Putting structures in place to facilitate cultural activities, public entertainment and public amenities like libraries, museums, sporting facilities.
    - Ensuring county transport such as roads, street lighting, public road transport, ferries and harbours is efficient and well maintained.
    - Ensuring animal control and welfare. This is through licensing of dogs and provision facilities for the accommodation, care and burial of animals.
    - Regulating county planning through land survey, mapping, housing, electricity, gas and energy regulation.
    - Having in place legislation to promote and regulate education at the primary, polytechnic, craft and child care levels.
    - Implementing specific national government policies on natural resources and environmental conservation including soil and water conservation and forestry.
    - Ensuring that the fire fighting services and disaster management centres are available and working in the county and having legislation to regulate their services.
    - Put in places measures to control drug abuse and access to pornography in the county.
                                                              (any 6x2 = 12mks)

22. (a) Five sources of the Kenyan law.
    - African customary laws.
    - Sharia Islamic laws.

- Acts of Parliament.
- Constitution of Kenya.
- By laws of county governments.   (any 5x1 = 5mks)

(b) The structure of the judicial system in Kenya.
   - The highest court in Kenya is the Supreme Court.
   - Below is the high court presided over by judges appointed by the president
   - Next is the chief magistrate court headed by chief magistrate court based in counties?
   - District magistrates / Kadhis court are under the resident magistrates courts and are the lowest courts.
   - Specialized courts deal with special court cases e.g. martial, industrial, commercial courts; rent tribunals, professional tribunals etc.   (5x2 = 10mks)

23. (a) The composition of the Defense Council in Kenya.
   - The Cabinet Secretary for defense as Chairperson.
   - Chief of the Defense forces.
   - The three commanders of the defense forces.
   - Principal Secretary in the ministry responsible for defense.   (3x1 = 3mks)

(b) Challenges facing the Kenya Defense Forces.
   - Fraudulent practices e.g. in recruitments.
   - Tribalism and nepotism which demoralize hardworking officers.
   - Inadequate funds for equipping of the forces.
   - Officers are not provided with opportunities to acquire further education.
   - Use of conservative regulations e.g. gender based discrimination.
   - Piracy and militia attacks Kenyan borders.
   - Invasion of Kenya's territorial waters.
   - Human encroachment on areas of KDF e.g. the Eastleigh Moi Air Base.
   - The challenges of allegation on violation of human rights as they maintain law and order.
                                                                          (any 6x2 = 12mks)

History Sample Paper 2 (1)

311/2 -MARKING SCHEME

1. Give **one** aspect of human activities studied in economic history.   (1mk)
    -   Hunting and gathering
    -   Fishing
    -   Agriculture / farming / keeping of animals and crops cultivation.
    -   Trade
    -   Transport
    -   Metal working
    -   Pottery working
    -   Metal working / blacksmithing
    -   Mining
    -   Cloth making
    -   Boat / canoe making
    -   Beekeeping   (1 x 1 = 1mk)

2. Give **two** shortcomings of oral tradition as a source of History.   (2mks)
    -   May contain exaggerations.
    -   Omissions of facts due to failure in memory.
    -   It may be inconsistent and inaccurate due to handling from generation to generation.
    -   It does not give correct dates.
    -   It is expensive and time consuming method.
    -   Some information is based on dominant groups such as believers and may be biased.

                                                                          (any 2x1 = 2mks)

3. Name **two** species belonging to the Australopithecus.   (2mks)
    -   Boisei
    -   Africanus / Gracilis
    -   Anamensis
    -   Afarensis
    -   Robustus   (any 2x1 = 2mks)

4. State **two** reasons why the camel replaced the horse as the beast of burden in the trade across the Sahara desert.   (2mks)
    -   It can travel for several days without water / food.
    -   Its hooves are adapted to the desert allowing it to move fast without sinking in the sand.
    -   Its nostrils have flaps which keep out sand even in a sand storm.
    -   Has thick fur that protects it from sweltering desert by the day and keeps it warm during cold nights.   (any 2x1 = 2mks)

5. State **one** result of the invention of the wheel in Mesopotamia.   (1mk)
    -   It was used to move war chariots.
    -   Let to development of roads.

- Led to making of high quality pots.
- Used to carry agricultural produce.   (any 1x1 = 1mk)

6. In what ways has brain drain undermined scientific revolution in Africa?
   - It has deprived African countries of trained personnel.   (1 x 1 = 1mk)

7. State **two** factors that facilitated the growth of Asante Kingdom   (2mks)
   - Able leaders like Osei Tutu.
   - United by the Golden Stool.
   - Had a large army.
   - Strong agricultural base.
   - Wealth from the Trans-Saharan trade.   (any 2x1 = 2mks)

8. State the main contribution of the discovery of chloroform in the field of medicine   (1mk)
   - It reduced pain during operation.   (1 x 1 = 1mk)

9. Name **two** materials where messages were written before invention of papers.   (2mks)
   - Clay tablets
   - Dried skin
   - Barks of trees
   - Scrolls
   - Parchments   (any 2x1 = 2mks)

10. Mention **two** ways in which the railway facilitated industrial development in Europe.   (2mks)
    - Industrial products were transported to markets.
    - Industrial workers reached the work place easily.
    - Raw materials could easily be transported to industries.   (any 2x1 = 2mks)

11. State **one** way in which European nationality contributed to the colonization of Africa   (1mk)
    - Countries competed for colonies to prove that they were powerful.
    - France wanted to restore her past glory after her defeat in the France-Prussian war of 1870 – 71.   (1 x 1 = 1mk)

12. Name **two** leaders of West Africa who collaborated with the French against Samori Toure in 1896.   (2mks)
    - King Tieba of Sikasso.
    - Seko Ahmadi of the Tokolor Empire.   (any 2x1 = 2mks)

13. State **one** method used in the direct rule in Zimbabwe to maintain law and order.   (1mk)
    - Use of company military force.
    - Use of African chiefs to administer justice in local areas.
    - Use of repressive laws.   (any 1x1 = 1mk)

14. State **one** problem faced by African nationalists in Ghana. (1mk)
    - Lack of adequate funds to finance nationalistic activities.
    - Disunity among Africans.
    - Arrest of African nationalists by the colonial government.
    - Rivalry among political parties e.g. CPP and UGCC. (any 1x1 = 1mk)

15. Why was the Economic Community of West African States (ECOWAS) formed? (1mk)
    - To promote peace in the region.
    - To promote industrial development among member states.
    - To promote economic cooperation among West African states.
    - To promote cultural interaction among member states. (any 1x1 = 1mk)

16. Identify **one** main political challenge which Zaire has faced since independence. (1mk)
    - Coup-de-tats / military coup-de-tats. (1 x 1 = 1mk)

17. State the Composition of the Congress in the United States of America (USA) (2mks)
    - The Senate / Upper House.
    - The House of Representatives / Lower House. (2 x 1 = 2mks)

SECTION B

18. (a) Identify the culture of early man during the Old Stone Age period. (5mks)
    - Man lived in small groups.
    - Simple tools called Oldowan tools were made.
    - Man ate raw meat, bird eggs and insects.
    - Slept on tree tops to avoid attack by animals.
    - Man had not developed language.
    - He had no clothes, as the body was hairy.
    - Hunting was done by using stones and digging pits. (any 5x1 = 5mks)

    (b) Explain **five** ways through which early man adapted to the environment during Old Stone Age. (10mks)
    - Making of clothes to warm their bodies.
    - Development of upright posture using hind limbs. This improved man's ability to hunt and see danger.
    - Gradual use of front limbs (hands) for holding objects enabled man to make tools which made his act easier.
    - Increased brain capacity to above 1500c.c. enhanced man's level of creativity.
    - Domestication of plants and animals ensured prolonged supply of food reducing nomadic life for sedentary life.
    - Discovery of language enhanced exchange of ideas.
    - Weapon making enhanced survival by reducing insecurity. (any 5 well explained x 2 = 10mks)

19. (a) Give **three** limitations of using fire and smoke to convey messages during pre-colonial period. (3mks)

- Messages could only be sent over short distances.
- Range of messages passed was limited.
- Only relevant when one was on look out.
- Not possible to send long or complicated messages.
- Smoke signals could easily be misinterpreted.
- Smoke sometimes may be interfered by weather conditions, wind, clouds, mist, and rains.

(b) Explain <u>six</u> negative effects of modern telecommunication in the society today.   (12mks)
- Telecommunication has undermined   the traditional way of life.
- Criminals use the efficient communication networks to commit crimes i.e. international.
- Most telecommunication devices are not accessible to many people due to their high cost.
- They promote violence when children watch violent television shows e.g. wrestling.
- The ease and speed with which ideas spread all over the world has encouraged international social crimes such as fraud, drug trafficking and terrorism.
- Some people get addicted to the systems such as internet, television and radio can cause sound pollution.
- Prolonged exposure to a computer screen affects the eyes adversely.
- Pornography on videos and internet is a threat to morals among the youths. (any 6x2 = 12mks)

20. (a) Give <u>three</u> pull factors for the scramble for Africa.   (3mks)
- Presence of a well developed trade – easy movements for European colonizers
- Good harbours along the vast coast line.
- Vast resources like minerals, ivory, attracted them.
- Weakness of African societies – decentralized /no unity.
- Many inter-tribal wars weakened African societies.
- Diseases and natural calamities made Africans weak thus easily vulnerable.   (any 3x1 = 3mks)

(b) Explain <u>six</u> results of the Chimurenga War of 1896 – 1897.   (12mks)
- Africans lost their political independence – British rule established over their territory.
- Led to destruction of property because of war.
- Africans lost their land to settler white farmers and were pushed to infertile areas / reserves e.g. Hawaii and Shangani.
- Introduction of forced labour on European farms and mines.
- Introduction of taxation.
- Led to spread of Christianity, Africans had lost confidence in their traditional religions.
- Some Ndebele Indunas were recognized as headmen.
- The Shona local police were withdrawn from Ndebele land.
- The war led to starvation, during war Africans could not engage in farming.
- Led to the discredibility of the colonial office due to poor administration.
- African leaders of the war were arrested and killed e.g. Nahanda Kakubi and Singimamatshe.

(any 6x2 = 12mks)

21. (a) State <u>five</u> methods used by nationalists in Mozambique to struggle for independence.   (5mks)

- Mass media.
- Formation of political association e.g. MANU.
- Use of strikes by workers.
- Formation of political movements e.g. FRELIMO.
- Got help from other countries e.g. Tanzania.
- Use of guerilla movements.
- FRELIMO built schools and health centres as a way of getting support.   (any 5x1 = 5mks)

(b) What were the differences between the British policy of indirect rule and French policy of Assimilation?
- French colonies ruled as provinces of French while those Britain were ruled as separate political entities.
- The French Assimilated Africans in their administration while the British used traditional chiefs.
- French colonies were represented in the chamber of deputies in France while British colonies were not represented in the house of councils.
- Laws used in French colonies were made by their respective legislative councils while British send representatives to make laws at legislative councils.
- French colonies assimilated Africans to become French citizens with full rights while those in British colonies remained subjects.
- British colonies upheld Africa culture while assimilation undermined it.
- Many French officers were military men unlike the British colonies who were civilians
                                                                                                                       (any 5x2 = 10mks)

22. (a) Give the names of **three** founders of Pan-Africanism.   (3mks)
- Booker T. Washington.
- W.E.B. Dubois.
- Marcus Garvey
- George Padmore.   (any 3x1 = 3mks)

(b) Explain why Pan-Africanism Movement was not active in Africa before 1945.   (12mks)
- African representatives in the movement were very few up to 1945. They were also outside Africa, some studying and others in exile.
- Colonial authorities did not allow Africans to organize movements that were opposed to colonial rule.
- Africans were more concerned with issues that affected them rather than the movement e.g. economic and social problems.
- Ethiopia and Liberia who were not colonized did give little attention to the movement.
- Africans in Africa did not have the machinery to communicate ideas / there was no communication between the different African colonies.
- The divide and rule policy used by the Europeans undermined African unity.
- Africans who returned home were not allowed to organize movements that opposed colonial rule.   (any 6 well explained x2 = 12mks)

23. (a) State **five** causes of the Cold War. (5mks)
    - Ideological differences i.e. capitalism and communism.
    - Formation of military alliances and military support to opponent's enemies.
    - The disagreement over disarmament created tension between two blocs.
    - The UN domination by western powers created tension between the super powers.
    - Economic rivalry created hostility between the two super powers.
    - Differences over Germany after the Second World War. The western allies desired a strong Germany while Soviet Union wanted a divided Germany. (5 x 1 = 5mks)

    (b) Describe **five** political results of the Second World War. (10mks)
    - Led to the rise of super states e.g. USA and USSR.
    - Led to the spread of communism to half of Europe / division of Europe into two blocs.
    - Led to the Cold War between Western and Eastern blocs;
    - Western Europe received financial assistance from USA.
    - Led to the formation of United Nations Organizations U.N.O.
    - Led to the division of Germany into two capitalist West and Communist East.
    - It led to the creation of the state of Israel to resettle the Jews.
    - It led to the production of atomic weapons nuclear weapons which led to destruction.
    - It facilitated decolonization in Africa and Asia.
    - USA got involved in European affairs. (any 5x2 = 10mks)

24. (a) Give **five** sources of the British Constitution. (5mks)
    - Act of parliament e.g. Magna Carta of 1911
    - Decisions made by the British Law Courts.
    - Legal publications by reputable authorities.
    - Royal prerogatives / powers of King / Queen e.g. to declare war / sign treaties.
    - The Hansard – official verbatim report of proceeding in parliament. (any 5x1 = 5mks)

    (b) Explain the importance of the monarchy to the British people. (10mks)
    - The presence of the monarchy helps to give some continuity to the executive policy.
    - The queen / King acts as a counselor to government leaders.
    - It is a symbol of British Unity for the larger Commonwealth of Nations.
    - It sets standards for social life in Britain and arouses interest in various activities and development efforts.
    - Its existence is an inspiration to the heads of government and instills a sense of responsibility and dignity.
    - The royal family pays state visits to foreign governments and undertakes tours in other countries of the commonwealth hence contributing to better understanding between Britain and other nations. (any 5x2 = 10mks)

The Barons

History Saple Paper 2 (2)

311/2 -MARKING SCHEME

1. Two types of sources of information on History and Government.
    -   Primary source / unwritten.
    -   Secondary source / written.
    -   Tertiary source.   (2x1 = 2mks)

2. Two characteristics of Kenyapithecus.
    -   Had small canines.
    -   Walked on four.
    -   Weighed 18 – 36kgs
    -   Had bigger brain than the earlier fossils.   (2x1 = 2mks)

3. Two contributions of William Harvey to scientific revolution.
    -   Discovered blood circulation with the heart as the pump.
    -   Causes of blood poisoning.   (2x1 = 2mks)

4. Main policy making body of Commonwealth.
    -   Heads of State Summit.   (1 x 1 = 1mk)

5. One social condition for membership to non-aligned movement.
    -   Interested countries to adopt an independence of co-existence.
    -   Member state to consistently support the movement for national independence. (1 x 1 = 1mk)

6. The main reason why nationalism developed in Ghana during the colonial period.
    -   Presence of a large group of educated Africans / Elites.   (1 x 1 = 1mk)

7. Two places in Africa where Cold War was witnessed.
    -   DRC
    -   Angola
    -   Ethiopia
    -   Mozambique   (2x 1 = 2mks)

8. The first president of FRELIMO.
    -   Edwardo Mondlane.   (1 x 1 = 1mk)

9. Two major events which made 1917 the decisive year for the end of World War 1.
    -   Russia's withdrawal from the war.
    -   The declaration of war by U.S.A.   (2x1 = 2mks)

10. Two social classes that made up the Buganda society in the pre-colonial period.
    -   Royal family of Kabaka.
    -   Chiefs.
    -   Peasants / commoners

-   Slaves   (any 2x1 = 2mks)

11. The main role of ECOMOG in West Africa.
    -   Promote peace by sending peace keepers to affected countries.   (1 x 1 = 1mk)

12. Any two political parties in India.
    -   Congress Party.
    -   Bharatija Janata Party.
    -   The Communist Party of India.
    -   The National Congress.   (2x 1 = 2mks)

13. Two regions that were declared mandate territories after Versailles treaty of 1919.
    -   Tanganyika.
    -   Togoland.
    -   Namibia
    -   Rwanda
    -   Burundi   (any 2x1 = 2mks)

14. Two ways through which Mobutu Sese Seko displayed dictatorship.
    -   Made Congo one party state.
    -   Controlled the economy of the government.
    -   He stripped the parliament of its powers.
    -   Changed the constitution to suit him e.g. abolishing the federal system.   (any 2x1 = 2mks)

15. How Bismarck and the rise of Germany led to scramble for colonies in Africa.
    -   Bismarck encouraged France to seek for colonies in Africa as compensation and consolation for her losses in Europe and Africa.   (1 x 1 = 1mk)

16. The reason why Soviet Union / Russia rejected the Marshall plan.
    -   The Russians felt that it represented American interference in the internal affairs of other states.   (1 x 1 = 1mk)

SECTION B

17. (a) Three factors which influenced the evolution of man.
    -   Natural selection.
    -   Mutations.
    -   Adaptation to changing environments.
    -   Isolation.   (1 x 3 =3 mks)

(b) Six reasons why studying History and Government is important.
    -   To develop a sense of belonging and foster pride.
    -   To understand and appreciate their past way of life which help predict future events.
    -   To acquire the capacity for political thinking as they analyze the historical information.

- To appreciate culture of other people.
- To attain a career and get employment e.g. teaching.
- To prepare students for a life and the way they should react to future challenges.
- To attain knowledge and the pleasure for reading and finding out new information.

(any 6x2 = 12mks)

18. (a) Five traditional forms of water transport.
    - Tree trunk
    - Rafts.
    - Canoes e.g. Dug out / Kayak etc.
    - Oar-driven boats.
    - Sailing ships.   (5 x 1 = 5mks)

(b) Contributions of TV to economic development.
    - Has encouraged business and trade through advertisement.
    - Created employment opportunities.
    - Has generated revenue for the government through taxation.
    - Has educated masses on economic issues.
    - Colour circuit has enhanced security in business premises.
    - Has provided a variety of entertainment through various entertainment programmes thus generating income.
    - Has facilitated cultural development / borrowing through music / drama etc viewed over the TV programmes.   (any 5x2 = 10mks)

19. (a) Reasons why Samori Toure resisted the French for long.
    - Use of scorched earth policy.
    - Religion inspiration.
    - Well equipped army.
    - Had his own army / workshop for repair / manufacture.
    - Use of guerilla warfare tactics.
    - Use of Diplomacy / Peace treaties to buy time.   (any 5x1 = 5mks)

    (b) Five results of the resistance against the French.
    - Loss of lives.
    - Inspired African nationalist in West Africa.
    - Disruption of economic activities.
    - Capture / deportation of Samori Toure.
    - Displacement of people / families.
    - Famine / starvation.   (any 5x2 = 10mks)

20. (a) Why the British used direct rule in Zimbabwe.
    - The indigenous / local political institutions based on Induna system had been destroyed during the British occupation of Zimbabwe.

- They desired to control the economy of Zimbabwe to maximize profits.
- To ensure complete control of the Africans / to end African's resistance.
- Existence of the British South African personnel on the spot which were familiar with the area as well s the British system of administration.
- The British South Africa company had enough finance to pay administrative officers.
- The Chamurenga uprising 1896 – 1897 had eroded European confidence in traditional African leadership in the colony.   (any 3x1 = 3mks)

(b) Effects of British rule in Zimbabwe.
  - Alienation of African land by white settlers resulting to displacement of Africans.
  - African traditional rulers lost their political autonomy and served as puppet of British.
  - Africans were subjected to heavy taxation.
  - It undermined African traditional economy as some Africans worked in white farms.
  - It led to the development of transport network.
  - It led to introduction of new crops in the region.
  - It undermined African culture.
  - Africans were subjected to forced labour.
  - Africans were denied freedom of movement by being confined to the reserves and required to carry identity cards.   (any 6x2 = 12mks)

SECTION C

21. (a) Three provisions of the Arusha Declaration.
  - Self radiance on local resources.
  - Ujamaa (socialism) establishment of a socialist state.
  - Equality of all citizens / avoidance of dissemination.
  - Nationalization of resources.   (any 3x1 = 3mks)

(b) Six economic reforms introduced in Tanzania since 1985.
  - Ujamaa policy was ended.
  - Nationalism policy was abolished.
  - Markets have been liberated with limited government control of prices.
  - Tanzania currency was also devalued to reduce inflation.
  - Disposal of unprofitable governments firms.
  - Has also enhanced her bilateral and multilateral economic relations with neighbours and the West.
  - She has also embraced World Bank and IMF aid contributions to attract foreign aid investment.
  - Has also improved infrastructure through construction of more roads.   (any 6x2 = 12mks)

22. (a) Five aims of Pan-African movement.
  - To unite all the people of African origin,
  - To challenge the ideology of white supremacy / to fight and end colonialism.

- To improve the African conditions all over the world.
- To create a forum to fight colonialism and racialism.
- To fight neo-colonialism in Africa.
- To preserve African culture. (any 5x1 = 5mks)

(b) Achievements of Pan-African movement by 1960s.
- It created a sense of unity and solidarity among the people of African origin.
- It laid foundation for interest in research on African cultures, literature, music, religion, medicine.
- It encouraged nationalist struggle in Africa.
- It enabled African leaders to be more committed to African issues e.g. black caucus in the USA that challenged apartheid in South Africa.
- The Movement was the forerunner of the Organization of African Unity (OAU) which later became African Union (AU).
- It condemned Mussolin's attempt to colonize Ethiopia in 1935 by organizing protests in major towns e.g. Brussels, Paris, London etc.
- It created awareness about African community origin, problems and destiny.
- Forums for discussing common problems affecting Africans and chance for cooperation among African leaders. (any 5x2 = 10mks)

23. (a) The objectives of the League of Nations.
- To prevent war from ever breaking out again by settling international disputes before they got out of hand.
- To maintain peace through collective security, member of the league to act together to restrain the aggressor through economic or military sanctions.
- To solve global economic and social problem through international cooperation.
- To promote and respect the sovereignty of member states.
- To act towards disarmament and discourage the production of weapons of mass destruction.
(any 5x1 = 5mks)

(b) The failures of the League of Nations.
- The Sino-Japanese disputes: Japan invaded and took over the Manchuria region of China and the league failed to stop Japan. Japan pulled out of the league.
- In 1935 Benito Mussolini of Italy invaded Ethiopia and when the league recommended Italy's withdrawal from Ethiopia. Italy pulled out of the league.
- The league failed to stop Germany from violating the terms of peace conference in Paris e.g. Germany embarked on remilitarization programme and invaded Poland.
- It failed to raise enough funds to implement some of its programmes.
- The league failed in the task of persuading member states to reduce armaments as stipulated in the covenant. (any 5x2 = 10mks)

Bibliography

Anderson, D. (2005). *Histories of the Hanged: The Dirty War in Kenya and the End of Empire.* London: Weidenfeld and Nicolson

Andrew, P. and Martin, L. (1987). *Cladistic Relationships of Extant and fossil hominoids.* Journal of Human Evolution

Appiah, K. A., Gates, H.L. Jr. (1999). *Africana: The Encyclopedia of the African and the African American Experience,* New York: Basic Books.

Basi, M. (2005). *Decisions in the Shade, Political and Juridical Processes among the Oromo-Borana,* Red Sea Press.

Columbia Encyclopedia (2007). *Mozambique "History,"* Sixth Edition

Denis Richcard, M. A. (1979). *An Illustrated History of Modern Europe 1789 -1974,* Hong Kong: Longman Group.

Evans-Pritchard, E. E. (1965). *The Political Structures of the Nandi-Speaking People of Kenya,* In the *Position of Women in Primitive Societies and Other Essays in Social Anthropology.*

Fage, J. D., Eds. (1979). *Cambridge History of Africa Vol. 2.* Cambridge University Press.

Farwell, B. (2001). *The Encyclopedia of Nineteenth Century Land Warfare: An Illustrated World View*

Gilbert, E and Jonathan T. (2008). *Africa in World History: From Pre-history to the Present,* Pearson Education.

Ilife, J. (197). Organization of the Maji Maji Rebellion. The Journal of African History Vo. 8 No. 3

Jone, S., Martin, R. and Pilbeam, Eds. (1992). *The Cambridge Encyclopedia of Human Evolution.* Cambridge University Press.

Kipkorir, B. E and Melbourne, F. B. (1973). *The Marakwet of Kenya: A Preliminary Study,* Nairobi, Kenya: East African Literature Bureau.

Makira, F. E. (1978). *An Outline History of the Babukusu.* Nairobi. Kenya: Kenya Literature Bureau.

M'manyareya, A. M. (1992). *The Restatement of Bantu Origin and Meru History.* Nairobi: East African Education Publishers.

Moss, J. and Wilson, G. (1991). *People of the World: Africa South of Sahara.*

Morell, V. (1996). *Ancestral Passions: the Leakey Family and the Quest for Humankind's Beginnings.* Simon and Schuster.

Mauta, T. (2010). *Retracing the Footsteps of Ameru and their Sub-tribal Differences,* Nkubitu Publishing Company.

Mwanzi, A. A. (1977). *A History of the Kipsigis,* Nairobi, Kenya: East African Literature Bureau.

Ochieng' W. R. (1975). *An Outline History of the Rift Valley of Kenya,* Nairobi, Kenya: East African Literature Bureau.

___ (1991). *Kenyan History,* Nairobi, Kenya: East African Education Publishers.

Ogot, B. A. (1978). *The Kalenjin, Kenya before 1900: Eight Regional Studies,* Nairobi: East African Publishing House.

Orchardon, I. Q. (1971). *The Kipsigi, Nairobi,* Kenya: East African Literature Bureau.

Tattersal, I. (1992). *The many faces of Homo habilis.* In Evolutionary Anthropology, Vol. 1

Toweek, T. (1979). *Oral traditional History of the Kipsigis,* Nairobi, Kenya: Kenya Literature of Bureau.

Rightmire, G. P. (1993). *Variations among early Homo crania form Olduvai Gorge and the Koobi for a region,* In American Journal of Physcal Anthropology, Vol. 90.

Robert, M. (1994). *An Introductory History*, Nairobi, East African Educational Publishers.

Robert, O. C. (2006). *The Southern Sudan in Historical Perspective*, Transaction Publishers.

Robert, W. P. and Reynolds, J. T. (2008). *Africa in the World History from Pre-history to the Present*. Pearson Education Ltd.

Rupiya, M. (1998). *Historical Context: War and Peace in Mozambique*.

Swynnerton, R. J. M. (1955). The Swynnerton Report: *A Plan to Intensify the Development of African Agriculture in Kenya*. Nairobi: Government Printer.

UNESCO, (1999). *General History of Africa Vol. VI: Africa in the 19th Century Until 1880's*.

UNESCO. (1985). *General History of Africa, Vol. VII: Africa under Colonial Domination, 1880 – 1935*.

Walker, A. and Shipman, P (2005).*The Ape in the Tree: An intellectual and Natural Hisotry of Proconsul*. Cambridge, Massachusetts, London England: The Belknap Press of Harvard University Pres

Young, L S. (1991). *Mozambique's Sixteen Years of Bloody Civil War*.

Glossary of Terms Used in the Text

Absolute Monarchy by any form	A system of government in which the monarchy or ruler is unchecked of parliament, and in which his own wishes are law
Age group	A group of peers or age mates initiated together.
Age set	A group of people who were initiated together, but vary in age because circumcision takes length periods.
Agrarian revolution	Rapid changes and improvement in agriculture
Alloy	Mixture of different metals
Annex	To take control of a country or region by force
Appeasement Policy	Was a policy whereby some Western powers, for example Britain gave into German demands after the World War I
Arbitration	System of settling disputes, not by fighting but by appointing somebody to choose between the two parties to the dispute
Arbitrary imprisonment	Imprisonment at the will of the ruler without reference to the law
Authenticity Programme	A programme launched by Mobutu of Zaire to return the Congolese people to their original cultural traits.
Aristocracy	System of government where the highest social class wields authority
Barter trade	Direct exchange of goods for goods
Bicermal Legislature	A legislature having two chambers or houses e.g. Upper House and Lower house
Capitalism	An economic system in which means of production are owned by the people and what is bought or sold is determined by market forces.
Centralized government	System of political organization with a centralized authority
Citizenship	Legal right of a person to belong to a particular country
Civil Rights	Privileges enjoyed by the people which are guaranteed and protected by the government
Cold War	Refers to the rivalry that emerged after the World War II between the capitalist West and the communist East. This war did not involve the actual confrontation in the battle fields
Communism	Belief that system of private ownership of land, factories, railways, banks etc. should be replaced by public ownership
Concession	Something that you allow to do or have, in order to end an argument or to make a situation less difficult
Conflict	This is a disagreement which can arise, for example between individuals or a group.
Constitution	A set of agreed principles and rules which are used to govern a state
Constitutional Monarchy	Monarchy where the king has little powers, but is bound by the terms of a constitution to accept parliament's advice
County	An area within a country that has its own government
Coup d'etat	Seizure of power
Convention	Agreement in documentary form
Decentralized government	System of political organization without a central authority

The Barons

Democracy	System of government in which the masses have some control of policy, usually in the form of electing their representatives to some kind of parliament
Devolution	The act of transferring some power from central government to a local authority or government
Devolved government	A form of government in which power and authority is transferred from the central government to the local government
Dictatorship	System of government in which one man or one group has complete power
Dual citizens	Kenyans who have acquire citizenship of other countries
Electoral College	The electoral body in USA which chooses the president and vice president in the country
Evolution	Gradual development of plants and animals over many years as they adapt to changes in their environment
Federal Government	Government comprising several states that have agreed to unite
Federation	System whereby many states group together to form a bigger state to which they surrender some, but not all of their powers
Franchise	The right to vote in a country's election
Hansard	An official verbatim report of proceeding in the parliament
Hominid	A human or a creature that lived in the past which humans developed from
Guerrilla Technique	Method of warfare involving surprise attack or ambush
Hominoid	A creature related to humans
Homo	A genus of primates that includes early and modern humans
Imperialism	Belief in building up or holding a colonial empire
Indirect Rule	British colonial policy where they retained the existing indigenous administrative systems and rulers in pursuit of their colonial interest
Industrial Revolution	Radical changes which took place in the field of manufacturing since the mid 18th century. It involved changes which took place in the process, organization and sources of power among others
Kabala	Title of the Baganda king
Katikiro	Prime Minister in the traditional Baganda society
Legislation	Law-making
Legislature	A group of people in a country or state who have the power to make and amend the laws
Lukiko	The law making body in the Baganda society
Monarchy	The type of government headed by the king or queen
Multipartism	A political system that allows for the existence of more than one political party
National integration	Process of mixing people who have previously been separate, usually because of race, tribe or religion to act as one.
Nationalism	Desire to see the nation organized powerfully and free from oppression by other nations

Natural citizens	People who are granted Kenyan citizenship because they were born in Kenya or have Kenyan parents.
Natural Selection	A process resulting in the survival of organisms - in a population of others, that is able to adapt to the environmental changes
Naturalized	citizens Women who are granted citizenship because they are married to Kenyan men and have accepted to continue staying in the country
Non-alignment	Freedom to support or withdraw support for any other country on any issue. This was a policy adopted by third world countries to avoid getting involved in conflict between the two superpowers
Palaeontology	The study of fossils to determine the structure and evolution of extinct animals and plants, and the age and conditions of deposition of the rock strata in which they are found
Pan Africanism	A belief in the uniqueness and spiritual unity of black people. It acknowledges their right to self determination in Africa and treatment of Africans with dignity as equal people to other races.
Plebiscite	Vote by all citizens on some important issue
Promulgate	To announce a new law or system officially or publicly
Propaganda	Ideas or statements that may be false or exaggerated and that are used in order to gain support for a political leader or party.
Referendum	Referring of a matter of national importance to the people to decide
Registered citizens	People who have applied for Kenyan citizenship and the request is granted
Representative Democracy	A political system in which officials are elected by the people to make government decisions on their behalf e.g. elected members of parliament
Revolution	A great change in condition, ways of working, beliefs that affects a large number of people
Scorch earth policy	destroying everything as you retreat to deprive your enemy of essential supplies
Socialism	Belief that the state, not private persons, should control the means of production (land, factories, etc.), distribution (Railway) and exchange (Banks)
Sovereignty	Complete power to govern or rule a country
Suffrage	Right to Vote
Stratigraphy	Is the study of rock layers
Triangular trade	Commercial exchange which took place between traders from Europe, America and West Africa during the 17th century across the Atlantic Ocean
Trans Saharan Trade	Trade across the Sahara desert that took place between 8th to 16th century
Unitary Government	Government administered through the central government and backed by the provincial administration

The Barons

Veto | Power to prevent legislation or action proposed by others e.g. USA, Britain, France, Russia and China can prevent other members of UNO from performing certain actions

Subject Index

The Barons

The Barons

The Barons

www.ingramcontent.com/pod-product-compliance
Lightning Source LLC
Chambersburg PA
CBHW062058090426
42741CB00015B/3263